DATE DUE

DE 11 '96			
FE 26 '97			
JE 26 '97			
DE 10 '97			
AP 2 '98			
AP 25 '98			
MY 20 '98			
MY 30 '98			
MY 27 '99			
MY 1 00			

DEMCO 38-296

BETWEEN
THE
LINES

BETWEEN THE LINES

Interpreting Welfare Rights

R. Shep Melnick

THE BROOKINGS INSTITUTION
Washington, D.C.

Copyright © 1994 by

THE BROOKINGS INSTITUTION

igton, D.C. 20036

ion data:

ghts / R. Shep Melnick. p.   cm.
dex.
    ISBN 0-8157-5664-X (cl : alk. paper) — ISBN 0-8157-5663-1 (pa : alk. paper)
    1. Public welfare—Law and legislation—United States.   2. Welfare recipients—Legal
status, laws, etc.—United States.   3. Political questions and judicial power—United
States.   4. Entitlement spending—United States.   I. Title.
KF3720.M45   1994
344.73′03—dc20
[347.3043]   93-45457
                                                                CIP

9 8 7 6 5 4 3 2 1

The paper used in this publication meets the minimum requirements of the American
National Standard for Information Sciences—Permanence of paper for Printed Library
Materials, ANSI Z39.48-1984

Typeset in Sabon

Composition by AlphaTechnologies/mps
Mechanicsville, Maryland

Printing by R.R. Donnelley and Sons, Co.
Harrisonburg, Virginia

THE BROOKINGS INSTITUTION

The Brookings Institution is an independent organization devoted to nonpartisan research, education, and publication in economics, government, foreign policy, and the social sciences generally. Its principal purposes are to aid in the development of sound public policies and to promote public understanding of issues of national importance.

The Institution was founded on December 8, 1927, to merge the activities of the Institute for Government Research, founded in 1916, the Institute of Economics, founded in 1922, and the Robert Brookings Graduate School of Economics and Government, founded in 1924.

The Board of Trustees is responsible for the general administration of the Institution, while the immediate direction of the policies, program, and staff is vested in the President, assisted by an advisory committee of the officers and staff. The by-laws of the Institution state: "It is the function of the Trustees to make possible the conduct of scientific research, and publication, under the most favorable conditions, and to safeguard the independence of the research staff in the pursuit of their studies and in the publication of the results of such studies. It is not a part of their function to determine, control, or influence the conduct of particular investigations or the conclusions reached."

The President bears final responsibility for the decision to publish a manuscript as a Brookings book. In reaching his judgment on the competence, accuracy, and objectivity of each study, the President is advised by the director of the appropriate research program and weighs the views of a panel of expert outside readers who report to him in confidence on the quality of the work. Publication of a work signifies that it is deemed a competent treatment worthy of public consideration but does not imply endorsement of conclusions or recommendations.

The Institution maintains its position of neutrality on issues of public policy in order to safeguard the intellectual freedom of the staff. Hence interpretations or conclusions in Brookings publications should be understood to be solely those of the authors and should not be attributed to the Institution, to its trustees, officers, or other staff members, or to the organizations that support its research.

For Kate

Foreword

IN RECENT YEARS judges' interpretations of federal laws have had an enormous effect on the design and operation of government programs. In areas as diverse as civil rights, environmental regulation, education, and welfare, the federal courts have issued far-reaching, controversial decisions based on their reading of federal statutes. Statutory construction by judges can expand or contract programs, strengthen Congress and its committees or augment the prerogatives of the executive branch, and extend the reach of the federal government or protect the authority of state and local governments. Although Congress always has the option of revising these court rulings, enacting legislation on controversial issues is seldom easy.

In this book, R. Shep Melnick examines statutory interpretation in three entitlement programs: aid to families with dependent children, food stamps, and education for the handicapped. He places court decisions within their political context, reveals the crucial assumptions made by judges, and traces the long-term consequences of court action. Although these three programs differ in important ways, Melnick finds that for all three, judicial interpretation expanded program benefits and costs and increased federal control over state and local governments. He also shows that in each program Congress eventually passed legislation reversing or modifying major court rulings. His analysis demonstrates that statutory interpretation is not a narrow, technical undertaking; rather, it raises fundamental questions about federalism, the separation of powers, and the nature of rights in the welfare state.

vii

Melnick, a former research associate in the Brookings Governmental Studies program, is professor of politics at Brandeis University. He is indebted to Martha Derthick and Sidney M. Milkis for their extensive comments on several drafts of the manuscript. He also received invaluable comments and advice from Donald L. Horowitz, Robert A. Katzmann, Martin A. Levin, Thomas E. Mann, Paul E. Peterson, and Martin Shapiro. Elizabeth Bussiere, Michael Paris, and Michael Sparer provided both research assistance and critical analysis. Vicky Macintyre and Nancy Davidson edited the manuscript, and Alison Rimsky verified its factual content. Ingeborg K. Lockwood provided secretarial assistance, Susan L. Woollen prepared the manuscript for typesetting, and Max Franke prepared the index.

The Brookings Institution would like to thank the John M. Olin Foundation, Inc., for its support of this project, and the author would like to thank The Lynde and Harry Bradley Foundation for support given through the Harvard Program on Constitutional Government. The views expressed here are those of the author and should not be ascribed to any of the persons or organizations mentioned above, or to the trustees, officers, or staff members of the Brookings Institution.

BRUCE K. MAC LAURY
President

January 1994
Washington, D.C.

Contents

PART V CONCLUSIONS

PART I

Issues and Context

CHAPTER ONE

Statutory Interpretation in American Politics

The process of construction . . . is not an exercise in logic or dialectic: The aids of formal reasoning are not irrelevant; they may simply be inadequate. . . . The area of free judicial movement is considerable. . . . What exactions such a duty of construction places upon judges, and with what freedom it entrusts them!
—Justice Felix Frankfurter, 1947

ONCE CONFINED to the dusty corners of law libraries, statutory interpretation hit the headlines in the 1980s. Court decisions based on the reading of federal statutes resolved a number of highly charged issues and served as catalysts for further political action on many others. In 1983, for example, the Supreme Court construed the tax code to prohibit the Internal Revenue Service from granting tax-exempt status to private schools that discriminate on the basis of race. The Court conceded that the religious schools in question fit the statutory definition of institutions operated for religious or educational purposes. But since racial discrimination is "contrary to established public policy," the Court decided that granting tax-exempt status to these schools would frustrate the underlying purpose of the statutory provision.[1] A year later the Court moved in a different direction, narrowing the scope of a federal law that prohibits gender discrimination in educational institutions. A four-year battle ensued, at the end of which Congress finally overrode President Ronald Reagan's veto and enacted the "Grove City bill" to reverse this Supreme Court decision.[2]

Statutory interpretation was also at the heart of a running dispute between the Reagan administration and the federal courts over disability insurance in the early 1980s. Responding both to a 1980 law mandating a review of the program and to the Reagan administration's fervent desire to cut federal spending, the Social Security Administration (SSA) engaged in a large-scale effort to purge its rolls of those it considered no longer eligible for benefits. The courts overturned agency determinations for

3

more than 200,000 claimants. The courts of appeal read the disability statute to require the SSA to prove that a recipient's medical condition had improved before it could cut off benefits. The SSA argued that since the statute itself made no mention of this "medical improvement standard," it could apply to current beneficiaries the same standard it applied to new applicants.[3] Although the SSA restored benefits to the specific individuals who had won in court, it refused to change its general policy to conform to the predominant judicial interpretation of the law. This led a number of judges to threaten the agency with contempt of court. After a two-year struggle to resolve this dispute, Congress passed the Disability Benefits Reform Act of 1984, which codified the courts' "medical improvement standard" without following their practice of placing the burden of proof on the SSA to demonstrate such improvement.

The political significance of statutory interpretation was made even more evident by the events leading to passage of the Civil Rights Act of 1991. In 1989 the Rehnquist court announced five statutory rulings that made it harder for employees to win employment discrimination cases against their employers. The most important decision, *Wards Cove Packing Co. v. Antonio*,[4] involved the standard for proving racial or gender discrimination under title VII of the Civil Rights Act of 1964. In *Wards Cove* the Supreme Court modified its interpretation of title VII in a previous case, *Griggs v. Duke Power*.[5] According to the so-called Griggs standard, once a plaintiff has established that an employment practice has a "disparate impact" on racial minorities or women, the burden shifts to the employer to prove that the practice in question bears a "demonstrable relationship to successful performance" of the job. The *Wards Cove* decision, in contrast, held that under title VII "the plaintiff bears the burden of disproving an employer's assertion that the adverse employment action or practice was based solely on a legitimate neutral consideration."[6] These rulings received harsh criticism from civil rights groups and many members of Congress, some of whom believed that the American public could no longer look to the courts for leadership on civil rights.

In 1990 the House and Senate approved legislation to reverse *Wards Cove* and a number of other Supreme Court decisions. President George Bush vetoed the measure, arguing that it "creates powerful incentives for employers to adopt hiring and promotion quotas."[7] The stalemate finally ended shortly after the Clarence Thomas–Anita Hill hearings when President Bush agreed to a compromise. The final version of the legislation stated that once a plaintiff shows that "a particular employment practice causes a disparate impact on the basis of race, color, religion, sex, or national origin," the employer must "demonstrate that the challenged practice is job related for the position in question and consistent with business necessity." Although this was seen as a major victory for those favoring the Griggs standard, the new law did not explain what the key terms "job related" and "business necessity" mean, nor did it explain which of the many judicial decisions fleshing out the *Griggs* standard Congress meant to endorse. As *Congressional Quarterly* noted, "the vagueness was part of the compromise."[8]

All parties realized that it would be many years before Congress would again go through the trauma of writing legislation on this controversial topic. In the meantime the courts would define the crucial statutory phrases. The final debate over the bill gave the president and members of Congress their last opportunity to lobby the judicial branch. Not surprisingly, the deep divisions that characterized the two-year struggle to enact the bill were evident here as well.

A key part of the deal negotiated by the White House and Senate leaders was an agreement that a two-paragraph memo placed in the *Congressional Record* by Senator John Danforth would constitute the "exclusive legislative history" on the crucial burden-of-proof issue. This memo explained that "the terms 'business necessity' and 'job related' are intended to reflect the concepts . . . of *Griggs* v. *Duke Power Co.* and other Supreme Court decisions prior to *Wards Cove Packing Co.* v. *Antonio.*" The agreement began to unravel almost immediately. Senator Edward Kennedy, the most visible and forceful sponsor of the original bill, offered an elaborate interpretation that would make discrimination easier to prove in court. So did Representative Don Edwards, chairman of a key House Judiciary subcommittee, and Representative William Ford, chairman of the Education and Labor Committee. Senator Orrin Hatch and Representative Henry Hyde submitted explanations intended to do just the opposite. Senate Republican leader Robert Dole placed in the record a lengthy legal memorandum written by White House lawyers.[9]

Senator Danforth, the principal author of the compromise, decried these subsequent efforts "to doctor the legislative history and influence the future course of litigation." He warned that "a court would be well advised to take with a large grain of salt floor debate and statements placed into the *Congressional Record* which purport to create an interpretation for the legislation that is before us."[10] Shortly thereafter the

Senate passed an amendment that gave formal recognition to the "exclusive legislative history."[11] When President Bush placed his signature on the bill a few days later, though, his signing statement announced that the executive branch would treat Senator Dole's floor statements as "authoritative interpretive guidance" on the key section of new law.[12] What the federal courts will eventually make of all this is anybody's guess.

These examples provide a number of important lessons about statutory interpretation in contemporary American politics. First, at the core of each of these disputes was an ambiguous statutory phrase—"business necessity," "permanently and totally disabled," "charitable organization." In announcing their decisions the courts were not simply enforcing the dictates of laws passed by Congress. Rather, they were reading between the lines in order to give specific meaning to vague legislative language.

Second, federal judges have at their disposal no generally accepted, authoritative methods for interpreting statutes. In *Wards Cove*, the Supreme Court significantly modified the analysis offered in *Griggs*. In its decision on tax-exempt status, the Court rejected a literal interpretation of the tax code, relying heavily on its understanding of the purpose of the provision and the dictates of good "public policy." In the *Grove City* case, it did just the opposite, insisting on a literal interpretation of title IX. As the following chapters show, one reason statutory interpretation has become so controversial is that the Supreme Court has altered its practices in recent years. It has placed less emphasis on the general purpose and legislative history of laws and more emphasis on what it often calls the "clear meaning" of specific statutory provisions.

Third, many of the issues that come before the courts involve highly charged issues that divide Democrats and Republicans, liberals and conservatives, Congress and the White House. Affirmative action, spending on entitlements, public policy toward fundamentalist Christian groups—these are among the most contentious issues in contemporary American politics. One reason legislation on these issues contains ambiguous language is that Congress has yet to develop a consensus on how to handle them.

Fourth, while it takes a constitutional amendment to overturn a court's interpretation of the Bill of Rights or the Fourteenth Amendment, Congress can reverse decisions based on statutory interpretation merely by passing new laws. Congress frequently does just that—witness the Civil Rights Act of 1991 and the *Grove City* bill. Passing new legislation, though, is seldom easy and it usually takes several years. Those who favor the courts' interpretation can often block remedial legislation or demand concessions. By altering the policy status quo, the courts inevitably affect the bargaining power of various legislative factions.

Fifth, given the inherent difficulties of passing specific legislation, legislators (including the president, to whom the Constitution gives an important role in the legislative process) will search for other means to influence the outcome of court decisions. Most obviously, they will try to build legislative histories that reflect their positions on controversial issues. Given the autonomy of federal judges and the paucity of accepted rules about statutory interpretation, influencing or even predicting court decisions is tricky business.

A variety of studies of welfare and regulatory programs attest to the importance of the federal courts' reading of statutes. In 1971 the D.C. Circuit adopted an interpretation of the twenty-four-year-old Federal Insecticide Fungicide and Rodenticide Act that revolutionized national regulation of pesticides.[13] Another lower court judge relied on bits and pieces of legislative history to create an extensive national air pollution control program. A third established a sweeping program regulating waterborne toxins. Hundreds of decisions interpreting the National Environmental Policy Act of 1969 have created an elaborate federal common law of "environmental impact" assessment.[14] Federal judges have read the Endangered Species Act to bar a variety of projects and activities, including logging in old-growth forests populated by the spotted owl. Judicial interpretation of the Voting Rights Act has had a profound influence on how state and local governments draw electoral districts.[15] Federal antitrust policy is virtually coterminous with the courts' interpretation of the Sherman and Clayton Antitrust acts. Important elements of American labor law flow from the Supreme Court's reading of the National Labor Relations Act. As chapters 4 through 10 of this book show, judicial interpretation of entitlement statutes has substantially enlarged programs for the poor and the handicapped. In fact, one would be hard-pressed to find a major domestic policy area in which statutory interpretation by the federal courts did not play a significant role in shaping the activities of government.

Despite the political significance of statutory interpretation, the political science literature contains only a handful of works on the subject, and many of these are now outdated.[16] Statutory interpretation remains the preserve of legal scholars, who are very good at describing the changing fashions of statutory construction and debating the proper methods of interpretation, but who make little effort either to place this judicial activity in political context or to explore the long-term consequences of court action. The purpose of this book is not to identify the best "canons of interpretation," but to explore the way in which the federal courts' interpretation of statutes has affected the development of public programs and the operation of government institutions. Parts II, III, and IV examine the rationale and the consequences of statutory rulings on three programs: aid to families with dependent children (AFDC), education of the handicapped, and food stamps. These case studies pay special attention to the political struggles that predate court action and to the way federal administrators, members of Congress, state governments, and interest groups respond to court decisions.

Statutory Interpretation and the American Constitution

Studying the politics of statutory interpretation requires an understanding of how the unique features of the American constitutional system affect the issues that come to court, the way judges conceive their role, and the opportunities other actors have for modifying court rulings. Long ago Aristotle observed that there are always "matters as to which the laws are quite unable to pronounce with precision because of the difficulty of making a general rule to cover all cases."[17] Public officials in every country in the world face the problem of applying general words to particular circumstances. But judges do not do all or even most of this work. Here and abroad, much of the task of interpreting legislation is done by administrators. Contemporary welfare and regulatory programs would be impossible to run without a specialized bureaucracy armed with the authority to issue binding rules and to make a variety of determinations about their application.

Political systems differ not only in the type of legislation they produce, but also in the way power is distributed between judges and administrators. In a number of subtle ways, the central features of the U.S. political system—the separation of powers, bicameralism, federalism, a comparatively weak national bureaucracy, and the presence of a written, enforceable constitution—conspire to multiply the number of statutory issues that come before judges, to encourage judges to look beyond the letter of the law, and to reduce (but not eliminate) the possibility that judicial decisions will be overturned by subsequent legislation.

To understand the link between political structure and statutory interpretation, it is useful to contrast British and American practices. Two broad principles guide British judges in their construction of statutes. First, administrators rather than judges are considered the primary interpreters of national laws: while English courts "will occasionally intervene against the most openly illegal conduct of local authorities," they "exercise very little supervision over the massive discretionary powers of the central government."[18] Second, judges are expected to focus on the ordinary meaning of the words of the statute and not rest their decisions on analysis of its history, purpose, or spirit.[19] As Patrick S. Atiyah and Robert Summers demonstrate in their comprehensive comparison of the two legal systems, English judges generally take "a more textual, literal approach" than American judges, who adopt "a more purposive, and, therefore, substantive approach."[20] The two principles of British law are related: judges willing to delegate policymaking to administrators need not consult legislative histories in order to determine the exact meaning of broad statutory language. British judges limit their role to preventing clear violations of statutory commands, not turning general laws into specific policies.

American judges, in contrast, have long maintained that "it is emphatically the province and duty of the *judicial department*, to say what the law is."[21] While the extent of judicial deference to administrative agencies has waxed and waned over the past fifty years, American judges have seldom been as willing as British judges to accept administrators' reading of statutory language. When "the only or principal dispute relates to the meaning of [a] statutory term," Justice William O. Douglas stated in 1970, "the controversy must ultimately be resolved, not on the basis of matters within the special competence of the [agency], but by judicial applications of canons of statutory construction."[22] A more recent Supreme Court opinion announced that "a pure question of statutory construction" is one "for the courts to decide."[23]

Not content to accept administrators' policies, American judges have searched far and wide for other guides. They do not hesitate to "go deeply into any legislative history for evidence of any actual legislative intent not evident on the face of the statute, and also into other purposes and policies whether or not evidence of any legislative intent is forthcoming."[24] The words of the statute are only "the starting point" for interpretation. The judge must then "look to the provisions of the whole law, and to its object and policy."[25] What a statute says, Justice John Paul Stevens maintained in a recent case, is not always an adequate indication of what Congress meant: "'The reports are full of cases' in which the will of the legislature is not reflected in a literal reading of the words it has chosen."[26] In such cases, he argued, the courts should ensure the triumph of the legislative will.

A century ago the Supreme Court stated the "familiar rule that a thing may be within the letter of the statute and yet not within the statute, because not within its spirit, nor within the intention of its makers."[27] This language has been cited many times by the Supreme Court in recent years, most notably in Justice Brennan's majority opinion in *Steelworkers* v. *Weber*, the controversial 1979 decision upholding affirmative action plans for private employers.[28] In another majority opinion, Justice William J. Brennan, Jr., stated, "Where the literal reading of a statutory term would 'compel an odd result,' we must search for other evidence of congressional intent to lend the term its proper scope." Brennan quoted Judge Learned Hand's advice that judges should "not . . . make a fortress out of the dictionary" but should "remember that statutes always have some purpose or object to accomplish, whose sympathetic and *imaginative discovery* is the surest guide to their meaning."[29]

It is not unusual for American judges to put more emphasis on imagination than on discovery. As can be seen in the case studies examined later in this volume, American judges are not shy about reading their own policy preferences into statutes. In the words of former Yale Law School dean Guido Calebresi, himself a advocate of relatively freewheeling judicial interpretation, "The development of theories and practices of judicial interpretation of statutes would make even the proverbial Jesuit blush if they were viewed as attempts to discern any kind of legislative intent."[30]

The contrasting interpretive styles of British and American judges are closely related to the political structures of the two countries. In Britain, the combination of parliamentary government, strong political parties, and a cohesive, respected senior civil service has allowed the prime minister and the cabinet to dominate the House of Commons. Not only is legislation drafted by the ministries, but it is ordinarily passed in much the same form as presented. In this political context, it is difficult to argue that the executive has ignored "legislative intent." The legislation that emerges from Parliament also tends to be more coherent and drafted with more care than is the legislation passed by Congress. Moreover, since Parliament seldom refuses to pass bills requested by the prime minister (a circumstance American presidents can contemplate only in their dreams), many of the types of policy disputes that the courts handle in the United States are quickly resolved by the majority party in Britain before anyone has had time to file suit. Any judicial inclination to disregard an interpretation offered by the bureaucracy is tempered by judges' awareness that a minister annoyed by a judicial decision can quickly steer corrective legislation through Parliament. In short, the highly centralized British political system neither encourages nor tolerates judicial reconstruction of the statutes approved by Parliament.[31]

The American legislative process is far more fragmented and less predictable. American legislation must ordinarily receive the assent of three institutions—the House, the Senate, and the president—each with its independent electoral base. Within Congress, party discipline is weak. Congressional committees are multiple and powerful. Rarely is legislation passed in the form originally submitted by the executive branch. Most controversial legislation is revised again and again in order to garner enough support to pass both chambers. It is not surprising, therefore, that many American statutes lack coherence, fail to resolve key controversies, or even incorporate inconsistent requirements. Describing the statute before the Court as "a child born of the silent union of legislative compromise," Justice John Harlan noted that Congress frequently has "voiced its wishes in muted strains and left it to the courts to discern the theme in the cacophony of political understanding."[32]

Presidents and administrators argue that the formidable task of resolving statutory ambiguity and conflicts should be left to them, not to judges. In a system of separated powers, though, such claims invite a ready response: How can the *executive* branch be trusted to show proper respect for the intent of *Congress*? The inevitable conflicts and jealousies between the legislative and executive branches seem to call out for resolution by the third. Nor have American civil servants ever commanded the respect accorded their peers on the other side of the Atlantic. Judge Skelly Wright echoed a common theme when he wrote that the duty of the judiciary is "to see that the important legislative purposes, heralded in the halls of Congress, are not lost or misdirected in the vast hallways of the federal bureaucracy."[33] Disagreement between the two branches over the interpretation of statutes is likely to increase when one party controls the Congress and the other the presidency, a condition that has prevailed for twenty of the past twenty-five years.

The difficulty of maneuvering legislation through the fabled obstacle course on Capitol Hill has two additional consequences for statutory interpretation. First, it reduces the likelihood that a court's interpretation will be overturned by subsequent legislation. The courts, after all, have legislative inertia on their side. The more controversial the issue, the greater the possibility of stalemate and the less courts need to worry about legislative reversal. Second, the slowness of the legislative process at times leads judges to believe that only they are capable of reforming obsolete statutes or reconciling inconsistent ones. The need to keep the law up to date is a recurrent theme in American statutory construction. Ironically, the features of the Constitution that promote cautiousness in the legislative process seem at the same time to breed assertiveness in the judicial.

Federalism, too, has important implications for statutory construction. Since the early days of the Republic, settling disputes between the states and the federal government has been a central part of the job of the federal courts. Does this state law conflict with that federal statute? Did Congress mean to preempt this entire field, or did it intend to ratify existing state legislation? Called upon to harmonize two sets of statutes, judges have often resorted to inquiry into the broad purposes of these laws, the expectations of legislators, and the practical consequences of different interpretations.

Over the past fifty years, the proliferation of programs administered jointly by state and federal governments has brought a new and more complex set of federalism issues before the courts. Because it is often difficult for federal administrators to control the behavior of state officials, recipients and interest groups have looked to the courts for enforcement of federal requirements. Federal judges, after all, can do one thing that administrators cannot: issue direct orders to state officials, backed with the threat of fines and even imprisonment. This puts judges in a strong position to insist on their interpretation of a statute. But, as subsequent chapters illustrate, it also means that the courts must decide a large number of policy issues with very little statutory guidance.

Another distinctive feature of American government, of course, is judicial review. In *Marbury* v. *Madison*, Chief Justice John Marshall argued that because the Constitution is a fundamental law, the courts must invalidate any statute that conflicts with it. One year later Marshall enunciated a corollary to this principle of judicial review: to minimize conflict with the other branches of government, judges should construe statutes to avoid violations of the Constitution.[34] In 1895 the Supreme Court established the "elementary rule" that "every reasonable construction must be resorted to, in order to save a statute from unconstitutional-ity."[35] In recent years this doctrine has been broadened so that the mere assertion that a case "would raise serious constitutional problems" allows the court to choose any interpretation that is not "plainly contrary to the intent of Congress."[36] Even Justice Brennan, certainly no foe of creative judicial interpretations, has complained that under this rule "the Court can virtually remake congressional enactments."[37]

The centralized British political system establishes a relatively simple and clear chain of legal command. No written constitution limits the sovereignty of Parliament. Parliament, according to the old saw, can do anything but change a woman into a man or a man into a woman—a limitation now made anachronistic by the wonders of modern science. The leaders of the majority party control not just the House of Commons but the ministries as well. It is not surprising, therefore, that British judges seldom question the authoritative nature of statutory language or the interpretive authority of administrators.

The fragmented American political system, in contrast, produces a welter of conflicting legal claims. Litigants ask American judges to make sense of the various commands issued by competing institutions: federal laws, state laws, federal administrative rules, state administrative rules, state court decisions, federal court interpretations of the Constitution, House reports, Senate reports, presidential signing statements—even Indian tribal law.[38] Not surprisingly, American judges feel free to pick and choose among these competing sources of legal authority, and they see their role as providing the disjointed U.S. polity with at least one far-sighted, integrative force. Of course, since more than 800 judges are busy interpreting scores of federal statutes and since only about fifty of these statutory interpretation decisions reach the Supreme Court each year, consistency is by no means assured. In practice the courts add to the cacophony of legal authority as often as they produce coherence.[39] Moreover, the openness and messiness of the legislative process in the United States ensures that when judges scrutinize a statute and its history, they will seldom discover a single, coherent purpose or intent. These features of the American political system make statutory interpretation legally troublesome—but also politically fascinating.

From Laissez-Faire to Programmatic Rights

In practice, how has the American judiciary used statutory interpretation to shape the activities of government? Over the past 200 years interpretive fashions have come and gone, often reflecting the political views of appointing presidents and confirming Senates. To be sure, few politicians have strong views on the proper canons of construction. But questions of statutory interpretation are often closely related to the central political issues of the day.

Before the Civil War, for example, the principal issue dividing the political parties was the distribution of power between the states and the federal government. Committed Federalists such as Chief Justice John Marshall were more likely to read a federal statute as precluding state regulation than were followers of Jefferson and Jackson. At the turn of the century, judges distrustful of economic regulation and the welfare state often used both statutory construction and constitutional interpretation to rob progressive legislation of its vitality. To achieve this goal, judges invoked the maxim that "statutes in derogation of the common law should be narrowly construed." Federal judges also interpreted antitrust laws so as to thwart labor union activity. This practice particularly infuriated friends of labor, who eventually succeeded in passing legislation to curb the courts. Viewed within this broader context, statutory interpretation is more than the ad hoc application of arcane canons of interpretation. It is an important arena for the definition of the powers of public institutions and the rights of American citizens.

Current disputes over the proper role of the courts in the interpretation of statutes have their roots in the 1930s. At that time the Roosevelt administration made concerted efforts to tame the federal judiciary, which it understandably saw as hostile to the New Deal. President Franklin D. Roosevelt insisted upon appointing judges who not only adopted a broad reading of the constitutional powers of the federal government but also shared his view that "the day of enlightened administration has come."[40] This meant above all that they would readily defer to the rulings of administrative agencies. In 1941, for example, the Supreme Court upheld an agency's reading of the Bituminous Coal Act, announcing that unless an administrative ruling "is so unrelated to the tasks entrusted by Congress to the Commission as in effect to deny a sensible exercise of judgement, it is the Court's duty to leave the Commission's judgment undisturbed."[41] A few years later the Court accepted the National Labor Relations Board's definition of the term "employee," explaining "it is not the court's function to substitute its own inferences of fact for the Board's, when the latter have support in the record."[42] James Landis,

FDR's resident expert on statutory construction, presented the issue in no uncertain terms: "Strong judges are always with us; no science of interpretation can ever hope to curb their propensities. But the effort should be to restrain their tendencies, not to give them free rein in the name of scientific jurisprudence."[43] If Roosevelt's conception of his job turned the president into something approaching the British prime minister, so too did members of the Roosevelt court begin to resemble British judges in their approach to interpreting statutes.

In the 1960s and 1970s another surge in government activity coincided with a swing toward a more assertive role for the courts. At the very time that Congress and the president were creating new agencies, distributing more public benefits, and imposing more controls on the states and the private sector, the federal courts were becoming increasingly suspicious of claims of bureaucratic expertise. The courts began to rely more heavily on legislative history and their understanding of statutes' purposes. This new judicial activism did not reflect a desire to protect the private sector or the states from new intrusions by the federal government. To the contrary, most of these doctrinal changes were tied to efforts to *increase* the federal government's activity—to extend benefits to those meeting statutory criteria, to force administrators to perform nondiscretionary duties, and to secure greater federal control over the states.[44]

Chapter 2 of this book explores several of the political factors that have contributed to the changing patterns of statutory interpretation. Suffice it to say here that in the late 1960s and early 1970s—the years of defeat in Vietnam and scandal in the White House—popular trust in government in general and bureaucracy in particular declined precipitously. This was especially true among intellectuals, who in prior years had carried the New Deal message of faith in public administration. In addition, divided government—the combination of a Republican presidency and a Democratic Congress—became a regular feature of American politics. Years of divided government not only intensified conflict between the executive and legislative branches over the meaning of statutes but impelled Congress to reorganize itself. The reformed Congress of the 1970s passed a large number of laws opposed by Republican administrations and created an elaborate record of the intent of Congress—or at least the intent of its increasingly numerous and powerful subcommittees. In a variety of ways, Congress encouraged the courts to scrutinize the activities of the executive branch. They wrote liberal judicial review provisions, eliminated jurisdictional barriers, made it easier for plaintiffs to receive attorneys' fees, and at times gave courts rather than agencies the primary responsibility for carrying out new programs.

Just as important, the successes of the civil rights movement in the 1960s increased federal judges' confidence in their ability to create effective, moral public policies and demonstrated to a variety of interest groups the advantages of conceiving their goals in terms of rights that can be defined and enforced by the courts. Congress passed a number of rights-based statutes, and the courts interpreted them liberally to require large-scale change in public and private practices. Concern for protecting the rights of "discrete and insular minorities" was most readily apparent in the constitutional rulings of the Warren Court, but it also had a profound influence on how the federal courts as a whole read legislative enactments. The call for equality and justice is not easily confined.

A principal feature of the current dispute over the role of the courts— in constitutional law and statutory interpretation alike—is the reversal of the New Deal's institutional patterns. For three decades liberals have championed the judicial activism that Roosevelt and his allies condemned. Conversely, in the 1970s and 1980s conservatives called for greater deference to the executive—a stance they bitterly opposed while "that man" was in the White House. What has changed over the years is not just a matter of which party controls the presidency (as important as that shift may be), but the nature of the rights defended by the federal courts. No longer protectors of private property against government intrusion, the federal courts have created a new set of "personal" rights.

Some of these personal rights—most notably the right to privacy—emanate from the Constitution or its ill-defined "penumbras." Others— which I have elsewhere called "programmatic rights"—have been discovered in the words, purposes, and spirits of federal statutes.[45] These rights to government benefits, services, and protections are usually the joint product of legislative, administrative, and judicial action. For example, in the 1970s the lower courts ruled that disabled children have a constitutional right to a "free appropriate public education." Before the Supreme Court had reviewed the matter, Congress passed the Education for All Handicapped Children Act, providing a statutory basis for this right. Subsequently, hundreds of federal court decisions and thousands of administrative determinations have spelled out the contours of this "appropriate public education." In the 1960s the courts granted citizens the right to require federal agencies to give "adequate consideration" to the environmental consequences of their actions. When Congress passed the National Environmental Policy Act, the courts grafted these "adequate consideration" and public participation requirements onto the statute and substantially expanded their scope. The disability insurance program discussed above provides another example of how the courts have expanded the boundaries of the "new property" established by the entitlements programs created by Congress and the president.

In substance, these programmatic rights bear a striking resemblance to the long-term policy goals of Roosevelt and his supporters. FDR may have sought a subservient judiciary, but he also announced an Economic Bill of Rights to supplement the "sacred Bill of Rights of our Constitution." His "Second Bill of Rights" included "the right to earn enough to provide adequate food and clothing and recreation"; the right to "adequate medical care," "a decent home," and "a good education"; and "the right to adequate protection from the economic fears of old age, sickness, accident and unemployment." Each of these rights, Roosevelt added, "must be applied to all our citizens, irrespective of race, creed or color." "What all this spells," he explained in 1944, "is security."[46]

Eighteenth-century liberalism promised security from civil war, anarchy, and arbitrary government action. Its cornerstone was the protection of a realm of private autonomy from government intervention. Contemporary liberalism promises a broader security—security against the vagaries of the business cycle and other hazards created by dynamic capitalism, against the prejudices of private citizens and the consequences of three centuries of racism, against the risks of congenital handicaps and inevitable old age, and against the consequences of poverty and of family decomposition. Not content to stand by idly while legislators and administrators built the welfare state, the courts did their part to strengthen this new form of security.

To protect traditional rights, the courts had to restrain the growth of government. The new understanding of rights, in contrast, has led the judiciary to enlarge public responsibilities and to increase the power of the national government. Using statutory as well as constitutional interpretation, the courts have put new issues on the public agenda and enlarged the programs created by the other branches of government. Because they so often took these steps under the guise of legislative intent, their contribution to the development of the welfare state has not been sufficiently appreciated.

One of the reasons statutory interpretation has attracted so much attention in recent years is that the Supreme Court has revised some of the judicial practices that contributed to the growth of programmatic rights in the 1960s and 1970s. Particularly important in this regard is the Court's 1984 decision in *Chevron* v. *NRDC*. In language reminiscent of Supreme Court opinions of the 1940s, it instructed federal judges to show greater deference to the interpretations of administrators:

> If the statute is silent or ambiguous with respect to the specific issue, the question for the court is whether the agency's answer is based on a *permissible* construction of the statute. . . . [A] court may not substitute its own construction of a statutory provision for a reasonable interpretation made by the administrator of an agency.[47]

The lower courts—and even the Supreme Court itself—have not always followed this guideline. But the frequently cited *Chevron* opinion has certainly made federal judges more hesitant to overrule agency determinations.[48]

This is not the only interpretive change effected by the Rehnquist court. It has refused to impose federal mandates on state and local governments unless the statute contains a "clear statement" of federal requirements. The Court has also been reluctant to find "implied private rights of action" in statutes or to deem administrative duties "nondiscretionary."[49] On a number of occasions a majority of justices have sided with Justice Antonin Scalia, who has declared war on the use of legislative history, which, he maintains, is "inserted, at best by a committee staff member on his or her own initiative, and at worst by a committee staff member at the suggestion of a lawyer-lobbyist."[50] Scalia has argued that judges must "interpret laws rather than reconstruct legislators' intentions." This means they should look exclusively to the "plain meaning" of statutes rather than to their purpose, spirit, or history.

Justice Scalia's outspokenness on statutory interpretation has made him a lightning rod for criticism by those dissatisfied with the Supreme Court's shift in direction. Testifying before a congressional subcommittee in 1990, Patricia Wald, chief judge of the D.C. Circuit, warned that Scalia's doctrines on statutory interpretation are "inherently executive enhancing" and thus have "important implications for the balance of power in an ever ongoing tug-of-war among the three branches in our constitutional system."[51] Justice Stevens, a frequent sparring partner of Scalia's, has claimed that "when the Court has put on its thick grammarian's spectacles and ignored the available evidence of congressional purpose," Congress has promptly overruled the Court.[52] Members of Congress, too, have taken note of this controversy. Senator Arlen Spector has warned that if Scalia's views prevail, "there [will] be a lot of resentment about it."[53] At the opening of hearings he convened on statutory interpretation, Representative Robert Kastenmeier explained, "This is more than just an academic debate." Changing judicial doctrines of statutory interpretation "may have a profound effect on the way Congress should be drafting legislation."[54]

Studying Statutory Interpretation

Despite all its implications for government institutions and public policy, statutory law languished in the intellectual doldrums for many years. Legal scholars have long been preoccupied with justifying or discrediting various "canons of interpretation." Those who bothered to examine the legal literature were confronted with multivolume tomes listing scores of canons that manage somehow to be both vague and contradictory. Perhaps the best-known article on statutory construction ever published is Karl Llewellyn's demonstration that "there are two opposing canons on almost every point." Llewellyn's examples include the following: "a statute cannot go beyond its text," but "to effect its purpose a statute may be implemented beyond its text"; "statutes in derogation of the common law will not be extended by construction," but "such acts will be liberally construed if their nature is remedial"; "expression of one thing excludes another," but "the language may fairly comprehend many different cases where some only are expressly mentioned by way of example."[55] It is little wonder that Justice Felix Frankfurter once told an assembly of fellow lawyers, "I confess unashamedly that I do not get much nourishment from books on statutory construction, and I say that after freshly examining them all, scores of them."[56]

The past few years have witnessed what one writer calls "a renaissance of scholarship about statutory interpretation."[57] Just as controversial affirmative action decisions such as *Steelworkers* v. *Weber* and *Wards Cove* were demonstrating the importance of the subject, Justice Scalia and his allies began to challenge the prevailing legal orthodoxy. The law reviews sprang to the defense of practices they had long taken for granted. Although legal commentators experimented with new approaches to the subject—ranging from deconstructionism to public choice analysis—they retained the traditional focus on the judge. With few exceptions the legal literature devotes itself to parsing the arguments presented by judges and offering advice to judges on how to improve their performance. Little effort is made to examine what happens outside the courtroom, either before or after the judge announces his or her decision.[58]

As mentioned earlier, this book presents a different approach. It explores the political significance of statutory interpretation by examining three federal programs in detail: AFDC, education of the handicapped, and food stamps. Each of the case studies begins with a description of the programs and the pattern of political conflict before the courts entered the picture. Federal court decisions—not just those of the Supreme Court, but those issued by federal district and circuit courts as well—are presented within this context. The discussion then turns to the policy changes wrought by the court decisions and the responses of interest groups, administrators, and members of Congress. In each of the case studies the central question is not "Did the courts correctly interpret this statute?" but rather "What difference did it make that the courts adopted this interpretation rather than competing ones?" In particular, "How would these programs have developed if the courts had adopted the highly deferential approach characteristic of British and New Deal judges?"

The three programs differ in important ways. AFDC provides income support for poor, single-parent families. States bear half the cost and retain considerable control over benefits and eligibility standards. AFDC was created in 1935 by a little-noted section of the Social Security Act. Controversy erupted in the second half of the 1960s, when the number of recipients grew very rapidly. Although AFDC has always had many critics, they have seldom been able to agree on how to revise the underlying statute.

The food stamp program serves a similar clientele, but has been much more popular than AFDC. The current food stamp program took form in the early 1970s and grew rapidly in that decade. Today it provides benefits to one out of every ten Americans. Unlike AFDC, the food stamp program has nationally uniform eligibility standards and benefits levels. The federal government foots the entire bill.

The program established under the Education for All Handicapped Children Act is run jointly by the state, local, and federal governments. Its clientele is obviously much different from that of AFDC and food stamps, and it provides services rather than cash or scrip. This act was passed during the first year of the post-Watergate Congress. Since 1975 it has ensured each disabled child a "free appropriate public education" based on a written plan worked out by the child's teachers and parents. Despite its cost, special education has developed strong political support both in Congress and in the states.

One of the few thing these three programs have in common is that they have all been affected by statutory rulings of the federal courts. The courts have issued thousands of decisions on eligibility and on benefit levels. But in this respect the three are hardly unusual.

Two sets of questions guide the examination of these cases. The first involves the operation of government institutions: How did the courts affect the balance of power between the states and the federal government, between the Congress and the president, between Congress as a whole and its committees? Is Judge Wald correct when she claims that Scalia's "textualism" is inherently "executive-expanding"? Does heavy reliance on legislative history, as Justice Scalia has argued, threaten to convert "a system of judicial construction into a system of committee-staff prescription"? If different institutional patterns appear in different policy areas, how can one explain the variation?

The second group of questions involves the ideas that have guided the development of welfare policy over the past fifty years. In a number of articles, legal scholars Cass Sunstein and William Eskridge have emphasized that broad "interpretive principles," "background norms," and "public values" have a decisive influence on judges' application of seemingly technical canons of interpretation. To take one of the most obvious examples, the now-discredited canon that "statutes in derogation of the common law are narrowly construed" reflected judges' faith not only in the wisdom of the judiciary, but in laissez-faire economics. Similarly, the rule that judges should impose federal mandates on the states only when Congress makes a "clear statement" to this effect reflects the belief that federalism is a central tenet of the Constitution.

What basic beliefs about the welfare state, the obligations of the government to provide for its needy citizens, and the obligations of citizens to provide for themselves are reflected in court decisions interpreting the AFDC title of the Social Security Act, the Food Stamp Act, and the Education for All Handicapped Children Act? To what extent do members of Congress share these views? How have the assumptions made by members of Congress and judges changed over time? These are some of the questions that will recur in the following chapters.

Judges are adept at hiding their policy choices. Their legitimacy in statutory interpretation cases comes from their claim to know what others—legislators—have already decided or at least previously intended. Legal scholars freely acknowledge the large amount of maneuvering room available to judges but then offer prescriptions that disguise their own policy preferences. After all, those who seek to gain the ear of the judiciary cannot afford to ignore the rules of the game played by judges. The purpose of this book, in contrast, is to highlight rather than obscure the nature of the policy choices embedded in courts' interpretation of statutes. Its goal is not to offer new ammunition to those who must use the canons, but to present a more accurate picture of how American welfare programs have come into being and how public policy is made in our exceptional polity.

CHAPTER TWO

The New Political Context

TWO POLITICAL TRENDS that began in the mid-1960s have had a profound effect on the courts' interpretation of federal statutes. The first is the enormous expansion of the responsibilities of the federal government. After years of deadlock, the national government finally took decisive action to protect the civil rights of black Americans. It also launched a war on poverty, created medicare and medicaid, expanded social security, substantially enlarged its role in education, and initiated massive efforts to protect the environment, improve the lives of the disabled, and promote gender equality. Not only are there many new statutes for the courts to interpret, but these laws touch nearly every aspect of people's lives.

At the same time that American politics was being nationalized, power at the national level was becoming more fragmented than ever. For many years those who favored the creation of the welfare state and a mixed economy believed that centralization of power was a prerequisite of reform. Some hoped to use strong national parties to overcome the effects of federalism and the separation of powers; others pinned their hopes on energetic liberal presidents. Remarkably, this growth of federal responsibilities has gone hand in hand with a *dispersal* of political power rather than a concentration of power in parties or the presidency. Americans "have attempted to articulate and implement the socially transformative policies of an activist, regulatory-welfare state through the legal structures of a reactive, decentralized, nonhierarchical government system."[1]

This dispersal of power is most evident in Congress. In the 1970s subcommittee government replaced the rule of the committee barons.

Then, the popular refrain "Why don't we do it on the floor" began to undercut the authority of the subcommittees.[2] But this is only one part of a larger story. The long-term decline of party structure and party identification led to the proliferation of candidate-centered campaign organizations. The New Deal coalition came apart, and divided government became the norm rather than the exception. Presidents bemoaned their inability to control the rest of the executive branch, and the Supreme Court found it increasingly difficult to give direction to the rest of the federal judiciary. Interest groups multiplied, and the power of peak associations declined. Even the big three television networks saw their influence decline when modern technology created new sources of information and entertainment.

No longer could presidents cut deals with committee leaders and expect everyone else to go along. No longer could the inhabitants of cozy subgovernments work their will without outside interference. A variety of new actors demanded to be included in the writing of legislation and stood ready to file suit if displeased by the way agencies carried out new programs. This not only increased the number of cases before the courts, but also made it more difficult for judges to determine what had been agreed upon by increasingly individualistic legislators.

The federal judiciary both contributed to these developments and was affected by them. The courts played a leading role in enlarging the responsibilities of the federal government. Constitutional rulings on segregation and other forms of racial discrimination helped place civil rights on the national agenda. Before *Roe* v. *Wade*, abortion was considered an issue for the states, not the federal government. Thereafter abortion was an issue national officials could not ignore (much as many of them tried). The federal courts were also the first to set national standards for state mental hospitals, prisons, and institutions for the retarded.

During the 1970s and 1980s the federal courts exhibited the same factiousness that characterized other public institutions. The Burger Court put an end to some of the experiments of the Warren court, but was unable to establish any clear themes of its own. The internally divided Supreme Court had great difficulty controlling the 800 members of the federal lower courts, many of whom had been weaned on the activism of the Warren court. Supreme Court justices who could not agree on constitutional issues found they could at times reach a compromise by adopting an innovative reading of statutory language. And lower court judges discovered that the Supreme Court would be less likely to

scrutinize and overrule their interpretations of statutes than their interpretations of the Constitution. In this way, dynamics internal to the
judiciary reinforced the external forces pushing statutory interpretation
onto center stage.

In recent years a substantial body of scholarly work has examined
what has variously been called "the new American political system," the
"new politics of public policy," and the "remaking of American politics."[3] This literature describes in great detail the institutional changes
mentioned above. The purpose of this chapter is to examine how these
many changes have affected the nature of federal statutes and the behavior of the judges who interpret them.

Civil Rights and the Expanded Agenda

Before World War II, few Americans paid income tax. The social
security withholding tax was so small as to be virtually invisible politically. Well into the 1960s few people—even retirees—relied entirely on
entitlements. Before 1970 business people did not have OSHA and EPA
to kick around. James Q. Wilson has observed:

> Once politics was about only a few things; today, it is about nearly every-
> thing. . . . Once the "legitimacy barrier" has fallen, political conflict takes a
> very different form. New programs need not await the advent of a crisis or an
> extraordinary majority, because no program is any longer "new"—it is seen,
> rather, as an extension, a modification, or an enlargement of something the
> government is already doing. . . . Since there is virtually nothing the govern-
> ment has not tried to do, there is little it cannot be asked to do.[4]

When Tip O'Neill entered the House of Representatives in 1952 it was no
doubt still true that "all politics is local." By the time he stepped down
from his position as Speaker, the aphorism was an anachronism.

For the first 175 years of the American Republic, nothing did more to
balkanize American politics and to frustrate efforts to expand the scope
of government than the issue of race. From the writing of the Constitution to the filibuster against the 1964 Civil Rights Act, the slogan of
states' rights was invoked to allow the South to perpetuate first slavery
and then an oppressive racial caste system. In 1964 the federal government finally committed itself to eliminating discrimination in education,
private employment, and public accommodations. A year later Congress
adopted the Voting Rights Act, which intruded even more deeply on

traditional state functions. In two short years the political logic of race had been reversed: previously objections from southerners had prevented the federal government from touching matters—such as education and welfare—with racial implications; now race became the rationale for federal control of the most fundamental elements of state government—including election laws and spending patterns. Once this imposing threshold had been passed, further policy breakthroughs—including environmental and consumer protection and recognition of the rights of women, the handicapped, the elderly, and linguistic minorities—came more easily.

Those who had for years opposed expansion of the federal role saw their power dwindle. The roots of the congressional reforms of the 1970s lay in the civil rights battles of the 1960s. The decline of the "control" committees in the House began with Speaker Sam Rayburn's efforts to stack the Rules Committee, which for years had been a graveyard of civil rights bills and other liberal initiatives. The same distrust of the southern committee barons that led proponents of the 1964 Civil Rights Act to bypass James Eastland's Judiciary Committee culminated in a thoroughgoing attack on the Senate's inner club and on the authority of committee chairmen. The remarkable surge in black voting that followed in the wake of the Voting Rights Act eventually replaced old-time segregationists like Eastland and House Rules Committee Chairman "Judge" Smith with congressmen who owed their election to a coalition of blacks and liberal-to-moderate white Democrats. Southern Democrats lost their predominance within the Democratic party and at the same time came to look much more like their counterparts from the North and the West.

Conservative southern Democrats also lost influence in the national party's presidential nomination process. The effort to oust "lily white" southern delegations was the beginning of repeated moves by the national Democratic party both to establish its control over state and local parties and to open up the nominating process to racial minorities, women, the young, and others. With only two exceptions—southern governors Jimmy Carter and Bill Clinton—the nominees produced by the reformed system fared poorly in the South and lost the general elections. Starting in 1964, the solid South became solidly Republican in presidential elections. Thus the same factors that helped northern and western liberals gain control of Congress allowed Republicans to capture the White House on a regular basis.

The Civil Rights Act was in part a political ratification of the Supreme Court's decision in *Brown* v. *Board of Education*. The fact that school desegregation did not begin in earnest in the Deep South until 1967 exposed the courts' weakness in implementing their decisions. But the fact that the Supreme Court had dared to take a stand while others dithered gave the judiciary a moral stature that few other institutions could match. It also convinced many judges that they had the capacity to tackle tough problems not resolved by other institutions.

If *Brown* set the standard for the courts, the National Association for the Advancement of Colored People (NAACP) and its enormously successful litigation strategy set the standard for a multitude of newly organized public interest groups. The disabled, welfare rights activists, consumer advocates, environmentalists, and pro-choice groups all saw the advantages of presenting their positions in terms of rights and of using litigation as a central (but seldom exclusive) element of their political strategy.

The legislation enacted after 1964 reflects these political patterns. Not surprisingly, a variety of new laws were modeled on the 1964 Civil Rights Act. These include the 1968 Fair Housing Law, section 504 of the Rehabilitation Act of 1972, the 1990 Americans with Disabilities Act, the Education for All Handicapped Children Act, title IX of the Education Amendments of 1972, the Age Discrimination Act, and the Pregnancy Discrimination Act. One characteristic of these laws is that they grant substantial discretion to the federal courts to define discrimination and to devise appropriate remedies.

Many other laws passed during these sessions of Congress sought to open up the political and administrative processes to allow participation by unconventional groups. Prominent examples include the "maximum feasible participation" requirement of the 1964 Economic Opportunity Act; the Freedom of Information Act; the National Environmental Policy Act, which required an environmental impact statement for major federal projects; the Moss-Magnuson Warranty—Federal Trade Commission Improvement Act, which provided "intervenor funding" for consumer groups; and the Civil Rights Attorneys Fees Awards Act. Too numerous to mention were the new laws that placed new strings on the states' use of federal grants or that created mandates the states must carry out regardless of whether they receive federal funds. In 1963 the federal government stood by while many states clearly and continually violated the Fifteenth

Amendment by disenfranchising black citizens. Fifteen years later it insisted that old, financially strapped cities install elevators for the handicapped in existing subway systems.[5] There had indeed been an enormous change in the role of the federal government.

Divided Government and the New Factionalism

The link between presidential leadership and expansion of the national agenda was never more apparent than in 1964–65 when Lyndon Johnson, consciously modeling himself on Franklin Roosevelt, achieved legislative successes that rivaled those of FDR's first one hundred days and second New Deal. Yet by 1967 LBJ's relations with Congress had soured, and the next year marked the beginning of more than two decades of divided government. Before 1968 only one president had come into office with the opposition party in control of both houses of Congress. In contrast, Presidents Richard Nixon, Gerald Ford, and George Bush never saw Republican control over either house. Despite the fact that the GOP held the presidency for twenty-eight of the forty years between 1952 and 1992, it has not held a majority in the House since 1954, and it held a slight lead in the Senate for only six of those years. Divided government, in short, was a prominent feature of American politics during the second half of the twentieth century.

Remarkably, this period of divided government included years of frenetic legislative activity. In the late 1960s and early 1970s Congress restructured itself to improve its capacity to produce new initiatives without the cooperation of the president. Northern and western liberals had become the dominant force within the Democratic party in Congress just as the party was losing control of the executive branch. Led by the Democratic Study Group, they sought both to break the power of the conservative coalition within Congress and to regain many of the powers Congress had ceded to the president since 1932.[6]

The most important change in Congress was the increase in the number, power, autonomy, and staff of its subcommittees. Already a decentralized institution, Congress became even more decentralized. Only this time it was the younger, more entrepreneurial members, not their more conservative adversaries, who controlled the key units. Efforts to make these powerful subcommittees representative of Congress as a whole were abandoned as each member sought a piece of the action and was allowed to choose the type of action he or she favored. The influence of the more cautious and balanced "insider" committees, especially Appropriations, declined. Using subcommittee resources, members initiated new programs and revised old ones, challenging the president for the title of "chief legislator." No longer would Congress write vague legislation asking the executive to "do something." Now it was writing detailed statutes that frequently deviated significantly from the president's program.

Federal administrators often found themselves caught between the competing demands of congressional subcommittees who had fought for new legislation and officials in the White House and the Office of Management and Budget who had opposed it. Virtually all the environmental and consumer protection legislation of the 1970s was the product of congressional initiation. The same was true of programs for the disabled. Republican presidents tried to reduce spending on entitlements, the Democratic Congress to expand it. In a variety of policy areas Democrats in Congress advocated putting more strings on grants to the states, while Republican presidents argued for converting categorical grants into block grants with fewer federal requirements. Program advocates on subcommittees insisted that administrators should not just comply with the letter of their newly minted statutes, but should also be guided by the spirit envisioned by the legislation's principal sponsors.

Convinced that administrators were more loyal to congressional committees than to the White House, President Nixon strengthened the Office of Management and Budget (OMB) and selected subcabinet officials on the basis of ideological consistency with the administration. Ronald Reagan later perfected the administrative mechanisms introduced by Nixon. For both, the goal of the administrative presidency was clear: to ensure that the bureaucracy would take its orders from the White House, not congressional subcommittees.[7]

Members of Congress in turn scrambled to find new methods of ensuring agency fidelity to their conception of legislative intent. The Congressional Budget and Impoundment Control Act of 1974 put an end to unilateral presidential impoundments, which had constituted the most obvious and painful attack on congressional power. It replaced permanent, open-ended authorizations with detailed, short-term authorizations. Committees with jurisdiction over regulatory programs struggled for years to limit OMB review of agency rules. Committees increased their oversight activities, held more hearings, issued more reports, hired more staff, and created inspectors general within executive departments.[8]

Congress enacted more than 250 legislative vetoes—and continued to do so even after the Supreme Court had ruled them unconstitutional.[9]

These changes in Congress reflect a broader weakening of integrative forces in American politics. Most obvious is the decline of political parties. Rampant ticket splitting has attenuated the ties between the legislative and executive branches. Recognizing that parties can do little to help them, members of Congress have developed their own campaign organizations and personal electoral bases. Similarly, umbrella organizations such as the AFL-CIO, the American Farm Bureau Federation, and the Chamber of Commerce have lost a good deal of their political influence as the number and activity of single-issue groups, trade associations, and professional organizations have increased. Not only do "peak associations no longer guide the process," but once-dominant groups such as the American Medical Association no longer exercise "quasi-monopoly powers" over particular policies.[10] This means that few groups can cast a *liberum veto*, and that majorities must constantly be built anew. In the words of Robert Dole, "Putting a majority together is like a one-armed man wrapping cranberries: You can't get them all in the wrap."[11] The process is time-consuming, unpredictable, and fraught with political perils.[12]

Fragmentation of power and legislative-executive conflict made the task of creating coherent public policy agonizingly difficult just as the demand for policy integration was on the rise. Hugh Heclo's term "policy congestion" aptly describes the effect of the accumulation of government responsibilities:

> The point is not simply that the federal government is doing more things, but that it is doing more things that affect one another. . . . During the 1960s sensitivity to the interrelatedness of issues began to increase—poverty problems and economic management; civil rights and the workings of labor markets and educational bureaucracies; housing and transportation programs, financial markets, and urban decay. Crowding onto the public agenda during the 1970s were issues—energy, inflation, economic revitalization—with even more intense crosscutting qualities.[13]

Boundaries between programs dissolved. Agencies whose mission was to promote economic development and energy independence suddenly had to protect the environment as well. School systems were not just to teach reading, writing, and arithmetic, but to promote integration, provide services for the disabled, and guarantee equal treatment of male and female students.

On several occasions Congress clearly proved itself incapable of establishing coherent policy—most notably energy policy in the 1970s and the budget in the 1980s. Members of Congress are highly responsive to their constituencies, which on these matters have divergent interests. To add to the problem, many of the new issues the federal government has had to face cut across committee jurisdictions. Although Congress has experimented with mechanisms for coordinating policymaking by its committees and subcommittees, these efforts to centralize power seldom sit well with rank-and-file members, who for years have sought to seize and protect a piece of the action. Just as tinkering with the rules of the presidential nomination process has done little to make the national political parties more autonomous, influential, or united, so the refining of congressional rules has only marginally ameliorated the fragmentation of authority that has been taking place for the past twenty-five years.

Implications for the Design of Statutes

All these political changes have left their mark on federal statutes. For example, legislation enacted in recent years presents a strange amalgam of specificity and ambiguity. On the one hand, many of these statutes follow the New Deal pattern of leaving key terms undefined and delegating policymaking responsibility to others. The core of the Education for All Handicapped Children Act, for example, is the requirement that states provide every handicapped child with a "free appropriate public education." What does this mean? Neither the act nor rules published by the Department of Education provide much guidance. In practice, content is provided by state and local officials and federal judges. The Clean Air Act directs the Environmental Protection Agency to establish air quality standards that "protect the public health with an adequate margin of safety." Many other regulatory statutes require the installation of "available" and "feasible" control technology. Section 504 of the Rehabilitation Act of 1973 declares that "no otherwise qualified handicapped individual . . . shall solely by reason of his handicap . . . be subject to discrimination under any program or activity receiving Federal financial assistance." Judges, legislators, administrators, and advocates for the disabled have spent years arguing about what "otherwise qualified," "solely by reason of his handicap," "discrimination," and even "program" mean in this context.

Resolving such issues is never easy in a legislative body lacking central-ized authority. Diffusion of power in Congress has at times amplified the body's tendency to paper over disagreements. Policy entrepreneurs in Congress often resort to broad legislative mandates with powerful sym-bolic appeal but little more.[14] In addition, many of the complex issues now before the federal government seem to defy codification. Some of the most important bureaucratic tasks—such as teaching students, conduct-ing relations with foreign countries, and maintaining order in urban areas—simply cannot be achieved by following general rules.[15]

On the other hand, the statutes passed since the 1960s tend to be much more detailed than those passed during the New Deal. In the 1930s Congress was willing to say to the president, "Here's the problem, now go solve it." But certainly the 93d Congress did not show the same confidence in Richard Nixon, nor the 100th in Ronald Reagan. The new regulatory statutes included specific procedures, deadlines, and perfor-mance standards. A study completed in 1985 found that fifteen federal environmental statutes contained a total of 328 deadlines for regulatory action, most of which applied to the Environmental Protection Agency.[16] The same statute that fails to say what constitutes "safe" air quality also states that in some rural areas sulfur dioxide increases shall not exceed an annual arithmetic mean of two micrograms per cubic meter.[17] As the case studies in this book demonstrate, entitlement law grew in length and specificity as programs underwent periodic reauthorization. Critics of Congress used to fault it for excessive delegation of authority to the executive. Now they routinely attack Congress's "micromanagement."

In some instances members of Congress are simply looking for new ways to "bring home the bacon" to the constituents whom they so assiduously court. But the hundreds of rules, procedures, deadlines, and other specifications contained in these laws also reflect the profound distrust that has characterized relations between the executive and legisla-tive branches of government. By writing detailed, ambitious, even utopian statutes, the members of Congress could take credit for new programs, place their own mark on policymaking, and blame the president for failing to produce clean air or to protect the rights of the disabled.

Another characteristic of post-1964 statutes is that they place more demands on the states than had previous federal laws. For many years federal grants provided money for those types of projects the states already wanted to undertake. Federal requirements were few, and those that existed were ignored as often as enforced. "Over the past two decades," the Advisory Commission on Intergovernmental Relations reported in 1984, "there has been a dramatic shift in the way in which the federal government deals with states and localities." While Congress continued to fund traditional subsidy programs (at least until the Reagan years), it also created "new, more intrusive, and more compulsory *regulatory* programs."[18] One leading student of federalism writes "that the new regulation has brought with it a spirit of coercion markedly different from the cooperative attitudes thought to be more characteristic of American intergovernmental relations."[19]

These new regulatory controls have taken several forms. Some are direct orders backed by the threat of civil and criminal penalties, such as the ban on employment discrimination by state and local governments and the prohibition on ocean dumping of sewage sludge by cities. A second form is the crosscutting requirement that attaches new conditions to all federal grants, as seen in title VI of the Civil Rights Act, which prohibits racial discrimination in any federally funded program. A third type of control, crossover sanctions, threatens to revoke funding in one program (for example, highway funds) if the state refuses to comply with federal policy in another (for example, environmental standards). Still another regulatory strategy, partial preemption, allows states to administer particular programs, but requires them to abide by federal standards. Having taken on these program responsibilities, the states are arguably required to carry out all the tasks mandated by the federal government.

The enforcement mechanism most readily available to federal administrators, the funding cutoff, has seldom proved to be effective. Years of experience have demonstrated that injunctions issued by the federal courts are much more likely to bring states into compliance with federal rules. Many of the statutes regulating state and local governments fail to make clear, however, whether they authorize private parties to file suit to enforce federal rules. Contributing to the uncertainty over the extent of federal and judicial authority is the fact that for years congressional Democrats have advocated greater federal control and Republican presidents have sought to reduce the number of federal strings. This means that when judges resolve disputes over the extent of judicial authority and the content of federal mandates, they are usually arbitrating disputes between Congress and the White House, between Democrats and Republicans.

Many recent laws also reflect the layering and overlap that springs from policy congestion. Perhaps the best example is the National Environmental Policy Act, which tries to force such agencies as the Corps of Engineers, the Bureau of Land Management, and the Federal Highway Administration to think about the environmental consequences of their actions. The same is true of the Endangered Species Act. Sometimes rules established in one program (for example, the food stamp program rule that all government benefits be counted as income) conflict with the goals of another program (for example, the effort of the low-income energy assistance program to increase the purchasing power of poor people with high fuel costs). As programs collide, so do federal bureaucracies and congressional committees. Although federal agencies are barred from suing one another, private parties usually find ways to bring such disputes to court. Federal judges must then try to sort out the conflicting legislative mandates. As policy congestion increases, judges assume the role of traffic cop.

Finally, Congress has become more inclined to encourage litigation in a number of ways. The Voting Rights Act, the Endangered Species Act, the Clean Air Act, the Federal Water Pollution Control Act, the Energy Policy and Conservation Act, the Noise Control Act, and the Futures Trading Act all explicitly authorize suits by private parties to enforce regulatory requirements. The Toxic Substances Control Act, the Consumer Product Safety Act, and the Occupational Safety and Health Act create liberal standing requirements for those challenging agency rules.[20] In 1988 Congress finally repealed a provision that for more than fifty years had precluded judicial review of benefits determinations by the Veterans Administration. Congress has also expanded the availability of attorneys' fees, reduced jurisdictional requirements, and protected the Legal Services Corporation from White House attacks. If New Deal statutes tended to insulate agencies from judicial review, more recent laws have encouraged the courts to take a "hard look" at administrative decisions. Clearly, many members of Congress and interest groups consider litigation a normal and at times beneficial part of the policymaking process.

At the same time, House, Senate, and conference reports—the most important parts of the legislative histories examined by courts—have grown longer and more detailed. For example, the House report on the 1977 amendments to the Food Stamp Act was 860 pages long and contained advice on such matters as how late intake offices should be open and which court decisions had identified the proper method for counting the income of migrant workers. The House report on the 1990

Clean Air Act is nearly 700 pages long and no less detailed. The young staffers who have filled one new office building after another have written elaborate floor statements, staff reports, and dissenting views for their bosses. The primary audience of these statements has not been judges but administrators who usually have first crack at determining congressional intent. But everyone knows that if litigation does ensue—as it so often has—it will never hurt to have one's policy preferences displayed prominently in the record.

A Judiciary in Flux

A number of years ago Robert Dahl argued that "the policy views dominant on the Court will never be out of line for very long with the policy views dominant among the law-making majorities of the United States. . . . It would be most unrealistic," he explained, "to suppose that the Court would, for more than a few years at most, stand against any major alternatives sought by a law-making majority."[21] According to Dahl, the constitutional crisis of 1937 was mainly a result of Roosevelt's "unusually bad luck." FDR did not appoint a justice until his fifth year in office. Once vacancies began to appear, FDR turned the "nine old men" into the "Roosevelt court," which quickly ratified and eventually enlarged the New Deal.

While Dahl's argument is not without its flaws, it serves to highlight a peculiarity of the past twenty-five years: there is no dominant "law-making majority" capable of giving definition to the judiciary.[22] The "Reagan revolution" may have sounded the death knell of the New Deal coalition, but no lasting Republican majority emerged. Nowhere is this more evident than in the appointment of Supreme Court justices. If the bitter struggle over the nominations of Robert Bork and Clarence Thomas has shown anything, it is that Republican presidents and Democratic senators have much different views on the meaning of the Constitution and the proper role of the courts.

Over the past two decades the federal judiciary has mirrored the political system as a whole in an important way: it is seriously divided internally. As Martin Shapiro has pointed out, Chief Justices Warren Burger and William Rehnquist "could not muster sufficient troops to create a dominant new bloc of Republican appointees even if they had been sure what to do with it." As a result, "no central value emerged to replace the Warren Court's eroded but far from eliminated commitment to equality."[23] In addition, many lower court judges embraced the Warren court's style of activism just as Republican presidents were appointing to the bench more proponents of judicial restraint. As a result, some courts of appeal have become even more fractious than the Supreme Court.[24] In this context statutory interpretation became a particularly useful judicial tool: not only did it provide a means of keeping alive the reform impulse of the Warren era, but it offered a mechanism for forging compromises between activists and proponents of judicial restraint.

The Supreme Court: From Crusading Reform to Ad Hoc Balancing

The Warren court (1953–69) was a period of unprecedented judicial innovation. From desegregation to reapportionment, from freedom of speech to rights of the accused, from the "due process revolution" to prayer in school, the Court used "constitutional adjudication . . . [as] an instrument of reform."[25] Critics and supporters agreed that for the Warren court reform usually meant the pursuit of equality. This was particularly clear on matters related to race. Reform also meant increasing the political power of a variety of groups previously excluded from the political process and reducing the effect of disparities in wealth.

Before 1937 judicial activism almost always meant restricting the power of government. Now it required more aggressive government action, especially at the federal level. Federal courts restructured a wide variety of state and local institutions, including schools, prisons, housing authorities, and mental hospitals. In doing so they expanded rather than narrowed the responsibilities of government. In its "commitment to the centralization of governmental authority," the Warren court "moved farther and faster than any Court that came before it."[26]

The innovations of the Warren court were by no means confined to constitutional law. It adopted an aggressive, antibigness reading of the Sherman Antitrust Act, called for greater judicial scrutiny of administrative agencies, and expanded the jurisdiction of the courts. These new policies were cheered by some and condemned by others. But no one could question their sweep or their boldness.

Richard Nixon was one of the few presidents to make criticism of the Supreme Court a major campaign theme. His successor, Gerald Ford, had led the effort to impeach Justice William Douglas. Although Presidents Nixon and Ford appointed five men to the Supreme Court, they only partly succeeded in changing the direction of the federal judiciary. The Burger court retreated somewhat on the constitutional rights of the accused and the definition of protected speech, and it refused to use the equal protection clause to create substantive welfare rights, to restructure state financing of education, or to require city-to-suburb busing. Yet it was also the Burger court that decided *Roe* v. *Wade,* presided over extensive court-ordered busing in the North as well as the South, made gender a "semi-suspect classification," broadened the rights of religious dissenters, placed a lengthy moratorium on capital punishment, and expanded or approved a variety of affirmative action programs.

The mixed nature of the Burger court's rulings reflected the fact that the Burger court lacked a continuing, coherent majority. Coalitions shifted from year to year and from one issue to another. According to Vincent Blasi, the "rootless activism of the Burger Court" arose from the judicial style and pivotal voting position of the Court's centrists:

[A] curious dynamic has governed the fashioning of constitutional doctrine. Normally, the intellectual leadership of a court comes from the extremes. The "swing" justices typically determine how the cases come out, but not what important new ideas emerge from those cases. . . . The Burger Court's activism, however, has been generated as well as moderated by the pragmatic men of the center. That activism has been inspired not by a commitment to fundamental constitutional principles or noble political ideals, but rather by the belief that modest injections of logic and compassion by disinterested, sensible judges can serve as a counterforce to some of the excesses and irrationalities of contemporary government decision-making. In other words, in the hands of the Burger Court judicial activism has become a centrist philosophy—dominant, transcending most ideological divisions, but essentially pragmatic in nature, lacking a central theme or an agenda.[27]

For this Court, policymaking through statutory interpretation had special appeal. Giving new meaning to federal statutes seems more cautious, more pragmatic, and more politically prudent than explicit constitutional innovation. It allows judges to deal with social or political problems without resorting to sweeping pronouncements about the requirements of equal protection and due process. It avoids open and prolonged confrontation with elected officials. If the decision proves more controversial than expected or if unintended consequences appear, then Congress can always change the law. As Donald Horowitz has put it, "Judges who recoil at innovation in constitutional lawmaking may not see the same dangers at all in the interpretation of statutes."[28] The justices could thus continue to pursue reform while responding to their critics' calls for greater judicial caution.

The shift toward statutory construction also made coalition building easier within the Court. Pragmatic centrists such as Justices Lewis Powell, John Paul Stevens, Byron White, and Potter Stewart could often garner the votes of Justices William Brennan, Thurgood Marshall, and William Douglas by pointing to the policy consequences of their opinions. At the same time, they could placate Chief Justice Burger or Justice Rehnquist by refusing to break new constitutional ground—or even overruling lower courts that did. The result was a hodgepodge of policies and canons of interpretation, a reflection of the style and the internal divisions of the Court.

With the appointment of Justices Sandra Day O'Connor, Antonin Scalia, Anthony Kennedy, David Souter, and Clarence Thomas, the Supreme Court has begun to shift once again. The Rehnquist court has not just whittled away at *Roe* v. *Wade* and the rights of the accused but has at times adopted a narrow reading of civil rights statutes, instructed the lower courts to show more deference toward federal administrators, and demonstrated renewed interest in protecting the autonomy of state governments. But, as subsequent chapters show, the Supreme Court remains divided—and inconsistent—on many issues. The absence of clear directives from the Supreme Court vests substantial discretion in the lower courts, which decide the vast majority of cases on the meaning of particular federal laws.

The Restive Lower Courts

The scholarly attention lavished on the Warren court has obscured the fact that the reform impulse was as strong in the district and circuit courts as in the Supreme Court. Judges of the Fifth Circuit spearheaded the desegregation of southern schools and initiated extensive busing. The Supreme Court responded with a rather confused nod of the head. District court judges such as Frank Johnson of Alabama, author of the influential *Wyatt* v. *Stickney* decision, broke new ground in defining the rights of the institutionalized and the disabled.[29] These district court judges were particularly active in experimenting with complex remedial decrees designed to overhaul prisons, housing projects, schools, and mental health facilities.[30] The "reformation" of American administrative law was largely a product of the Court of Appeals for the District of

Columbia Circuit. In this area the Supreme Court's major contribution was to issue an occasional (and ineffective) reprimand to the circuit court for going too far.[31] The Supreme Court, in short, did not impose a new legal order on a staid judicial branch. Often it merely ratified or silently condoned changes initiated by the lower courts.

If the Supreme Court was becoming more cautious and more centrist during the 1970s, the lower courts seemed to be moving in the opposite direction. The reason for this is not clear. Most likely, changes in legal education, coupled with the moral force of such landmark cases as *Brown* v. *Board, Reynolds* v. *Sims, Gideon* v. *Wainwright,* and *Griswold* v. *Connecticut,* altered the legal culture in fundamental ways. The politics of the appointment process also had its effect. Presidents Nixon and Ford made less effort to change the ideological composition of the lower courts than of the Supreme Court, usually leaving nominations of lower court judges to Republican senators. President Carter appointed no members of the Supreme Court, but he placed 264 judges on the federal bench—more than any president until Reagan. Carter's appointments were, if anything, even more committed to an active, reformist judiciary than those on the bench before 1969. The Reagan administration was much more aware of the importance of the lower courts than were previous Republican administrations. It was intent upon appointing conservatives to the lower courts and generally succeeded in doing so. More than half of all federal judges are now Reagan or Bush appointees. As a result, the "appeals courts have become judicial battlegrounds, with ideological warfare waged between conservative Reagan-Bush appointees and their more liberal Carter colleagues."[32]

A divided Supreme Court that sits atop a judicial branch of 800 strong-willed judges and decides fewer than 150 cases a year cannot hope to control every area of the law. It did not require much astuteness for lower court judges to realize that their decisions would receive less scrutiny from the Supreme Court if they relied on statutory rather than constitutional arguments. Four justices of the Supreme Court would undoubtedly grant *certiorari* to review a lower court decision establishing a constitutional right to an adequate diet. But how many justices would notice or care if a circuit court read the Food Stamp Act to guarantee a "right to an adequately nutritious diet"? In 1975 the answer was none.[33] The Supreme Court might eventually accept a Food Stamp Act case if there was a continuing split among the circuit courts or if the solicitor general complained of a particularly objectionable pattern of statutory interpretation. But this could well take years, by which time the new policy would already be established. Simply put, by relying on statutory interpretation lower court judges can substantially increase their autonomy.

Nor was this lesson lost on the new types of litigants who appeared in the 1960s and 1970s. Civil rights groups had fared well during the Warren years. Scores of new groups, many of them sponsored by private foundations and funded in part by the federal government, followed their example of using litigation to achieve policy change. Lawyers working for organizations such as the NAACP Legal Defense Fund, the Natural Resource Defense Council, the American Civil Liberties Union, the Food Research and Action Center, the National Association for Retarded Citizens, and the Legal Services Corporation are sophisticated repeat players with long-range litigational strategies. Since they are often the party initiating litigation, they have the opportunity to engage in forum shopping to argue before the most sympathetic judges. These groups were well aware of the risks of Supreme Court review, especially on constitutional issues. They adapted their arguments to the new judicial terrain, stressing statutory rather than constitutional arguments and putting more emphasis on winning a string of cases in the lower courts than one big case in the Supreme Court.

The new politics of the post-1965 era placed new demands on the federal courts. Not only did statutes increase in number and complexity, but policy congestion and a restructuring of state-federal relations led many participants to look to the courts for help. Increased access to the legislative process, heightened legislative-executive conflict, rampant distrust of administrative expertise, frequent disagreements among federal agencies, and unprecedented federal regulation of the states all made the task of interpretation a daunting one. At the same time, statutory interpretation offered new opportunities to judges wary of constitutional experimentation but eager to do good.

CHAPTER THREE

The Law of Entitlements

Receipt of welfare benefits may not at the present time constitute the exercise of a constitutional right. But among our Constitution's expressed purposes was the desire to "insure domestic tranquility" and "promote the general Welfare." Implicit in those phrases are certain basic concepts of humanity and decency. One of these, voiced as a goal in recent years by most responsible governmental leaders, both federal and state, is the desire to insure that indigent, unemployable citizens will at least have the bare minimums required for existence without which our expressed fundamental constitutional rights and liberties frequently cannot be exercised and therefore become meaningless.
—Federal District Court Judge Walter R. Mansfield in
Rothstein v. Wyman, 1969

NOTHING ILLUSTRATES the expansion of federal responsibilities better than spending on entitlements. Between 1965 and 1990 the cost of social security (including old age, survivors, and disability insurance) rose from $17 billion to $250 billion. Spending for medicare and medicaid soared from zero to $150 billion. The combined cost of aid to families with dependent children, food stamps, and supplemental security income was $3 billion in 1965 and $40 billion in 1990. The share of the federal budget devoted to these programs doubled during this period, from 17 percent to 35 percent. In 1965 their total cost was 2.9 percent of GNP; by 1990 it was 8.1 percent. The entitlement budget is now half again the size of the defense budget and twice as large as the total for domestic discretionary spending.[1]

This spending growth has engendered substantial political conflict. In the 1970s Presidents Nixon and Ford vetoed unprecedented numbers of spending bills and repeatedly accused Congress of fiscal irresponsibility. Congress overrode many of these vetoes, limited the president's ability to impound appropriated funds, and in 1974 established a new budget process designed to establish congressional budget priorities. In 1981 Ronald Reagan persuaded Congress to approve controversial spending cuts and even larger tax cuts, which produced a deficit that has shaped political debate in Washington for the past decade.

Budget politics played a central role in the reconstruction of Congress described in chapter 2. Liberals sought to expand domestic programs by strengthening authorizing committees—which tend to be dominated by program advocates—and weakening the more conservative appropriations committees. No longer would authorizing committees rest content to pass broad, ambiguous legislation, trusting the president and his subordinates to fill in the details and allowing the economy-minded appropriations committees to set budget ceilings. Now, authorizing committees insisted on writing legislation that would not just *permit* new expenditures but *mandate* payments to all eligible individuals and subnational governments. Once an entitlement statute is enacted, administrators cannot refuse to spend the specified funds, nor can an appropriations bill set spending ceilings that reduce the obligations of the government. Spending totals, in fact, are never chosen, but result from millions of individual eligibility determinations. According to the Congressional Budget Act, since "entitlements constitute a binding obligation on the part of the Federal Government," "eligible recipients have *legal* recourse if the obligation is not fulfilled."[2]

At the same time that Congress and the president were creating new programs, expanding eligibility, and raising benefits, the federal courts were rewriting judicial doctrines on entitlements. In its most famous decision on the subject, *Goldberg* v. *Kelly*, the Supreme Court announced, "It may be realistic today to regard welfare entitlements as more like 'property' than a 'gratuity.' " According to Justice William Brennan's opinion,

> We have come to recognize that forces not within the control of the poor contribute to their poverty. . . . Welfare, by meeting the basic demands of subsistence, can help bring within the reach of the poor the same opportunities that are available to others to participate meaningfully in the life of the community.[3]

In *Goldberg* the Court ruled that the Constitution requires due process hearings before the termination of welfare benefits. In another well-known case, *Shapiro* v. *Thompson*, the Court held that state residency requirements for welfare programs violate the Constitution.[4] The courts have struck down eligibility restrictions related to gender, illegitimacy, and marital status.[5]

These constitutional rulings were the most visible part of a broader development. Before 1966 the Supreme Court rarely heard cases on entitlements. Over the next eight years the Court decided thirty-nine cases on income transfer programs. Many of these were brought by the newly created Legal Services Program, which won a remarkable 62 percent of its cases.[6] Almost half of these Supreme Court decisions were based on statutory construction. During the same period lower courts decided hundreds of entitlement cases, resolving the bulk of them through statutory interpretation.

In the late 1960s the Warren court seemed to be moving toward an interpretation of the due process and equal protection clauses of the Fourteenth Amendment that would create a substantive constitutional right to welfare. The Burger court quickly put an end to this constitutional experimentation.[7] But the federal court continued to issue innovative rulings on federal jurisdiction, legal remedies, and the meaning of particular statutes. These statutory decisions not only expanded the role of the courts in reviewing federal and state policies but broadened eligibility standards and raised benefit levels for many programs.

The Demise of the Rights–Privilege Distinction?

That a sea change occurred in the courts' treatment of welfare programs during the second half of the 1960s is widely recognized. According to the conventional wisdom, this shift can be attributed to the new understanding of "rights" and "privileges" laid out in *Goldberg* v. *Kelly*. The story—repeated frequently in the legal literature—runs as follows. Before the mid-1960s common law property received extensive judicial protection, but government largess such as driver's licenses, public employment, social security checks, and public housing was treated as privileges that could be granted or withheld as legislators and administrators saw fit. As citizens became more dependent on government benefits, arbitrary denial of these privileges threatened to undermine personal autonomy and security. Consequently, the courts expanded their concept of property to include government benefits. Judges required agencies to conduct due process hearings before depriving citizens of this "new property," and they prevented the government from imposing restrictions on First Amendment rights as a condition of receiving government benefits. Just as important, judges carefully scrutinized the eligibility rules and benefit levels of programs to ensure they were consistent with statutory provisions. Courts and commentators announced the "demise of the rights-privilege distinction" and all danced on its grave.[8]

This commonly offered explanation suffers from two serious flaws. First, in entitlement cases, the rights-privilege distinction never had much of a life before its alleged death. It was applied almost exclusively to public employment cases. There was nothing particularly novel in the assertion that citizens denied promised benefits should have redress in court. Throughout the nineteenth century the federal courts heard cases on veterans' pensions and land grants, occasionally issuing writs of mandamus requiring administrators to deliver the contested benefits. After World War I the courts became heavily involved in the war risk insurance program, expanding benefits far beyond those initially granted by administrators. The 1935 Social Security Act not only allowed disappointed claimants to challenge administrative rulings in court but waived the usual $10,000 jurisdictional requirement.[9] Indeed, the idea that social security benefits should be paid as a matter of right was a guiding tenet of the system. In the words of Arthur Altmeyer, long-time commissioner of social security and one of the program's founding fathers, "Because of contributions there were certain rights, statutory rights, that had to be recognized and achieved, and we had an obligation [to pay them]."[10]

During the 1940s and 1950s the federal courts heard hundreds of social security cases. Typically, the claimant would argue that the board's reading of "covered employment," "widow," or "fully insured individual" was too narrow. With monotonous frequency the courts upheld the board. What is most striking about these cases is not the deference to agency expertise—this was a staple of New Deal jurisprudence—but the lack of any reference to the "rights-privilege distinction."[11]

The second problem with the conventional argument is that it seriously exaggerates the extent to which statutes clearly delineate the boundaries of the "new property" discovered and protected by the courts. In the disability insurance controversy mentioned in chapter 1, the courts ruled that recipients remain eligible for benefits unless the Social Security Administration can demonstrate "medical improvement," a requirement that did not appear in the statute at the time. Similarly, in a large number of cases the courts interpreted the AFDC section of the Social Security Act to invalidate state eligibility requirements not explicitly authorized by federal law. Not only did the courts have no statutory basis for this policy, but they reversed an assumption about the states' role that had prevailed for more than thirty years. The judiciary was not simply defending rights defined by legislators but was insisting upon new definitions that substantially expanded eligibility.

The changes in court doctrines that have affected entitlement programs are considerably more complicated than the demise of the rights-privilege distinction suggests. Four factors help explain the new pattern of judicial behavior:

—The federal courts became significantly less willing to defer to administrators' interpretations of entitlement statutes. They insisted upon adding their own gloss to ambiguous statutory phrases. This decline in judicial deference to administrative expertise was not confined to welfare policy, but was evident in many other areas as well.

—Federal judges were particularly aggressive in curtailing the discretion of state officials. In effect, they turned conditions attached to federal grants—previously enforced only through the termination of federal aid—into individual rights enforceable through court injunctions. This constituted a major change in federal-state relations.

—Judges became much more inclined to rely on legislative history and broad statements of statutory purpose in order to expand benefits and ease restrictions on eligibility.

—Most important—but hardest to pin down—is a subtle change in judicial presumption about entitlement statutes. Replacing the presumption of administrative regularity was the presumption that administrators must justify deviations from the principle of "actual need." Time and again federal judges would strike down state rules and federal regulations not because they transgressed clear statutory language, but because they failed to take into account the actual need of potential beneficiaries.

Although not developed simultaneously, these four elements fit together quite well. The first two give the courts a bigger role in interpreting statutes. The fourth provides a substantive rule of thumb for such interpretation. And the third offers convenient methods for attributing the resulting policies to Congress. The remainder of this chapter examines each of these elements in greater detail. Subsequent chapters will show how they were applied to particular programs.

The Decline of Deference

In virtually all entitlement cases the judge's task is to evaluate prior determinations of federal or state administrators. Those prior decisions usually take one of three forms. First, a federal agency may use the rule-making authority granted to it by statute to establish general eligibility requirements, which will specify and define the pertinent criteria (such as earned income, work expenses, unemployment, and assets). Second, the parameters of joint state and federal programs may originate in state laws or state administrative rules. The states set benefit levels for AFDC, for example, and have substantial control over the kinds of medical services available to medicaid recipients. Federal officials must then decide if state plans conform to federal requirements. Third, in many programs eligibility and benefit levels depend on highly subjective determinations made by lower-level gatekeepers. Physicians, for example, must take the first step in determining whether an applicant is "totally and permanently disabled"; special education teachers must determine what constitutes an appropriate "individualized educational program" for handicapped students.[12]

The basic elements of the American welfare state were established during the New Deal, when faith in administrative expertise was at its apex and the legitimacy of the courts at its nadir. The agency overseeing the largest income maintenance programs, the Social Security Administration (SSA), was one of the most respected in the country. It is not surprising, therefore, that for years federal judges accepted the determinations of the agency "unless the Act itself or the unambiguous legislative intent thereof [was] obviously misapplied."[13]

In the second half of the 1960s, administrative law—the array of statutory provisions and judge-made rules that guide the judicial review of agency action—changed drastically. What Richard Stewart called "the reformation of American administrative law" has usually been examined in the context of regulatory policy.[14] But these changes left their mark on welfare programs as well. Even the prestigious SSA found its judgment repeatedly questioned in federal court.[15]

The first phase of this reformation focused on procedures. The courts increased the opportunities for civil rights advocates, environmentalists, consumer advocates, welfare rights organizations, and other public interest groups to participate in agency decisionmaking. For example, in 1970 the D.C. Circuit ordered the Department of Health, Education and Welfare (HEW) to allow the National Welfare Rights Organization to intervene in hearings on the adequacy of two state AFDC plans. Organizations claiming to represent beneficiaries, the court held, can be excluded from such hearings only if there is "clear and convincing evidence" that Congress intended to exclude them.[16] The courts have instructed agencies to solicit comments from all these interested parties and to respond to all significant comments. The agency must explain to the reviewing court why it accepted some suggestions and rejected others, how it evaluated technical evidence, and why it made its final decisions.[17] In the first half of the 1970s the courts substantially reoriented the judicial review of agency action "so that its dominant purpose is no longer the prevention of unauthorized intrusions on private autonomy, but the assurance of fair representation for all affected interests in the exercise of the legislative power delegated to agencies."[18]

In the second phase of the reformation, roughly between 1975 and 1980, the courts shifted their emphasis from demanding more participation to requiring agencies to arrive at "correct" decisions. Once the courts perfected agency procedures, it seemed but a small matter to insist "that the agencies persuade them that they had made the substantively best policy."[19] Guaranteeing that agencies came to the right decision meant ensuring that they accurately construed the underlying statute. To use the catch phrase of the new administrative law, judges took a "hard look" not just at the agency's evidence and explanation, but also at its reading of the statute.

Whereas New Deal administrative law was in large part an attempt to rein in judges who in previous years had placed a heavy burden on agencies seeking to regulate private entities, the new administrative law frequently required federal agencies to be *more* aggressive in regulating business firms and state governments. In one of the most famous administrative law decisions of the 1970s, Chief Judge David Bazelon of the D.C. Circuit announced that in this "new era in the long and fruitful collaboration of administrative agencies and reviewing courts" the "fundamental personal interests in life, health, and liberty" would have "a special claim to judicial protection, in comparison with the economic interests at stake in a ratemaking or licensing procedure."[20] Judge Bazelon's claim that this had "always" been the case was disingenuous. Previously the courts had seen their primary role in administrative law as protecting private property from unwarranted government intrusion. Those who hoped to benefit from government regulation often lacked standing to demand greater protection. The fact that health had replaced property in the pantheon of judicially protected rights shows that the courts were often more interested in helping the potential beneficiaries of government programs than in protecting the vested interests of those who would bear the costs.

From Grants-in-Aid to Individual Rights

In many of the entitlement cases that come before the federal courts, beneficiaries challenge the decisions of state governments, not federal administrators. As a rule, the role of the state is substantially larger in means-tested programs (such as AFDC and medicaid) than in contributory programs (such as social security and medicare). These means-tested programs also tend to entail more administrative discretion than do contributory programs.

Over the past twenty-five years the federal courts have been more willing to overturn state rules—regardless of whether they take the form of state laws or regulations established by state agencies—than federal regulations. Race played a major role in undermining the credibility of the states. Many of the state policies challenged in federal courts in the late 1960s and early 1970s came from the South and had a disproportionate impact on blacks. Attorneys affiliated with Legal Services made a concerted effort to acquaint judges with the implicit racism of state welfare practices. The federal courts intervened frequently, not just to strike down such suspect rules but also to increase the uniformity of means-tested programs. In order to do so, they had to revise a number of long-standing rules about the jurisdiction and powers of the federal courts.

Grant-in-aid programs such as those established by the AFDC and medicaid provide matching funds to states that comply with federal requirements. The supervising federal agency has the authority to terminate funding for states whose programs are not in "substantial compliance" with these rules. But this is an unusual step, which the agency can only take after conducting a compliance hearing. Before the 1970s federal courts seldom intervened in negotiations between state and federal officials. In the early 1950s, for example, the D.C. Circuit ruled that it had no jurisdiction in a case challenging HEW's disapproval of a state plan.[21]

In grant-in-aid programs federal money does not go directly to welfare recipients, but first to the states, which then distribute it according to rules laid out in approved plans. In a sense, welfare recipients are third-party beneficiaries of the agreement between the state and the federal government. Under rules in effect before 1964, federal courts would entertain suits by third parties only if such suits had been explicitly authorized by statute. In practice this meant no judicial control over state programs since "seldom does Congress explicitly authorize suits by beneficiaries against either the grantee or the federal grantor."[22]

In a celebrated 1964 decision, *J. I. Case* v. *Borak*, the Supreme Court made it far easier for judges to discover in federal statutes "implied private rights of action," that is, jurisdiction to hear cases brought by third-party beneficiaries.[23] In *Borak* the Court noted that the Securities Exchange Act "makes no specific reference to a private right of action" for investors. But one of the act's "chief purposes is 'the protection of investors,' which certainly implies the availability of judicial relief where necessary to achieve the result." The Court reasoned that a private right of action is a "necessary supplement to [Securities and Exchange] Commission action." Breaking with years of precedent, the Court concluded that it had the duty "to provide such remedies as are necessary to make *effective* the congressional *purpose*."[24]

The history of private rights of action is a long and winding one. After the Supreme Court announced its new policy, lower courts recognized private rights of action with increasing frequency.[25] By the mid-1970s the Supreme Court had begun to move in the opposite direction, reinstituting a presumption against implied private rights of action. Shortly thereafter, however, the Supreme Court read a provision of a Reconstruction era civil rights act, 42 U.S.C. 1983, as creating a generic private right of action against state and local officials.[26] Within a few years the Court began to reverse direction on the applicability of section 1983, too.

Such indecision at the top allowed the lower courts to go their own way. In a 1979 case, Justice Powell complained that while the Supreme Court "consistently has turned back attempts to create private actions," "other federal courts have tended to proceed in exactly the opposite direction." In the preceding four years, Powell stated, "no less than 20 decisions by the Courts of Appeals have implied private actions from federal statutes."[27] Despite the Supreme Court's "sharp reversal" on private rights of action, "some lower federal courts have continued to create private remedies, although the controlling standards are obscure and conflicts among the courts are common."[28]

Private rights of action have been particularly important in shaping joint federal-state programs because the alternative enforcement mechanism—the funding cutoff—has so seldom proved effective. Before the courts allowed recipients to sue state governments in federal court, the federal government was a paper tiger. Thereafter it became a stern disciplinarian. In the process, the locus of federal policymaking shifted from agencies to the judiciary.

Equally important is the remedy federal judges found appropriate for a state's failure to comply with federal rules. They did not terminate federal funding, but issued injunctions ordering state officials to comply with all federal requirements. If judges had ruled that the appropriate relief for violation of federal rules is the termination of funding, few recipients would have found litigation an attractive strategy. As lawyers affiliated with the Legal Services Corporation argued in one early case, enjoining the expenditure of federal funds "would be precisely that injurious, self-destructive remedy which has proven so ineffective over the years." Granting this form of relief would "substantially undermine the remedy for the vindication of federal rights" and result in a "tragically pyrrhic victory."[29] The potent combination of private rights of action and injunctive relief opened a new chapter in state-federal relations.[30]

The extent to which the courts were willing to revise or even ignore jurisdictional rules in order to scrutinize state welfare rules was evident in early litigation over AFDC. The generic statute on the jurisdiction of the federal court, 28 U.S.C. 1341, established a $10,000 minimum for federal cases. Very few AFDC cases approached this sum, and class action rules did not permit the aggregation of benefits in cases of this sort. In its first decision on AFDC, *King* v. *Smith*, the Supreme Court dismissed the problem in a brief footnote. Since the lower court had found a constitutional violation, this made the case one in which a citizen had allegedly been deprived of a "right, privilege, and immunity secured by the Constitution and laws," thus allowing the plaintiff to bring her case under section 1983. Once the case was before the court, the Supreme Court ruled, judges could decide the statutory issues even if they dismissed the constitutional challenge. The Court refused to say "whether and under what circumstances suits challenging state AFDC provisions *only* on the ground that they are inconsistent with the federal statute may be brought in federal courts."[31]

Despite the fact that constitutional claims virtually disappeared from AFDC litigation over the next few years, few federal judges found they lacked jurisdiction. Then in 1974 the Second Circuit ruled that it had no jurisdiction over AFDC cases because Legal Services attorneys were using "insubstantial constitutional claims" merely as a pretext for gaining access to the federal courts. The Supreme Court thought otherwise.

Noting that for six years it had "either assumed that jurisdiction existed under section 1343 or so stated without analysis," the majority explained that to be "insubstantial" a claim must be "obviously frivolous," "no longer open to discussion," and "so attenuated and unsubstantial as to be absolutely devoid of merit." In other words, a case could be dismissed on jurisdictional grounds only if the state could show that its practice "was so patently rational as to require no meaningful consideration."[32] This peculiar formulation—one must wonder what it means to be "patently rational"—protected the federal courts' jurisdiction in most cases.

In 1990 Alan Houseman, former director of the Legal Services Corporation's Research Institute, reviewed the accomplishments of poverty lawyers during the previous quarter century. In the late 1960s, he noted, Legal Services attorneys "developed innovative theories on federal statutory issues that the courts had not considered previously." According to Houseman,

> Today, advocates take for granted that individuals can assert rights under federal statutes and regulations that were designed to protect or assist them, but when *King* v. *Smith* was decided [in 1968], this was novel. *King* radically changed poverty law by providing remedies in federal and state courts for decisions by administrators of AFDC, public housing, and other public benefit programs. *King* and its progeny also federalized and legalized the AFDC program and other federal statutory programs.[33]

Transforming grants-in-aid into entitlements required some fancy judicial footwork, but judges, aided by Legal Services, were usually willing and able to demonstrate such dexterity.

The Search for Meaning

Having made clear their determination to force federal administrators and subnational governments to comply with national legal standards, judges now had to find ways to squeeze specific mandates out of vague statutory phrases. This was no easy task. Even in the years stretching from Watergate to Irangate, few clear-cut violations of entitlement statutes came before the federal courts. The doctrinal changes described above would have had little practical significance had not the federal courts also begun to rely heavily on two methods for ascertaining "legislative intent": combing legislative history and identifying the overriding statutory purposes of statutes. In large part because of the persistent criticism of Justice Scalia, the first has become highly controversial. But the second has been even more important in statutory interpretation over the past twenty years.

In the United States as well as in Britain and Canada, the usual rule of statutory construction is that judges should look to legislative history only when statutory language is ambiguous. In the United States, however, this rule is honored principally in the breach. Indeed, in one frequently cited opinion Justice Thurgood Marshall stood the rule on its head. "Because of this ambiguity" in the legislative history, he explained, "it is clear that we must look primarily to the statutes themselves to find legislative intent."[34]

Studies of the Supreme Court have shown that the use of legislative history increased dramatically in the 1970s. In 1939 Supreme Court opinions contained only 19 references to legislative history. In the 1940s and 1950s the Court averaged between 100 and 200 a term. This rose to about 200 a term in the 1960s. In 1973 and 1974, though, the number of references exceeded 400 and remained at an elevated level throughout the 1970s.[35] In her survey of the 1981 Supreme Court term, Judge Patricia Wald found "No occasion for statutory construction . . . exists when the Court will *not* look at the legislative history." In addition, "the Court has greatly expanded the types of materials and events that it will recognize in the search for congressional intent."[36] In the Court's 1988–89 term, about half of the 133 signed opinions involved statutory interpretation, "and in 53 cases—almost three-fourths of those involving statutory construction and over one-third of all the opinions of the Court—legislative history was relied upon in a substantive way to reach the Court's decision."[37] As subsequent chapters show, a similar trend was evident in the lower courts.

This reliance on legislative history has exposed the courts to two criticisms. First, current practices may give judges a skewed image of the legislative process. The most important piece of legislative history, the committee report, today is usually written by staff under the direction of a subcommittee chair. No vote is taken on the report once it leaves committee. The next most important piece of legislative history is the floor statement of the bill's manager, which is often written by the program's strongest advocate and addressed to a nearly vacant chamber. The use of legislative history may also undermine the president's constitutional role in the legislative process. As Justice Robert Jackson explained in a famous concurring opinion, "It is only the words of the bill that have

presidential approval, where that approval is given. It is not to be sup-
posed that, in signing a bill, the president endorses the whole Congressional Record."[38] The second criticism of legislative history is that it can
be used to justify virtually any policy a judge wants. Even Judge Wald, a
consistent advocate of the use of legislative history, has concluded that
"consistent and uniform rules for statutory construction and use of
legislative materials are not being followed today," and that "there
appear to be few, if any, restrictions on what judges may look at to
discern legislative intent or purpose."[39]

Despite this criticism, many judges see reliance on legislative history as
the only alternative to turning interpretation over to the executive
branch. According to Judge (and former member of Congress) Abner
Mikva, a statute's meaning frequently "is not going to be discerned at all
if the judges and courts do not look at the legislative history." Consequently, "if judges are to make *congressional* primacy meaningful, they
cannot afford to ignore those obvious tools which members of Congress
use to explain what they are doing."[40] Those who tend to favor "congressional primacy" over administrative discretion are less inclined to see
committee reports and floor debate as product of rogue staff or unrepresentative subcommittees than are critics such as Justice Scalia, who also
advocate greater deference to administrators.[41]

A related trend—one that has generated less controversy—is the use of
prefatory language to determine legislative purpose. Many federal laws
grandiloquently proclaim that their purpose is "to protect and enhance
the quality of the Nation's air resources" (Clean Air Act) or "to alleviate
. . . hunger and malnutrition" (Food Stamp Act). The canons of interpretation discourage judges from putting much weight on these broad statements. Yet federal judges have often evaluated challenged policies by
asking whether they further or retard these purposes. In a 1973 case
involving benefits under the federal work-study program, for example, a
district court judge found that the purpose of the underlying statute was
"to break [the] bonds [of the cycle of poverty] upon the untrained poor."
"The Court," it concluded, "will not allow the defendants to defeat this
beneficent purpose by their own interpretation of the law, especially
when that interpretation, *however faithful it may be to the letter of the
law*, totally defeats the spirit of the law."[42]

This line of argument has been particularly important for lawyers
representing welfare recipients. According to Sylvia Law, who worked
with Legal Services and welfare rights organizations for many years,

Public benefit programs are enacted with generally benevolent purposes (or, at least, generally benevolent purposes are announced), and lawyers for the poor rely on these intentions in their arguments that particular restrictive regulations violate this intent. If so little weight is accorded to the intent and context of the statute [as Justice Scalia suggests], the welfare recipients challenging a restrictive regulation have little on which to base their arguments.[43]

The Supreme Court's recent emphasis on the "clear meaning" of particular phrases rather than on the purpose of the act as a whole, she warns, "is an ominous portent to public assistance advocates."

Members of Congress usually have a number of goals in mind when they pass new laws. They want to help the needy but not spend too much money, encourage people to work yet provide aid to those who cannot, protect the environment without hurting the economy. A bill's preface will usually trumpet the program's goals while ignoring its costs. When judges rely heavily on statements of purpose they subtly shift the burden of proof in favor of those who support the expansion of federal programs.

The Two Meanings of "Entitlement"

The combined effect of these changes was to increase the role of judges in defining entitlements. What ideas and presumptions guided their search for the meaning of federal statutes? To answer this question, it is necessary to compare two understandings of the term "entitlement." An exploration of judges' use of this ambiguous term shows that many of them were not simply trying to discover the boundaries of the "new property" established by Congress, but were superimposing a much broader understanding of "entitlement" on the statutes passed by legislators.

On the one hand, "entitlement" can simply mean any benefit provided to an individual or organization under a program not subject to annual appropriations ceilings. This is how the term is used by students of the budgetary process. According to this view—described as "formalistic" and "positivist" by its critics—entitlements are entirely the creation of the legislative process. In the words of a 1970 Senate Finance Committee report highly critical of a number of Supreme Court decisions,

Welfare is a statutory right, and like any other statutory right, is subject to the establishment by Congress of specific conditions and limitations which may be altered or repealed by subsequent congressional action. . . . The "right to welfare" implies no vested, inherent or inalienable right to benefits. It confers no constitutionally protected benefits on the recipient. To the contrary, the right to welfare is no more substantial and has no more legal effect, than any other benefit conferred by a generous legislature.

The committee noted that "it is the ability to change the nature of a statutory right which distinguishes it from a property right or any right considered inviolable under the Constitution."[44]

In legal circles this narrow view is often associated with Chief Justice Rehnquist, who insists that Congress has broad latitude not just to define eligibility standards and benefit levels but also to establish procedures for terminating benefits. In a well-known 1974 opinion, Rehnquist wrote, "Where the grant of a substantive right is inextricably intertwined with the limitations on the procedures which are to be employed in determining that right, a litigant . . . must take the bitter with the sweet."[45] Even Justice Brennan, the author of *Goldberg* v. *Kelly* and one of the Court's leading proponents of a more expansive understanding of entitlements, has at times endorsed this view. In a 1985 food stamp case he wrote, "Where 'new' property interests—that is, statutory entitlements—are involved, however, claimants have an interest only in their benefit level as correctly determined under the law, rather than in any particular preordained amount."[46]

Straightforward as it may at first seem, this understanding of entitlements has some surprising implications. In *Goldberg* v. *Kelly*, the Supreme Court ruled that recipients facing "brutal need" are entitled to a due process hearing before benefits are terminated. This requirement came not from the statute, but from the due process clauses of the Fifth and Fourteenth amendments. Seven years later Congress enacted an amendment to the Food Stamp Act limiting eligibility to three-month certification periods. At the end of each period recipients must reapply and again prove their eligibility. Those dropped from the rolls at the end of the certification period, the amendment makes clear, have no right to a pretermination hearing since the "property" created by the statute incorporated a specific expiration date. The circuit courts that reviewed this provision all found it constitutional. One described the claim that this procedure violates *Goldberg* v. *Kelly* as "utterly without merit."[47]

The Supreme Court, which in recent years has gravitated to the narrow definition of entitlements in constitutional cases, let these rulings stand.[48] Several legal commentators have pointed out that as the courts return to this narrow understanding of entitlement they destroy the underpinnings of some of the innovative court rulings of the late 1960s and early 1970s.[49]

The second, broader view of "entitlement" is more difficult to describe since it is rarely defended fully or explicitly. It is perhaps best captured in the words of Charles Reich, the Yale law professor who coined the phrase "the new property": "The idea of entitlement is simply that when individuals have insufficient resources to live under conditions of health and decency, society has obligations to provide support, and the individual is entitled to that support as of right."[50] In the section of the influential law review article paraphrased by Justice Brennan in *Goldberg* v. *Kelly*, Reich explained,

> Today we see poverty as the consequence of large impersonal forces in a complex industrial society. . . . It is closer to the truth to say that the poor are affirmative contributors to today's society, for we are so organized as virtually to compel this sacrifice by a segment of the population. Since the enactment of the Social Security Act, we have recognized that they have a right—not a mere privilege—to a minimal share in the commonwealth.

For this reason, Reich concluded, "public welfare should rest upon a comprehensive concept of actual need spelled out in objectively defined eligibility [standards] that assures the maximum degree of security and independence."[51]

As explained in subsequent chapters, the idea that eligibility and benefit levels should reflect "actual need" is repeated in judicial opinion after opinion. Frequently judges emphasize those factors that should *not* affect eligibility or benefit levels since they do not reflect actual need. Most obviously, benefits should not depend on the color of one's skin. Nor should they depend on the location or duration of one's residence, or on the circumstances of one's birth—especially whether a child is legitimate or illegitimate. In calculating benefits, welfare agencies should consider only income "actually available" to recipients, not income "deemed" available by program guidelines. Perhaps most important, requiring that benefits should be based on actual need means that they should not be affected by certain types of behavior—for example, by whether a mother observes the sexual norms of the community, whether recipients live in a traditional nuclear family, whether adults in the household accept employment offered to them, or whether they cooperate with caseworkers. According to this view, it would be particularly egregious for the government to reduce benefits to *children* on the basis of the conduct of their *parents*. It should be noted that fully adopting this understanding of entitlements would have enormous implications for the American welfare system, which offers benefits to certain categories of the poor—the elderly, the disabled, and single-parent families—but denies them to others who face identical financial need.

Although these themes reappear regularly in court opinions, judges have seldom explained the underpinnings of this broader understanding of entitlements. Laurence Tribe has pointed out that "the best way to understand" a number of nettlesome Supreme Court rulings on welfare is to see them as halting attempts to establish the principle that "welfare criteria must be closely related to need" and to impose a "heightened level of evenhandedness, requiring disregard of non-need related factors."[52] To arrive at this conclusion, though, it is necessary to extrapolate from several elusive Supreme Court opinions.

Statutory interpretation has been central to the development of this broad understanding of entitlement. The argument typically follows this pattern: since the purpose of the statute is to aid the needy (here the court cites the act's title or preamble), Congress is presumed to have made financial need the primary grounds for eligibility; additional restrictions are therefore invalid unless explicitly authorized. As Chief Justice Warren stated in *King* v. *Smith*, "to assume that Congress, at the same time that it intended to provide programs for the economic security of *all* children also intended arbitrarily to leave one class of destitute children without meaningful protection . . . would be most unreasonable, and we decline to adopt it."[53] In another AFDC case a lower court similarly refused to believe "that Congress intended to leave the needy child without any means of subsistence if the mother was unwilling to name the father. Indeed, if Congress had intended so drastic a result, there is good reason to suppose that it would have made its intent more explicit."[54] In 1981 a federal district court judge explained that the courts "have routinely invalidated presumptions which . . . 'result in the denial of benefits to eligible individuals without reference to actual need.' "[55] Judge Henry Friendly of the Second Circuit found in the accumulated federal cases "a kind of common law of the AFDC statute that the sins of the mother . . . shall not be visited upon the children."[56] This meant that even "egregious" behavior by the mother could not result in termination of benefits to the family.

Among the most prominent and candid judicial advocates of this understanding were Justices Brennan, Marshall, and Douglas. They made no secret of their willingness to read their views on the right to welfare into particular statutes. In both *Dandridge* v. *Williams* and *Jefferson* v. *Hackney*, for example, the two major Burger court decisions curtailing constitutional review of welfare programs, these dissenting justices suggested that a creative reading of entitlement statutes would produce the same result as a broad interpretation of the equal protection clause.

Justice Marshall was particularly frank in linking statutory interpretation to his frequently repeated conviction that the Constitution creates substantive welfare rights:

> In my view, every citizen who applies for a government job is entitled to it unless the government can establish some reason for denying the employment. This is the "property" right that I believe is protected by the Fourteenth Amendment and that cannot be denied "without due process of law." And it is also liberty—liberty to work—which is the "very essence of the personal freedom and opportunity" secured by the Fourteenth Amendment.[57]

For Marshall this meant that the burden of proof is on the *government* to show why benefits should be *denied*, not on the private citizen to explain why they should be granted. Similarly, when interpreting statutes establishing public assistance programs, Marshall argued that courts should recognize restrictions on eligibility only when the statute makes them crystal clear. "Because the recipients of public assistance generally lack substantial political influence," he argued, legislators may "single out politically unpopular recipients of assistance for harsh treatment." The courts can counteract this by requiring a "clear statement of authorization" before allowing states "to impose additional conditions of eligibility."[58] Thus when Justice Marshall read a provision of the Social Security Act relating to foster care, he started with the presumption that the "program was designed to meet the particular needs of all eligible neglected children." Consequently, states "may not deny assistance to persons who meet eligibility standards defined in the Social Security Act unless Congress clearly has indicated that the standards are permissive."[59]

For years Justice Brennan argued that the government cannot make receipt of benefits contingent upon acceptance of conventional views of proper behavior. In 1973, for example, the Supreme Court found unconstitutional a provision making "hippie communes" ineligible for food stamps. Writing for the Court, Brennan explained that "a bare congressional desire to harm a politically unpopular group cannot constitute a *legitimate* governmental interest."[60] A few years later the Supreme Court found a conflict between the federal AFDC statute and a New York law requiring "lodgers" (usually the male friends of women receiving AFDC) to contribute to rent payments. Brennan explained that "[the] State may not seek to accomplish policies aimed at lodgers by depriving needy children of benefits."[61] "The very pervasiveness of modern government," Brennan warned in 1987, "creates an unparalleled opportunity for intrusion on personal life. In a society in which most persons receive some form of government benefit, government has considerable leverage in shaping individual behavior." To protect individual liberty, the courts must strike down—or interpret very narrowly—rules that interfere with "family living arrangements."[62]

If belief in legislative supremacy is the foundation of the narrower understanding of entitlements, then a particular view of the causes of poverty underlies the second, more expansive view. Henry Aaron's description of a view of welfare popular in the late 1960s and early 1970s catches the essential elements of the understanding of poverty that informs many court decisions:

> If poverty is believed to be the resultant of forces exogenous to the poor, then the attachment of unpleasant conditions to assistance is a gratuitous cruelty inflicted upon the already victimized. Indeed, this conception of poverty suggests that welfare should be regarded as a right—as a form of just compensation for a kind of casualty loss, the accident of poverty. This view, or something very much like it, lay behind the drive . . . in the early 1970s, to deliver welfare payments in dignified settings, with rights of appeal and the assurance of due process, and without any coercion or requirements that the recipients of aid do anything in return for it. . . . These contentions all came to the same thing: Cash should be provided on the basis of economic need and without strings.[63]

It was this substantive understanding of "welfare rights"—not the far simpler belief that the courts should ensure that citizens receive all the benefits promised by statutes—that underlay the sea change in judicial behavior noted by students of the courts.

A Battle on Two Fronts

Judges were hardly alone in embracing this view of poverty and entitlements. In the 1965–72 period, Congress and state legislatures were knocking down barriers to eligibility, simplifying application processes, and increasing benefits levels. Congress came close to approving the nationally uniform, noncategorical family assistance plans proposed by Richard Nixon and Jimmy Carter. Aaron notes, though, that "the idea that economic status alone should determine eligibility for aid flickered only briefly and guttered out." Reformers never "seriously threatened the dominance of the traditional American view that only certain groups among the poor deserve welfare."[64]

Key elements of the "actual need" approach conflict not just with the structure of existing welfare programs but also with important elements of American political culture. Most important, the American welfare system makes a fundamental distinction between those expected to work and those not expected to work. Benefits for the latter tend to be relatively generous. The former, in contrast, receive no assistance or very low benefits, regardless of their "actual need." Indeed, the primary purpose of the American categorical welfare system is to distinguish between those who cannot work—because they are too old or disabled or must provide care for young children—and those who can. Most studies of public opinion and elite opinion in the United States have found strong opposition to government programs that provide benefits to those who are capable of working but do not.[65] As pollster Daniel Yankelovich has put it, "The public's emphasis on work and on helping people to become self-supporting can hardly be over-emphasized."[66]

The broader understanding of entitlements eventually came under attack not just in Congress but in the federal judiciary as well. Influential as this view was in the late 1960s and early 1970s, it never achieved judicial hegemony. For years it remained a recurring theme rather than a controlling principle. Soon after the courts began to reshape welfare programs, judges appointed by President Nixon (and later Reagan) started to weaken key precedents. By the mid-1980s each element of the judicial transformation described in this chapter was under attack from the Rehnquist court. The *Chevron* decision ordered lower courts to show more deference to administrative agencies.[67] A number of Supreme Court opinions—many of them written by the new chief justice—made it more difficult for federal judges to impose regulation on the states.[68] The Court recognized fewer and fewer "implied private rights of action."[69] Justice Scalia's "new textualism" discouraged judges from looking at either legislative history or broad statements of legislative purpose. The Court, in short, moved toward a more formal, less substantive understanding of the "new property."

Support for competing views on entitlements thus do not break down cleanly along institutional lines. The expansive "actual-need" approach has supporters and critics in each branch of government. Interbranch alliances have shifted from issue to issue and from time to time. The following chapters show how the politics of entitlement played out in three much different programs: AFDC, food stamps, and education of the handicapped. Chapter 13 will return to the question of why the actual-need formula has more political appeal in some contexts than in others.

PART II

Aid to Families with Dependent Children

CHAPTER FOUR

The Reform Agenda

The welfare recipients' lawyer started his struggle in 1965 not merely as a technician whose function was to help the welfare system conform to what the elected representatives of the majority had decreed it should be. His mission was to utilize the legal process to help change the very nature of the welfare system and, thereby, to change the ground rules of American society. No mere legal technician, he was a grand strategist.

—Edward Sparer, 1971

FEW PROGRAMS have received as much criticism as aid to families with dependent children. AFDC began as a little-noted provision in the Social Security Act of 1935, designed to help financially pressed states fund "mothers' pension programs." It eventually became the major source of support for many of the nation's poorest families, as well as the principal gateway to benefits such as medicaid and social services. By 1991 AFDC was providing over $20 billion to 12 million children and parents.[1] As the program grew larger and more visible, nearly everyone—liberals and conservatives, legislators and administrators, state and federal officials, taxpayers and recipients—called for reform. Presidents Nixon and Carter proposed comprehensive welfare reform measures that garnered substantial support in Congress, but not quite enough to be enacted. Meanwhile, Congress passed a number of incremental revisions. And in the late 1960s the federal courts announced a novel interpretation of the AFDC title of the Social Security Act that effected major changes in welfare practices.

To those on the left, AFDC is a prime example of how decentralized and incomplete the American welfare system remains. In their view, American public assistance programs are "ungenerous by international standards and uneven in their coverage across the states and population groups at risk."[2] Certainly, AFDC fits this description. Both eligibility requirements and benefit levels vary greatly from state to state. In 1992 a mother with three children and no income received $800 a month in California but only $150 a month in Mississippi and Alabama. Moreover, AFDC is available to only one category of the needy: single-parent families with children under the age of eighteen. Single individuals, childless couples, and most two-parent families are ineligible for benefits.[3]

For years conservatives have charged that the program creates a number of perverse incentives. Not only does it subsidize immorality by providing benefits to illegitimate children, they charge, but it treats unmarried parents better than married ones. By making welfare more attractive than work it creates a form of dependency that is allegedly passed from one generation to another. In short, this side contends, AFDC and related programs create "incentives to fail."[4]

Not surprisingly, AFDC became a prime target of welfare-rights lawyers in the 1960s and early 1970s. At first, attorneys affiliated with Legal Services concentrated on challenging the constitutionality of a wide array of welfare practices. After winning two dramatic constitutional law cases involving AFDC, *Shapiro* v. *Thompson* and *Goldberg* v. *Kelly*, these poverty lawyers hit a brick wall in the Supreme Court.[5] A five-justice majority on the Burger court declared in 1970 that "the Constitution does not empower this court to second-guess state officials charged with the difficult responsibility of allocating limited public welfare funds among the myriads of potential recipients." "The intractable economic, social, and even philosophical problems presented by public welfare assistance programs," Justice Stewart announced in *Dandridge* v. *Williams*, "are not the business of this Court."[6]

This was hardly the end of judicial involvement in AFDC. In 1970 a flurry of Supreme Court decisions on AFDC indicated that the Court intended to expand the "new property" through statutory interpretation rather than through constitutional law. In that year the Supreme Court—which until 1968 had never decided a case involving AFDC—issued four rulings on the program. Two weeks after announcing *Goldberg* v. *Kelly*, the Court decided *Rosado* v. *Wyman*, a complicated interpretation of title IV that both expanded the jurisdiction of the federal courts and allowed the lower courts to review the level of AFDC benefit provided by the states.[7] The same day the Court handed down its *Dandridge* opinion. Two weeks later, it invalidated on statutory grounds California's man-in-the-house rule.[8]

The central issue in most of these statutory cases was the role of the states in setting eligibility requirements and benefit levels. For more than thirty years, welfare administrators, members of Congress, judges, and reformers had all worked under the assumption that under the AFDC section of the Social Security Act the states retained authority to run their own programs, subject only to the handful of limitations listed in the act—such as the bans on waiting lists and residency requirement longer than one year. In a series of cases starting with *King* v. *Smith* in 1968, the Supreme Court suddenly reversed this presumption.[9] Now state eligibility rules were invalid unless they were explicitly authorized by the federal statute or were deemed consistent with the courts' understanding of the underlying purpose of the program. As the Court stated in 1972, the act does not allow states "to vary eligibility requirements from the federal standards without express or clearly implied congressional authorization."[10]

This novel interpretation of the Social Security Act in effect called upon the lower courts to scrutinize hundreds of state rules on eligibility and benefit levels. Federal circuit and district court judges responded with "surprising eagerness" to invalidate state restrictions on eligibility.[11] Although the Supreme Court later voiced reservations about this line of interpretation, inconsistencies in its own ruling left the lower courts free to follow their own inclinations. Between 1968 and 1981 the federal judiciary did more than any other institution to reduce state control over AFDC.

The scope and complexity of AFDC case law as well as the vacillation of the Supreme Court are best understood in light of the central irony of AFDC litigation: reformers seeking to make AFDC more nationally uniform, more generous, and more widely available turned to the courts because their efforts had repeatedly met with failure in Congress; the courts then justified their policies by claiming that this is what Congress had intended all along. The sudden shift in presumptions was a boon to AFDC recipients and their lawyers. Because the states had always run the program, the federal statute contained little guidance on eligibility standards or benefit calculations. The courts' novel reading of the statute placed a heavy burden on the states to justify a multiplicity of rules. But it also left judges in the position of making up policy in an ad hoc manner as they reviewed the details of fifty state programs. Adding to the uncertainty and complexity of litigation was the Supreme Court oscillation between its new reading of the statute and a more candid recognition of Congress's deference to the states.

The Frustration of Reform

The keystone of the American welfare state is the Social Security Act of 1935. The act created four income-maintenance programs: old age and survivors insurance, unemployment insurance, public assistance for the aged, and AFDC. AFDC received almost no attention in 1935. President Roosevelt viewed the two social insurance programs as the most important elements of the legislation. Congress reserved its enthusiasm for old age assistance. AFDC was created largely because the Committee on Economic Security (CES) decided to include title IV in the bill it drafted for the president. According to the committee's executive director, "Nothing would have been done on this subject if it had not been included in the report of the Committee on Economic Security."[12] For many years the program's only significant political constituency was state governments looking for a few extra federal dollars.

Unlike the New Deal's earlier, temporary relief programs, which had aided all needy families and individuals regardless of the cause of their poverty, the Social Security Act created a series of *categorical* programs. The CES explained that this array of programs would "segregate clearly distinguishable large groups among those now on relief" and "apply such differentiated treatment to each group as will give it the greatest practical degree of economic security."[13] Only those who had contributed through the withholding tax were eligible for old age insurance and unemployment compensation. The elderly poor not covered by social insurance could qualify for old age assistance. AFDC provided benefits to children in single-parent households.

Although presidential adviser Harry Hopkins warned that such a system would leave some needy families unprotected, especially those experiencing prolonged periods of unemployment, both the president and the CES rejected suggestions for a more inclusive program.[14] The legislation drafted by the CES limited eligibility to children "deprived of support" due to "the death, continued absence from the home, or physical or mental incapacity of a parent." Since widows constituted almost 90 percent of the caseload of the existing state mothers' pension programs, AFDC was expected to "wither away" as more widows and their families were covered by social insurance.[15]

Battle Lines, 1935–67

Only one aspect of AFDC captured congressional attention in 1935: the extent of federal control of state programs. The bill submitted to Congress by the Roosevelt administration required that state AFDC and old age assistance payments be sufficient to provide "a reasonable subsistence compatible with decency and health." Both the House Ways and Means Committee and the Senate Finance Committee found this provision too intrusive. The most vocal opposition came from two devoted segregationists, Representative Howard Smith and Senator Harry Byrd (Democrats of Virginia). Southerners clearly did not want to be told how to treat poor blacks. In addition, members of Congress from poor states were reluctant to commit themselves to paying whatever federal administrators determined was "reasonable." The bill was amended to require states to furnish assistance only "as far as practicable under the circumstances of such State." Wilbur Cohen later described this change as "the bill's most significant long-range loss."[16]

Under the Social Security Act that emerged from Congress, the federal agency was to "approve any plan that fulfills the conditions specified." These conditions were few in number: residency requirements were not to exceed one year; the program was to operate statewide; a single state agency was to administer the plan; and all those "whose claim with respect to aid to a dependent child is denied" were to have an "opportunity for a fair hearing before such State agency." The only other condition of eligibility was that the "dependent child" had to be under sixteen, living with specified relatives, and "deprived of parental support." To emphasize that this list only set the outer boundaries of eligibility, both committee reports announced that a state could "impose such other eligibility requirements—as to means, moral character, etc.—as it sees fit."[17] According to the Senate report, title IV would provide "less Federal control" than "any recent Federal aid law." AFDC "does not represent an attempt to dictate to the States how they shall care for families of this character, but is recognition of the fact that many States need aid to carry out the policies which they have already adopted."[18]

Responsibility for overseeing state programs fell to the newly created Bureau of Public Assistance (BPA) within the Social Security Board (later to become the Social Security Administration). AFDC was the board's least favored program. Within the social security fraternity it became an article of faith that "a program for the poor is a poor program."[19] Not only was AFDC based on the "despised" means test, but neither its benefit levels nor eligibility requirements were nationally uniform.

Soon after passage of the act, the board recommended a series of legislative changes aimed at limiting the discretion of the states. In 1939 it persuaded Congress to require the states to institute merit selection for welfare personnel and to protect the confidentiality of clients' files. In

1950 it persuaded Congress to bar the use of waiting lists and to make grants available to caretaker relatives as well as children. Further than this Congress would not go. Although the board "never missed an opportunity to urge federal and state liberalization of residence standards," Congress always said no.[20] It also refused to insist on statewide standards of need or to provide federal matching funds for general assistance.

Federal administrators also suffered two legislative setbacks during the 1950s that illustrate their differences with Congress. With the number of families on AFDC due to desertion and illegitimacy growing rapidly, conservatives in Congress succeeded in 1950 in passing a provision that required welfare officials to notify the police whenever they discovered that a father had deserted his family. Public assistance administrators opposed the addition of any eligibility requirement—in this case that mothers identify the father of their children—not related to need. Shortly thereafter Congress demonstrated its reluctance to allow the board to impose a funding cutoff. In 1951 the board had taken the unusual step of terminating public assistance funds to Indiana, which had violated the act's confidentiality provision by requiring county officials to make public the names of welfare recipients. Congress responded by attaching a rider to a tax bill limiting the confidentiality requirement to disclosures made for political or commercial purposes. This made the board even more reluctant than ever to use the funding sanction.[21]

Rather than fight quixotic battles in Congress, the Social Security Board and the Bureau of Public Assistance chose to pursue reform through administrative persuasion. The key to this strategy was to build a professional bureaucracy in each state that would supply state administrators with detailed guidance and help them use the threat of funding cutoffs to extract concessions from state legislatures. According to Martha Derthick,

> Had they [federal administrators] been free to make federal policy by themselves, that policy surely would have gone farther toward preventing state and local efforts to impose upon the poor officially defined standards of right conduct. . . . Congress, however, has been sympathetic to the moralistic practices of state and local governments. . . . Lacking support from Congress, federal administrators have had, in attacking moralism in particular states, to rely upon their powers of persuasion and such fragments of authority as the Social Security Act supplied.[22]

A handful of state agencies managed to develop programs that the BPA considered satisfactory. But most did not. In the South racial politics made welfare particularly controversial, substantially reducing the autonomy of welfare professionals. Much as they hoped to create a more uniform, generous, and professional AFDC program, federal administrators were well aware of their limited authority over the states and the proclivity of Congress to oppose further federal control.

The Flemming Ruling and the Limits of Federal Power

The limits of federal power became apparent in 1960 when the state of Louisiana adopted a severe "suitable home" rule. Many of the states that had established mothers' pension programs before 1935 provided benefits only to those mothers whom local officials deemed morally "fit" or capable of providing children with a "suitable home." This practice continued after passage of the Social Security Act. Not surprisingly, virtually all of the mothers declared fit were white, even in the South, where poverty was rampant among the black population. In states providing general assistance, a two-tier system developed, with "fit" parents receiving AFDC and those less favored receiving the lower general assistance payments. In states without general assistance—again, primarily in the South—those families not favored by local administrators were left to fend for themselves.

Federal administrators opposed such fit-parent and suitable-home rules, but found they had little power to abolish them. In the mid-1940s the BPA recommended that state agencies work for the repeal of such legislation. The Social Security Board vetoed this approach as too politically risky. The BPA then wrote a letter to the states expressing its general opposition to suitable-home requirements and warning against their discriminatory application. Although the BPA continued to oppose such laws and encouraged local administrators to ignore them, it grudgingly approved state plans with suitable-home provisions.[23]

The strategy of gentle persuasion failed. Between 1950 and 1960 nine states instituted suitable-home requirements, and only one state discontinued the practice. In 1960 Louisiana brought the issue to a head by passing a suitable-home law that removed from AFDC 24,000 children, 95 percent of whom were black. The Louisiana law presented federal administrators with a sticky problem. Not only had the state legislature declared all homes containing an illegitimate child per se unsuitable, but it had placed responsibility for purging the rolls in the hands of local lay boards rather than establish welfare agencies. Federal administrators had no one to negotiate with. Nor did they have clear statutory authority to cut off funds. Although the Louisiana crisis received worldwide attention, HEW (the new home of the Social Security Administration) at first did nothing to address the problem.

Under ordinary circumstances, the BPA would have worked patiently behind the scenes to persuade state legislators to repeal the law. But it could not do so in this instance because of the public outcry against Louisiana's policy. Shortly after the presidential election, lame-duck HEW Secretary Arthur Flemming announced what came to be known as the Flemming ruling. It stated that suitable-home provisions were consistent with the terms of the Social Security Act, but that when states found homes unsuitable they would have to take steps to place the children in foster homes. States that failed to remove children from unsuitable homes would lose federal funds.

Although the Flemming ruling solved the immediate problem, it suffered from two flaws. The first was that alternative pretexts were readily available to the states. Some southern states classified men living with AFDC mothers—or even those having casual relations with them—as "substitute parents" whose incomes were "available" for the support of the children. Shortly after HEW issued the Flemming ruling, Louisiana added such a clause to its statute.

The second problem was that Congress balked at accepting even the carefully circumscribed rule announced by Flemming. In 1961 Congress delayed the effective date of the ruling until September 1962. In 1962 the Senate Finance Committee warned HEW not to expand its attack on suitable-home provisions: "No such payment may be withheld . . . by reason of any action pursuant to such a State statute if adequate care and assistance are otherwise provided for such child under State law."[24] Far from rejecting the states' rights thrust of title IV, Congress grudgingly accepted HEW's policy, offered the states more time to comply, and cautioned against excessive federal intervention. In view of the outcome of the suitable-home issue, "neither Louisiana nor any other state had reason to feel that the federal leash was shortening."[25]

A New Era Begins

Despite the attention paid to poverty during the Kennedy and Johnson administrations, the AFDC experienced little change. At the urging of the

Kennedy administration, Congress authorized states to provide benefits to two-parent families in which the father was unemployed, but it refused to make the unemployed-parent policy mandatory. Less than half the states exercised the option. Correctly sensing that AFDC was a political land mine, LBJ steered clear of the program. His war on poverty focused on education, training, and public participation rather than on income maintenance programs.

The war on poverty did, however, have a substantial indirect effect on AFDC. Community action programs helped mobilize the poor, who became more aggressive—both individually and collectively—in claiming welfare benefits. A much larger percentage of those eligible for benefits now chose to apply for them. This, combined with changing demographic patterns—the migration of millions of poor blacks from the rural South to the urban North, an increase in the number of young women of childbearing age, and a surge in the number of children born out of wedlock—produced rapid growth in the welfare rolls. From 1967 to 1971 the number of AFDC recipients grew at an annual rate of almost 20 percent. By 1972 the number of recipients was almost 11 million, five times what it was in the mid-1950s and twice what it was in 1967.[26] This sudden rise in recipients and spending created a pervasive sense that the program was a "mess" and in "crisis."

Contributing to the growth of the program, the pressure for reform, and the political visibility of welfare in general was the reorientation of the civil rights movement. Having won passage of the Civil Rights Act of 1964 and the Voting Rights Act of 1965, civil rights leaders turned their attention to the economic plight of black Americans. President Johnson captured this shifting emphasis in his famous 1965 speech at Howard University: "It is not enough just to open the gates of opportunity. All our citizens must have the ability to walk through those gates." Noting that "Negroes are trapped—as many whites are trapped—in inherited, gateless poverty," the president promised to "attack these evils through our poverty program," which was "aimed at the root causes of this poverty."[27] In 1968, shortly after the assassination of Martin Luther King, Jr., civil rights leaders organized the Poor Peoples' Campaign to focus attention on the continuing problem of poverty. The link between civil rights and welfare reform was hard for federal judges to miss: two days after Resurrection City appeared on the Washington Mall in Washington, D.C., the Supreme Court heard oral argument in the most important AFDC case, King v. Smith.

The surge of interest in poverty emboldened those who had long sought welfare reform. The reform agenda became formal in 1966 with the publishing of the recommendations of the Advisory Council on Public Welfare, a body established by Congress and dominated by those long associated with the BPA and the SSA. The council urged that AFDC-UP (for unemployed parents) be made mandatory and more inclusive, that the federal government establish a minimum benefit level, that need be established as the sole criteria of eligibility, and that a simple declaration form be substituted for lengthy and intrusive eligibility investigations. At the same time, federal administrators started taking a tougher line with the states. They criticized "midnight raids" and substitute-parent laws and recommended that states institute the declaratory system for determining eligibility favored by the advisory council.[28]

In 1967 Daniel Patrick Moynihan presciently observed that a quarter century of "nonpolitical professional direction" of federal welfare policy was coming to an end. On the one hand, Moynihan noted, militants were "seeking to transform welfare recipients into a powerful interest group that will no longer be forced to accept whatever bargain the welfare establishment could strike with the larger society." On the other hand, backlash was setting in: "terms such as 'welfare mothers' and demands for residency requirements . . . emerged as effective forms in which to exploit anti-Negro sentiment among voters to whom raw racism would appear vulgar, even immoral."[29] The old federal welfare establishment quickly crumbled. In 1968 HEW Secretary John Gardner abolished the BPA, replacing it with a new organization that stressed income support, placed little emphasis on social services, and demoted those with social work credentials.[30] Under these pressures, Martha Derthick noted, "professional, bureaucratic dominance was bound to give way."[31]

If there was a pervasive sense that something had to be done, there was little agreement on what. When Congress undertook a comprehensive review of the program in 1967, the amendments it finally produced after long and acrimonious debate were, as one observer put it, "a curious mixture of provisions to contract and liberalize the program."[32] The most controversial sections of the new law penalized those states that failed to reduce the percentage of AFDC children born out of wedlock and required mothers with school-aged children to register for work. According to the *Washington Post*, these provisions took the states "back to barbarism." Moynihan called the law "the first purposively punitive welfare legislation in the history of American national government."[33] Yet it also provided more family planning services, allowed recipients to retain more of their earnings, expanded day care funding, and included a one-shot cost-of-living adjustment. Reducing welfare dependency was the top priority for most members of Congress, and they were willing to experiment with a number of approaches.

Rising welfare costs, Ways and Means Committee Chairman Wilbur Mills warned, would spark a taxpayer "revolution": "Unless the trends in these programs are reversed, and their administration made more sensible and more in the public interest, the taxpayer is going to insist that they be eliminated."[34] The sense of crisis led Congress to exert more control over the states. Members were at least as concerned about states such as New York—which they considered too lenient—as about Mississippi, Alabama, and Louisiana—which combined low benefits with racially discriminatory eligibility requirements. As welfare became politicized, the old battle lines over federalism faded. But a new program and a new coalition failed to emerge.

From Professional Norms to Welfare Rights

One of the earliest and most significant innovations of President Johnson's Office of Economic Opportunity was the creation of Legal Services. Attorneys working for Legal Services brought almost all the AFDC cases that came before the federal courts over the next three decades. Legal Services' litigational strategy was devised by a handful of lawyers at the Columbia Center for Social Welfare Policy and Law (CSWPL), which eventually became a Legal Services "backup center." The center's first director, Edward Sparer, instilled in an entire generation of Legal Services attorneys an understanding of the operation of the welfare system, the goals of the welfare rights movement, and the tactics of test-case law reform. It was at the CSWPL that an older generation of welfare reformers passed the torch to a new generation of welfare rights advocates.[35]

This transition was led in part by Elizabeth Wickenden, a member of the old guard, "who, together with Wilbur Cohen, had long constituted a kind of inner club of public assistance specialists."[36] Wickenden came up with the idea of creating a legal advocacy center at Columbia and enlisted Sparer to head it. Wickenden began her career in the New Deal's Federal Emergency Relief Administration. Later she served as a lobbyist for the

National Social Welfare Assembly and was at the center of efforts to stop Louisiana from carrying out its suitable-home rule. Her influential circle of friends included Arthur Altmeyer and Wilbur Cohen of the Social Security Administration and Supreme Court Justice Abe Fortas. Although she was not a lawyer, Wickenden wrote a widely circulated 1963 paper titled "Poverty and the Law: The Constitutional Rights of Assistance Recipients," which laid out the key elements of a legal strategy for achieving a more uniform and more generous welfare system.[37]

Sparer represented the new law-oriented side of the welfare rights movement. Long devoted to progressive causes, he had previously served as legal director of the Mobilization for Youth, a controversial precursor of community action agencies. Sparer's training in welfare matters came from his contacts with social workers and community organizers, and he tried to persuade welfare administrators and social workers that their cause was the same as that of poverty lawyers. Both groups, he argued in many of his law review articles, have an interest in eliminating residence requirements, guaranteeing fair procedures, and "reducing arbitrary decision-making."[38] Although lawyers and public assistance administrators often find themselves at opposite ends of the table, legal advocacy "increases the administrator's potential for effecting humane policy." This is because the line administrator "no matter what his personal excellence, almost invariably has to bargain and compromise. He does not and cannot call his own shots, developing his own policies in the manner that his best professional instincts may dictate."[39] By eliminating many of the constraints imposed by legislators and other elected officials, lawyers can free administrators to follow their professional norms. In short, Sparer, like Wickenden, saw welfare rights litigation as a novel method for achieving goals that had long eluded welfare reformers.

The Goals of the Legal Reformers

In his most comprehensive statement on the goals of poverty law, Sparer described the litigational campaign spearheaded by the CSWPL as part of a "struggle to establish a legal right to an adequate welfare grant, without onerous conditions and with fair administration, for all persons in need of financial assistance."[40] Although the "initial legal and organizational strategy" was "directed against exclusions of needy citizens who fall *within* the federal categories," the "long-range goal of welfare legal strategy during the 1965–1970 period was to end the categorical nature of the welfare system."[41] Because achieving this goal required a fundamental change in the American welfare system, it was vital for the welfare lawyer to "understand the highly political nature of welfare litigation." His task was not just to change the decisions of the Supreme Court—as the NAACP and the ACLU had done—but to combine litigation with a broad mobilization of the underprivileged.

Sparer divided his plan into four parts. The simplest—and the one most quickly achieved—was to assault "the state and local character of the welfare system" by eliminating residency requirements. This was one matter on which welfare professionals, poverty lawyers, and the Supreme Court agreed unequivocally. Sparer viewed the Court's decision in *Shapiro* v. *Thompson* as the first step toward the elimination of "state and locally funded welfare systems": "In the long run, the constitutional requirements of *Shapiro* will, for better or worse, help collapse this structure and force the issue of a single federal system."[42]

Sparer's second goal, to create the right to a "minimally adequate grant," was another long-standing objective of welfare professionals. "Increasing the amount of the money grant," he explained, "is a prime order of business in the struggle for welfare rights." His strategies for achieving this goal included invalidating "false assumptions of income," organizing "special needs campaigns," using a little-noticed provision in the 1967 amendments to force the states to adjust benefits for inflation, and, most ambitiously, using the equal protection clause to strike down a number of funding inequities. The first three strategies produced some tangible results in the first few years of litigation. The fourth was thwarted by the Supreme Court's decision in *Dandridge* v. *Williams*.

A third, more complex goal was to ensure that recipients "not be dependent upon agency whim." Although the hearings mandated by *Goldberg* v. *Kelly* helped reduce such dependence, procedural change by itself was not enough. It was just as important to eliminate eligibility requirements "so vaguely stated as to make impossible a determination by objective standards."[43] Many such rules—especially "man-in-the-house" rules—also intruded upon the most private of matters. In Sparer's view, the civil liberties of welfare recipients, as of all citizens, should include not just the right to travel guaranteed by *Shapiro*, but "the right to privacy and protection from illegal search[es]," the right "to refuse work relief without suffering penal or other improper consequences," and "the right to choose one's own standards of morality."[44] One of the fundamental tenets of the welfare reform effort was that the behavior of welfare recipients be no more the object of government control than the behavior of other citizens.

Finally, Sparer sought to establish the right to welfare aid "for all persons in need of financial assistance" by eliminating "the innumerable tests for aid and exclusions from aid, most of which were unrelated to need." Need alone, not family composition, age, or physical capacity, should determine eligibility and benefits:

> Surely the rationality and fairness of the federally supported categories are doubtful. For example, is it not arbitrary to give aid to needy children whose fathers desert them and refuse aid to needy children whose fathers refuse to desert them although they cannot find work?[45]

This, of course, was an argument that many reformers had been making since 1935 but that Congress had never endorsed.

From Goals to Tactics

To achieve these goals, Sparer pushed Legal Services to adopt a centralized test-case litigational strategy. Legal Services should not simply respond to the requests of clients but should devote its energies to winning a small number of cases that would change national welfare policy. After an initial period of infighting, the director of Legal Services adopted what he called the Wickenden-Sparer model for law reform.[46] The CSWPL circulated to local attorneys lists of state rules ripe for challenge and extensive directives on how to present their cases. At least for a few years the center's prestige and expertise gave it substantial control over which cases came before the federal courts and how they were argued.

In an article addressed to local Legal Services offices and subtitled "a plea for planning," Sparer's successor, Lee Albert, explained that in properly planned test cases

> the locale, court, regulation, and plaintiff were carefully selected. Litigation strategy and tactics were the determinants and the Center rendered a fairly comprehensive service in such cases. That strategy represents the erosion theory of litigation: the worst example of a practice or rule, the gross or excessive form, so to speak, in the most highly suspect social setting, was chosen as the subject of challenge.[47]

In planning its attack on employment rules, the center chose to start with a Georgia rule that assumed all mothers were "employable" during harvest season. Its first case challenging substitute-parent rules pitted a hard-working widow against segregationist Governor George Wallace.

Warning that "welfare litigation is, even now, generally new and unfamiliar to the courts" and that premature litigation can produce disastrous precedents, Albert called on poverty lawyers to "educate the courts to the nature of welfare administration in America, to the fundamental level of human needs on which it operates and to the impact various rules and practices have on the life of the poor in America" and to "dispel the myth of the unworthy poor drinking deeply at the public trough."[48] Legal Services attorneys knew they had to appeal to judges' hearts and consciences as well as their legal minds. They had to acquaint judges not only with the racial motivation behind many welfare rules but with the "brutal necessity" facing many recipients. Attorneys following this strategy looked for the case that would strike "at a gut level—one that was easy to be outraged at."[49]

Sparer urged poverty lawyers to look beyond legal victories and to see "litigation as one element among several that may be required to induce a particular change in welfare policy." For example, the decision to take *Goldberg* v. *Kelly* all the way to the Supreme Court "was part and parcel of the *organizing* strategy of the welfare rights movement, designed to amplify the organized forces—particularly the organized welfare recipient forces—of the movement." A prior hearing would enable recipients to "talk back and resist and still have some protection."[50] Practicing what he preached, Sparer worked closely with George Wiley, the driving force behind the National Welfare Rights Organization.[51]

Despite such efforts, welfare rights activists failed to build a grassroots political movement. The National Welfare Rights Organization collapsed shortly after Wiley's death, and nothing took its place. Unlike the legal reformers who focused on food stamps and education for the handicapped, the lawyers who brought AFDC cases never developed close ties with congressional committees. As a result, many of their victories in court were overturned in Congress.

Because they concentrated on attacking existing rules rather than establishing new ones, legal rights advocates could sidestep many of the dilemmas that bedeviled the reformers actively involved in writing legislation and administrative regulations. For example, they never squarely faced the problem of work incentives. For years, they opposed both mandatory work rules and the negative income tax strategy contained in

Nixon's family assistance plan. Sparer's response to the problem of work incentives was to call for radical change in the economic system:

> Suppose a welfare system offered an adequate grant to all those in need (with income below it), and a right to refuse work which paid less than the welfare grant. If, as a result, private business and government were forced to reorganize the economy to ensure that it provided purposeful and well-paying work, would not this be desirable?[52]

Those who engaged in legislative bargaining on welfare policy could not take refuge in such vague and unlikely possibilities.

Similarly, welfare rights advocates were never forced to resolve the tension between their insistence that welfare payments reflect the economic need of participating households and their opposition to means-tested programs. Administrators cannot determine a household's need without first calculating its income. And they cannot determine income without establishing the legal obligations of absent parents, step-parents, grandparents, boyfriends, and siblings. As judges hearing AFDC cases soon discovered, calculating need inevitably involves defining family obligations—a task that is often both intrusive and "moralistic."

Enemies and Allies

The initial victories of the CSWPL and Legal Services did not go unnoticed. Vice President Spiro Agnew decried "tax funded activism [that] transfers great power in community affairs from elected officials to self-appointed ones." Paying someone to sue yourself, Senate Finance Committee Chairman Russell Long declared in one of his many tirades against Legal Services, is "the absolute extreme of idiocy." In his first term as governor of California, Ronald Reagan engaged in a running battle with California Rural Legal Assistance and sought to prohibit Legal Services from suing federal, state, or local agencies. Years later, Reagan described Legal Services attorneys as "a bunch of ideological ambulance chasers doing their own thing at the expense of the poor who actually need help."[53]

The new poverty lawyers had many admirers as well. In 1967 the Senate Labor and Public Welfare Committee urged Legal Services to devote *more* attention to "test cases and law reform." According to committee member Walter Mondale, Legal Services "has probably caused more hope and trust in the system and more basic legal reform per dollar than any other program."[54] Senator Fred Harris wrote that "welfare recipients and lawyers associated with federally funded legal services programs have compiled a remarkable record of services to poor people."[55]

Legal reformers also had important allies in HEW. Before the Supreme Court heard *Goldberg* v. *Kelly*, the department issued new regulations requiring the states to provide pretermination due process hearings. Promulgating these rules shortly before President Nixon's inauguration, lame-duck Secretary Wilbur Cohen both fulfilled a promise he had made to the Poor Peoples' Campaign in 1968 and revealed HEW's growing commitment to a more legalistic, rights-based orientation.

> Today there is a growing recognition of the legal right to the receipt of public assistance, a legal right to insist that it be fairly designed and fairly administered—and a legal right to invoke the Constitution to assure the fairness of the system. What lies ahead is the task of applying these rights, point by point, so that the poor may come to stand truly equal before the law.[56]

Surprisingly, both Cohen's midnight regulation and the broader welfare-rights orientation of HEW survived the first phase of the Nixon administration. Not only did Nixon's initial appointees to HEW include such liberal Republicans as Robert Finch, John Veneman, and Elliot Richardson, but the department's Office of General Counsel began to recognize that litigation could help the department exert control over the states. In 1970 the deputy general counsel noted that in the previous few years, "instead of the legislative and executive branches providing the initiative for the creative development of new rules, it has been the courts that have supplied the initiative and, in some measure, the creativity."[57] Such intervention by the federal courts "permitted a sort of four-sided game of leapfrog." "If for any reason the federal administrators were inhibited in the development of new rules—perhaps because of the disapproving views of members of an appropriation committee—the courts could assume the lead in developing new legal requirements." Federal administrators could embed a judicially developed policy in their rule book, "perhaps even embellishing it a bit." Reform "could thus proceed in an ever-ascending spiral with no single participant in the process having the capacity to block progressive development."[58] Changes HEW officials had long sought through legislative revision and jawboning with the states were now being delivered through litigation.

Congressional defenders of the old order understood this dynamic and tried to stop it. In 1970 the Senate Finance Committee announced that it was "unwilling to accept the implication of these activities: that the Legal

Services lawyers are better qualified than the Congress to, in effect, determine national policy regarding the poor." The committee's majority charged that HEW had "attempted through regulation to make substantial legislative changes in the welfare provisions of the Social Security Act." It also proposed legislation terminating federal funding for "any individual who in any way participates in action relating to litigation which is designed to nullify Congressional statutes or policy under the Social Security Act."[59] The committee's bill passed the Senate but never became law. Two years later the committee complained that the combined actions of the courts and HEW made it very easy for an individual—"ineligible as well as eligible—to find his way onto welfare" and created "a mystic maze making it very difficult for the welfare agency to get him off of welfare even if ineligible."[60] Nevertheless, Congress again failed to agree on any changes in the AFDC law.

These events served to highlight a central feature of reformers' new litigational strategy: once the courts had expanded eligibility, the burden shifted to their opponents to pass legislation reestablishing the status quo ante. This meant that reformers did not need to build a majority coalition in Congress. Given the extent of disagreement in Congress over welfare matters, it was seldom possible—at least until after the 1980 elections— for any side to pass broad legislation on AFDC. Of course, reformers first had to win their cases in court. The nature and extent of their legal victories is the subject of chapter 5.

CHAPTER FIVE

Welfare Reform in Court

*Federal public welfare policy now rests on a basis considerably more sophisti-
cated and enlightened than the "worthy-person" concept of earlier times. . . .
Congress has determined that immorality and illegitimacy should be dealt with
through rehabilitative measures rather than measures that punish dependent
children, and that protection of such children is the paramount goal of AFDC.*
— Chief Justice Earl Warren, *King* v. *Smith*, 1968

WHEN POVERTY LAWYERS first tried to persuade a federal court to invalidate restrictive AFDC practices, they received a sharp rebuke. The judge
ruled that since the payment of benefits is "absolutely discretionary,"
there is no judicial review of the manner in which the states exercise this
discretion.[1] Legal reformers had few precedents to rely upon. Thirty-three
years after passage of the Social Security Act the Supreme Court had yet
to decide a case involving AFDC. Indeed, there was but one recorded
federal case on the subject: a state unhappy with the Department of
Health, Education and Welfare's disapproval of part of its plan tried—
unsuccessfully—to overturn the department's decision.[2]

The situation changed drastically in the ensuing years. From 1968 to
1975 the U.S. Supreme Court decided eighteen AFDC cases. Legal Services attorneys achieved an "unusual degree of success" in this forum.[3]
During this period the lower courts issued hundreds of decisions touching
nearly every aspect of the program, from residency requirements and
man-in-the-house rules to work expense calculation, pregnancy benefits,
and cost-of-living adjustments. The Columbia Center for Social Welfare
Policy and Law did not exaggerate when it claimed that these decisions
heralded "a new age of federal law and order for . . . needy citizens."[4]

Twice the Supreme Court found that state and federal welfare practices violated the Constitution. In *Shapiro* v. *Thompson* the Court found
the residency requirements authorized by title IV unreasonably burden-
some to the constitutionally protected "right to travel."[5] In *Goldberg* v.
Kelly, the Court required administrators to conduct due process hear-

ings before terminating welfare benefits.[6] After *Dandridge* v. *Williams*, though, efforts to use the Constitution to reform public assistance programs ground to a halt.[7] Statutory interpretation then became the chief tool of judicial reformers.

In three statutory decisions handed down between 1968 and 1972— known as the *King-Townsend-Carleson* "trilogy"—the Supreme Court reversed the long-standing presumption of state control over AFDC eligibility standards.[8] Before 1968 state control over benefit levels and eligibility standards was the norm, and federal regulation the exception. The *King, Townsend,* and *Carleson* cases, in contrast, established the principle that states' restrictions on eligibility were invalid unless explicitly authorized by Congress. This novel interpretation threw nearly all state eligibility rules into doubt.[9]

In 1975, however, a divided Supreme Court made a halting attempt to rein in the forces that it had unleashed less than a decade before. It overturned the decisions of five circuit courts that had seen fit "to establish a special rule of construction applicable to Social Security Act provisions governing AFDC eligibility." The lower courts' "departure from ordinary principles of statutory interpretation" was "not supported by the Court's prior decisions."[10] Four years later, though, the Supreme Court was maintaining that "a participating State may not deny assistance to persons who meet eligibility standards defined in the Social Security Act unless Congress clearly has indicated that the standards are permissive."[11] With the Supreme Court unable to make up its mind on which set of precedents to apply, the lower courts were left to follow their own inclinations. Not until the mid-1980s did the Court clearly revert to its previous practice of deferring to state and federal administrators. For almost two decades the federal courts scrutinized virtually every detail of welfare policy, yet failed to explain in a consistent manner the principles that would guide this judicial oversight.

The New Jurisprudence of Title IV

In the fall of 1969 a lawyer charged with defending welfare practices in California told the Supreme Court, "I can't defend the welfare system. I don't think anyone can. It is indefensible."[12] So widespread was this sentiment in the late 1960s that even Richard Nixon proposed replacing AFDC with a uniform federal program covering all families in need. "We can't go on with the present system," he told a group of senators. While conceding that his family assistance plan was a "possible disaster," Nixon argued that the existing welfare system was a "certain disaster."[13] The same combination of pessimism and willingness to experiment was evident in the Supreme Court's early AFDC decisions.

King v. Smith: Easy Cases Make Uncertain Law

Few court cases are as carefully planned as *King v. Smith*. Legal Services attorneys searched for a case that would shock the conscience of judges by pitting a sympathetic client against malicious state officials. They found such a client in Mrs. Sylvester Smith, a hard-working, widowed black woman with four children. Mrs. Smith had been removed from AFDC solely because an anonymous informant told her caseworker that she had occasional sexual relations with a Mr. Williams, who lived elsewhere and had nine children of his own to support. This was one of many cases in which Alabama welfare officials had invoked a 1964 rule that defined a "substitute parent" as any man who "lives in the home" with the mother of an AFDC child or who "visits frequently for the purpose of cohabitating." Children with such a substitute parent lost their eligibility for AFDC. As a result of this rule, 16,000 children—more than 90 percent of them black—were dropped from the program. Among them were the children of Mrs. Smith. The fact that the case came from Selma and involved a rule issued by Governor George Wallace made the racial element of the story unmistakable.[14]

HEW refused to approve the substitute-parent regulation, claiming it was a de facto suitable-home provision and thus violated the Flemming ruling. But neither did it find Alabama's program out of compliance with federal law. Legal Services then filed suit. A three-judge panel found the state rule unconstitutional. The goal of discouraging immoral behavior, the court maintained, "is wholly unrelated to any purpose of the AFDC statute." To assume that such a policy will reduce illegitimacy is "utterly unrealistic." So arbitrary was the rule that it violated the equal protection clause of the Fourteenth Amendment.[15] When Georgia and Mississippi lost similar cases in the lower courts, they prudently chose to adjust their rules rather than appeal. But George Wallace was not one to avoid a confrontation with "pointy-headed" federal judges. He chose to fight.

Shortly after the Supreme Court agreed to hear the case, Mrs. Smith's lawyers decided that a statutory ruling would have broader ramifications than a constitutional one. If the Court based its decision on the equal protection clause, then in future cases poverty lawyers would bear the burden of proving that the challenged rule was discriminatory in its intent or effect. A statutory ruling, in contrast, could prohibit the states from imposing certain restrictions on eligibility without a finding of discrimination. "If the decision goes off as the lower court's did," plaintiff's attorney Martin Garbus told the Court in oral argument, "then very little will have been accomplished. Even if we win in Alabama, HEW will not stop similar practices in other states." A statutory argument, though, "would give us all we wanted" and provide "a way in which the narrowest of rulings would have the broadest of implications." Garbus asked the justices to "give us a decision interpreting the Social Security Act as having rejected the concept of a worthy and an unworthy poor."[16]

A unanimous Supreme Court did just that. Chief Justice Warren's opinion ignored the constitutional arguments of the three-judge panel and relied instead on novel arguments about the meaning of the Social Security Act. These arguments guided the development of AFDC law for the next two decades.

Warren conceded that Alabama's argument "would have been quite relevant at one time," but claimed that "subsequent developments clearly establish that these state interests [in discouraging illicit sexual relations and illegitimacy] are not presently legitimate justifications for AFDC disqualification." Because the "social context" of legislative activity in 1935 was the general acceptance of the distinction between the "worthy" poor and the "undeserving poor," Congress had left the states free to impose "moral character" requirements. Society, Warren argued, had subsequently rejected this outmoded orientation. Not only had Congress ratified the Flemming ruling, but in 1962 it adopted a "services" approach to welfare that further corroborated "that federal welfare policy now rests on a basis considerably more sophisticated and enlightened than the 'worthy-person' concept of earlier times."[17]

Warren was right to see Alabama's substitute-parent provision as an attempt to circumvent the Flemming ruling. For years HEW officials had recognized that the ruling was a stopgap measure that dealt with only one part of a larger problem. Warren's description of the "mood of Congress" in the 1960s, however, was misleading. Neither Congress's grudging acceptance of the Flemming ruling nor the conceit that the 1962 "services" amendment would reduce the welfare rolls provides evidence that national legislators had embraced the progressive views described by the Court. The chief justice ignored the best-publicized sections of the 1967 amendments, which Congress had approved only a few months before the Court issued its decision. The amendments added a new work requirement and penalized states that failed to reduce the number of illegitimate children on AFDC. Liberal reformers decried these measures. Senator Robert Kennedy complained that "the man-in-the-house rule emerges from the conference strengthened rather than weakened" and joined with other liberals in an unsuccessful attempt to kill the conference report.[18]

The Supreme Court's opinion in *King* v. *Smith* did much more than breathe new life into the 1960 Flemming ruling. After arguing that it was the codification of the Flemming ruling that made Alabama's substitute-parent rule unacceptable, Warren claimed that Alabama had violated the 1935 act as well. Congress had already defined the term "parent" and had determined that *all* "needy, dependent children" were entitled to receive AFDC benefits. The states could not substitute their own definitions of "parent" for the definition used by Congress, nor could they serve only a select subset of needy, dependent children.

Because Congress had said so little about eligibility in 1935, Warren had to comb the legislative record to discover what Congress could have meant by the term "parent." AFDC, he argued, "was designed to meet a need unmet by programs providing employment for breadwinners." Mr. Williams did not provide support for Mrs. Smith's children, nor did he have any legal obligation to do so. Consequently, he could not have been "the type of breadwinner Congress had in mind." Congress, Warren argued, "must have meant by the term 'parent' an individual who owed to the child a *state-imposed duty to support*."[19]

To buttress this argument, Warren added the following statement, which was frequently cited in later cases:

> A contrary view would require us to assume that Congress, at the same time that it intended to provide programs for the economic security and protection of *all* children, also intended arbitrarily to leave one class of destitute children without meaningful protection. . . . Such an interpretation of congressional intent would be most unreasonable, and we decline to adopt it.[20]

The implication was that any state or federal rule that left some children "without meaningful protection" violates the Social Security Act. Yet, as Harry Hopkins pointed out to President Roosevelt in 1935 and as critics of AFDC have complained ever since, the act left at least two classes of destitute children without protection: those living in households with two parents but little income and those living in states with extremely low benefits. If Congress had intended to provide "meaningful protection" to "all" children, it would have created a nationally uniform, noncategorical welfare program, something it had declined to do—not just in 1935, but also in 1950, 1970, 1972, and 1978.

Thus, in its search for a rationale for putting an end to Alabama's substitute-parent rule, the Supreme Court came up with several possible interpretations of title IV:

—The states ordinarily set eligibility standards but cannot establish rules whose sole purpose is to reduce "immorality" or "illegitimacy."

—States cannot consider the income of any person to be "available" to the AFDC family unless that person has a *legal* duty to support the family.

—States cannot deny support to *any* "needy, dependent" children unless such restrictions are clearly authorized by the act.

In *King* v. *Smith*, the Court emphasized the first and second. In later cases, both the Supreme Court and the lower courts presented the third as the guiding principle of judicial interpretation of title IV.

Of MARS and Men

Shortly after the Supreme Court announced *King* v. *Smith*, the director of the Columbia Center wrote, "As some liberal northern states are but now learning to their surprise, the scope of the holding affects longstanding budgetary, family unit and income assumption rules which few if any perceived to be at stake in the challenge to Alabama's substitute father rule."[21] Legal Services attorneys flooded the courts with challenges to a wide variety of state practices. The next cases to come before the Supreme Court were not ones to shock the consciences of the justices. All came from northern or western states and involved issues far more mundane than Alabama's substitute-parent rule. Yet in these cases the Supreme Court adopted the broadest possible reading of *King* v. *Smith*.

In the late 1960s most states, even relatively liberal ones such as New York and California, had some form of man-in-the-house rule. In most instances these rules did not completely disqualify the family, but placed some financial responsibility on the man in question. According to California law, for example, a "man assuming the role of spouse" (MARS) owed the family any income in excess of that needed to support himself and his own children. Income over this amount was subtracted from the family's AFDC grant. The "lodger" rule adopted by New York in 1974 reduced the family's AFDC grant by an amount equal to the man's prorated share of the AFDC housing allowance. The assumption behind both rules is that men taking on some of the attributes of parenthood—living in the house, having sexual relations with the mother—bear some obligation to help meet family expenses.

The Supreme Court took a hard line against such practices and enshrined the principle of "actual availability." This means welfare agencies cannot attribute to the family the income of a "man assuming the role of spouse," a "lodger," or any other person who has no legal obligation to support the family unless the agency can prove that such income is "actually available" to the family. In practice it is very difficult (and intrusive) to prove actual availability.[22] By extending this principle to a variety of forms of income, many of which are not connected to men in the house, the courts decreased the amount of income attributed to AFDC families and consequently increased benefits.

The California law challenged in *Lewis* v. *Martin* placed a legal duty on men assuming the role of spouse to provide support for the families with whom they resided.[23] HEW announced that the California rule was invalid since the legal obligation was not "of general applicability"; that is, it applied only to men living with AFDC families, not to all men living with families. But HEW, true to form, did not terminate federal funds. When Legal Services attorneys asked the lower court to enforce the HEW regulation, the court agreed with California. Congress, it found, had never imposed the general applicability condition announced by HEW.[24]

The Supreme Court disagreed. HEW, it ruled, may "reasonably conclude that an obligation to support under state law must be of 'general applicability' to make that obligation in reality a solid assumption on which estimates of funds actually available to children on a regular basis may be calculated." *King* v. *Smith* "held only that a legal obligation to support was a *necessary* condition for qualification as a 'parent'; it did not also suggest that it would always be a *sufficient* condition." HEW was free to add conditions consistent with the act's "basic purpose of providing aid to 'needy' children."[25]

In *Van Lare* v. *Hurley*, the Court struck down a more limited state rule without any help from HEW. The New York law labeled "a non-legally responsible relation or unrelated person in the household" a "lodger," and assigned to this "lodger" a prorated share of the family's housing allowance. A divided panel of the Second Circuit upheld the rule. But the

Supreme Court ruled that New York's law violated the Social Security Act because it was "based on the assumption that the nonpaying lodger is contributing to the welfare household, without inquiring into whether he in fact does so."[26] Actual availability rather than deference to federal administrators had become the touchstone of AFDC law.

What had led the Court to equate Alabama's heavy-handed, racially motivated substitute-parent rule with New York's rule that a man in the house or even a relative living with an AFDC family should contribute a small amount toward housing? Since the court fashioned this policy in small steps—first resting its decision on a strained reading of legislative intent, then on deference to administrative expertise, and finally on the rule of actual availability—its reasoning is not easy to discover. Hints, though, are provided both by Justice William Brennan's majority opinion in the *Van Lare* case and by Circuit Court Judge James L. Oakes's dissenting opinion in *Van Lare* when it was heard by the Second Circuit.

Justice Brennan pointed out that "lodgers" may refuse to pay their share of the housing allowance, leaving some needy children with reduced benefits. This is impermissible since "the State may not seek to accomplish *policies aimed at lodgers* by depriving needy children of benefits."[27] In other words, the real policy behind the "lodger" rule was, to use Judge Oakes's phrase, "to punish the welfare family for using its own resources in a manner of which the Commissioner disapproved." According to Judge Oakes, *King* v. *Smith* prohibits states from using AFDC as "a lever . . . to compel compliance with local standards of moral conduct."[28] *Any* reduction in benefits for families without two legally responsible adults in the house constitutes a "morality tax" that the court would not sanction. As Justice Brennan later explained in a dissenting opinion, "On those occasions that the Government deeply and directly intrudes on basic family relationships, there must be a powerful justification for doing so."[29]

Completing the Trilogy

At the same time that the Court was expanding its attack on man-in-the-house rules, it was strengthening the presumption against all other types of state-imposed restrictions on eligibility. In the 1971 case of *Townsend* v. *Swank*, the second leg of the "trilogy," Justice Brennan used sweeping language to resolve a minor dispute. Amendments passed in 1964 allowed—but did not require—states to extend AFDC benefits to children between the ages of eighteen and twenty-one who attend high school or vocational school. The next year Congress expanded the optional coverage to include eighteen- to twenty-one-year-olds enrolled in a four-year college. The issue before the Court was whether Illinois could cover students in high school and vocational school but not those in college. Figuring that half a loaf was better than none, HEW had approved the practice.

Writing for a unanimous court, Justice Brennan disagreed. In words that came to be repeated frequently by lower court judges, he explained that

> *King v. Smith* establishes that, at least in the absence of congressional authorization for the exclusion clearly evidenced from the Social Security Act or its legislative history, a state eligibility standard that excludes persons eligible for assistance under the federal AFDC standard violates the Social Security Act and is therefore invalid under the Supremacy Clause.[30]

Legislative history, he added, did not support the proposition "that Congress also gave to the individual states an option to tailor eligibility standards within the age group, and thus exclude children eligible under the federal standards." Deference to administrative expertise was "inapplicable" because "the regulations are inconsistent with the requirement . . . that aid be furnished 'to *all eligible* individuals.'" Steering some children away from college "channels one class of people, poor people, into a particular class of low-paying, low-status jobs." This "plainly raises substantial questions under the Equal Protection Clause." His broad reading of the act allowed the Court to "avoid the necessity of passing upon the equal protection issue."[31]

The next year the Court heard a challenge to another California law, this one denying benefits to the family of a soldier serving in Vietnam. Although the family was needy, California denied benefits because the father had not deserted his family. HEW approved the practice of excluding the families of servicemen who continue to function as "providers of maintenance" for their children. In *Carleson* v. *Remillard* a unanimous Supreme Court disagreed.

Justice Douglas argued that "war orphans" should be treated no differently than other orphans. The *Townsend* decision had established the principle that states cannot "vary eligibility requirements from the federal standard without express or clearly implied congressional authorization." Absent from the home meant "absent for any reason." Douglas repeated Chief Justice Warren's statement that "Congress intended to provide programs for the economic security and protection of *all* children," adding that he was "especially confident Congress could not have designed an Act leaving uncared for an entire class who became 'needy children' because their fathers were in the Armed Services defending their country."[32]

Thus in four cases coming from states with relatively generous welfare programs—California, New York, and Illinois—the Court went even further than it had in *King* v. *Smith*. All eligibility qualifications unrelated to need became suspect. Only those limits clearly announced in the federal statute would survive judicial scrutiny. All doubts would be resolved in favor of eligibility. Indeed, the *Carleson* case indicated that even two-parent families could qualify for aid. Not only was the Supreme Court turning a state-run program into one with nationally uniform eligibility requirement, but it was slowly expanding a categorical program so that it offered benefits to *all* needy families with children.

Anomalies

Despite its remarkable record in the Supreme Court, Legal Services lost two AFDC cases in the early 1970s. At the time no one knew whether to consider these cases mere quirks or portents of a reinterpretation to come. In the first, *Wyman* v. *James*, Legal Services attorneys challenged a New York rule requiring AFDC recipients to submit to warrantless "home visits" by caseworkers.[33] Because Mrs. James refused to allow a caseworker into her home, her family's AFDC benefits were terminated. The lower court ruled that New York had violated the Fourth Amendment. Much to everyone's surprise, the Supreme Court upheld New York's practice.

Wyman was the mirror image of *King* v. *Smith*: not only was the plaintiff unlikely to engage the justices' sympathies, but her lawyers foolishly chose to rely exclusively on constitutional arguments. Eager to expand search and seizure protections under the Fourth Amendment, they refused to present a statutory argument based on *King* v. *Smith*. The early years of the Burger court, it turned out, were not an auspicious time to argue for a broad reading of the Fourth Amendment.

Writing for the majority, Justice Harry A. Blackmun described the plaintiff's "failure ever really to satisfy the requirements for eligibility," her "constant and repeated demands," and her "occasional belligerency." He hinted that Mrs. Wyman might be guilty of neglecting her child and painted a surprisingly benign picture of the welfare system in New York. The home visit, he explained, is made by a caseworker of "some training whose primary objective is, or should be, the welfare, not the prosecution, of the aid recipient for whom the worker has profound responsibility. . . . The caseworker is not a sleuth but rather, we trust, is a friend to one in need." Blackmun noted that home visits are "not required by federal statute or regulation" but failed to discuss the implications of this statement or even to cite *King* or *Townsend*.[34]

In his dissenting opinion, Justice Thurgood Marshall criticized the majority for its failure to follow these precedents. He and Justice Brennan argued that the Court should have struck down the New York rules as being contrary to HEW regulations and the Social Security Act. Ironically, those who favored vigorous judicial scrutiny of state programs could dismiss the *Wyman* decision as "merely" a constitutional ruling. In fact, the Supreme Court seldom cited *Wyman* in other AFDC cases.[35]

The Court's 1973 decision in *New York State Department of Social Services* v. *Dublino* cast further doubt on its attachment to the arguments it had made in *King, Townsend,* and *Carleson*.[36] The issue before the Court was whether states could reduce benefits when a parent refused to participate in state work programs. The work incentive (WIN) program established in 1967 required all parents (except those with children younger than six) to register for work and, if offered a job, to accept employment. Those who refused could have their benefits substantially reduced. Since WIN programs were not available in most counties, many states established supplemental programs. Making registration for state-created programs a condition of eligibility clearly conflicted with the rationale of *King, Townsend,* and *Carleson*. Yet by a 7–2 vote the Supreme Court held that Congress had intended to allow the states to take reasonable additional steps to promote employment.

The description of Congress presented by the Court in *Dublino* was undoubtedly more realistic than the one presented by Justice Warren in *King*. Yet one cannot help but be struck by the cavalier manner in which the *Dublino* decision pushed aside the Court's previous pronouncements on title IV. The lower court's invalidation of state work rules, Justice Powell argued, "is a sweeping step that strikes at the heart of state prerogatives under the AFDC program." Because the "problems confronting our society in these areas are severe," state governments "must be allowed considerable latitude in attempting their resolution." Quite remarkably, Powell reversed the presumption established in earlier cases:

"This Court has repeatedly refused to void state statutory programs, absent congressional intent to pre-empt them. If Congress had intended to preempt state plans and efforts . . . such intentions would in all likelihood have been expressed in direct and unambiguous language."[37] Justices Brennan and Marshall, in contrast, followed the logic of the trilogy and voted to invalidate the state program.

Dublino left state and federal administrators understandably bewildered. In 1974 the Department of Health, Education and Welfare announced that "because of the number of Court actions in this area in the last few years and the complexity of the issues involved," it would issue new general regulations "to reflect directly the recent decisional law in this area." HEW noted that the broad language of *Townsend* was "inconsistent with the Court's earlier actions in *Wyman* v. *James*," and that the Court's *Carleson* decision "failed to clarify the inconsistency." "Thus, questions remained with respect to the authority of the States to impose their own conditions of eligibility upon individuals eligible for assistance under the standards set forth in the Act." The *Dublino* decision, HEW claimed, reaffirms "the fundamental principle that States have considerable latitude in establishing the conditions which individuals must meet in order to be eligible." HEW did a masterful job of embedding the contradictory Court doctrines in its guidance to the states:

> The States may exclude one or more such groups from the scope of coverage under their programs only where the Act or its legislative history authorizes such an exclusion. The States may, however, impose their own conditions of eligibility which, if not satisfied, result in denial or termination of aid, if these conditions either assist the State in the efficient administration of their assistance programs or further an independent State welfare policy and are not inconsistent with the provisions and purposes of the Act.[38]

In the following months, HEW received many complaints that this language was "too imprecise to help States in complying with the Social Security Act and regulations and avoiding litigation." But it published the guidelines without amendment.[39] The states, in effect, were left to fend for themselves in the federal courtroom.

A Pyrrhic Victory on Benefits

Expanding eligibility was one of the two major goals of AFDC reformers. The other was to increase benefits. In both *Dandridge* v. *Williams* and *Jefferson* v. *Hackney*, they tried unsuccessfully to use the equal protection clause to force the states to raise benefit levels. To switch from constitutional adjudication to statutory interpretation was especially difficult on this issue because in 1935 Congress had removed every hint of a nationally uniform benefit level. Title IV required states to provide assistance only "as far as practical under the condition in such state."

The act requires every state to establish a "standard of need" for welfare recipients, that is, to estimate how much it costs families of various sizes to live in the state. But it does not require states to pay this full "standard of need." Over the years, states had used several means to keep welfare costs down. Some failed to adjust their "standard of need" for inflation. Others established a "family maximum," that is, an upper limit on benefits that applies regardless of family size. Still others paid only a percentage of the "standard of need." Federal administrators urged states to update their standard of need on a regular basis, to repeal "maximums," and to eliminate percentage reductions. But they had no legal authority to do more than encourage. Year after year, Congress refused to mandate higher benefits.[40]

Poverty lawyers and the newly organized National Welfare Rights Organization (NWRO) responded to these difficulties by fastening on a statutory provision of the legislation passed in 1967. Section 402(a)(23) states that

> by July 1, 1969, the amount used by the state to determine the needs of individuals will have to be adjusted to reflect fully changes in living costs since such amounts were established, and any maximums that the state imposes on the amount of aid paid to families will have been proportionately adjusted.

This became the statutory hook for a litigation campaign to increase benefits. Although poverty lawyers technically won their case in the Supreme Court, the 1970 *Rosado* v. *Wyman* decision proved to be a great disappointment for legal reformers. The fact that real AFDC benefits fell significantly in the 1970s provides graphic evidence that the courts were not nearly as willing to increase benefits as to expand eligibility.

Section 402(a)(23) had a complex legislative history. In 1967 Lyndon Johnson became the first president in more than thirty years to recommend that states be required to pay 100 percent of their "standard of need." The legislation he submitted also required that the standard of need be updated annually. The House Ways and Means Committee ignored the administration's proposal, but the Senate Finance Committee adopted two of its elements, annual recalculation of the standard of need and cost-of-living adjustments for all maximums. Senators George

McGovern and Robert Kennedy offered a floor amendment requiring a four-dollar monthly increase for all AFDC recipients, but they lost by voice vote. The conference committee eventually split the difference between the House and Senate bills, endorsing the cost-of-living adjustment but making it a one-time event. Soon after passage of the amendments, HEW conceded that the states could nullify the cost-of-living adjustment simply by switching to a "percentage reduction" system. Secretary of HEW Wilbur Cohen, the legislative strategist who had guided the provision through Congress, argued that at least the provision would place the burden of action on those at the state level who opposed cost-of-living increases.[41]

The little-noted provision took on new significance when New York, the state with the largest and most vocal welfare population, began to recalculate its standard of need in order to eliminate its controversial "special grant" program.[42] The NWRO and its attorneys argued that states could eliminate special needs grants only if the new system offered a *real* increase in benefits. HEW was sympathetic, but stuck by its previous position. NWRO and Legal Services then went to court.

Three district court judges agreed that Congress had intended to force the states to raise their payments.[43] According to Judge Jack Weinstein, who heard the New York case, the new provision created a "floor under present levels of benefits by prohibiting further cuts in welfare payments and by requiring . . . at least one increase." The narrow reading suggested by HEW would "render the statute virtually meaningless." "By encouraging states to switch to percentage reduction systems," Weinstein warned, HEW's approach "is likely to lead to lower payments."[44]

The Supreme Court was not willing to go this far. Writing for a six-man majority, Justice Harlan discovered two "broad purposes" in section 402(a)(23): to "require States to face up realistically to the magnitude of the public assistance requirement" and "to prod the States to apportion their payments on a more equitable basis." The statute did not, he argued, establish a floor for benefits. To mandate such an "extensive alteration in the basic structure of an established program" could not be justified by "ambiguous language that is not clarified by the legislative history." As amended, Harlan explained, the statute merely required that states make a conscious decision on whether to adopt a "percentage reduction" system. States should not be allowed to sit by quietly while inflation eats away at welfare benefits, but should be forced to bring "to light the true extent to which actual assistance falls short of the minimum acceptable" and "accept the political consequences of such a cutback."[45]

In the years following *Rosado*, Legal Services devoted enormous effort to using section 402(a)(23) to raise benefit levels, but ended up with little to show for their efforts. As Judge Weinstein had predicted, many states responded to rising AFDC costs by instituting "percentage reduction" systems. In effect, the states paid for expanded eligibility by reducing actual benefits. Legal strategist Edward Sparer concluded that "*Rosado* had the outer attributes of a major welfare recipient victory; in fact it was a disaster. It is one thing to force a state to raise its 'standard of need'; it is another to prevent a state from lowering its actual payment level."[46] Prevented from using litigation to raise benefits directly, Legal Services placed new emphasis on changing state rules on deductions and income accounting to increase the benefits received by their clients.

Activism in the Lower Courts

For an appellate body that decides only 150 cases a year and devotes much of its time to constitutional law, the Supreme Court has decided a remarkably large number of AFDC cases. Even so, when dealing with complex statutes it can only announce general themes. The job of working out the details and applying judicial doctrines to the diverse programs of the fifty states falls to the lower courts. Since 1968 federal district and circuit courts have issued hundreds of rulings on such matters as what constitutes available income and resources, whether states can cut off recipients who refuse to identify the father of children in the household or accept employment, and whether states must consider a striker to be unemployed or a fetus to be a child.

The lower federal courts were even more aggressive than the Supreme Court in striking down state-created barriers to eligibility. One of the unusual features of early welfare reform litigation is that the Supreme Court broke new doctrinal ground by *affirming* the decisions of the lower courts. Of the eight lower court decisions in cases similar to *Goldberg* v. *Kelly*, for example, six held that the Constitution required pretermination hearings. Similarly, the decision in *Shapiro* v. *Thompson* came after nine of eleven lower courts had held residence requirements unconstitutional.[47]

Most federal judges were quick to adopt a broad reading of *King* v. *Smith*. In 1971 a district court judge in Mississippi announced an interpretation of the act that presaged that of the Supreme Court in *Townsend* and *Carleson*:

> It is the opinion of the Court that the Act creates the right to a grant of assistance and aid to a needy and dependent child, once such need and dependency have been established, and a participating agency may not withhold the granting of such aid by the promulgation of an additional eligibility requirement.[48]

By 1975 the Supreme Court had begun moving in the opposite direction. As result, the lower courts, which were still extending the logic of the trilogy, eventually found themselves at odds with the Supreme Court.

The activism of the lower courts was especially evident in the issue of the eligibility of mothers who refused to identify the father of their children. In 1950 Congress required state and local welfare workers to notify law enforcement officials whenever the child of a deserting parent received AFDC. Alarmed at the rapid increase in illegitimacy and desertion, Congress later required states to create programs to establish the paternity of illegitimate and deserted children and "to secure support" for them.[49] Many states responded by terminating benefits to AFDC mothers who failed to cooperate with state efforts to collect support payments from absent fathers. None of these rules withstood judicial review.

The first court to decide the matter explained that although "Congress has said that state plans must make provision for establishing paternity and obtaining support from absent fathers," it did not intend "to leave the needy child without any means of subsistence if the mother was unwilling to name the father." The name of the child's father "is absolutely irrelevant to the question of AFDC eligibility." If Congress had intended to allow states to terminate benefits on these grounds, "there is good reason to suppose that it would have made its intent more explicit."[50] Of the fifteen lower court decisions on this issue, only one upheld state regulations—and it was soon reversed by a circuit court. These decisions invalidated regulations in states stretching from New York to California, Florida to Oregon. The Supreme Court affirmed these decisions without opinion.[51]

No issue generated more court rulings than state rules for calculating the amount of income available to the AFDC family. The lower courts went even further than the Supreme Court in limiting the states' ability to take into account the income of a "man in the house." For example, in

1969 a district court in Connecticut ruled that the income of nonadopting stepparents cannot be deemed available to the family since they have no legal obligation to support the children.[52] The Tenth Circuit determined that a state cannot attribute to an AFDC family half the income of a stepfather residing in the home even though state law makes half the stepfather's income the property of the mother.[53] The First Circuit found that a New Hampshire statute requiring stepparents to support stepchildren when they are "in need" does not constitute a "law of general applicability" since it does not apply to nonneedy stepchildren.[54] The Eighth Circuit argued that a stepfather who has not adopted his stepchildren cannot be required to disclose his income. In this case Minnesota had argued that gathering such information was necessary for determining how much the stepfather had made "available" to the family. The court replied that it would be improper for the state to presume that some of the income would flow to AFDC recipients.[55]

The courts also ruled that many types of income received by a sibling or caretaker cannot be considered "available" to others in the AFDC household. Among those payments not "available" to the AFDC family are social security or SSI payments made to a parent or a caretaker; child support payments made on behalf of one child; the earnings of a sibling; income from work-study programs; and educational loans, even if they exceed school costs.[56] When two AFDC families share the same residence, the state may not lower benefits under the presumption that they share the rent. To do so, one judge argued, would be to assume without proof that one family made part of its income available to pay the rent.[57] Even tax refunds received by an AFDC family cannot be considered income since they are not available "on a regular basis."[58]

The courts also applied the doctrine of "availability" to resource limits. In an important 1976 opinion, the D.C. Circuit struck down HEW regulations establishing nationally applicable resource limitations. The department's decision to employ the gross market value rather than the equity value (market minus encumbrances) ran afoul of the judicially created principle. The department's method for valuing assets, the court concluded, "must fail because it conflicts with the spirit of the AFDC program."[59] Following a similar logic, a district court invalidated a state transfer-of-assets rule that required recipients to show that they had received "fair value" for property they had sold. Such a rule, the court held, arbitrarily presumes that the "fair value" is "actually available" to recipients.[60]

Many other AFDC cases involved state work requirements. One of the earliest cases initiated by the Center for Social Welfare Policy and Law involved Georgia's "employable mother" rule. In some Georgia counties, welfare officials took recipients off the rolls during harvest time, arguing that full-time work was available to all who would take it. Recognizing that it was likely to lose in court, Georgia toned down its rule.[61] Thereafter, most of the litigation on employment rules involved the issue of whether state rules on employment conflicted with the federal work incentive program.

In the initial round of litigation, the lower courts struck down a number of work requirements.[62] Despite the fact that the Supreme Court approved supplemental state programs in its *Dublino* decision, the lower courts continued to invalidate state rules. One district court struck down a ninety-day period of ineligibility for recipients who had refused to accept work, ruling that the period of ineligibility could last no longer than the refusal to work.[63] In another case the court was asked to decide whether an unemployed father who refused to participate in the WIN program should be subject to the penalties set out in the WIN section of the act or the more severe penalties established in the AFDC-UP section of the act. Finding that the "limited sanction would tend to promote the overall purpose of the AFDC program generally which is to provide aid to needy children," the court chose the former, overturning the state's policy.[64] Several judges ruled that states must consider striking workers "unemployed" and thus eligible for AFDC-UP.[65] Seven courts ruled that the Social Security Act prohibits states from placing an upper limit on work expenses.[66] One district court went a step further: it prohibited a state from requiring those who take work-expense deductions to provide written verification.[67]

Few facets of AFDC policy escaped review by the lower courts. Among the state and federal practices invalidated in the 1970s were the following: federal rules establishing nationally applicable "quality control criteria"; state laws penalizing recipients for fraud; laws and regulations denying benefits to aliens; and a variety of rules on verification procedures, foster care, and emergency assistance.[68] In the wake of the Supreme Court's *Rosado* decision, many federal courts also took a close look at states' determination of the standard of need and in several instances asked states to change their calculations substantially.[69]

The most remarkable example of the federal lower courts' use of statutory interpretation to expand eligibility came in a series of cases on benefits for pregnant women. Title IV of the Social Security Act makes no reference to pregnancy. For many years HEW had allowed states the option of considering a fetus a "dependent child," thus making pregnant women eligible for AFDC and increasing the grants of those already eligible. In the early 1970s Legal Services mounted an extensive legal campaign to make this coverage mandatory. Of the fourteen district courts to rule on the issue, ten discovered that Congress intended to include the unborn in the act's definition of dependent children. Five of the six circuit courts reviewing these decisions agreed.[70]

That the courts would read "child" to include a fetus is somewhat odd, to say the least. The statute requires the child to be "living with" a particular relative and bases residency on the child's "place of birth." Moreover, shortly before this dispute arose the Supreme Court announced in *Roe* v. *Wade* that a fetus is *not* a person. After all, if a fetus were a child, then abortion would be murder.

In essence, the argument advanced by the lower courts was that the term "child" is at least somewhat ambiguous and that all ambiguity should be resolved in a way that furthers the act's goal of helping the needy. The First Circuit argued that "protection of needy children" is the "paramount goal" of the program and that "payments to the unborn are an appropriate, if not essential, means to that end." The Fifth Circuit stated that "payments to expectant mothers are consistent with the purposes of the Act" because "proper prenatal care is vital to the physical and mental health of the child." The Seventh Circuit could not "discern a rational basis for denying pregnant women the same assistance" granted to new mothers since "need may be greater" for those about to give birth.[71]

The argument that benefits should reflect "actual need" permeated lower court opinions. In 1976 one district court judge announced that "a state cannot, consistent with the Act and regulations, reduce payments without a guarantee that those minimal needs [of each child] will in fact be satisfied."[72] Six years later, well after the Supreme Court had backed away from the trilogy, another district court judge announced:

> If anything, congressional failure to specify that states should deny benefits for a specific reason under the AFDC program is evidence of its intent not to allow states to deny benefits for that reason. . . . *King* v. *Smith* and its progeny have erected a fundamental principle of AFDC jurisprudence: that the Social Security Act will not countenance depriving needy children of benefits because of factors beyond their control, and unrelated to need.[73]

In short, the broad understanding of entitlements described in chapter 3 continued to hold sway even after the Supreme Court shifted gears.

The Supreme Court's Second Thought

The lower courts' rulings on pregnancy benefits were too much for the Supreme Court. By a lopsided vote of 7–1, the Court overturned this expansive reading of the Social Security Act. Justice Powell's opinion took aim not just at the outcome in the pregnancy cases, but at the general approach of the lower courts in AFDC cases. The five circuit courts reversed in *Burns* v. *Alcala*, Powell explained, had taken the position that "persons who are arguably included in the federal eligibility standard must be deemed eligible unless the Act or its legislative history clearly exhibits an intent to exclude them from coverage, in effect creating a presumption of coverage when the statute is ambiguous." Such a "departure from ordinary principles of statutory interpretation," he argued, "is not supported by the Court's prior decisions." Powell insisted that "the method of analysis used to define the federal standard of eligibility is no different from that used in solving any other problem of statutory construction."[74] The Court accepted HEW's interpretation that pregnancy benefits are optional but not mandatory. Only Justice Marshall disagreed.

The Vacillation Continues

Although the *Burns* decision was a serious blow to Legal Services, the Supreme Court was not in full retreat. That very year it struck down New York's "lodger" rule, with only Justice Rehnquist dissenting. Over the next several years the Court invalidated a number of other state laws, focusing on the meaning of particular words and avoiding broad statements about the authority of the states. One example of this ad hoc approach is *Shea* v. *Vialpando*.

In a unanimous decision the court struck a down state-imposed ceiling on the work-expense deduction. The act requires states to "take into consideration . . . any expenses reasonably attributable to the earning of . . . income." Setting an upper limit on the amount "taken into consideration" reduces benefits for some recipients and makes some others completely ineligible. Four district courts and three circuit courts had previously struck down standardized work-expense deductions. Justice Powell agreed:

> In light of the evolution of the statute and the normal meaning of the term "any," we read this language as a congressional directive that no limitation, apart from that of reasonableness, may be placed upon the recognition of expenses attributable to the earning of income. Accordingly, a fixed work-expense allowance which does not permit deductions for expenses in excess of that standard is directly contrary to the language of the statute.[75]

On this matter, he maintained, "Congress has spoken with firmness and clarity."

In a decision handed down shortly after *Burns*, the Court held that states cannot deny AFDC-UP to families that also qualify for unemployment benefits. The AFDC-UP section of the act *requires* states to deny benefits to families "with respect to any week for which such child's father receives unemployment compensation."[76] Since in this instance AFDC benefits were higher than unemployment compensation, the plaintiff refused to accept the latter and requested the former. Justice Rehnquist's opinion for a unanimous Court argued both that there is a difference between being *eligible* for aid and actually *receiving* aid and that Congress had "demonstrated an awareness of the difference."[77]

To get a sense of the conflicting signals administrators, recipients, and the lower courts were receiving from the Supreme Court after 1975, it is instructive to compare two cases involving the emergency assistance (EA) subtitle of the act. In 1978 the Supreme Court upheld an Illinois law that created a "special-needs" program limited to AFDC recipients, stating that no statutory language "can reasonably be understood as imposing uniform standards of eligibility on every state EA program."[78] Four years later, the Court invalidated a New York law that limited emergency assistance to impoverished families *not* receiving AFDC. Justice Marshall found "strong support in the legislative history" for HEW's "conclusion that the automatic exclusion of AFDC recipients from an EA program is inequitable in light of the purposes of the EA program."[79]

With one hand the Court granted broad discretion to the states, but with the other it insisted that state programs be "equitable" in light of the vaguely defined purposes of the program. The Supreme Court simply could not decide where it stood. Four years after the Court had denied that any special rules apply to the interpretation of title IV, Justice Marshall wrote that a "participating State may not deny assistance to persons who meet eligibility standards defined in the Social Security Act unless Congress clearly has indicated that the standards are permissive."[80] Despite the fact that the *Burns* decision had rejected this view, no one dissented.

The Courts in the Reagan Era

The 1980s brought important changes to AFDC. First, a large number of legislative revisions enacted in 1981, 1982, and 1984 restricted eligibility and reduced benefits. Many of these changes were designed to overturn previous court decisions, and almost all resulted in some form of legal challenge. Second, the Department of Health and Human Services (HHS) was now in the hands of Reaganites who were much more likely than their predecessors to agree with the states. Third, Reagan's judicial appointments slowly changed the character of the Supreme Court. From 1984 to 1990 the Supreme Court heard five cases, all of which Legal Services lost. After 1986, when Justice Scalia joined the Court, Justices Brennan and Marshall—the most outspoken advocates of judicially managed welfare reform—dissented from every decision. The tide had decisively turned against an expansive reading of title IV.

Each of these changes is evident in the extensive litigation over the work-expenses deduction. In 1981 Congress overturned the Court's decision in *Shea* v. *Vialpando* and set a $75 work-expense ceiling. HHS instructed the states to treat state and federal withholding taxes as "work expenses" subject to this cap. Legal Services argued that the states should completely exclude taxes from income rather than consider them "work expense." This was more than a small accounting dispute. HHS estimated that its interpretation would reduce benefits to 45,000 families in California alone, with the reduction averaging about $80 a family.[81]

The lower courts split on the issue: five district courts and one circuit court agreed with Legal Services; three district courts and three circuit courts agreed with HHS.[82] At stake in the case before the Supreme Court was not just the issue of how to count taxes, but how the courts would apply the judicially developed doctrine of available income to legislation specifically designed to overturn previous court rulings.

In *Heckler* v. *Turner*, the Court showed great deference to HHS and warned the lower courts against placing too much weight on the principle of "actual availability." This doctrine, the Court argued, not only lacked statutory basis but served the limited purpose of preventing the states "from conjuring fictional sources of income and resources by imputing financial support from persons who have no obligation to furnish it."[83] The Supreme Court was critical of the lower courts' heavy reliance on vague statements about the purpose of the legislation. The task of the Supreme Court, Justice Blackmun warned, is not to assess "the wisdom of the course Congress has set," but "only to determine that the Secretary has identified it correctly."[84]

As the Supreme Court backed away from *King* v. *Smith* and its progeny, the dissenting justices placed renewed emphasis on constitutional law. This was evident in two cases involving a new statutory provision creating a "standard filing unit." After several years of prodding by the Reagan administration, Congress approved legislation in 1984 that included in the AFDC filing unit all parents, brothers, and sisters living together. Under this provision, the income of each member must be attributed to the entire filing unit. One part of the compromise arranged in the conference committee was that $50 in child support payments could be exempted from the calculation of income each month and thus "passed through" to the family.

In the first round of litigation, Legal Services lawyers challenged an HHS rule that social security insurance benefits paid to the family on behalf of a child are not "child support payments" subject to the $50 "pass through." The Fourth Circuit disagreed with HHS, arguing that any benefits designed to help a child are child support payments. Again the Supreme Court sided with HHS. Writing for the majority in *Sullivan* v. *Stroop*, Chief Justice Rehnquist found that "the Secretary's construction is amply supported by the text of the statute which shows that Congress used 'child support' . . . as a term of art referring exclusively to payments from absent parents." The lower court, he noted, had reached a different conclusion "in part because it felt the construction we adopt would raise a serious doubt as to its constitutionality." Rehnquist curtly responded, "This sort of statutory distinction does not violate the Equal Protection Clause if any state of facts reasonably may be conceived to justify it." In his dissenting opinion, Justice Blackmun stopped short of calling HHS's policy unconstitutional, but he did find that it "results in an arbitrary and irrational reduction of welfare benefits to certain needy families."[85]

The constitutional issues lurking beneath the surface in *Sullivan* v. *Stroop* were at the core of another Supreme Court decision on child support payments, *Bowen* v. *Gilliard*.[86] A federal district court judge in North Carolina declared that the standard filing unit rule violated the

Fifth and Fourteenth amendments because the government had in effect "taken" support payments from the child without offering "just compensation." By a vote of 6–3, the Supreme Court reversed the lower court.

Justice Stevens's majority opinion was a relatively straightforward application of the deferential standard of review established in *Dandridge*. While "suffering is frequently the tragic by-product of a decision to reduce or modify benefits to a class of needy recipients," Stevens argued, "under our structure of government . . . it is the function of Congress—not the courts—to determine whether the savings realized, and presumably used for other critical governmental functions, are significant enough to justify the costs to the individuals affected by such reduction." The statute did not "take" payments made on behalf of the child as the lower court had alleged, but had only reduced the AFDC benefits granted to the family. "Congress is not, by virtue of having instituted a social welfare program, bound to continue it at all, much less at the same benefit level."[87]

Justices Brennan, Marshall, and Blackmun refused to accept this narrow understanding of entitlements. The HHS rule on child support payments, Justice Brennan wrote, is unconstitutional because it "intruded deeply into [children's] relationship with their parents." The pervasiveness of modern government "creates an unparalleled opportunity for intrusion on personal life." In a society in which most persons receive some form of government benefit, the government has considerable leverage in shaping individual behavior. Sometimes this intrusion "is so direct and substantial that we must deem it intolerable if we are to be true to our belief that there is a boundary between the public citizen and the private person." By "directly and substantially" interfering with family living arrangements, the statute puts an unconstitutional burden on "the child's fundamental interest in living with its mother and being supported by its father." Such intrusion requires "a powerful justification"—more than simply the desire to save public funds.[88]

Justice Brennan had put forth similar arguments in *Van Lare* v. *Hurley* and *Townsend* v. *Swank* but had couched them in terms of statutory interpretation. Like much of the legislation passed in the 1980s, the child support provision was much more specific than the statute on the books in 1968. Since the Court's majority was unwilling to engage in exotic forms of statutory construction, Brennan had little choice but to make his basic constitutional argument explicit.

The fact that welfare recipients fared poorly in the Supreme Court in the second half of the 1980s does not mean that the federal courts have wholly retreated from the policy area. Between 1985 and 1990, the lower courts issued the following decisions.

—Almost twenty courts found that HHS could not use AFDC's "standard filing unit" rules when determining recipients' eligibility for medicaid.[89]

—The First Circuit invalidated HHS rules limiting child support exemptions to $50 a month (rather than $50 per monthly payment), relying in part on its understanding of the purpose of the 1984 amendments.[90]

—The Second Circuit ruled that HHS had violated the statute when it limited correction of underpayments to those currently receiving benefits.[91]

—The Ninth Circuit decided that the State of Hawaii had erred when it counted disability insurance payments as "unearned" rather than "earned" income.[92]

—A district court in Nevada overturned a policy established by the state and endorsed by HHS that private loans should be considered "income" rather than "resources"—despite the fact that the Supreme Court had deferred to HHS on a similar issue just one year before.[93]

—A district court in Michigan ruled that a state could not penalize a recipient who had worked in a WIN program for two days and then quit since the statute only allows states to sanction those who refuse "to accept employment."[94]

In the early 1990s the states began to attach a new set of conditions to receipt of AFDC. Wisconsin and New Jersey, for example, have denied benefits for illegitimate children born while their mother is on welfare. Several states have imposed penalties for truancy; others have required teenage mothers to live with their parents.[95] All of these rules will most likely be challenged in court. Some, it is safe to assume, will not survive judicial review.

Recognizing that their chances of prevailing in federal court are not nearly as good as they used to be, Legal Services has placed more emphasis on litigation in *state* courts. In the early 1970s California state courts issued a number of decisions that required the states to raise benefits. In 1987 the Supreme Judicial Court of Massachusetts, relying on a 1913 state statute, ordered the state to raise AFDC benefits to meet the rising cost of housing. State welfare officials estimated the cost of compliance at $700 million a year. Courts in such varied locales as New York, Hawaii, New Hampshire, and Florida have issued rulings directly affecting benefit levels. This judicial activity in welfare policy is just one manifestation of a broader trend toward activism among state courts.[96]

AFDC and the Judicial Process

The convoluted story of litigation over AFDC provides at least five lessons about the consequences of using "creative" statutory interpretation to effect major policy change:

EXTREME AND NORMAL CASES. In *The Courts and Social Policy*, Donald Horowitz notes that because judges must wait for private parties to bring cases to them, there is

> no guarantee that the litigants are representative of the universe of problems their case purports to present. In fact, the guarantees are all the other way. As a matter of litigation strategy, plaintiffs' lawyers are likely to bring not the most representative case but the most extreme case of discrimination, of fraud, of violation of statute, of abuse of discretion, and so on.[97]

The effect of extreme cases was particularly apparent in the early stages of AFDC litigation. Following the "erosion theory of litigation," the Center for Social Welfare Policy and Law presented judges with "the worst examples of a practice or rule, the gross or excessive form . . . in the most highly suspect social setting."[98] Clearly, the extraordinary story presented in *King* v. *Smith* shocked the conscience of the justices and induced them to search for a novel interpretation of the statute.

Soon more mundane issues and less attractive plaintiffs came before the federal courts. In some of these cases (such as *Townsend* and *Carleson*), judges enlarged judicial doctrines by applying in normal circumstances rules developed for the extreme. In others (such as *Wyman* and *Dublino*), they showed more willingness to defer to state and federal administrators and chipped away at precedents like *King* v. *Smith*. For years both lines of reasoning coexisted uneasily.

SEPARATING POLICIES THAT ARE INHERENTLY CONNECTED. Horowitz also notes that "the lawsuit is the supreme example of incremental decisionmaking," and that litigation tends to "isolate what in the real world is merged."[99] This is particularly evident in the separate lines of decisions on eligibility—where the courts were aggressive—and on benefits—where they were not.

Originally, welfare rights lawyers had viewed benefit increases and elimination of eligibility restrictions as equally important goals. As they frequently asked, what good does it do to make more people eligible for the meager benefits paid by states like Alabama? When the courts left the states the option of lowering benefits, the fiscally strapped states found they could offset their losses in eligibility suits by reducing benefits to those already on the rolls. To increase benefits for their clients, Legal Services challenged a plethora of arcane accounting rules. By the 1980s, hardly anyone was willing to defend the resulting system as the best way to target scarce public resources to the most needy.[100]

THE HAZARDS OF RELYING ON LEGISLATIVE SILENCE. The Supreme Court's reinterpretation of the Social Security Act in *King, Townsend*, and *Carleson* was in one respect very clever. By reversing the long-established presumption of state control, the Court converted Congress's silence on eligibility issues into a federal ban on most barriers to eligibility. If Congress wants to exclude certain categories of "needy, dependent children," the Court in effect said, then let it do so explicitly. There was no "smoking gun" in the statute itself to indicate that this was an incorrect reading of the federal law.

As a practical matter, this put in legal limbo hundreds of state rules. Take the question of how to determine the amount of income available to an AFDC household. In *King* v. *Smith* the Court indicated that states cannot count the income of an occasional visitor as "available" to the household. What about a live-in boyfriend? A stepfather? A stepfather with a legal obligation to support his stepchildren? All these issues came before the courts. (The answer in each case was no.) What about rules designed to punish fraud—can a state disqualify someone previously convicted of welfare fraud? Can a state reduce benefits in one month in order to recoup overpayments caused by the misreporting of income in a prior month?[101] In drawing the line between acceptable and unacceptable rules, the lower courts had very little to go on. Statutory guidance was scarce, and Supreme Court opinions were contradictory. It is little wonder that on many issues lower court decisions revealed "massive judicial uncertainty over the appropriate preemption framework."[102]

This uncertainty had serious consequences for the day-to-day operation of state programs. Some changes demanded by the courts—such as the recalculation of the "standard of need" mandated by *Rosado*—seemed pointless to administrators. According to a study commissioned by the Joint Economic Committee,

> Litigation means that caseworker time which would normally be spent serving recipients must be spent gathering data for the courts. Loss of a court fight means adjusting operations to comply with the court order. . . . In sum, the constant legislative changes, litigation, and internal reorganization contribute greatly to dysfunction in welfare administration.[103]

In the words of one administrator, the problem "is not so much whether we win or lose in court, but the severe strain which litigation places on the State's assistance payments system."

FROM WARREN TO BURGER TO REHNQUIST. Supreme Court rulings on AFDC passed through three phases, which correspond roughly to the Warren, Burger, and Rehnquist courts. During the first period (1968–72), the Court expanded the presumption of federal control. Most of these opinions were written by Justices Brennan, Douglas, and Warren, members of the Court's liberal bloc. In the third period (1984 to the present) the Court demonstrated a much greater willingness to defer to state administrators and to the federal Department of Health and Human Services, which, during the Reagan years, generally sided with the states.

In the middle years, the Court adopted what could charitably be called an ad hoc approach. A number of the opinions in this phase were written by Justice Powell, the quintessential pragmatic moderate. The Court avoided broad statements about how to read the act, focusing instead on the wording of particular statutory phrases. AFDC thus provides a graphic illustration of what Vincent Blasi has described as the Burger court's "belief that modest injections of logic and compassion by disinterested, sensible judges can serve as a counterforce to some of the excesses and irrationalities of contemporary governmental decision-making."[104] With the Supreme Court unable to formulate clear rules, discretion flowed to lower court judges, most of whom continued to take a hard line against the states.

FROM GRAND PRINCIPLES TO WOODEN RULES. Behind the early decisions of the Supreme Court lay a particular understanding of how welfare programs should be operated. Benefits should be based on need, not behavior. Recipients should not be penalized for violating "middle-class morality." Eligibility standards should not vary from state to state. In order to justify their decisions, judges invented rules of thumb for interpreting the AFDC statute. The most prominent rule was the presumption of federal preemption. Another was the doctrine of "actual availability." Originally conceived as an effort to "prevent the States from conjuring fictional sources of income," the principle was later employed to judge the legality of a wide array of complicated accounting procedures, such as the decision to treat withheld taxes as "work expenses."

Explicit discussion of overarching issues about welfare policy appeared in the opinions of the Warren court as the justices struggled to provide a rationale for the interpretive rules they were creating. Such debate then disappeared for more than a decade, replaced with arid discussions of rules ripped from their context. To some extent, this discussion of broad principles reappeared when Justices Marshall and Brennan objected to the deferential approach of the Rehnquist court. In the vast majority of AFDC cases, though, dialogue about constitutional principles and values is conspicuously absent. Judges' need to pretend that Congress had really created the "sophisticated and enlightened" welfare system envisioned by Chief Justice Warren put serious limits on the quality of the debate before the courts.

CHAPTER SIX

The Congressional Response

Court decisions have played a major role in the phenomenal growth of the welfare rolls in the last three years. . . . If the welfare statutes are inadequate, and there is little disagreement on this point, then the proper forum for improving them is the legislative branch of our Government, not the judicial.
— Senate Finance Committee report, 1970

Significant court decisions have begun to nudge the welfare system toward a more equitable and enlightened program. Cruel and demeaning regulations, irrelevant to the purposes of the Social Security Act, have been overturned in the courts.
— Senator Fred Harris, 1970

THE TRANSFORMATION of law regarding aid to families with dependent children coincided with the first major political debate over American welfare policy since 1935. In 1969, little more than a year after the Supreme Court announced *King* v. *Smith*, President Nixon unveiled his family assistance plan (FAP) to a nationwide television audience. Congress argued about FAP for the next three years. Twice the House passed legislation incorporating the main features of the Nixon plan; each time the Senate failed to concur. Five years later the Carter administration submitted its version of comprehensive welfare reform. After another lengthy and often acrimonious debate, Carter's Program for Better Jobs and Income (PBJI) met the same fate as Nixon's FAP.

What drove these efforts at comprehensive welfare reform was the pervasive sense that welfare was in crisis. By expanding eligibility and increasing welfare costs, the federal courts clearly added to the sense that immediate action was needed. For example, one hour after the Supreme Court overturned state residency requirements in *Shapiro* v. *Thompson*, Secretary of HEW Robert Finch told reporters, "This makes inevitable national minimum welfare standards."[1] Although Finch seriously overestimated FAP's appeal, *Shapiro* and many other court decisions unquestionably increased the fiscal pressures on high-benefit states such as New York and California and led the "intergovernmental lobby" to become a leading proponent of comprehensive reform.

As different as they were in detail, the reform proposals of the 1970s shared four key features. First, they created a minimum national benefit level, narrowing or eliminating the large differences between the states and providing more adequate benefits to recipients in the low-benefit states of the South. Second, they set uniform national eligibility standards and provided for federal administration of the new program. Third, they extended eligibility to two-parent as well as single-parent families, making benefits a function of family income, not family composition. Fourth, they tried to increase and rationalize work incentives. Those who designed these programs—many of whom were economists—believed that properly designed financial incentives would reduce welfare dependency without resorting to coercion or creating a large administrative apparatus.

The first three features, of course, were long-standing goals of welfare reformers. The fourth element, work incentives, created a dilemma that eventually led some reformers—including the National Welfare Rights Organization and its allies in Legal Services—to urge Congress to "zap FAP." To preserve work incentives without producing huge increases in welfare costs, these plans set initial benefit levels—that is, benefits for those without any earned income—quite low. Under Nixon's first plan, the benefits received by many recipients in states such as New York and California would have dropped significantly. Raising the initial benefit level meant either raising the income level at which recipients would "exit" the public assistance program or reducing work incentives. The first option alarmed conservatives, who strenuously objected to making more people eligible for government benefits. The second option weakened FAP's chief selling point.

Putting together a welfare reform coalition broad enough to overcome the many veto points in the legislative process proved impossible.[2] Members of Congress might agree that welfare was "a mess," but they could not agree on why or on what should be done to remedy the situation. Some thought welfare should be reformed because benefits were too low, especially in the South. Others thought benefits were too generous (at least in the Northeast) and costs to the federal government too high. Some wanted to expand eligibility by putting an end to categorical programs; others wanted to reduce welfare "dependency" by shrinking the rolls. Some wanted to use federal money to bail out states like New York; others wanted to use federal funds to increase benefits for the poor in the South. Some favored work incentives to deliver welfare benefits to the working poor; others wanted to force the welfare poor to work.

Because political factions are multiple and passions run high in this policy area, there are always some groups who prefer the status quo to the proposed change and who will do whatever they can to block legislative action. Given the deep ideological divisions within Congress, it is quite remarkable that FAP and PBJI came as close to passage as they did. As House Ways and Means Committee Chairman Dan Rostenkowski observed, "No issue is more divisive or difficult than welfare."[3]

The features of the political system that subverted presidentially initiated reforms insulated judicially initiated ones from legislative revision. A dedicated group of congressional conservatives—usually led by Senate Finance Committee chairman Russell Long—tried to reverse the court decisions. Other members of Congress saw the court rulings as a step in the right direction. An even larger group preferred to avoid the unpleasant subject of welfare altogether. For more than a decade Congress was no more capable of repudiating the court-initiated policies than it was of embracing or expanding them.

Nothing lasts forever—not even stalemate in Congress. A two-pronged conservative attack on welfare practices took shape in the early 1970s and eventually bore fruit in the early 1980s. Both the Senate Finance Committee and Governor Reagan's administration in California put together detailed proposals to cut AFDC rolls, to increase the financial responsibilities of parents, to force those on welfare to accept employment, and to eliminate what they called "waste, fraud, and abuse." Both groups knew that their policies were at odds with court precedents. Consequently, they denounced the courts, tried to overturn their decisions, and even (in the case of Governor Reagan) disobeyed court orders. By the time Reagan became president, his aides had developed close relations and a common agenda with a coalition of Republicans and conservative Democrats on the Senate Finance Committee. In both 1981 and 1982 they used new budget procedures and the president's popularity to overcome opposition from House Democrats and finally take their revenge on the courts.

This chapter considers why Long, Reagan, and their allies found a variety of court rulings objectionable, why they achieved few victories in the 1970s, why they prevailed on a number of issues in the early 1980s, and why some changes wrought by the court remain in place. Legislation passed in the early 1980s, for example, allowed the prorating of rent for "lodgers" (overturning the Supreme Court's decision in *Van Lare* v. *Hurley*), put an end to the open-ended work-expense deduction (overturning *Shea* v. *Vialpando*), and prohibited the families of servicemen from qualifying for AFDC benefits (overturning *Carleson* v. *Remillard*). Yet it did not bring back the more extreme substitute-parent or man-in-the-house rules struck down in *King* v. *Smith*. And the legislation of the 1980s tended to *increase* rather than diminish the federal government's control over the programs of the state. Congress inched toward a more nationally uniform program without embracing the "sophisticated and enlightened" policies envisioned by Chief Justice Warren.

The Political Lessons of the Guaranteed Income

The extensive debate of the 1970s provides insight into the complex response to court decisions. For one thing, it shows that Congress did not defeat welfare reform because it was unwilling to spend more money on means-tested programs. Indeed, measured in constant dollars, spending for the poor *doubled* between 1968 and 1975. The food stamp program and medicaid grew by leaps and bounds. In 1972 Congress federalized the old age assistance program. Within three years, the budget for the renamed supplemental security income program more than doubled. In 1975 Congress quietly enacted the earned income tax credit. Federal outlays started at $1.2 billion and by the early 1990s approached $10 billion.[4] Although means-tested programs sustained substantial cuts in the early Reagan years, by the end of the decade they had recovered their losses and were growing again.[5]

The Decline of States' Rights

Another lesson of the long debate over welfare reform was that Congress was growing impatient with the states. As explained in chapter 4, states' rights had been the hallmark of AFDC policy for many years. Social welfare professionals and liberal Democrats in Congress advocated greater uniformity and federal control, but to no avail.

The welfare crisis of the late 1960s shook the faith of those who had traditionally supported state autonomy. In 1970–71 the two most important members of the House Ways and Means Committee, Chairman Wilbur Mills and ranking Republican John Byrnes, were frustrated by the federal government's lack of control over spending and advocated federalizing AFDC and old age assistance. "Any time you have a government program that each year doubles in cost," Mills argued, "you know there is something wrong."[6] Mills complained that the free-spending state of New York "has got us under the present program . . . like the fellow who has the bear by the tail going downhill."[7] The chairman was particularly upset with what he saw as the states' reluctance to enforce the work requirements established by the 1967 amendments. Byrnes concurred. Asked "Why he, a conservative, was willing to support federalizing welfare," Byrnes replied, "Hell, we can't trust the states. We can't depend upon them to carry out the philosophy of our program—to enforce the work and training requirements."[8] No longer was support for a nationally uniform program limited to those who wanted to make welfare more generous. Now many in Congress saw uniformity as a way to control costs and to mandate work.

The states, too, were starting to throw in the towel. In both 1969–72 and 1978–79 the states were the most important advocates of welfare reform. Secretary of HEW Joseph Califano told President Carter that "most members of Congress would still prefer not to deal with the subject at all," but that "the states are our natural allies in welfare reform."[9] It is hardly surprising that New York sought a federal bailout throughout the 1970s. Much more remarkable is the fact that in 1972 the governor of Texas supported a federal takeover of welfare.[10] States' rights was becoming a policy without a constituency.

Family Ties

From Alabama's substitute-parent rule of the mid-1960s to the standard filing unit provision of the mid-1980s, federal judges have shown particular interest in how AFDC affects the stability and privacy of the welfare family. Protecting and strengthening the family was also a primary goal of those supporting the Nixon and Carter proposals. Liberals had long argued that AFDC forced unemployed fathers to leave home in order to help their children. Conservatives maintained that AFDC subsidized illegitimacy and allowed fathers to escape financial responsibility for their families. Both sides agreed that the categorical nature of AFDC—the fact that it was limited to single-parent families in most states—constituted a perverse antifamily policy.[11]

By eliminating an incentive widely viewed as pernicious, welfare reformers thought they had achieved a result everyone wanted—stable two-parent families—without using coercion to enforce "middle-class morality." An incentive-based approach promised to achieve "what most people wanted without insisting that it was what God wanted, or what religion wanted, or what was best for people and their community."[12] This is one reason why FAP initially had appeal for all bands of the political spectrum.

Guaranteed income proposals suffered a stunning setback, however, when the result of income maintenance experiments in Seattle and Denver (called the SIME-DIME findings) indicated that income guarantees significantly *increased* the rate of family breakup, especially for racial minorities. These unexpected findings received a great deal of attention and gave pause even to some of the most ardent supporters of FAP and PBJI. Senator Daniel Patrick Moynihan, who by 1977 was chairing the Finance Committee's Subcommittee on Social Security and the Family, claimed that the findings were "as important as anything I have seen in my lifetime to the formation of making judgments about a large social problem." The new evidence, he reluctantly conceded, "discredited fifteen years of social policies that I had been trying to press."[13] Subsequent studies indicate that SIME-DIME may have exaggerated the extent of family breakup. Yet the fact that welfare reform would not promote family stability—and might even make matters worse—robbed reformers of one of their most appealing arguments and shook their faith in social engineering.

Two other changes of the 1970s and 1980s broadened the ranks of those willing to join conservatives in taking a harder line against parents who fail to support their children. The first was the growing strength of the women's movement. If poverty was becoming "feminized," it was in large part because too many men were leaving children and their mothers without financial support. Locating absent fathers and forcing them to pay child support was now seen as a matter of gender equity rather than as a punitive measure against the poor. The second development was the continued growth in the number of single-parent families, particularly in black communities. More welfare administrators, civil rights leaders, and writers became willing to talk about this subject, which had long been taboo. Although no one is sure how to inculcate "family values," by 1990 scholars and policymakers were more willing than in 1970 to say that trying to do so is a legitimate job for government.[14] Certainly, few members of Congress accepted the "nonjudgmental" approach to welfare that underlay many court decisions.

The Pivotal Issue of Work

The other big selling point of the Nixon and Carter proposals was their promise of carefully calibrated work incentives. Proponents argued that low marginal benefit reduction rates would be more effective than mandatory work rules for getting recipients off welfare and into jobs. They also claimed that properly engineered incentive structures would provide more equitable treatment for the working poor. When the Carter administration began putting together its reform package, it established the principle that "no non-working family will have higher income than a comparable working family."[15] Although this sounded attractive in the abstract, the difficulty of providing adequate benefits to those who could not be expected to work (because they were disabled or had small children in the home) while maintaining low marginal benefit reduction rates proved to be the Achilles' heel of welfare reform.

A conspicuous feature of the welfare legislation passed by Congress over the past two decades is the inclusion of *explicit* work requirements.[16] In 1967 Congress established the work incentive program, requiring states to create work training programs. In 1971 the Talmadge amendments made work registration mandatory for all recipients except those with young children. In 1981 Congress authorized the states to require some recipients to "work off" part of their benefits. The Family Support Act of 1988 required sixteen hours of unpaid work a week from parents in AFDC-UP families and set specific participation targets for state-run work and training programs.

These enactments show that most members of Congress believe that incentives alone are not enough: those who receive welfare have an obligation to work when work is available, and the law should punish those who do not. A 1970 study of congressional opinions on welfare concluded that "policies that provide unearned income run counter to widely held and deeply felt American values, such as achievement, work, and equality of opportunity."[17] Members "did not believe that their middle-class and working-class constituents . . . would support guaranteed income." One member explained that his constituents "tell me they bust their butts over their jobs and they're not about to have someone living off the fruits of their energies." Here again, Congress's inclination to insist upon behavioral prerequisites for welfare put it at odds with the "actual-need" approach of reformers and many federal judges.

THE CONGRESSIONAL RESPONSE

The Unintended Consequences of Congressional Reform

One consequence of AFDC's inclusion in the Social Security Act of 1935 was that the program fell within the jurisdiction of the House Ways and Means and the Senate Finance committees. For years neither committee showed much interest in AFDC. Their agenda was dominated by such high-visibility issues as taxation, trade, social insurance, and health care. The revenue committees did not usually attract members committed to expanding social welfare programs. Such members gravitated toward the House Education and Labor Committee and the Senate Human Resources Committee, which encouraged program advocacy and policy entrepreneurship.

In the early 1970s the Ways and Means Committee valiantly attempted to construct a middle-of-the-road package that could pass the House. Unlike the Senate Finance Committee, Ways and Means included a number of members from urban areas with large welfare populations. As the most powerful and respected committee in the House, it was a particularly important—if generally unappreciated—ally of those who sought to create a nationally uniform, noncategorical public assistance program.

A number of the congressional reforms of the 1970s reduced the influence of Ways and Means. In 1974 the Democratic caucus stripped the committee of its power to make committee assignments, opened its meetings to the public, required it to establish subcommittees, and reduced its authority to bring bills to the floor under closed rules. The committee's turnover rate was high during the 1970s, and many of the new Democrats were "strong liberals with well-defined policy goals."[18]

The weakened committee never again played the central coalition-building role it played in 1970–72. In 1977–78 it was forced to share jurisdiction over welfare reform with two other committees. The bill it helped to write never reached the floor because party leaders decided it could not muster a majority.[19] In 1981 the House rejected the committee's recommendation on a large number of spending and revenue measures, replacing them with an omnibus bill written by the Reagan administration. The Democrats on the reconstructed Ways and Means Committee could at times bottle up welfare legislation they opposed, but rarely could they enact the legislation they favored.

The decline of Ways and Means strengthened the hand of the more conservative Senate Finance Committee. Senate Finance has had few members from urban states and a surfeit of members from southern and mountain states. In the Nixon years the Democrats on the committee were "more conservative and less partisan than their fellow Senators."[20] Senate liberals attacked the committee and tried to build their own coalitions on the floor. They soon discovered that Senate Finance had an uncanny ability to kill welfare reform legislation either by keeping it off the floor or by opposing it in conference committee.

The leader of the Finance Committee's conservative coalition on welfare issues was Chairman Russell Long. At first considered "unpredictable," "flighty," and "erratic," Long eventually "developed a reputation for power in the Senate."[21] He had strong opinions on welfare. Few members of Congress were more vocal or vehement in denouncing the federal courts and Legal Services. Long hired able staff members who shared his views, and he adeptly used his control over the committees's schedule to influence the course of legislation. He made a habit of attaching his own welfare proposals to popular bills coming to the floor at the very end of the legislative session. With these resources, Long played an important role in every congressional debate over AFDC from 1967 until his retirement in 1986. As Ways and Means declined in influence, Long's star rose—hardly the result congressional reformers had in mind.

The First Attack on the Courts: Long's March

In both 1970 and 1972 the Senate Finance Committee rejected the welfare reform bills passed by the House. In 1970 it sent to the floor a bill overturning a large number of court rulings and authorizing a test run of a guaranteed income. A floor amendment to eliminate the former lost by a margin of 42–27.[22] The bill eventually died in conference when it became enmeshed in a controversy over an unrelated matter. Two years later the Senate Committee endorsed an elaborate "workfare" program sponsored by Senator Long. This bill, too, included provisions to reverse a variety of court decisions. Unable to agree on any welfare reform proposal, the full Senate voted to test three different plans. The House refused to go along. Although Senate Finance failed to change AFDC law in these years, it did establish a remarkably resilient agenda for conservative welfare reform.

The Anticourt Manifestos

The 1970 and 1972 Senate reports demonstrated that key actors on the Finance Committee had an impressive understanding of the role the courts had played in reshaping welfare—and of how Congress could reverse their policies. The 1972 report noted that the federal courts had used "the very broadness of the Federal statute (intended to allow States more latitude) against the States by saying sometimes that anything the Congress did not expressly prohibit it must have intended to require— and sometimes that what the Congress did not expressly permit it must have intended not to permit."[23] Charging that the combined efforts of the courts, HEW, and Legal Services had seriously distorted the original intent of title IV, the committee sought not just to reestablish the previous interpretation of the law, but to reduce the authority of all three of the offending institutions.

The committee—or, to be more precise, the ten-member majority that usually sided with Senator Long—emphasized its intent to strengthen rather than weaken "the states' control of the AFDC program."[24] It laid out a few federal eligibility requirements and explicitly left all other decisions to the states. These provisions were presented not as changes in the statute but as "clarification of congressional intent regarding welfare statutes."[25]

Particularly controversial was the committee attempt to resuscitate man-in-the-house rules. Senator Long had strong opinions on this subject. In a 1971 floor speech he attributed "a significant part of today's welfare mess" to decisions such as *King* v. *Smith* and *Lewis* v. *Martin*. "Persuading the Supreme Court to strike down the man-in-the-house rule, probably was the supreme achievement of the poverty lawyers working for the Office of Economic Opportunity." But, Long warned, "no equitable system of family support can make any sense—so long as we permit the father to remain outside the family unit without requiring any of his income to be made available to his children."[26] The Finance Committee's proposal allowed the states to determine whether a man was a "parent" after conducting a "total evaluation of his relationship with the child." The bill spelled out ten factors that would constitute "positive indications of the existence of such a parent relationship." The list included such factors as "the individual and the child are frequently seen together," "the individual is the parent of a half-brother or half-sister," "the individual exercises parental control," and "the individual makes frequent visits to the place of residence of the child." When Senator Fred Harris tried to prevent the committee from "resurrecting the onerous man-in-the-house rule," the Senate backed the committee.[27]

The committee also expressed its opposition to lower court rulings that had prevented the states from forcing mothers to identify the father of their children. The 1970 report claimed that Congress had "clearly established in legislation its belief in the importance of making every reasonable effort to establish the paternity of a child born out of wedlock."[28] The 1970 and 1972 reports contained lengthy excerpts from the dissenting opinion in the Second Circuit's *Doe* v. *Shapiro*.

Among the other decisions attacked by the committee in 1970 and 1972 were the Supreme Court's rulings on residence requirements and due process hearings;[29] a variety of decisions on cost-of-living adjustments; and numerous lower court decisions expanding AFDC-UP, providing benefits to pregnant women, limiting the states' ability to recoup overpayments and exclude aliens, and prohibiting states from requiring home visits by caseworkers. As other court decisions were handed down, they too were added to the committee's "hit list." The committee subsequently recommended reversal of the Supreme Court's decisions on "lodgers," standardized work-expense deductions, and the eligibility of the families of servicemen and those qualifying for unemployment compensation, as well as lower court decisions on the eligibility of strikers, resource limitations, and quality control.

Chipping Away

As chairman of the committee with jurisdiction over taxation, trade, and social security, Russell Long was able to bring his welfare proposals to the floor on a regular basis. According to Gilbert Steiner, when Long controlled the committee's agenda,

> HEW, the Finance Committee, the White House, and welfare groups negotiated, traded, and otherwise bargained according to a well-known if imperfectly understood pattern whereby either an important trade or tax bill or some such esoteric measure as one to change the duty on synthetic rutiles can become the vehicle, as necessary, either for speeding the passage of particular welfare-related items, or making them veto proof. Those items most earnestly sought by the administration are . . . most likely to be held for their hostage value.[30]

Nearly every year one or more of the AFDC proposals contained in the 1970 bill would come before the full Senate. Long won a few bouts in the 1970s. But it took the combination of Reaganism and budget reconciliation procedures to achieve major changes in AFDC policy.

Conservatives on the Senate Finance Committee had their first taste of success in 1971 with passage of the "Talmadge amendments." This legislation was nearly identical to the committee's 1970 proposal to increase substantially the number of recipients who must register for work programs. The Talmadge amendments ran into little opposition, passing both houses by wide margins. Although they never produced the employment results promised by their sponsors, they underscored the breadth of congressional support for mandatory employment programs.

In 1973 Senator Long and his staff began placing special emphasis on federal efforts to force absent parents to pay child support. The committee sent to the floor a bill that, among other things, mandated that mothers who refuse to help locate absent fathers should lose their AFDC benefits. Attached to a social security bill, this legislation passed the Senate but was dropped in conference. The next year the Finance Committee attached similar provisions to a bill capping federal matching funds for social services. This time it persuaded the House conferees to go along.[31] Despite the fact that the new law reinstated rules long decried as punitive by welfare rights advocates, it faced virtually no opposition in the Senate, even from liberals. Senator Walter Mondale, for example, described the failure of fathers to support their children as "intolerable" and sided with Chairman Long. Ironically, the only resistance came from the Nixon and Ford administrations, which opposed involving the federal government in domestic relations. Increasingly, child support enforcement was viewed not as an attack on welfare beneficiaries, but as a women's issue—one way to force irresponsible fathers to help women escape poverty.

Long's next target was the open-ended work-expense deduction. Long had first tried to limit the deduction in 1973, only to be stymied by the House. HEW tried to achieve this goal administratively, but the Supreme Court's decision in *Shea* v. *Vialpando* banned uniform work-expense ceilings. The Ford, Carter, and Reagan administrations all proposed placing a cap on this deduction. Twice, in 1977 and 1979, the Senate Finance Committee attached the cap to bills on other subjects. Each time, House conferees refused to accept it.[32]

This was but one manifestation of the standoff between the House and Senate on welfare issues. The House Subcommittee on Public Assistance and Unemployment Compensation was nearly as predictable in its opposition to these changes as the Senate Finance Committee was in its advocacy. But as the House became more budget-conscious in the late 1970s, the Ways and Means Committee faced stiff challenges on the floor. In 1979 a Republican plan similar in many respects to the 1972 AFDC proposals of the Senate Finance Committee was defeated by a mere five votes. In both 1979 and 1980 riders establishing stringent "quality-control" standards passed the House. For liberals, this was a warning of things to come.

The Second Attack on the Courts: The Reagan Experience

At the same time that Senator Long and the Senate Finance Committee were burying FAP, Ronald Reagan was putting together the California Welfare Reform Act of 1971 and defending it—often unsuccessfully—in the courts. When Reagan was elected governor in 1966, California had one of the most liberal AFDC programs in the country. With costs going up rapidly, Reagan made revision of the program a top priority. As Fred Doolittle has shown, his strategy was to create "an alternative model for national welfare reform." Under Reagan, "California cut back aid to the working poor, decreased financial work incentives, imposed work requirements for some recipients, increased the responsibility of family and household members to support the needy, and tightened administration to lessen fraud and overpayments to recipients."[33] When he came to Washington in 1981, President Reagan brought a list of changes for the AFDC program and a cadre of trusted aides who had helped develop his California program.

If ever there was an opponent of the view described by the Supreme Court as "sophisticated and enlightened," it was Ronald Reagan. When almost everyone else was calling for fundamental change in AFDC, Reagan spoke of the virtues of the program created in 1935:

> If there is one area of social policy that should be at the most local level of government possible, it is welfare. It should not be nationalized—it should be localized. If Joe Doaks is using his welfare money to go down to the pool hall and drink beer and gamble, and the people on his block are paying the bill, Joe is apt to undergo a change in his lifestyle.[34]

Testifying against Nixon's program in 1972, Reagan concluded that "the basic original structure of the welfare system was sound," that "able-bodied adults were expected to support themselves, their children, and their aged parents to the extent of their capabilities," and that "the system was meant to be administered by the states and counties with the federal government sharing the cost."[35]

The key to Reagan's success in garnering Democratic support for his California welfare reform package was linking restrictive eligibility and accounting rules with an across-the-board cost-of-living adjustment. Benefits rose for two-thirds of all AFDC families in the state. Among the third whose benefits fell were the working poor. In response to charges that he was discouraging people from working, Reagan proposed mandatory "workfare," by which he meant requiring recipients to "work off" benefits in public service jobs. He also advocated more aggressive enforcement of child support laws and the use of income accounting rules that assume, for example, that stepparents and "men assuming the role of spouse" were providing support for children in the home.

Not surprisingly, Reagan often found himself at odds with federal and state judges. Several key Supreme Court cases, including *Lewis* v. *Martin* and *Carleson* v. *Remillard*, came from Reagan's California. According to Fred Doolittle, Reagan

> confronted lawsuits on issues that previous governors could have decided with little challenge from judges, federal officials or recipients. . . . With the liberal Warren Court setting the tone, and the even more liberal California Supreme Court also hearing recipient challenges, Reagan's arguments asserting state authority to limit welfare eligibility were consistently rejected. These defeats reenforced Reagan's hostility to welfare rights litigators and courts that accepted their arguments and must have encouraged his later willingness to ignore court orders and HEW interpretations of program requirements.[36]

One reason Democratic legislators accepted several of Reagan's proposals was that they knew the courts would strike them down.[37]

Reagan and his aides learned three lessons from their California experience. The first was that court decisions had banned many of the practices they advocated. The second was that attacking—and even disobeying—the courts could be good politics. The third was that in the long run the courts' position would prevail unless the federal law was amended.

Three key Reagan aides—Robert Carleson, David Swoap, and John Svahn—played a key role in effecting those statutory changes. Carleson and Svahn helped write and implement the California Welfare Reform Act of 1971. Soon thereafter they traveled to Washington to push these policies at the national level. Carleson first worked as a special adviser to Senator Long, then moved to HEW, where he eventually became commissioner of welfare. Svahn and Swoap also served in HEW and helped shape the Nixon administration's post-1972 effort to "crack down" on a welfare system it had failed to reform legislatively.[38] After the 1980 election, Swoap became undersecretary of HHS, Svahn administrator of the Social Security Administration, and Carleson head of the HHS Transition Task Force and special assistant to the president for policy development. By the time Reagan became president, all three were ready to go forward with their version of welfare reform. They knew they could count on Reagan's wholehearted support.

1981–82: Welfare's Thermidor

The 1980 elections put into place all the pieces necessary for significant changes in the AFDC statute. Not only did Ronald Reagan achieve a surprisingly broad victory, but Senate Republicans—who had backed Russell Long's welfare proposals—took control of the upper chamber. Office of Management and Budget Director David Stockman seized upon the reconciliation procedures established by the Budget Act of 1974 as a mechanism for forcing a quick up-or-down vote on the budgetary program of the then-popular president. The unusual politics of 1981 not only put the principal proponents of conservative welfare reform in a position to set the legislative agenda but reduced the ability of House committees to block legislation endorsed by the Senate.[39]

Shortly after his inauguration, President Reagan approved a package of AFDC amendments put together by Carleson. Carleson originally envisioned them as part of a separate welfare reform bill. The purpose of the changes, he told an interviewer, "was policy, not to save money but to reduce dependency and redirect funds to the truly needy."[40] When Stockman began to prepare his omnibus budget bill, he and Carleson found that each had something to offer the other. Carleson's proposals would reduce federal spending by more than $1 billion a year, savings Stockman desperately needed to achieve his $40 billion target. Carleson reportedly told Stockman, "Here is something that has already been approved. All you have to do is plug it in. It's like a cassette."[41] Like many of the policy changes included in the Omnibus Budget and Reconciliation Act of 1981, this welfare legislation was not developed within the bureaucracy or even approved by the department secretary.

Once placed in the reconciliation bill, the welfare proposals became nearly impossible to defeat or even to amend. In the Senate, the new Republican majority voted in unison to protect the President's program. In the House, a coalition of Republicans and "boll weevil" Democrats first endorsed a closed rule and then approved the administration's proposal. Recognizing that some reductions in spending were inevitable in the new fiscal and political environment, Ways and Means proposed reductions that would save about $600 million, half as much as the administration's. Even this scaled-down version went down to defeat on the floor.

The largest budget savings—and the greatest opposition—came from the proposals to reduce aid for the working poor: ending the income disregard after four months; capping work expenses; and limiting eligibility to those whose gross income is less than 150 percent of the state standard of need. HHS Secretary Richard Schweicker argued that AFDC should aid only the "truly needy"—those incapable of working—and should not become an income supplement for the working poor.

The open-ended work-expense deduction was a product of the Supreme Court's *Shea* decision. The 150 percent gross income ceiling was a rule enacted by several states in the 1970s but struck down by the courts as unrelated to the purpose of the act.[42] The income disregard was a product not of court action but of the 1967 amendments. Various court rulings, though, had made the disregard more generous.

Another component of the Reagan administration's 1981 welfare package was the insistence that "before the first dollar of aid is paid, all other sources of income should be pursued and all available income counted." Secretary Schweiker told the House subcommittee:

Under the current law many actual and potential sources of income to AFDC recipients are ignored. . . . We will also require that income of stepparents or those assuming the role of stepparents be counted as available to children living in the same household. The proposal will prevent those situations in which the children receive AFDC even while they are an integral part of a family situation with substantial income.[43]

These efforts to count more income, increase the financial responsibility of family members, and tighten administration of the program involved a significant modification of court doctrines on the "actual availability" of income.

In 1982 the Reagan administration tried again. The Tax Equity and Fiscal Responsibility Act of 1982, the second omnibus reconciliation bill approved by Congress under Reagan, included provisions that allowed states to prorate benefits for households with "lodgers," exclude families when the husband is in the military, and impose stricter quality-control standards. This time, however, the House succeeded in blocking many of the administration proposals passed by the Senate. Dropped in conference, for example, were amendments to create a standard filing unit, to consider part of the income of grandparents and siblings as "available" to the welfare family, and to increase the penalty for failure to accept employment. Two years later, the omnibus Deficit Reduction Act of 1984 endorsed the standard filing unit provision long sought by the Reagan administration to prevent AFDC families from excluding income earned by family members.

Taken together, the legislative changes of the early 1980s overturned a surprisingly large number of court decisions. Among other things, Congress required states to count the income of stepparents, partly overturning *Lewis v. Martin*; overturned the Supreme Court's *Hurley* decision on lodgers; removed the open-ended work expense-deduction mandated by the Court in *Shea* v. *Vialpando*; reversed the *Townsend* decision on benefits for college students; reversed the *Carleson* decision on benefits to servicemen; prohibited the states from considering a fetus a "child," a policy mandated by many lower courts before *Burns*; broadened the definition of income available to the welfare family, overturning a large number of lower court decisions on the subject; modified the Supreme Court's expansion of AFDC-UP in *California* v. *Westcott* by limiting eligibility to families in which the "principal wage earner" is unemployed; required the Department of Health and Human Services to establish resource limits and quality-control guidelines similar to those struck down by the lower courts; and mandated retrospective budgeting and accounting, practices prohibited by the California courts.

By 1984 Congress was routinely responding to court decisions interpreting the legislation passed in 1981 and 1982. For example, the Deficit Reduction Act of 1984 made clear that "earned income" means gross income before taxes, not net income after taxes, as several courts had found. The Senate report presented these court decisions as clear mistakes. The House went along without controversy.[44] Not only was the

Reagan administration quick to identify court decisions that impeded its policies, but for several years reconciliation gave them a recurring mechanism for putting such matters before Congress.

Why were the policies established by the courts during the preceding decade subject to so much legislative revision? Two factors were particularly important. First, court decisions had created a number of anomalies that were easy targets for those intent upon cutting federal spending. Examples included welfare families with relatively affluent stepfathers, families with parents serving in the military, families with high work expenses, and families with employed older children. Court rulings on available income and their insistence upon complex, individualized calculation of deductions at times created a distorted picture of financial need. Such policies may have affected only a small percentage of recipients, but they channeled scarce funds to less needy families and increased public indignation about welfare "abuse."

Liberal Democrats did not put up much of a fight to protect these judicially initiated policies. When possible, they traded concessions in these areas for minor changes elsewhere. For example, the House accepted the standard filing unit in return for a $50 a month "pass through" for child support payments. More often, they simply accepted these changes as the least painful ways to cut spending. The new budget politics of the 1980s placed new importance on the efficient targeting of limited resources—a subject to which federal judges paid scant attention.

Second, the purpose of the Reagan proposal was not simply to cut costs, but to reduce welfare dependency by imposing norms of work and family responsibility—even if this meant leaving some families without assistance. Underlying these amendments was a view of welfare far removed from the conception of entitlements tacitly endorsed by the federal courts. In the words of Nathan Glazer, the Reagan administration rejected a "nonjudgmental, supportive" welfare system. Its approach was not to "encourage family stability by means of an incentive," but to "promote stability by *imposing a norm*—i.e., that a man living with a woman and her child had an obligation to support the woman with whom he lived as husband, the children with whom he lived as father."[45] Imposition of these norms is especially clear in such items as the workfare programs long advocated by the Reagan administration and included in the 1988 Family Support Act. It is also evident in the increasingly aggressive and intrusive child support enforcement mandated by Congress and in rules on lodgers, stepparents, and the standard filing unit. Those who violated these norms were penalized, sometimes to the extent of having their entire grant withdrawn.

As significant as these changes are, it is also important to note what Congress did *not* do even at the apogee of the "Reagan revolution." First, no attempt was ever made to reauthorize the extreme substitute-parent or suitable-home rules of the pre-1968 period. All that survived of the man-in-the-house rules incorporated in the 1970 and 1972 Senate Finance Committee bills were the mild rules on stepparents and lodgers. An administration proposal to include the income of all nonrelated adults living in the household was approved by the Senate in 1982 but dropped in the conference committee. New political realities in the South and changing sexual mores within society at large help explain Congress's lack of enthusiasm for such eligibility rules.

Second, despite administration rhetoric about returning welfare to the states, the legislative changes of the early 1980s did not always leave the states with more discretion. With the federal government intent upon saving money and promoting work, federal requirements tended to *grow* rather than shrink. Indeed, it was the administration that tried to force workfare programs on the states, and congressional liberals who defended state discretion. Moreover, as they struggled to write statutory provisions not susceptible to reinterpretation by the courts, administration officials and their allies in the Senate added more and more detail to title IV. The federal requirements added in the 1980s are, by previous standards, remarkable both in their number and in their complexity. Never before, for example, had Congress told the states how to calculate income or how to define the family unit. Not only had support for state control waned in the 1970s, but those who had previously championed state discretion now made reducing federal spending and combating welfare dependency higher priorities.

Finally, no attempt was made to limit judicial review of state or federal practices. One of the small ironies of AFDC history is that the welfare reform legislation filed by Nixon in 1969 sharply limited judicial review of state and federal rules, but the legislation submitted by Ronald Reagan in 1981–84 did not. The explicit attack on the courts that permeated the Senate reports of 1970 and 1972 is absent from the debates of the 1980s. Debate focused on the substance of welfare policy rather than on institutional issues.

A New Consensus?

In the fall of 1988 Congress passed yet another set of amendments to AFDC. The Family Support Act is notable for the way it combined the proposals of liberal and conservative welfare critics. The act extends transitional medicaid and child care benefits to those who leave AFDC to take a job—a striking reversal of Reagan policies reducing benefits to the working poor. Not only does the act increase spending by $3.5 billion over five years, but it requires all states to establish AFDC-UP programs, a goal long sought by liberals. At the same time, the act demands that one parent in each AFDC-UP family perform at least sixteen hours of unpaid work each week—a requirement that some liberals denounced as "slavefare."[46] The act also requires states to enroll specific percentages of recipients in education and training programs, and it creates more vigorous child support enforcement programs. According to the act's chief sponsor, Senator Daniel Patrick Moynihan, "Conservatives have persuaded liberals that there is nothing wrong with obligating able-bodied adults to work. Liberals have persuaded conservatives that most adults want to work and need some help to do so."[47]

Passage of the Family Support Act reflects a shift in thinking about welfare that is broader and more long-lasting than the Reagan administration's push to cut spending for poverty programs. Robert Reischauer reports that among "a broad spectrum of the policy establishment" the idea that "welfare is an entitlement that all eligible citizens may claim" has been replaced by "the concept of mutual obligation." In the 1960s and 1970s "policymakers shied away from making judgments about family living patterns." Today, in contrast, there is greater willingness "to discuss sensitive value-laden issues" in order to find ways to strengthen the family.[48] According to a study group assembled by the American Enterprise Institute, this "new consensus on welfare" is both "job-focused, taking as its premise the ideas that all able-bodied persons ought to work" and "obligational, requiring aid recipients to meet certain responsibilities in return for their benefits."[49] "The drift of antipoverty policy during the 1970s and 1980s," Lawrence Mead writes, "was away from social reformism of either the left or the right and toward efforts to reorder the personal lives of the poor."[50] Another prominent student of welfare policy, Joel Handler, described this change (which he decries) as "a reaction against the ideology of entitlement."[51]

The history of the Family Support Act shows that it is not always easy to move from a consensus on these abstract issues to agreement on program design. Disagreements over spending levels and participation rates for work programs nearly killed the legislation.[52] Differences between liberals and conservatives later reemerged as HHS struggled to write regulations required by the act.

If this "new consensus" has not provided a blueprint for welfare reform, it clearly represents a repudiation of both the incentive-based approach of FAP and PBJI and the broad, need-only understanding of entitlements embraced by many judges in AFDC cases. To most judges and legal commentators who wrote about welfare in the 1960s and early 1970s, progress meant jettisoning the heritage of the Elizabethan poor laws—the source of the localistic, moralistic, categorical American welfare system—and moving toward some form of guaranteed income paid in cash without strings or stigma. Over the past thirty years, members of Congress and the American public have become more willing to support nationally uniform welfare programs and less willing to tolerate overt racial discrimination. But they have not accepted the view that public assistance benefits should be based solely on economic need. On this matter public opinion did not follow elite wisdom. Rather, elite opinion returned to more traditional positions on the importance of establishing norms of work and family responsibility. The "sophisticated and enlightened" approach to welfare that Chief Justice Warren painted as the wave of the future today seems strangely—even quaintly—anachronistic.

PART III

Education for the Handicapped

CHAPTER SEVEN

A Bill of Rights Becomes a Law

Over the past few years, parents of handicapped children have begun to recognize that their children are being denied services which are guaranteed under the Constitution. It should not, however, be necessary for parents throughout the country to continue utilizing the courts to assure themselves a remedy. It is this Committee's belief that Congress must take a more active role . . . to guarantee that handicapped children are provided equal educational opportunity. . . . [This legislation] takes positive necessary steps to ensure that the rights of children and their families are protected.
—Senate Labor and Public Welfare Committee report, 1975

EDUCATION for the handicapped presents a vivid contrast to aid to families with dependent children. As the previous chapters show, the courts' understanding of "welfare rights" never took root in Congress. None of the Supreme Court's many rulings under title IV of the Social Security Act were ever explicitly endorsed by Congress. In the early 1980s the courts' opponents gathered enough support to overturn a number of judicial decisions. Moreover, the "new consensus" that developed in the late 1980s shifted attention from individual rights to family responsibilities. The Education for All Handicapped Children Act (EAHCA) of 1975, in contrast, recognized and expanded the right to a "free appropriate public education" first announced in two innovative lower court rulings. In the words of Senator Robert Stafford, "Those of us who drafted the [EAHCA] were influenced and instructed by these decisions. . . . The law codified the rights already spelled out in earlier court decisions."[1] This landmark legislation not only distributed billions of dollars to state and local school systems but created an elaborate mechanism for defining the contours of this right and for ensuring compliance by local school systems (see figure 7-1).

The Education for All Handicapped Children Act has had a dramatic impact on special education policy at the federal, state, and local level. It "transform[ed] special education practice across the nation by bringing all states up to the standard that some states, prompted by court action

Figure 7–1. *Major Provisions of the Education for All Handicapped Children Act*

Mandates school systems to provide a "free appropriate public education" to all handicapped children.

Requires teachers and administrators to hold yearly conferences with parents, and on this basis to establish an "individualized educational program" for each handicapped child.

Offers parents dissatisfied with this "individualized educational program" the opportunity to receive an "impartial due process hearing," first before a local independent hearing officer, then before a review board at the state level, and ultimately before a federal district court judge.

Requires schools to "assure that, to the maximum extent appropriate, handicapped children . . . are educated with children who are not handicapped."

Requires schools to provide handicapped children with "related services" such as occupational and physical therapy, recreation, psychological services, and counseling.

Prohibits school systems from changing the placement of handicapped children without a change in the "individualized educational program" approved by the parents.

Provides federal funding for a portion of the "excess cost" required for educating handicapped children.

---

and advocacy by handicapped rights groups, already had adopted."[2] Despite a decline in the total public school population, the number of children in special education rose from 2.3 million in 1968 to 4.3 million in 1986. The number of special education teachers increased from 179,000 in 1977 to 275,000 in 1986. Although accurate cost estimates are hard to find, the "excess" cost for special education (that is, the total cost minus the cost of educating an equal number of regular students) is probably between $25 billion and $30 billion a year. The federal government spends about $2 billion annually on special education (up from $92 million in 1972), making this the second largest program administered by the Department of Education.[3] Indeed, over the past decade and a half special education programs have been the fastest growing part of the budget for most state and local school systems. The United States now devotes considerably more resources to education of the handicapped than do most European nations.

The EAHCA also represented a major departure from previous patterns of policymaking for education. Education in the United States is even more decentralized than public assistance. State and local school districts provide 90 percent of the cost of elementary and secondary education. Not until 1965 did the federal government spend significant sums on primary and secondary education, and even then it was reluctant to exert any control over curricular matters. With education for the handicapped, federal regulation of state and local school systems has far outstripped the federal money provided by the act. The EAHCA, said to be "the most prescriptive education statute ever passed by Congress," establishes "with unusual exactitude the expectations for local school district officials."[4]

The extent and nature of federal regulation of state and local programs is evident in court rulings under the act. In 1989, for example, the First Circuit ordered a New Hampshire school district to provide special tutoring and physical therapy to a child with virtually no brain cortex. Despite the fact that the child sometimes could not even respond to familiar voices, the court found him to be educable. The court maintained "that education under the Act encompasses a wide spectrum of training, and that for the severely handicapped it may include the most elemental life skills." Other judges have required school districts to pay for twenty-four-hour care in psychiatric hospitals and for such "related services" as periodic catheterization and reinsertion of tracheotomy tubes.[5]

In a 1985 case, the Fourth Circuit barred a school system from expelling a student involved in drug dealing. The court found that the child's learning disability had made him particularly susceptible to peer pressure.[6] Three years later, the Supreme Court decided a case involving two emotionally disturbed children. One had choked a fellow student and "kicked out a school window while being escorted to the principal's office afterwards." The other had engaged in such behavior as "stealing, extorting money from fellow students, and making sexual comments to female classmates." The Court ruled that even when handicapped students engage in violent behavior they cannot be expelled or suspended for more than ten days.[7]

In another case, the Ninth Circuit upheld a lower court decision enjoining California from moving a state school for the blind. After forty-eight days of testimony, the trial court ruled that the new school had not complied with state rules on earthquake protection. Six dissenting judges (including now-Justice Anthony Kennedy) wrote, "This, in effect, extends to handicapped children a federal cause of action to redress a violation of *any* state requirement concerning education, even requirements that benefit all children generally."[8] These, of course, are extreme cases. But they demonstrate just how extensive federal regulation of state and local educational practices has become.

The Strategy of Rights

Previous efforts to expand the role of the federal government in education had required vigorous presidential leadership and extensive political mobilization. Both the Civil Rights Act of 1964 and the Elementary and Secondary Education Act (ESEA) of 1965 were enacted only after a powerful, determined president focused public attention on the issue in order to overcome the opposition of strategically positioned minorities in Congress. Passage of the Education for All Handicapped Children Act was much different. It never attained the visibility of either the Civil Rights Act or ESEA. To say that presidential leadership was not a central factor is an understatement. President Nixon repeatedly opposed the legislation, and President Ford signed it only after seeing that Congress would surely override a veto.

How did advocates for the handicapped manage to pass legislation transforming special education and substantially expanding the role of the federal government without the advantages of presidential leadership, party support, lobbying by established school interests, or a significant shift in public opinion? Much of the answer lies in the interaction between the courts and a newly reformed Congress. Unilateral judicial action put the issue on the national agenda. In 1972 two federal district courts ordered school systems to provide an "appropriate education" and "due process hearings" to handicapped children. Yet these two cases, *Pennsylvania Association for Retarded Children (PARC)* v. *Commonwealth of Pennsylvania* and *Mills* v. *Board of Education of the District of Columbia*, were shaky legal precedents.[9] One was a consent decree. The other was based primarily on local law in the District of Columbia. Soon after these two court rulings, the Supreme Court announced in *San Antonio* v. *Rodriguez* that the courts should not use the equal protection clause to establish novel educational policies.[10] If Congress had not passed the EAHCA, it is quite likely the two lower court decisions would have become exhibits in the museum of Warren-era initiatives abandoned by the Burger court. Since 1975 the courts have been active in special education policy, but only through statutory interpretation, not constitutional adjudication.

Of central importance to the development of federal policy is the fact that from 1972 onward members of Congress, federal administrators, state and local school personnel, parents, and special education professionals have all adopted the individual-rights framework first established by the courts. As David Neal and David Kirp have pointed out, the transformation of special education was accomplished by "distinctively legal" means. "The language of rights and the mechanisms of due process were introduced into an area that had previously relied on the professional discretion of teachers, psychologists, and school administrators."[11]

This approach is peculiarly American. When the British revamped their special education system after passage of the EAHCA, they consciously rejected the American model, choosing to protect professional judgment and bureaucratic discretion rather than to mandate adversarial proceedings and extensive parental involvement. Indeed, the chair of the Committee of Enquiry that reviewed special education policy for Parliament once said, "There is something deeply unattractive about the spectacle of someone demanding his own rights."[12] The attitude underlying the new American policies, in contrast, is that there is something deeply unattractive about allowing disabled students to be subject to the whim of school officials.

In recent years some scholars, administrators, and parents have questioned the wisdom of this rights-based approach to the problem of educating those with disabilities. This debate is likely to grow more heated as special education continues to increase its share of school budgets. The primary purpose of this chapter and the next is not to resolve this dispute, but to explain how the framework of individual rights combined with the separation of powers in an era of divided government to expand the program and extend federal control. In particular, these chapters develop four themes about the political significance of the language of rights.

First, in both the passage and implementation of the act, rights were more than mere symbols, but less than "trumps" (to use Ronald Dworkin's now-famous term). The focus on individual rights, both substantive and procedural, was the central feature of the 1975 act. Yet few of the key actors (including the most devoted advocates for the handicapped) believed that the costs of educational programs for the handicapped would be or even should be irrelevant. Questions of resource allocation were never far from anyone's mind. Rather, the focus on rights was the linchpin of a sophisticated political strategy that allowed these advocates to unite a highly diverse reform coalition, to use victories in the courtroom as leverage in other political forums, and to place themselves in an advantageous bargaining situation during implementation of the act.

Second, although the emphasis on rights was at first perceived by special education professionals as an attack on their expertise and discretion (a perception obviously shared by British officials), they soon realized that this approach could increase their control over special education policy. Indeed, the interest group most active in shaping the act was the Council for Exceptional Children (CEC), the principal national association of special education professionals. Leaders of the CEC argued that creating such legal rights would not only increase the resources going to special education, but would reduce the extent to which principals, superintendents, and school boards scrutinized the professional activities of the organization's members. This explains in part why "school personnel, particularly those in front-line positions, were enthusiastic about the law's reform objectives and sincerely dedicated to their realization."[13]

Third, despite the claims of the act's sponsors that federal legislation would reduce the role played by the courts, litigation has increased dramatically since the passage of the EAHCA. Congress has encouraged litigation not only by creating legal rights to a "free appropriate public education" and to "impartial due process hearings," but also by giving federal district courts substantial discretion to review the decisions of school administrators. Members of Congress feel comfortable with policymaking through litigation. Rather than jealously guarding their institutional prerogatives, they have sought to protect parents' opportunity to have their day in court.

Fourth, despite the influence of the federal judiciary, the Supreme Court left almost no imprint on policymaking. It never issued an opinion on the constitutional rights of handicapped students. For a number of years after passage of the EAHCA, "the U.S. Supreme Court remained a bystander, declining to enter the fray."[14] When it finally did issue an opinion on what constitutes "appropriate education," it endorsed a restrained, deferential role for the federal courts. But its dictates have been ignored or evaded by lower courts' judges. Moreover, in two instances the Supreme Court's narrow reading of the act was reversed by Congress. The real action has been in federal district and circuit courts and in state courts, where judges determine what constitutes an "appropriate education" for particular handicapped students.

Finally, what is most intriguing about education of the handicapped is that policy became more ambitious as it traveled from one institution to another. The conventional wisdom holds that federalism and the separation of powers create multiple veto points, leading to either the defeat or watering down of reform initiatives. Here the opposite was true: federalism and the separation of powers provided a number of opportunity points for reformers, who skillfully used victories in one forum to press for further action in another.

In Pennsylvania, for example, the federal court suit mentioned above spurred the incoming governor to increase the amount of money spent on special education. In Massachusetts, state court decisions and attendant media attention led the state legislature to pass a statute that became a model for the federal law. These states appealed to Congress for financial support. The sponsors of federal legislation argued not only that the states needed help but also that federal money should be tied to guarantees that the states were protecting the "constitutional" rights of handicapped children. Since no one knew precisely what these rights were, the federal legislation needed to spell them out in detail. Once the legislation was passed, the courts reentered the picture, insisting on a literal interpretation of some phrases (such as the requirement that states educate *all* handicapped children) and giving a liberal interpretation to others (such as "related services").

The result was incrementalism, credit taking, and blame avoidance of a peculiar sort. Each institution made incremental changes that seemed small when viewed individually but that constituted rapid and substantial change when put together. Additional steps were taken well before anyone could evaluate the consequences of previous steps. This complex interaction of separated institutions allowed elected officials to take credit for helping the handicapped while avoiding blame for imposing costs. "Don't blame me, the courts made me do it." "Don't blame me, the feds require it." "Don't blame me, that is what the statute says." These were the constant refrains of policymakers, who often understated the discretion available to them.

The Courts Set the Stage

The initial step in this process of racheting up federal requirements came in two 1972 cases, *Pennsylvania Association for Retarded Children (PARC)* v. *Commonwealth of Pennsylvania* and *Mills* v. *Board of Education of the District of Columbia*. Participants and academic commentators agree that these two cases were central to the development of the

Education for All Handicapped Children Act.[15] The influence of the decisions was twofold. First, the substance of the act was drawn from the court orders in *PARC* and *Mills*. The duty to provide all handicapped children with a "free appropriate public education," the requirement that schools work with parents in preparing a plan to meet the unique needs of each handicapped student, the elaborate "impartial due process hearings" requirements, and the preference for mainstreaming all came originally from the courts. In the words of Senator Harrison Williams, the act's chief sponsor, "Certainly the courts have helped us define the right to an education in the last few years. That is what we are trying to find, the means to carry out the fundamental law of the land."[16] The Senate report accompanying the bill added that "Court action and State laws throughout the Nation have made clear that the right to education of handicapped children is a present right, one which is to be implemented immediately."[17] Throughout the debate in Congress the rights recognized by the federal legislation were equated with the rights announced by the courts.

Second, the decisions led state governments to demand that the federal government help pay for the judicial mandates. As a result of *PARC*, *Mills*, several state court decisions adopting their reasoning, and the threat of further litigation, state expenditures for special education rose from $900 million in 1972 to more than $2.1 billion in 1975.[18] The goal of the plaintiffs in these cases had always been to use the courts to spur further legislative action. As one key advocate put it, the strategy was "to cook the school districts until they came to Congress demanding the funds that we [need] to provide appropriate programs."[19] This strategy worked: "Neither the pressures of interest groups nor the general receptivity of Congress would have been sufficient to pass the 1975 act without two court decisions that greatly altered the states' responsibility for education of the handicapped."[20]

PARC and *Mills*, though, were peculiar "landmark" cases. For one thing, the plaintiffs and the defendants did not disagree on much. In *PARC* the nominal defendant, the Commonwealth of Pennsylvania, settled the case after a single day of testimony by the plaintiff's witnesses. Local school systems later complained that the state had colluded with the plaintiffs to fashion a remedy that the local schools would be forced to implement. In the District of Columbia the school system was struggling to deal with a large number of problems, including a federal desegregation order. The beleaguered school board accepted the court's ruling in principle, but was slow to put it into practice. School administrators and the school board realized that a court decree increased their chances of winning increased appropriations from Congress.

In addition, the two courts addressed constitutional issues only in the most oblique fashion. They relied primarily on their interpretation of a variety of state laws, a task usually left to state courts. In *PARC* the court accepted "pendent jurisdiction" over matters involving state law because "the plaintiffs have established a colorable claim under the Due Process Clause" and because "the evidence raises serious doubts (and hence a colorable claim) as to the existence of a rational basis for such exclusions [of handicapped children]."[21] Because the federal courts for the District of Columbia at that time had jurisdiction over all matters involving the D.C. code, it addressed the constitutional issues more directly. Yet this discussion of constitutional mandates remained "remarkably cursory."[22]

None of this stopped the two courts from issuing extensive, detailed orders. The thrust of the two decisions was similar. First, the school systems were ordered to launch a concerted effort to locate handicapped students excluded from public school. Second, in the words of Judge Joseph Waddy of the U.S. District Court for the District of Columbia, school systems

> shall provide to each child of school age a free and suitable publicly-supported education regardless of the degree of the child's mental, physical or emotional disability or impairment. Furthermore, defendants shall not exclude any child . . . on the basis of a claim of insufficient resources.[23]

Third, defendants were required to notify a parent or guardian of "the proposed educational placement, the reasons therefor, and the right to a hearing before a Hearing Officer if there is an objection to the placement proposed." Parents were granted the right to be represented by legal counsel, to examine school records, and to cross-examine school officials. The hearing officer, Judge Waddy ruled, "shall not be an officer, employee or agent of the Public School System." Fourth, school officials "shall not suspend a child from the public schools for disciplinary reasons for any period in excess of two days without affording him a hearing . . . and without providing for his education during the period of any such suspension."[24] Finally, both courts expressed a preference for "mainstreaming," which meant placing handicapped students in classrooms with their nonhandicapped peers.

The Civil Rights Connection

The litigation in Pennsylvania and the District of Columbia made palpable the multiple links between the civil rights movement and the transformation of special education. In the early 1970s a number of civil rights organizations and lawyers involved in desegregation efforts became convinced that special education testing and tracking were being used to perpetuate racial segregation. The *Mills* case itself grew out of the massive District of Columbia desegregation case *Hobson* v. *Hansen*.[25] It was initiated and sustained by three public interest organizations—the National Legal Aid and Defenders Association, the Center for Law and Social Policy, and the Harvard Center for Law and Education, a Legal Services "backup" center—with ties to both the civil rights movement and the war on poverty. The lawyers affiliated with these groups argued not just that many minority students were mistakenly labeled "retarded," but that handicapped students were themselves a stigmatized, excluded minority deserving special judicial protection under the equal protection clause of the Fourteenth Amendment.

The *PARC* case was an offshoot of institutional reform litigation—judicial efforts to restructure such complex state institutions as mental hospitals and prisons—that had in turn grown out of the campaign to desegregate public school systems. The Pennsylvania Association for Retarded Children was originally concerned primarily with conditions at the Pennhurst State School and Hospital, a large residential institution for the retarded. In the late 1960s and early 1970s lawyers familiar with judicial efforts to restructure segregated school systems launched an attack on state facilities for the retarded and mentally ill.[26] The plaintiffs' lawyer persuaded the Pennsylvania association that its best legal attack would be on education, a subject more familiar to judges than the quality of treatment within state institutions. Establishing a constitutional right to education, he argued, would both give the association a foothold at Pennhurst and make deinstitutionalization more attractive to parents.[27] In short, the legacy of the civil rights movement went from desegregating schools to restructuring institutions for the retarded to reforming special education.

From Exclusion to Appropriateness

With education of the handicapped, as with desegregation, the courts started out with issues of "simple justice" and before long found themselves facing complex administrative and policy issues. The most compelling argument the courts heard in *PARC*, *Mills*, and similar cases around the country was that some children were receiving *no* education, either because they had been excluded as "uneducable" or because they had been suspended for behavior related to their disability. Not only did such exclusion violate state laws mandating public education for all those capable of benefiting from it, but it raised equal protection issues in a particularly stark way. In *Brown* v. *Board of Education* the Supreme Court held that "where the state has undertaken to provide" public education, it "must be made available to all on equal terms."[28] In *San Antonio School District* v. *Rodriguez*, the Supreme Court explained that it was willing to uphold Texas's school financing law because it did *not* result in "an *absolute deprivation* of a meaningful opportunity to enjoy that benefit."[29] Complete deprivation of a "fundamental interest" such as education or voting is hard to square with the equal protection clause or with widely shared beliefs about equality of opportunity.

The *PARC* trial began and ended with expert testimony on the educability of all retarded children. The state of Pennsylvania originally claimed that it excluded only the uneducable. The plaintiff's four experts countered that "there is no such thing as an uneducable and untrainable child."[30] In the middle of the trial the state suddenly reversed its position, announcing its agreement with these experts and offering to settle the case. The state Department of Education was eager to accept the controversial assertions of academic experts, and other state officials—especially the newly elected governor, Milton Shapp—were anxious to get rid of a case that made them appear heartless.[31]

More surprising than the defendants' quick capitulation on the issue of exclusion was the effortless way in which the parties and the court moved from nonexclusion to the right to an *appropriate* education. The due process hearings originally designed to prevent exclusion were given the additional task of establishing the appropriateness of instruction within the classroom. This is by no means a necessary progression. Regular students—who presumably have a similar right to an education—seldom receive an individualized hearing on the appropriateness of their education. Nor do they have the opportunity to appeal school decisions to an "impartial hearing officer." Appropriateness, after all, is precisely the type of judgment the Supreme Court has told judges to avoid.

Advocates for the handicapped, distrustful of local officials and concerned at least as much about the quality of special education as about exclusion, were adamant on the issue of "appropriateness." What good is merely sitting in a classroom, they argued, if the education provided by the state is not suited to the student? School officials, assuming that they would be the ones to determine appropriateness, had little reason to object.

Ironically, it later became clear that exclusion was not nearly as extensive a practice as advocates had claimed. The plaintiffs in *PARC* claimed the number of children receiving no education in Pennsylvania was 100,000. The Pennsylvania Department of Education put the number at 50,000. The extensive court-mandated effort to find these children turned up only 2,500 children who were not in any educational program.[32] Results were similar at the national level. The preamble of the Education for All Handicapped Children Act announced that "one million of the handicapped children in the U.S. are excluded entirely from the public school system." The Senate report put the number of handicapped children "receiving *no* educational services at all" at 1.75 million.[33] Yet from 1975 to 1985 the number of mentally retarded, severely emotionally disturbed, and multiply disabled students—those most likely to be excluded—actually declined by more than a quarter of a million. By 1981 both the General Accounting Office and the Office of Civil Rights concluded that the figures used by Congress were far too high.[34] But by then everyone's attention had shifted away from exclusion to the *quality* of special education.

The Reform Coalition

One of the central achievements of the litigation of the early 1970s was to bring together a broad coalition of groups dedicated to reforming special education. The *PARC* and *Mills* cases received a great deal of publicity, including front-page stories and editorials in the *New York Times*. Subsequent litigation gave state and local organizations concrete tasks and helped the CEC and the National Association for Retarded Children (NARC) build a national network of supporters. Most important, the emphasis on individual rights allowed a highly diverse coalition to come together and stay together. This coalition included parents of children with an array of disabilities, special educational professionals, civil rights groups, and other public interest lawyers.

The variety of disabilities that afflicts children of school age is enormous. They stretch from profound retardation to dyslexia, from autism to blindness, from emotional disturbances to spina bifida. Before 1970 parents tended to organize around particular disabilities—if they organized at all. Consequently, the blind, the deaf, the retarded, the physically disabled, and those with learning disabilities competed with one another for scarce resources. Even within these smaller groups there were disagreements about proper treatment—sign language versus lipreading for the deaf, home care versus institutionalization for the profoundly retarded, to cite but two examples. About the only thing everyone could agree upon was that each child should receive an education "appropriate" to his or her "unique capacities."

Robert Katzmann's discussion of the American Coalition for Citizens with Disabilities (ACCD), an umbrella organization concerned primarily with accessible transportation, applies equally well to the coalition put together by the CEC and NARC:

> If government defined federal policy toward the disabled as a matter of claims involving the allocation of finite resources, then presumably each of the many groups within the ACCD would have competed with the others to secure funds for its own constituency. But because the government defined the issue in terms of rights, questions of cost became irrelevant: each group could champion the demands of others without financial sacrifice.[35]

Indeed, the events examined by Katzmann—the passage and implementation of section 504 of the Rehabilitation Act of 1973—helped make clear to advocates for handicapped children the advantages of a rights-based approach.

The driving force behind most of the litigation and lobbying at the state and federal level was the Council for Exceptional Children. An association of more than 70,000 special education professionals, the CEC provided the expert testimony in *PARC* and wrote the model statute that was the basis for many state laws and, ultimately, the EAHCA. The CEC distributed pamphlets and held seminars on how to initiate court suits and how to use these suits as leverage for passing legislation. It took great pains to explain to its members how in the long run this litigation would enhance their position within the school system. Thomas Gilhool, the lead attorney in *PARC*, told a CEC conference, "We have with some ease adopted the agenda that you, the professionals, have set and we have taken it to court." He advised professionals not to interpret court suits as an attack on them: "The experience in the litigation has been that those named as defendants, if they are good professionals, welcome litigation as an opportunity to advance the agenda which they share."[36] A key CEC official emphasized this theme. With surprising candor, he wrote:

> Changes sought through litigation may be very similar to directions the party named as "defendant" has tried to achieve. . . . Litigation (or the threat of litigation) may be used as a lever to bring about the action desired by both the potential defendant and the plaintiff. . . . [In some cases] named defendants have spent days preparing defenses for the suit, and nights assisting the plaintiffs to prepare their arguments.[37]

Parents, lawyers, and professionals shared not only a common set of enemies but also a commitment to *individualized* treatment for each handicapped child. Individual needs, in the end, would be determined by special education experts now insulated from pressure by cost-conscious administrators and politicians. These factors brought parents, lawyers, and professionals together in early litigation and eventually produced a formidable alliance dedicated to protecting the EAHCA.

The Appeal to Congress

For all the brave talk about a constitutional right to a "free appropriate public education," the law on the subject was remarkably thin. Even the *PARC* decision contained the statement that "the settlement itself eliminates the need to make *any* constitutional decisions at all concerning these unclear state statutes."[38] Advocates for the handicapped won a few state court cases, most notably in Maryland and North Dakota. At the same time, they were losing other cases in federal courts.[39] The judicial steamroller pictured by congressional sponsors of the EAHCA began to run out of gas well before enactment of the legislation.

No one was more painfully aware of this tenuous legal position than lobbyists for the CEC and the lawyers with whom they worked. "They particularly feared that an increasingly conservative U.S. Supreme Court would reject a constitutional right to education for the handicapped. They chose their judges carefully and avoided appellate resolution of the issue."[40] And with good reason. One year after *PARC* and *Mills*, the Supreme Court announced that "it is not the province of this Court to create substantive constitutional rights in the name of guaranteeing equal protection of the laws." It added, "this Court's lack of specialized knowledge and experience counsels against premature interference with the informed judgments made at the state and local levels. Education, perhaps even more than welfare assistance, presents a myriad of 'intractable economic, social, and even philosophical problems.' "[41]

At the same time, all was not well in Pennsylvania and the District of Columbia. Although Pennsylvania had proceeded aggressively to locate excluded children, its effort to improve the quality of instruction had bogged down. The parties could not agree on such issues as mainstreaming. The cost of reform continued to mount. Overhauling a highly decentralized education system presented unanticipated implementation problems. Even the special master appointed by the court to oversee the *PARC* decree concluded that there "isn't much new educationally in Pennsylvania, as an outcome of this case." The situation in the District of Columbia was even worse.[42]

CEC's political genius was to convert a stalled judicial strategy into a successful legislative campaign. Working first at the state level, advocates discovered that legislators and governors were willing to appropriate more money for special education and to impose new regulations on local schools as long as they could lay the blame on the federal courts.[43] Before long, advocates for the disabled turned their attention to Congress. They joined with state and local officials to demand that the federal government help pay for the mandates of *PARC* and *Mills*. They also argued that federal legislation would put an end to the unnerving uncertainty created by pending litigation. As one advocate put it, "School officials hate judges even more than they do bureaucrats, even federal bureaucrats."[44] As it turned out, the federal legislation passed in 1975 forced them to deal even more frequently with both.

The Passage of Rights

For a bill that has been described as "one of the most important developments in the history of American education," "the most significant child welfare legislation of the 1970s," and a "Magna Carta" for parents of handicapped children, the EAHCA generated remarkably little opposition in Congress.[45] Not one interest group opposed the bill. Only the White House and HEW Secretary Caspar Weinberger spoke against it. The bill passed both houses by margins so lopsided that President Ford decided not to veto it. Republicans in the House made a half-hearted attempt to lower authorization levels, but quickly added that with minor changes "this bill would truly represent one of the finest Acts ever produced by Congress."[46]

Four factors help explain congressional support for education of the handicapped. First and most obvious is the entrepreneurial role of the two authorizing committees, the House Education and Labor Committee and the Senate Labor and Public Welfare Committee. These committees have been aggressive in their support for federal aid to education as well as assistance for the handicapped. In the early 1970s members of these committees were looking for an opportunity to expand the federal role in special education. *PARC, Mills*, and other court decisions created a fiscal problem for which these entrepreneurs had a ready policy solution.

Second, education of the handicapped is an issue that cuts across party lines. The best indication of this came in 1981 when the Republicans gained control of the Senate. Senator Lowell Weicker, the new chairman of the Subcommittee on Handicapped, was at least as vocal in his opposition to the Reagan administration on this issue as were Democrats on the panel. Weicker, to be sure, is hardly a typical Republican. But such atypical Republicans gravitate to the two education committees. Senators Robert Stafford, Jacob Javits, and Charles Mathias, as well as Representatives Albert Quie and James Jeffords, were all instrumental in the passage of the EAHCA. Just as important, their more conservative Republican colleagues made little effort to oppose them on the floor. Disabilities such as retardation, spina bifida, blindness, autism, and learning disabilities are universally viewed as tragedies that fall upon rich and poor, black and white, and residents of inner cities, suburbs, and farm districts—even members of Congress and their families.[47] This fact has made normal political cleavages—between Republicans and Democrats, liberals and conservatives, North and South, rural and urban—nearly irrelevant.

Third, although federal policy changed rapidly from 1970 to 1975, this change took the form of several small steps, none of which seemed significantly greater than the last. Initially Congress provided a small amount of money to the states. A few years later, state and federal courts imposed new requirements on school systems. Congress then strengthened these rules while claiming only to spell out requirements already imposed by the courts. What is surprising is how rapidly one increment was added to another and how little thought was given to their long-term, cumulative consequences.

Fourth, the benefits of the new federal program are clear and are of great importance to parents and professionals, but the costs are hard to trace. Only a small part of the cost of special education is borne by the federal government. Who pays for the services required by the EAHCA? Local taxpayers? State taxpayers? Teachers who are expected to take on extra duties? Regular students who receive fewer resources and experience the disruptive consequences of mainstreaming? No one can say for sure. This ambiguity—an ambiguity created largely by the rights-based structure of the act—has proved highly significant politically.

Handicapped to the Fore

The two committees with jurisdiction over education have long been known as liberal, policy-oriented, and entrepreneurial. In the 1960s and early 1970s the Senate Labor and Public Welfare Committee contained no southern Democrats and only two conservative Republicans. The House committee has been dominated by northern liberal Democrats ever since the 1958 election.[48] In 1965 committee members swallowed their pride and accepted *in toto* the version of the Elementary and Secondary Education bill negotiated by the Johnson administration and education interest groups.[49] Within a year, they were rushing to champion causes that they believed the executive branch had ignored.

In 1966 the House committee formed an ad hoc subcommittee on the handicapped. Over the objection of the White House and the Office of Education, Congress established a small authorization for education of the handicapped and created the Bureau of Education for the Handicapped (BEH). Committee leaders then pressured the administration to appoint the subcommittee's chief staff member as the bureau's first director. Four years later, Congress passed the Education of the Handicapped Act, which increased authorizations and earmarked federal aid for such activities as research on "specific learning disabilities," centers for the handicapped, and personnel training. The White House and the appropriations committees showed less enthusiasm for these programs. Appropriations never approached the $500 million annual authorization.[50]

This pattern of executive resistance and committee insistence became more pronounced under President Nixon. The Nixon administration sought to reduce both federal spending on education and federal demands on the states. Congress's response was to create more and large categorical programs. As Gary Orfield has pointed out, "In a remarkable reversal of the pre-1965 period, the Nixon era found Congress generally fighting to preserve the momentum of educational change against a President committed to reaction."[51] Education became both a Democratic and a congressional issue. The more education bills Nixon threatened to veto, the more Democrats presented themselves as the party of education. The more Democrats took credit for education programs, the more congressional Republicans backed away from Nixon and presented the issue as one between Congress and the president rather than one between Democrats and Republicans. The time was ripe for new initiatives in education.

Education for the handicapped was just one of many programs with enthusiastic congressional advocates. Some members of Congress wanted to increase general aid to education. Other wanted to target aid to the poor or to troubled urban school systems or to schools undergoing desegregation. Before *San Antonio* v. *Rodriguez*, it seemed possible that Congress would pass legislation to reduce the large financial disparities among state and local school districts. This initiative quickly lost steam after the Supreme Court handed down its decision.

Education for the handicapped received an important boost in 1970, when Senator Harrison Williams rose to the chairmanship of the Senate committee. Williams had previously had an undistinguished career in the Senate and was looking for an issue to call his own. He soon decided to make the handicapped his top priority. He used his position as chairman of the Subcommittee on Housing and Urban Affairs of the Committee on Banking, Housing, and Urban Affairs to push for accessible public transit. At the Labor and Public Welfare Committee he created the Subcommittee on the Handicapped.[52]

Chairman Williams and the rest of the committee soon discovered that this was an issue with a vocal clientele and significant political appeal. Over the next few years, Congress passed a number of important laws on the subject. These include section 504 of the Rehabilitation Act (which outlawed discrimination on the basis of handicap in any program receiving federal assistance), the Developmental Disabilities Assistance and Bill of Rights Act, the Civil Rights for Institutionalized Persons Act, and several pieces of legislation expanding transportation for the disabled.

The Act Takes Shape

In 1972 Senator Williams introduced S.6, the bill that eventually became the Education for All Handicapped Children Act. Previous education legislation had emphasized money and "capacity building," that is, creating a cooperative corps of reformist professionals at the federal, state, and local levels. S.6 departed from this tradition. Its detailed mandates on "free appropriate public education," "related services," and "due process hearings" were not written by older staff members with their ties to the Office of Education, but by an "alternative policy network" created by Williams. Jack Tweedie has described this network as "a 'progressive cohort' of personally and politically compatible legislative staff members and lobbyists."[53] Williams's staffers worked especially closely with the CEC, whose model statute formed the core of this bill. Strict enforcement and confrontation with the educational establishment replaced capacity building and cooperation as the goals of reformers.

S.6 was but one of many programs competing for money and floor time before the resurgent Congress of the mid-1970s. Of decisive importance to the bill's success was the fact that state officials lined up to testify that they needed help. State officials, committee members, and advocates for the handicapped created the image of a right-to-education juggernaut that would crush the states unless they received a massive injection of federal funds. The federal government, they argued, had already set standards for special education. Now it should put its money where its mouth was. The Nixon administration lamely replied that the states had more money in their coffers than did the federal government. The Democratic leadership realized that this created a golden opportunity for their party to come to the aid of the states.

The political change wrought by the court decisions was evident in the congressional action on the Education Amendments of 1974. On the floor of the Senate, Charles Mathias offered an amendment substantially increasing the authorization for education of the handicapped. Mathias explained that a successful class action suit in state court had dramatically increased the cost of special education for Maryland. He warned that "the set of conditions found in Maryland are replicated throughout this country in most States."[54] No one spoke against the amendment, which was passed by voice vote, accepted by the House in conference, and signed into law.

Added to the Mathias amendment was an unprinted floor amendment that, in the words of its sponsor, Senator Robert Stafford, "simply attaches guarantees to Mr. Mathias's amendment, which conform to the court decrees."[55] The Stafford amendment likewise faced no opposition on the floor or in conference. It established the goal of a "free appropriate public education" for all handicapped children. It required states to guarantee "procedural safeguards in decisions regarding identification, evaluation and educational placement of handicapped children." These procedures must include prior notice to parents, "an opportunity for the parents or guardian to obtain an impartial due process hearing . . . and obtain an independent educational evaluation of the child," and "procedures to insure that, to the maximum extent appropriate, handicapped children . . . are educated with children who are not handicapped."

What all this meant, of course, was left unclear. No one wished to challenge the contention that when states receive federal money they should protect children's constitutional rights. Moreover, these amendments were presented as a stop-gap measure designed to tide the states over until Congress could put together a more comprehensive response. Just as Stafford claimed in 1974 that he was doing little more than codifying court rulings, the following year Senator Williams and his cosponsors claimed that they were doing little more than providing additional money and guidance for carrying out the Stafford amendment.

The Final Hurdles

Legislation on education of the handicapped came into 1975 with considerable momentum. State and local education agencies and the two major teachers' unions supported the effort to increase the federal authorization substantially. Even in an ordinary year the prospects for increased funding and a concomitant increase in federal regulation would have been good. But 1975 was no ordinary year. The 1974 election had produced a "veto-proof" Congress with 291 Democrats in the House and 60 in the Senate. Democrats were already building a legislative record in anticipation of the 1976 presidential election. With the proven popularity of both education and assistance for the handicapped, with little organized opposition (other than that of President Ford, which probably *helped* advocates for the handicapped by making the issue a test of congressional resolve), and with committees that had already done their homework, passage of some variation on S.6 seemed assured.

The only real challenge to passage of the act came in the conference committee. Conferees faced two issues: money and compliance mechanisms. The House bill created a permanent authorization, but the Senate's authorization expired after 1979. By reducing the authorization level significantly for the 1976–82 period, the conferees gave the appearance of responding to President Ford's budgetary concerns. The post-1982 level remained similar to that in the House bill. Given the fact that actual appropriations have never approached authorization levels, this was not much of a concession on the part of either committee.

Disagreement over compliance mechanisms, in contrast, nearly produced a deadlock in the conference. Advocates for the handicapped insisted on elaborate appeals procedures, which the National School Board Association and other education groups strenuously opposed. Given the vagueness of the act's substantive mandate, compliance procedures in effect are a mechanism for deciding who sets federal policy. Advocates for the handicapped, many of whom had spent years battling school districts, understood this better than the lobbyists for school groups.

The original version of S.6 had required the federal Office of Education to review and approve all individualized education programs (IEPs). The federal bureaucracy was not enthusiastic about screening several million plans each year, and Senator Williams and his staff eventually discarded this approach as impractical. Their next solution was to require each state to create a new "entity for assuring compliance with the Act." This "entity" would be composed of special education experts and citizens with disabilities. It would "conduct periodic evaluations," review complaints, "make determinations with respect to alleged violations," and "take appropriate steps to assure that such violations are corrected."[56] The revised Senate bill pleased neither local agencies, which objected to state-level review, nor state agencies, which were "appalled at the elaborate system proposed in the Senate bill and the amplification of this procedure suggested by the advocacy groups."[57]

The House bill, in contrast, required local school districts to establish "grievance procedures" to consider complaints by parents. The state agency would review the facts of each disputed case and correct failures to comply with the act. A record of each grievance proceeding would be sent to the Office of Education, which was required to cut off funds for school districts that failed to comply with the act. The House bill established a deferential "substantial evidence" standard of judicial review. A major problem with the House bill was that it seemed to place this complex grievance procedure on top of the "impartial due process hearing" requirement of the Stafford amendment. Senate conferees considered it too cumbersome to be effective.

The architect of the conference committee's solution was first-term representative George Miller, who has made children's issues one of his major issues. Miller worked closely with the Children's Defense Fund

(CDF) and the California Rural Legal Assistance Foundation (CRLAF), both of which had been involved in litigation on behalf of handicapped students and were highly suspicious of the education "establishment."[58] The lengthy and detailed proposals written by CDF and CRLAF and put forth by Miller were weakened somewhat to make them more palatable to traditional education interest groups.

The final version of the EAHCA contained these provisions:

—A parent dissatisfied with an IEP can demand an "impartial due process hearing" at the local level. The hearing officer may not be "an employee of such agency or unit involved in the education or care of the child." Parties to the hearing have the right to be accompanied by legal counsel, to compel attendance by witnesses, to cross-examine witnesses, and to receive a verbatim record of the hearing and a written explanation of the hearing officer's decision.

—Either party may appeal the outcome of the first "impartial due process hearing" at the state level. The state agency "shall conduct an impartial review . . . and make an independent decision."

—Aggrieved parties can appeal this decision in federal district court. The court shall review the record of the prior hearings, "hear additional evidence at the request of a party," and "basing its decision on the preponderance of the evidence, shall grant such relief as the court determines is appropriate." The conference report added that the federal court should make an "independent" judgment as to the adequacy of the IEP.

Most commentators have stressed the legalistic and adversarial nature of this compliance mechanism. Not only does it give a significant role to the federal court—the "preponderance of the evidence" standard is much less deferential than the "substantial evidence" standard common in such statutes—but it makes each administrative hearing relatively formal and courtlike. Just as important (and less often noted) is the way control over IEP decisions shifted away from those who must bear the cost of complying with them. Hearing officers at each level are to be "independent," which means, above all, not readily subjected to reprisal by school administrators. Most independent of all are the federal judges who have the final say over what constitutes an "appropriate" education.

Why did school systems ultimately accept this intrusion into their traditional area of autonomy? The conference bill was less obnoxious than either the House or the Senate bill. State and local education agencies could choose the hearing officers, and the initial review was at the local rather than the state level. Moreover, the change from the

Stafford amendment with its vague "due process" requirement did not seem large. To be sure, the conference bill expanded the role of the courts. But hadn't the courts played a significant role even without federal legislation? Looming over everything else was the carrot of federal money. Why put authorizing legislation in jeopardy over procedural issues, especially since the courts might impose more stringent procedural requirements if the legislation were to fail?

On November 29, 1975, President Ford signed P.L. 94-142. He warned that "unfortunately, this bill promises more than the federal government can deliver" and that the bill's "vast array of detailed, complex, and costly administrative requirements" would "unnecessarily assert federal control over traditional state and local government functions."[59] In 1975 such arguments fell on deaf ears, which is probably why Ford declined to veto the bill.

The Ironies of Congressional Action

The history of the Education for All Handicapped Children Act is replete with ironic twists. Although advocates for the handicapped focused their efforts on Congress because they recognized that their constitutional arguments were weak, members of Congress constantly exaggerated the scope and the solidity of these court rulings. This allowed them to take credit for helping both the handicapped and financially pressed school systems while deflecting to the courts any blame for additional federal regulation. State and local officials supported the act in order to receive more federal money, but soon found that the cost of the new requirements was far greater than the amount of federal financial support. Familiar only with national programs that provided money with easily evaded strings, most state and local official only later realized that federal mandates could become "millstones."[60]

The legislation passed by Congress in 1975 was complex and detailed in its procedures, but surprisingly vague in its substantive mandates. State applications for federal money, local applications to the states, IEP meetings, due process hearings—all these were spelled out in elaborate statutory provisions. Yet the heart of the act, the right to a "free appropriate public education" and "related services," became the educational equivalent of the Holy Ghost: everyone considers them sacred, but no one really knows what they are. Members of Congress talked blithely about providing equal educational opportunity and allowing each individual to maximize his potential without giving serious thought to what this might mean in practice.

This combination of procedural precision and substantive ambiguity was a result of two conflicting policy imperatives. On the one hand, special education professionals, leaders of groups such as the CEC and NARC, and their congressional allies all argued that educational plans must be geared to the *unique* needs of each handicapped child. Special education, they claimed, should not be rule-bound, but remain sensitive to the subtle differences among the disabled. Given the huge variety of disabling conditions and the extent of disagreement over how to treat each one, it is difficult to see how Congress could possibly have laid out the proper treatment for each and every subcategory of handicapped child.

On the other hand, the principal sponsors of the act were highly suspicious of local school systems, which they accused of ignoring and mistreating the handicapped in the past. They strenuously opposed the traditional practice of providing state and local officials with more money and hoping they would spend it wisely: "Since these organizations were generally suspicious of what schools would provide for the handicapped, in developing the legislation they considered not only questions of broad purpose but what, under other circumstances, might have been regarded as administrative details."[61] How could one hope to change educational practices in 15,000 local school systems without providing substantive guidelines? Elaborate procedures seemed to provide the only way out of the dilemma.

In designing these procedures, groups like the CEC, NARC, CDF, and CRLAF had an important advantage. They had spent years fighting and suing school systems. As a result, they had a fairly good sense that procedures provided leverage against recalcitrant school officials. The Washington representatives of traditional education groups, in contrast, were far removed from such local confrontations, were accustomed to seeing financial issues as paramount, and thus were not nearly as sophisticated at estimating the likely consequences of procedural change. With the help of congressional allies such as George Miller and Harrison Williams, advocates for the handicapped won the day.

The procedures they created not only made proceedings within the schools more adversarial and courtlike but made it easy for federal judges to play an active role in policymaking under the act. A principal reason state and local officials supported the EAHCA was that they believed it would reduce the uncertainty and contentiousness of litigation. Sponsors of the federal law repeatedly reassured school officials that the legislation would take these matters out of the courts. But the opposite happened: the number of court cases grew enormously. Just as the Supreme Court was pulling the federal judiciary away from educational policymaking, Congress was pushing it back in.

CHAPTER EIGHT

Back in Court—Again

[The act] describes the problem which might cryptically be stated as the unsatisfactory educational opportunities found to be available to handicapped children . . . [and] announces that these handicapped children should have an "appropriate" education. . . . Whether or not any of these procedures created by the congressional delegation to the agencies and the states results in an appropriate education for a handicapped child cannot be determined by reference to any of the provisions of the law passed by the Congress. . . . The entire matter is to be decided, de novo, by a United States district judge [who] . . . is to determine on a case-by-case basis, what is the "appropriate" answer to the problem seen by the Congress to confront the country.
—Federal Appeals Court Judge Robert M. Hills, 1983

IMPLEMENTATION of the Education for All Handicapped Children Act was bound to be contentious. Throughout the legislative process members of Congress had acted under the assumption that what constitutes an "appropriate education" could be determined through a relatively straightforward application of professional judgment. Professional norms, though, proved far weaker than expected. It soon became apparent that in many instances "equally well-trained professional educators working in good faith and under the best of circumstances in a non-adversarial context, cannot agree on either the assessment or placement of handicapped children."[1]

On top of this, the act brought a variety of new actors into the policymaking process. Parents, teachers, school psychologists, and local administrators all work on individualized education programs. Hearing officers at the state and local level confront many of the most troublesome cases. Local school boards and state boards of education continue to make decisions that affect the availability of services. Both the Department of Education's Office of Special Education and Rehabilitative Services and the Office of Civil Rights in the Department of Justice have written extensive federal regulations on education of the handicapped. Last but not least, virtually every school district in the country has had at least one case wind up in court. Much of this litigation takes place in state court. The federal courts, though, have heard hundreds of cases. Six have gone all the way to the U.S. Supreme Court. One indication of the extent to which special education has been judicialized is the fact that an entire reporting service, the *Education of the Handicapped Law Reporter*, is devoted to publishing the opinions of judges, hearing officers, and state and federal agencies.

That the courts should be so involved in the administration of the act is, in retrospect, not surprising. Parents with severely disabled children have a great deal at stake: residential placement can cost $50,000 or more a year. In nearly every state there soon appeared private attorneys who specialize in education of the handicapped. Those district and circuit court judges who chafed under the Burger court's restrictive reading of the equal protection clause in education cases welcomed the opportunity to make an "independent" finding on the adequacy of educational plans.

As the quotation at the beginning of this chapter indicates, not all judges were happy about being handed hot policy potatoes.[2] Although the Supreme Court's most important decision under the act, *Hendrick Hudson District Board of Education* v. *Rowley*, came down squarely on the side of judicial modesty, the Supreme Court has not succeeded in persuading all the lower courts to comply with this directive.[3] Judicial review of state and local decisions has remained remarkably decentralized and ad hoc.

The Quiet Administrators

One reason the courts have played such an important role in defining the requirements of the Education for All Handicapped Children Act is that federal administrators have offered so little useful guidance on key issues. The usual role of the federal courts in administrative law is to review the decisions of administrators. Even during periods of judicial activism—such as the 1970s—the courts strike down agency decisions only if they find them unreasonable. Under the Education for All Handicapped Children Act, though, the courts are usually the *only* agent of the federal government to examine the appropriateness of particular education programs. Not only does the Department of Education lack authority to review individual cases, but it has studiously avoided explaining what constitutes a "free appropriate educational program." Ironically, the courts have generally left procedural matters to the agency and resolved substantive issues themselves.

One reason the Department of Education has been happy to leave difficult substantive issues to the courts is that for years it has been caught between two competing constituencies as well as between congressional committees and the White House. Soon after passage of the act, the Bureau of Education for the Handicapped (subsequently renamed the Office of Special Education and Rehabilitative Services) began a rulemaking procedure that in its scope and extent of public participation was unprecedented for the agency.[4] During this rulemaking process, "federal and state professionals were repeatedly at loggerheads."[5] State officials realized that complying with some of the new rules would require changing state laws as well as school practices. State officials, local officials, and advocacy groups disagreed on such matters as the content of notices to parents, who should pay for independent evaluations of handicapped students, what constitutes "nondiscriminatory" testing, who could conduct "impartial" hearings, and when in the appeals process new evidence could be introduced.

Caught between its traditional clientele—representatives of state and local school systems—and its newly adopted one—advocates for the disabled—the department adopted a strategy it called "minimum regulation–future rulemaking." Noting that "some commenters felt that more extensive regulations were necessary" and others "felt that the Office of Education had already over-regulated and should cut back on the rules," the department explained that the best approach would be "(1) to write minimum regulations at this point, and (2) to amend and revise such regulations in the future as need and experience dictate." It intended "to expand on the statutory provisions only where additional interpretation [seems] to be necessary."[6]

The BEH did manage to write elaborate rules on such matters as recordkeeping, schedules for holding individualized education program (IEP) conferences, and the type of information required in applications for federal funding. Each side won a few victories. For example, the 1977 regulations sided with school officials in finding that the IEP is not a legally binding contract between the school system and parents. Although the statute makes no mention of residential placement, the BEH required schools to absorb all nonmedical costs, including room and board, when such placement is deemed "appropriate." In a supplemental rule announced the day before the Carter administration left office, the department classified "clean intermittent catheterization" as a "related service."

Far from imperialistic, the BEH was happy to have other agencies help interpret and enforce the act. It agreed with the Office of Civil Rights that section 504 of the Rehabilitation Act of 1973 requires all states, even those not accepting EAHCA funds, to follow the mandates of the law. The rights specified in the act, it argued, are not just part of a contract between state and federal governments, but are basic rights "guaranteed under the U.S. Constitution." This conclusion has "been reiterated in a series of court rulings over the past six years." With two agencies enforcing federal rules, the BEH and the Office of Civil Rights could play "good cop–bad cop" with the states: the BEH could be cooperative, offering funding and advice; the OCR could be the one to threaten enforcement action against states whose policies it determined violate federal law. At times, the BEH would try to eat its cake and have it too, approving state applications while agreeing with the OCR's claims that the state plan failed to comply with the law.[7]

BEH also faced conflicting pressures from the president and Congress. This was particularly apparent in 1982, when Reagan appointees in the Department of Education tried to loosen regulations written during the Carter administration.[8] The new regulations were hardly earthshaking. They shortened reporting requirements and gave school officials a bit more leeway in making initial placements, dealing with disruptive behavior, and defining which services are "medical" (and thus exempt from the related services requirement). Most of these changes had been suggested by the National School Board Association and were consistent with the Reagan administration's effort to reduce federal control of state and local governments.

These proposed changes were angrily attacked in Congress and the press. The House and the Senate passed a nonbinding resolution expressing disapproval of the rules. Both houses also attached a rider to an appropriations bill to prevent the rules from taking effect. Although President Reagan vetoed the appropriations bill for other reasons, the department saw it was fighting a losing battle and withdrew the proposed regulations.[9] Just to make sure the department did not change its mind, Congress attached a provision to the 1983 reauthorization of the Education of the Handicapped Act prohibiting the department from implementing rules that "would procedurally or substantively lessen the protections provided to handicapped children under this Act, as embodied in regulations in effect on July 20, 1983 . . . except to the extent that such regulation reflects the clear and unequivocal intent of the Congress in legislation."[10] None of the groups that had originally pushed for the revisions came to the department's defense once the issue came to the attention of Congress and the media. Little wonder that the department has gracefully acquiesced to judicial primacy in interpretation of the act.

Judicial Rules and Themes

The extensive federal case law on education for the handicapped defies easy description. The typical federal case involves competing professional judgments about the treatment of a severely disabled child. Most often the parents ask for residential placement, tuition for private day school, or special services such as psychotherapy, a sign language interpreter, or catheterization. The school district claims either that a less expensive program would be equally appropriate or that the service in dispute is not mandated by the act. On the central issue of appropriateness and the amount of deference due to school officials, disagreements among federal judges have been serious and lasting. But on a few matters—the legality of the 180-day school year, the meaning of "impartiality," the outer bounds of "related services"—the courts have spoken clearly. A quick review of these issues will convey a sense of how judges have interpreted the act liberally to expand benefits to disabled children.

Extended School Year

Most states by statute limit the school year to about 180 days. When parents of some handicapped children asked for year-round educational services, most school systems balked. Providing an extended school year for handicapped children, they argued, would be very expensive and would constitute a form of affirmative action for handicapped students not required by the statute.[11] The National School Board Association was particularly aggressive in opposing the extended school year.

The courts unanimously opposed across-the-board limits on the length of the school year. According to the Third Circuit, refusing to provide more than 180 days of education is "incompatible with the Act's emphasis on the individual." Such a rule "imposes with rigid certainty a program restriction which may be wholly inappropriate to the child's educational objective."[12] The Fifth Circuit stated, "If a child will experience severe or substantial regression during the summer months in the absence of a summer program, the handicapped child may be entitled to year round services."[13] Since—as many of the judges hearing these cases have conceded—all children experience some regression over the summer, the real issue is not regression itself but its severity. Most federal courts have held that the school officials, hearing officers, and judges who make these complex determinations must be guided above all by the needs of handicapped students, not the cost of extended school year programs.[14] On occasion, judges have ordered school districts to provide extended school year programs, even when experts are divided over its usefulness for the child in question.[15]

Discipline

Disabled children, like other children, sometimes exhibit behavior punishable by suspension or even expulsion from school. Children with severe emotional problems are more likely than the average student to get into trouble. This raises the question of whether suspension and expulsion deny the student an "appropriate education" and whether such punishments conform with the requirement that "the child shall remain in the current educational placement until the local education agency and the parent agree on a new placement." In particular, can disabled students who engage in dangerous behavior be suspended unilaterally by administrators? These cases present in stark terms the issue of the authority of principals and teachers.

Most of the lower courts hearing these cases have enjoined schools from expelling students for misbehavior. Some set the limit on suspensions at five or even three days; others allowed suspensions of up to twenty-one days. Some judges tolerated suspensions only in emergencies, others allowed them in nonemergency situations.[16] The lower courts generally followed the lead of the Fifth Circuit, which argued that in discipline cases the EAHCA "should be broadly applied and liberally constructed in favor of providing a free and appropriate education to handicapped students."[17] For example, in *Kaelin* v. *Grubbs* the court reinstated a student who had refused to do assigned work and kicked and pushed his teacher.[18] In *Stuart* v. *Nappi* the court ruled that a school could not expel a student for participation in what it called a "school-wide disturbance."[19] The Fourth Circuit barred a school from expelling a student involved in drug dealing after the court found that the child's learning disability had made him particularly susceptible to peer pressure.[20] In another case, however, the Eleventh Circuit allowed a school to expel an emotionally disturbed student who had brought a razor blade and martial arts weapons to school and threatened to kill another student.[21]

In 1988 the Supreme Court resolved some of these disagreements by deciding a case involving two emotionally disturbed children who had exhibited violent behavior. The Court found the language of the statute "unequivocal" and refused to read a "dangerousness exception" into the "stay-put" provision. Although two justices dissented on the grounds that the case was moot, no one disagreed with Justice Brennan's conclusion that "Congress very much meant to strip schools of the *unilateral* authority they had traditionally employed to exclude disabled students, particularly emotionally disturbed students, from school." "In drafting the law," Justice Brennan noted,

> Congress was largely guided by the recent decisions in [*Mills* and *PARC*] both of which involved the exclusion of hard-to-handle disabled students. . . . Conspicuously absent from section 1415(e)(3), however, is any emergency exception for dangerous students. This absence is all the more telling in light of the injunctive decree issued in *PARC*, which permitted school officials unilaterally to remove students in "extraordinary circumstances." Given the lack of any similar exception in *Mills*, and the close attention Congress devoted to these "landmark" decisions, we can only conclude that the omission was intentional.[22]

The Court allowed a ten-day suspension as a "cooling down period," but required schools to go to court in order to exclude students for longer periods.[23]

Impartiality

The lower courts have been particularly aggressive in insulating due process hearings from political and administrative influence. The act provides that no hearing "shall be conducted by an employee of such agency or unit involved in the education or care of the child." This phrase was crafted during the conference committee's restructuring of the appeals process.

The courts have ruled that state commissioners of education and members of state boards of education are "employees" of state education agencies and thus cannot serve as hearing officers; that state boards of education cannot overturn the decisions of state-level hearing officers; that teachers employed by local school systems cannot serve as hearing officers at the state level; and even that state university personnel who helped formulate the state program for the handicapped cannot serve as hearing officers.[24] State and local school board members, the courts have reasoned, are too concerned with saving money to be impartial. Teachers and other local employees "might be concerned about retribution." And a university professor who had helped develop a state's program "could become sufficiently personally or professionally invested in the policy that he would find it difficult to reverse or modify it as a due process hearing officer."[25] Protecting the autonomy of street-level professionals has clearly been one of the courts' chief concerns.

Related Services

Few issues have been litigated as frequently or have involved as many unusual circumstances as related services. The act defines "related services" as

> transportation and such developmental, corrective, and other supportive services (including speech pathology, psychological services, physical and occupational therapy, recreation, and medical and counseling services, *except* that such medical services shall be for diagnostic and evaluation purposes only) as may to required to assist a handicapped child benefit from special education.[26]

This provision raises two issues of great importance to schools and parents: What services are required to assist a particular handicapped child benefit from special education, and what services are exempt because they are medical? At stake is not just the extent of services received by handicapped children but also the distribution of costs among state and local agencies. In many states, health and human service agencies have used the EAHCA to transfer to the schools responsibility for providing a variety of services the former had provided in the past.

The courts have generally taken an "inclusionary" approach to related services.[27] When residential placement and extensive programming are needed to deal with a child's severe psychological problems, these become related services because, in the words of an early court opinion, "the emotional needs of this plaintiff are closely interwoven with his educational needs."[28] According to the Third Circuit, "the concept of education is necessarily broad" with respect to persons with serious disabilities.[29] In a case involving a severely retarded child, the First Circuit explained,

"Where what is being taught is how to pay attention, talk, respond to words of warning, and dress and feed oneself, it is reasonable to find that a suitably staffed and structured residential environment providing continual training and reinforcement in those skills serves an educational service."[30] Judges have agreed that when residential placement is appropriate the school must pay *all* nonmedical costs. A school cannot even assess parents a $100 monthly maintenance charge.[31]

Judges and hearing officers have required schools to provide what one commentator has called "a bewildering array of services, including music therapy, 'therapeutic recreation,' myofunctional therapy, sign language training for parents, detoxification, and the assistance of a 'visual computer.' "[32] Although some judges have ruled that psychiatric treatment is a medical service since it is provided by a licensed physician, others have deemed extensive psychotherapy and group therapy to be "related services."[33] In the case of a boy whose body could not regulate its own temperature, the school and the reviewing court disagreed about the appropriate related service: the school proposed placing him in a temperature-controlled plexiglass cubicle; the court required the school to control the temperature of the entire classroom.[34] In another unusual case, the court ruled that reinsertion of a tracheotomy tube into a child's stomach is a service covered by the act, not a medical procedure.[35]

In its only decision on the subject, the Supreme Court followed the lead of the lower courts in adopting a broad reading of "related services." In *Irving Independent School District* v. *Tatro*, the Court ruled that "clean intermittent catheterization"—periodic reattachment of a catheter, a procedure required by those with spina bifida—is a related, nonmedical service. Chief Justice Burger ruled that services that can be provided by school nurses rather than solely by physicians do not fall within the medical exception. "School nurses have long been a part of the educational system, and the Secretary could therefore reasonably conclude that school nursing services are not the sort of burden that Congress intended to exclude as a 'medical service.' "[36] This decision did little to resolve disagreements among the lower courts on such matters as whether hospital treatment of emotionally disturbed children constitutes a related service. By focusing on the peculiar facts of the case before it, the Court limited its ability to give direction to the rest of the federal judiciary.

Defining an Appropriate Education

What constitutes an "appropriate education" for a child with a particular concatenation of disabilities? That is the question that has perplexed almost everyone touched by the EAHCA. The act allows parents to challenge adverse decisions of state and local hearing officers in federal district court. The district court must consult the administrative record, hear additional evidence, and "basing its decision on the preponderance of the evidence," "grant such relief as the court determines is appropriate." Most judges, following the 1975 conference report, have interpreted this to mean that they must make an "independent" decision on the merits.

In the late 1970s judges and commentators voiced confidence in the courts' ability to create a coherent "common law" on education of the handicapped. An influential *Harvard Law Review* note, for example, maintained that the act "has set the stage for judges and hearing officers to take an active role in the intimate details of educational decision-making." Eventually the "development of a 'common law' for decisionmaking under the Act would eliminate much of the ambiguity of the current standards." Although this task would be "exceedingly difficult," many times in the past "courts have risen to the challenge of turning vague language into meaningful guidelines for conduct. . . . In entrusting courts with the ultimate power to review the appropriateness of individual programs, Congress has placed great faith in such judicial virtues."[37] Twelve years and hundreds of cases later, judicially manageable standards of appropriateness remain elusive. The courts are still "struggling in the quicksand of conflicting educational research and practice."[38]

After remaining silent on the "appropriate education" issue for several years, the Supreme Court addressed the issue in its 1982 *Rowley* decision.[39] The Court instructed the lower courts to show more deference to school officials and hearing officers. Yet the *Rowley* decision has had surprisingly little effect on the district and circuit court judges. Few areas of the law provide as graphic an illustration of the limited control of the Supreme Court as special education.

Early Cases

During the initial period of judicial review of placement decisions (1978–82), the lower courts "split sharply over the precise type of equality they believed the statute guaranteed."[40] Some judges announced that they would overturn decisions of school officials and hearing officers only if they were "clearly erroneous" or failed to provide the handicapped student with "some educational benefit." In their opinion, school officials have more educational expertise than judges, and weighing the cost of alternative placements is an inevitable and legitimate part of a school administrator's job. The act, one federal district court judge maintained, does not create a right for parents "to write a prescription for an ideal education for their child and to have the prescription filled at public expense."[41] According to another, failure to consider the cost of IEPs "would ultimately work to circumvent congressional intention to educate *all* handicapped children as best as practicable" because "excessive expenditures made to meet the needs of one handicapped child ultimately reduce the amount that can be spent to meet the needs of the other handicapped children."[42] Other judges rejected this circumscribed role. They characterized the act's substantive standard in a variety of ways: equal educational opportunity, equivalent opportunity, the opportunity to meet one's maximum potential, or the education "in the best interest of the child." At times, they denied that administrators could take cost into account even when that cost was very high.[43]

What distinguished the latter set of judges was their insistence on scrutinizing the decisions of administrators to make sure that they had not rejected a promising placement simply because it cost too much money. "Congressional rejection of court deference to agency determinations," the Third Circuit stated, "is a salient feature" of the act.[44] One district court judge ruled that if a twenty-four-hour behavior modification program is the only treatment likely to help a child with multiple handicaps, then the school must foot the bill:

> The language and legislative history of that Act simply do not admit of the possibility that some children may be beyond the reach of our educational expertise. . . . Regardless of the financial and administrative burdens that may obtain . . . the Act imposes upon schools the singular obligation to provide a comprehensive range of services to accommodate a handicapped child's educational needs, and if necessary, to resort to residential placement.[45]

Since the act "is a remedial statute," another district court ruled, it should be "broadly applied and liberally construed in favor of providing an appropriate education to handicapped students."[46]

Perhaps the best example of this aggressive form of judicial review came in the case eventually heard by the Supreme Court. The case involved Amy Rowley, a highly motivated deaf girl with an IQ of over 120. Her school had placed her in a regular class and provided her with daily individual tutoring, a weekly session with a speech therapist, and an FM hearing aid that could pick up voices in the classroom through a wireless receiver. School administrators also took sign language classes to communicate with Amy's parents, who were themselves deaf. But the school refused to honor her parents' request for a sign language interpreter to accompany Amy in class.

The district court agreed with the Rowleys. Without the interpreter, the court found, Amy could understand only 59 percent of what was said in class; with the interpreter, she could understand 100 percent. In language that vividly presents the point of view of the more activist set of judges, the court found that whereas "the failures of other children can be attributed either to lack of intellectual potential . . . or to a lack of interest or energy, factors which can be controlled and which it is the purpose of a school to develop," Amy's educational shortfall "is inherent in her handicap and is precisely the kind of deficiency which the Act addresses in requiring that every handicapped child be given an appropriate education."[47] The Second Circuit issued a brief opinion stating that the trial court had "meticulously applied precisely the standard prescribed by Congress."[48]

The Supreme Court Speaks

By a vote of 6–3, the Supreme Court overruled the Second Circuit. Writing for the majority, Justice Rehnquist noted that the statutory definition of "free appropriate public education" "tends toward the cryptic. . . . Noticeably absent from the language of the statute is any substantive standard prescribing the level of education to be accorded to handicapped children." According to Rehnquist, the lower court had mistakenly concluded that this silence, coupled with the act's liberal judicial review provision, indicated a congressional intent for the court to fashion its own substantive standards. The mere use of the words "preponderance of the evidence," Rehnquist argued, is "by no means an invitation to the courts to substitute their own notions of sound educational policy for those of the school authorities which they review." Not only are the courts ill suited to engage in educational policymaking, but the lower courts' approach violates a key tenet of federalism. The authors of the act expected state and local education agencies to remain the dominant decisionmakers. If Congress had meant to impose on state and local education systems obligations such as those ordered by the district court, then it would have done so "unambiguously" rather than through definitional silence.[49]

To determine what constitutes an "appropriate" education, Rehnquist looked to the *PARC* and *Mills* decisions, which he read as dealing with the *availability* rather than the *quality* of education: "The intent of the Act was more to open the door of public education to handicapped children on appropriate terms than to guarantee any particular level of education once inside." All the act requires is "that the education to which access is provided be sufficient to confer *some* educational benefit upon the handicapped child." This means that "courts must be careful to avoid imposing their views of preferable educational methods upon the States."[50]

In contrast, Justice Byron White's dissenting opinion relied heavily on the act's legislative history, which, he pointed out, is full of references to "equal educational opportunity" and allowing each handicapped child to "achieve his or her maximum potential." According to White, the purpose of the act is "to eliminate the effect of the handicap, at least to the extent that the child will be given an equal opportunity to learn if that is reasonably possible." The change in judicial review provisions made by the conference committee "demonstrate[d] that Congress intended the courts to conduct a far more searching inquiry."[51]

The majority and dissenting opinions present a classic confrontation between judges who rely on legislative history to support judicial activism through statutory interpretation and those who rely on federalism and strict construction of statutes to justify judicial restraint. The *Rowley* decision also illustrates the Supreme Court's growing doubts about the ability of judges to resolve complex policy questions, its tendency to defer to administrators, and its willingness to allow them to balance program costs and benefits.

Is Anyone Listening?

The fact that Justice Rehnquist garnered more votes in the Supreme Court than did Justice White did not put an end to the debate within the judicial branch. The decision was roundly condemned by the authors of law review articles who, as is typically the case, advocated greater judicial aggressiveness and substantial program expansion. Before long, these commentators discovered that their initial alarm was unjustified. Instead of "minimizing the statutory obligation of the schools," the lower court responded to *Rowley* by "distinguishing it when they could, and minimizing it and finding other sources of guidance when they could not."[52] The Legal Services Corporation's *Clearinghouse Review* explained that although the lower courts "have been careful to say that they gave due consideration to the administrative record," these judges "have not been unduly constrained. They still make independent decisions based on all the evidence before them."[53]

This point is illustrated by several district court decisions that were in the process of being appealed when *Rowley* was announced. In *Doe v. Anrig*, the district court decision had explicitly relied on the standard of review subsequently rejected by the Supreme Court. Shortly after *Rowley* was announced, the First Circuit upheld the ruling of the trial judge:

> Though the district court's statement that the "administrative decision is entitled to no special deference" may seem at odds with the thrust of the *Rowley* requirement that courts give "due weight" to state proceedings, we find nothing in the record before us to suggest that "due weight" was not accorded. . . . The difference here between [district court] Judge Zobel and the school authorities was not a choice of educational *policy*, but resolution of an individualized *factual* issue as to the effect of John's handicap on his ability to benefit from the proposed school setting. This falls within the scope of the question which *Rowley* says is for the court.[54]

In other cases, too, decisions initially based on the reading of the statute rejected in *Rowley* were upheld by circuit judges claiming fealty to that ruling.[55]

The most common technique that lower courts have used for evading *Rowley* has been to stress the need for individualized consideration of the peculiarities of each case. According to the Fourth Circuit,

> *Rowley* recognized that no single substantive standard can describe how much educational benefit is sufficient to satisfy the Act. Instead, the Supreme Court left that matter to the courts for case-by-case determination. . . . While one might demand only minimal results in the case of the most severely handicapped children, such results would be insufficient in the case of other children.[56]

While the Fourth Circuit maintained that the Supreme Court's command of deference did not necessarily apply to children *less* disabled than Amy Rowley, the Third Circuit argued that it "is difficult to apply *Rowley*" when the student before the court is severely disabled. Finding that the

Supreme Court had contradicted itself and failed "to confront squarely the fact that Congress cared about the quality of special education," the court relied more heavily on Justice White's dissenting opinion than on the majority opinion of Justice Rehnquist. Conceding that to some extent "dicta in the [*Rowley*] opinion tend to undermine our substantive standard," the court found *Rowley* "distinguishable." The Supreme Court's ruling, it maintained,

> specifically limited itself to the facts before it, involving a hearing impaired child advancing from grade to grade in a "mainstreamed" classroom. Because the Court so self-consciously restricted the scope of its holding, we may (as we did above) reexamine the policies and the legislative history of the EHA to inform our decision.[57]

In other words, if Amy Rowley's case ever came before the Third Circuit, that court would follow the Supreme Court's lead; in all other cases it would read the statute however it saw fit.[58]

Another strategy has been to rely on the "least restrictive environment" and "related services" sections of the act rather than the "appropriate education" phrase already parsed by the Supreme Court. When a district court judge relied on *Rowley* to defer to a local school district on the question of which of two schools was best for a retarded child, the Sixth Circuit reversed. The court explained that while the *Rowley* case "involved a choice between two methods for educating a deaf student," the question in the case at hand "is not one of methodology but rather involves a determination of whether the school district has satisfied the Act's requirement that handicapped children be educated alongside non-handicapped children to the maximum extent appropriate."[59] Whether the school had complied with the statute's mainstreaming mandate was for the courts, not administrators, to decide. The circuit court did not explain how a trial judge could decide how much mainstreaming is appropriate without making an independent determination of what type of education is appropriate.[60]

Yet another way some judges have circumvented *Rowley* is by relying on state laws that seem to set a substantive standard more rigorous than "some educational benefit." Massachusetts law, for example, refers to the "maximum possible development of handicapped children." A New Jersey statute establishes the principle that all students "be assured the fullest possible opportunity to develop their intellectual capacities." The First, Third, and Ninth circuits have all argued that the EAHCA "incorporates by reference" such state laws. This incorporation of state law into the federal statute, said the First Circuit, is "bottomed on both the statutory language and authoritative legislative history."[61] The statutory basis cited by the court was the proviso that the IEP "meet the standards of the State educational agency." Ironically, the court used this phrase to justify its *rejection* of the state agency's position. The legislative history cited by the court was a floor speech by Senator Williams that touched on this issue only in the most oblique manner. However weak the justification, the consequence is that federal judges hearing cases in these states can revert to their aggressive pre-*Rowley* stance.[62]

This does not mean that all federal judges have ignored the Supreme Court's guidance in *Rowley*. Many judges were reluctant to second-guess school systems before the Supreme Court spoke and maintained their deferential approach after 1982. But the Supreme Court has done little to reduce the considerable variation among the federal courts. EAHCA cases will continue to be decided on an ad hoc basis by judges with widely varying understanding of federal requirements.

The Political Appeal of Legal Rights

When the courts announced their decisions on the extended school year, school discipline, related services, and residential placement, Congress reacted not at all—no hearings, no appropriations riders, no legislation. Even when the Supreme Court issued the *Rowley* opinion, which was roundly condemned by advocates for the disabled, Congress as a whole and its entrepreneurial subcommittees remained silent. This was not because members of Congress had lost interest in the subject or grown more conservative. In 1982–83, as already mentioned, Congress blocked Reagan administration efforts to relax regulations under the EAHCA. In 1986 Congress enacted legislation requiring states to begin special education at age three.[63]

Congress twice responded quickly and unequivocally to Supreme Court rulings. Both controversies involved the powers of the federal court, and in each instance Congress adopted the broader reading of judicial authority. In the first case, *Smith* v. *Robinson*, the Court ruled that plaintiffs who prevail in EAHCA cases cannot collect attorneys' fees.[64] This decision was a relatively straightforward application of the "American rule," which holds that courts will not award fees unless explicitly authorized to do so by Congress. In 1975, several months before the passage of the EAHCA, the Burger court had reaffirmed its commitment to the "American rule" in the highly publicized *Alyeska Pipeline* decision.[65] Congress responded to *Alyeska* by passing the Civil Rights Attorneys Fees Awards Act of 1976, which covered the Voting Rights Act, the Civil Rights Act of 1964, and the Fair Housing Act of 1968. Legislation passed in 1978 extended attorneys' fees to cases brought under section 504 of the Rehabilitation Act. No mention of attorneys' fees appears in the EAHCA, nor do either of these two attorneys' fees statutes refer to the EAHCA.

Soon after the Court announced *Smith* v. *Robinson*, the halls of Congress rang with denunciations of this "misinterpretation of Congress' intent," which "threatened the rights of handicapped children" and will have "a devastating effect on the ability of parents to secure free appropriate public education for disabled children."[66] "This is like the David and Goliath struggle," exclaimed Representative Mario Biaggi, except "this David does not have a slingshot."[67] According to Senator Lowell Weicker, "This conflict is one of the law versus those who want to save money at the expense of a population which they consider to be too weak to fight back."[68] Both houses unanimously passed legislation to authorize courts to award attorneys' fees to prevailing parties. The Handicapped Children Protection Act of 1986 did more than overturn *Smith* v. *Robinson*. It allowed these awards to cover attorneys' fees incurred in administrative as well as judicial proceedings.

In the second case, *Dellmuth* v. *Muth*, the Supreme Court ruled that in most circumstances federal courts cannot order state and local schools to reimburse parents for educational expenses previously incurred. According to Justice Anthony M. Kennedy's majority opinion, the Eleventh Amendment grant of sovereign immunity to state governments can be breached only when Congress makes its intention to abrogate sovereign immunity "unmistakably clear in the language of the statute."[69] Within a year Congress had passed legislation doing just that.[70] The bill encountered virtually no opposition.

Congress's reaffirmation of its commitment to adversarial procedures and its strengthening of the powers of the federal courts came at a time when some school officials, parents, and academics were attacking the act as a leading example of rights gone wrong. School officials decried the increase in paperwork, the amount of time spent at conferences and hearings, the cost of lawyers, and the harm done to the parent-teacher relationship by adversarial proceedings. As one administrator put it, "We really try and avoid these things like the plague."[71] Parents find the proceedings even more difficult. According to a major study of EAHCA procedures, parents consider the process "emotionally straining, overly formal, and primarily concerned with procedures and rules of law rather than issues of substance." Many found the experience "so intimidating and threatening" that they "felt unable to act on their own, feeling strongly the need for an attorney or advocate."[72] One mother stated, "I've been through seizures and everything else with her, and this has been the worst affair of my life." Said another, "It's been hell. Absolute hell."

Why, in light of these criticisms, has Congress reinforced rather than weakened its rights-based approach to special education? Part of the answer, no doubt, lies in the power of the policy legacy. Because the act was sold as a way to vindicate constitutional rights already recognized by the courts, Congress could not stray very far from the structure established in *Mills* and *PARC*. Congress is not inclined to alter the basic structure of a law that has built a broad and vocal constituency and produced clear—and often dramatic—improvements in the treatment of disabled children. Once the federal government had chosen to place so much weight on adversarial proceedings, it was hard to argue that parents should be responsible for huge attorneys' fees after prevailing in court.

The rights-based approach to special education also constitutes an ingenious form of client politics. Clearly, many disabled students, their parents, and special education professionals have benefited enormously from the act. For this, members of Congress can—and do—take credit. Of course, as a few commentators and many state and local officials have pointed out, most of the added cost is borne by state and local school systems. The question this raises is why members of Congress are willing to suffer criticism from the "intergovernmental lobby" in order to court the beneficiaries of special education. One might expect, for example, that school board members would carry a good deal of weight with their local member of Congress.

What Douglas Arnold has called the "traceability" of policy effects helps explain the weak opposition to the expansion of special education.[73] Special education professionals and parents' organizations attribute much of their success over the past decade and a half to the Education for All Handicapped Children Act and for that reason vehemently oppose anything smacking of retrenchment. But can the parents of a nondisabled child show that his education would have improved if a dyslexic student had not been treated so well? Can a school board member blame his representative or even Congress as a whole for a court decision ordering the school system to pay for psychiatric care for a severely disturbed child? Maybe the child desperately needed this help. Perhaps this was just example of a judge failing to consider the cost of the programs he has mandated. Who can know for sure? The very incoherence of substantive policy—which one can see in the Department of Education's laconic regulations as well as in the Supreme Court's inability to control the lower courts—allows members of Congress to accept credit for the act's accomplishments while protecting them from blame for its costs.

Although Congress could never establish in the statute what constitutes an "appropriate education" for each subcategory of handicapped child, certainly the act could be far more explicit than it is. It could, for example, explain which categories of "related services" schools must pay for, whether the federal law incorporates state standards, and who carries the burden of proof at each stage of the appeals process. Congress studiously avoids making these kinds of judgments because any decision is bound to anger one side or another. The political incentives are all on the side of leaving such hard choices to others.

For several reasons, the courts proved to be a particularly attractive place to lodge this discretion. The key sponsors of the act were serious about changing the practices of state and local educational systems. But advocates for the disabled did not trust the federal Department of Education much more than they trusted state and local school systems. The department had always emphasized the development of cooperative relations with local administrators. Moreover, its principal enforcement mechanism, the funding cutoff, was seldom effective. To make matters worse, the very Republican presidents who had sought to weaken the act were responsible for appointing the department's top executives. The courts, in contrast, had no close ties to the educational establishment, had an effective enforcement tool (the injunction), and (at least in the 1970s) were not in the thrall of conservative Republican presidents. In short, to advocates for the disabled, relying on the courts was about the only way to overcome the obstacles created by federalism and divided government.

Making such highly subjective, individualized judgments about the needs of particular students is a task federal judges have found difficult yet compatible with their conception of the judicial role. Having warned administrators against relying too heavily on rigid rules, they have avoided enunciating clear-cut rules themselves. The courts' emphasis on meeting the unique needs of individual students has not only reduced the authority of school officials but has also limited the control of appellate courts.

In this respect, the understanding of individual rights that developed in this policy area contrasts sharply with the understanding of rights enunciated by those who sought to restructure AFDC. In special education, recipients are entitled to the type and level of treatment considered appropriate by those professionals acquainted with the unique details of each case. The right to welfare, in contrast, meant the right to be *free* from the ad hoc judgment of social workers and administrators. Welfare rights advocates sought to construct a program with a relatively small number of clear rules that would reduce recipients' dependence on the whims of others. One of the ironies of welfare reform, of course, is that once these rules are in place they can easily be changed by administrators and legislators whose primary goals are to save money or impose new restrictions on eligibility. Special education costs are particularly difficult to control because so much discretion is in the hands of street-level administrators. In this sense—the extent to which rights involve the application of clear rules or consideration of the unique facts of each case—education of the handicapped and AFDC are polar cases of "rights" politics.

PART IV

The Food Stamp Program

CHAPTER NINE

The Surprising Success of Food Stamps

This program was hatched by the New Deal, revived by the New Frontier, grew under the Great Society, and has now been embraced and expanded by the Administration and the Congress beyond the wildest imagination of yesterday's liberals.

—Representative George Goodling, 1970

IN 1993 the number of people receiving food stamps reached an all-time high of 27 million—one of every ten Americans. Federal spending on the food stamp program climbed to $23 billion, making it the federal government's largest income maintenance program for the poor.[1] This precipitous rise in spending began during the 1970s, when the real annual growth rate for food stamps was 15.7 percent—five times the growth of the gross national product and twice the growth rate of government as a whole.[2] Although the food stamp program sustained substantial budget cuts in the early years of the Reagan administration, it rebounded quickly and fully as Congress expanded coverage in 1985, 1988, and 1991 (see figure 9-1). The 1993 budget legislation also increased spending by more than $2.5 billion for 1994–98.[3] Over the past two decades the program has become one of the most important and resilient elements of the "social safety net."

Just as important as the amount of federal money devoted to food stamps is the way it is distributed. The food stamp program is a rare bird in the American context: a nationally uniform, noncategorical, means-tested income maintenance program. Aid is available to all low-income households regardless of family composition. Consequently, food stamps provide assistance to several groups that fall between the cracks of categorical welfare programs: two-parent families, single adults, and childless couples. The low benefit-reduction rate—about 30 percent—allows the working poor to receive income support.

Figure 9-1. *Food Stamp Benefits and Participants, Fiscal Years 1965-92*

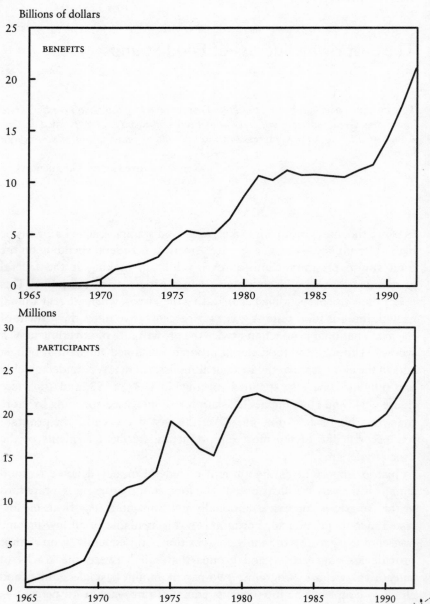

Billions of dollars

Millions

Sources: *The Food Stamp Program: History, Description, Issues, and Options.* Committee Print 99-32, Senate Committee on Agriculture, Nutrition and Forestry, 99 Cong. 1 sess. (Government Printing Office, 1985), p. 162; and U.S. Department of Agriculture, Food and Nutrition Service, Office of Governmental Affairs, "Food Stamp Program: Background Information" (January 1992).

Eighty percent of food stamp recipients also receive some other form of public assistance. The program not only supplements these often inadequate benefits but also promotes equality among the states. Because participants in states with low AFDC benefits receive more food stamps than participants in high-benefit states, the program has cut interstate variation in welfare payments roughly in half.[4] Program benefits and participation rates are highest in the South, which has always had the greatest poverty and least generous welfare system. In Alabama and Mississippi, the states with the lowest AFDC benefits, three-person households with no other income receive twice as much in food stamps (nearly $300 a month) as in AFDC (less than $150 a month). In California and Connecticut, in contrast, such households receive over $650 from AFDC but only $180 in food stamps. In Mississippi, 20 percent of the population receives food stamps, compared with 10 percent in New York and 7 percent in California. The seven states with the highest food stamp participation rates are all in the South.[5] The combination of these characteristics has led Richard Nathan to describe food stamps as "the most important change in public welfare policy in the U.S. since the passage of the Social Security Act of 1935."[6]

Food stamps became an important welfare supplement, "equalizer," and "gap filler" in the decade stretching from 1967 to 1977. In these years a $100 million program operating in a few counties grew to a $5 billion program serving residents of every part of the country. The 1970 Food Stamp Act created nationally uniform eligibility standards and substantially increased spending levels.[7] The 1977 amendments broadened eligibility and eliminated the requirement that recipients use a portion of their income to buy their allotment of stamps. During this decade public opinion on the subject was volatile, and congressional votes were often razor thin. In 1976, for example, Congress came close to enacting substantial cuts. A year later it approved changes that brought two and a half million more recipients into the program.

The years between passage of the 1970 and 1977 acts were also a time of extensive litigation over food stamps. The lower courts' interpretation of the 1970 law left a lasting imprint on the program. Federal district and circuit courts issued decisions on a wide variety of matters, ranging from the composition of the diet plan to the definition of household income, from the adequacy of the Department of Agriculture's "outreach" program to the process it uses to certify recipients. The main theme running through these court opinions was that in passing the 1970 act "Congress intended to assure that all needy families would be able to obtain a nutritionally adequate diet, regardless of administrative difficulties in implementing this objective."[8]

The judicial effort to protect the right to a "nutritionally adequate diet" ended almost as suddenly as it had begun. In 1977 the Supreme Court issued its first and only statutory interpretation on food stamps.[9] In a unanimous decision, it ordered federal judges to show greater deference to the Department of Agriculture. In that same year Congress eliminated nearly all the broad statutory phrases that had been at the heart of food stamp litigation. Committee chair Thomas Foley, the chief architect of this legislation, announced that the "pervasive purpose of this entirely rewritten food stamp law" was to "permit the program to be administered by the Department of Agriculture under oversight by the respective agriculture committees—always subject to legislative revision—rather than to be run by the Federal court."[10]

Looking back over the decade, lawyers at the Food Research and Action Center (FRAC), the public interest group that spearheaded most food stamp litigation, saw the 1977 amendments as a watershed. FRAC had won a large number of cases under the 1970 act "because of the amount of discretion given USDA and the broad purpose of the program." Legal victories under the 1970 law "resulted in significantly expanded eligibility and improved program benefits." But in 1977 "Congress was successful in eliminating legal handles for lawyers to challenge restrictive program requirements." Consequently, "few lawsuits challenging the Act or the regulations have been filed since 1977."[11] If the history of the Education for All Handicapped Children Act shows that Congress sometimes encourages litigation, the history of the food stamp program shows that on other occasions Congress is willing and able to reduce the influence of the judiciary.

Food Stamps and Special Education

The comparison with special education provides a useful window into the politics of food stamps. Both programs grew rapidly in the 1970s. Each is based on a simple, compelling moral claim: just as advocates for the disabled argued that children should not be denied public education simply because they are handicapped, food stamp advocates argued that hunger and malnutrition are unacceptable in a country that produces huge agricultural surpluses. This theme reappears in virtually every discussion of the program. In 1969, for example, Richard Nixon declared, "That hunger and malnutrition should persist in a land such as ours is embarrassing and intolerable."[12] Fifteen years later the Task Force on Food Assistance appointed by President Reagan stated, "It has long been an article of faith among the American people that no one in a land so blessed with plenty should go hungry."[13] Two Harris polls taken in 1976 and 1977—the period of greatest publicity about fraud and abuse in the program—found that while 90 percent of the sample agreed with the statement "too many people on welfare could be working," an even greater number, 94 percent, believed "it's not right to let people who need welfare go hungry."[14]

Like special education, food stamps attracted a dedicated and politically sophisticated group of advocates who labored for years to build the program. The "hunger lobby" (as it has been dubbed by journalists) is an informal collection of public interest groups, churches, labor unions, and prominent nutritionists dedicated to expanding a variety of nutrition programs.[15] Three small Washington-based organizations—the Food Research and Action Center, the Community Nutrition Institute, and the Center for Budget Policy and Priorities—have provided the political strategy and most of the staff work. Their role is similar to that of the Council for Exceptional Children and the National Association for Retarded Citizens (formerly the National Association for Retarded Children) for special education. The Field and Ford foundations provided these groups with direct financial assistance and funded efforts to identify and publicize the problem of malnutrition. The "hunger lobby" has also received invaluable support from the media: from 1969, when CBS aired its controversial documentary "Hunger in America," to the Reagan years, when newspapers and television reported an "epidemic" of malnutrition, the media have repeatedly given prominence to the issue.

Just as advocates for the disabled worked closely with the House and Senate education committees, food stamp advocates developed close ties with key members of Congress and their staff. Hunger first became a political issue in 1967 when a Senate subcommittee held well-publicized hearings on the subject. These hearings led to creation of the Select Committee on Nutrition and Human Needs chaired by Senator George McGovern. Lacking legislative jurisdiction, the Nutrition Committee devoted itself to pointing out the inadequacies of existing nutrition programs. The staff of the Nutrition Committee worked so closely with the "hunger lobby" that it was often hard to tell where one left off and the other began. In the House, food stamps advocates relied heavily on two influential patrons, Thomas Foley and Leon Panetta. Both were liberal Democrats who sat on the House Agriculture Committee and took a special interest in the program. And both rose to positions of power in Washington: Foley became chairman of the Agriculture Committee and later Speaker of the House; Panetta served as chair of the House Budget Committee and later became President Bill Clinton's director of the Office of Management and Budget (OMB). Foley, Panetta, and their staff used their considerable political clout and acumen to protect and expand the food stamp program.

Like the Council for Exceptional Children and the National Association for Retarded Citizens, the "hunger lobby" adroitly integrated litigation with lobbying. This ability to fight on two fronts—Congress and the courts—was central to the success of program advocates. Although poverty lawyers who focused on AFDC were more successful in court than their colleagues who focused on food stamps, the former never managed to build a political base in Congress. Real AFDC benefits fell in the 1970s, the period of fastest growth for food stamps.

One important difference between food stamps and education for the handicapped is that food stamps never became a political sacred cow immune from criticism and budget cuts. Throughout the 1970s the food stamp program was the subject of acrimonious debate. Congress's mood shifted from attacking hunger to preventing "waste, fraud, and abuse"— and then back again. After expanding the program in 1977, Congress approved a variety of cuts in 1980, 1981, and 1982. These quick shifts indicated that the rights orientation that continues to have such a pervasive influence on special education never took firm root with food stamps. Judicial intervention was short-lived. Congress succeeded in writing specific legislation that resolved the main disputes over the program's operation. This is something the authors of the Education for All Handicapped Children Act never even attempted to do.

Part IV of this book focuses on two questions raised by this comparison of food stamps and special education: How did judicial rulings contribute to the development of the food stamp program? Why did the Congress that passed the expansionary 1977 amendments go to such lengths to reduce future court intervention? Chapter 10 examines the court decisions of 1971–77 and the politics of the 1977 amendments.

This chapter provides the context for that discussion by highlighting three central features of the politics of food stamps.

First, while the food stamp program has been sold to the public as a nutrition program, it functions primarily as a welfare supplement, equalizer, and gap-filler. As the program matured, its announced purpose of providing low-income households "the opportunity to attain a nutritionally adequate diet"—a phrase upon which the courts repeatedly placed great weight—became less and less important.

Second, food stamp legislation is handled by the House and Senate Agriculture committees, whose members are more interested in farm bills than welfare programs. The lack of reliable committee support has led to protracted negotiations both within the committee and between committee members and party leaders. Moreover, the two authorizing committees had little previous experience dealing with the courts and were apprehensive about giving them much control over the program.

Third, the food stamp program provides a vivid illustration of how the politics of the late 1960s and 1970s differed from that of the New Deal era. The contemporary program was the product not of presidential leadership but of interbranch rivalry in a period of divided government. The "hunger lobby" constantly attacked the White House and the Department of Agriculture (USDA) for doing too little to combat malnutrition. Litigation was an integral part of this adversarial politics.[16]

The Two Faces of Food Stamps

"Since its inception," Richard Nathan notes, the food stamp program "has suffered an identity crisis. To some it is a feeding program; to others it is essentially an income transfer; and many, of course, see it as serving both purposes."[17] A central dynamic of food stamp politics is that the program's two principal objectives often pull in opposite directions. To the extent that the focus is on nutrition, the program will insist that beneficiaries' added purchasing power be devoted to food—perhaps even to food deemed particularly nutritious. To the extent the focus is on alleviating the shortcomings of other income maintenance programs, the emphasis will be on increasing the purchasing power of the poor and allowing recipients to decide for themselves which of their needs are most pressing.

To understand this conflict, it is necessary to review the basic structure of the program and the significance of the decision to eliminate the so-called purchase requirement. For many years the food stamp program has been based on the assumption that low-income households should not need to spend more than 30 percent of their available income on food.[18] Program benefits fill the gap between 30 percent of available income and the cost of a "nutritionally adequate diet." The USDA establishes the latter by computing the market price of a combination of foods it calls the thrifty food plan. In 1992, for example, the monthly cost of the thrifty food plan was about $200 for a family of two, about $300 for a family of three, and $370 for a family of four.[19]

Before 1977, 30 percent of net income constituted the food stamp "purchase price," that is, the amount the household would pay to the government in exchange for an allotment of coupons equal in value to the cost of the thrifty food plan. In 1977 Congress passed legislation eliminating the purchase requirement. Now participating households pay nothing to the government. They receive "bonus stamps" equal in value to the cost of the thrifty food plan minus 30 percent of net household income. This means that participating households are no longer required to convert 30 percent of their available income into stamps.

Assume, for example, that a family of four has a net income of $6,000 a year or $500 a month. It would be expected to spend $150 a month on food (30 percent of $500). This would not be enough to purchase an adequate diet, which according to the USDA will cost $370 a month. Before 1977 this family would have exchanged $150 in cash for $370 in stamps. After elimination of the purchase requirement, it would receive $220 ($370 minus $150) in stamps without making a payment to the government.

The food stamp program has never guaranteed that all participating households will receive an adequate diet, but only that if they spend their money very carefully they will be able to purchase the thrifty food plan without spending more than 30 percent of their income for food. The pre-1977 purchase requirement did, however, ensure that the total amount participating households spent on food would equal or exceed the value of the thrifty food plan and that the households would almost certainly spend more on food than they did before joining the program. With the purchase requirement, if a household had previously spent more than 30 percent of its income on food, it could decide either to continue to spend the same amount of cash and have more food or to use part of the money it had previously used for food to buy other things. For example, if the hypothetical family described above had previously spent $250 for food, participating in the food stamp program would allow it both to increase its food budget by $120 (from $250 to $370, its allotment of stamps) and to have an additional $100 ($250 minus $150) in cash available to use as it saw fit. A Congressional Budget Office study completed just before Congress eliminated the purchase requirement estimated that for every dollar of "bonus stamps" recipients increased their food expenditures by 57 cents.[20] In other words, before 1977 about half of the money the government spent on the program went toward food.

After the purchase requirement was eliminated in 1977, the hypothetical family would receive $220 in stamps and retain complete control over the $250 it originally spent on food. If it raised its total food expenditures to, say, $350 ($220 in stamps plus $130 in cash), it would have $120 ($250 minus $130) to spend on other items. No longer is there any assurance that participating households will either increase their food purchases or spend enough on food to purchase the thrifty food plan. While there are few reliable post-1977 studies on the subject, it is unlikely that under the current system additional food expenditures approach the 50 percent estimate of previous reports.[21]

When the food stamp program was expanded in the late 1960s, it substantially increased the purchasing power of the nation's poorest families. This undoubtedly helped to reduce malnutrition, particularly in desperately poor regions of the rural South. In recent years, though, benefit increases and reductions have had little demonstrable effect on dietary habits or public health. After reviewing the scientific literature on the link between food stamps and nutrition, a staff report prepared in 1984 for the President's Task Force on Food Assistance concluded that "the program does not have a pronounced impact on nutritional intake."[22] As one member of the task force, George Graham of the Johns Hopkins Medical School, has explained, "To the surprise and chagrin of many investigators, it has always proven extremely difficult to document benefits from food assistance programs. . . . Most authorities, nutritional or political, concede that food stamps are in reality an income supplement, and would not expect any meaningful evaluation of their nutritional effect to be possible."[23] In the words of one of the few comprehensive examinations of the program, "The naive view that food stamps are restricted, in-kind transfers is largely incorrect. . . . Instead, the program primarily provides general purchasing power."[24]

The extent to which the food stamp program should be tied to nutrition was the subject of extensive congressional debate in 1976–77. In 1976 the House Agriculture Committee voted to retain the purchase requirement, arguing that this was necessary to maintain the program's "character as a nutritional assistance program."[25] A year later the committee reversed its position. The 1977 House Report described elimination of the purchase requirement as an important first step "in the direction of meaningful welfare reform." The change would make administration of the program simpler, reduce black market trading in stamps, encourage more qualified households to participate, and increase the value of the benefits provided. With this change, the program would "more adequately provide to the needy working poor assistance unavailable from other programs" and "more effectively equalize the help available to welfare families whose benefits vary so substantially because of the wide variation in payment levels between states."[26] In short, Congress quite consciously shifted the focus from nutrition to income maintenance.

Paradoxically, while food stamp advocates have consistently argued that hunger is widespread in the United States and that programs such as food stamps, school lunch, and commodity distribution are essential for reducing malnutrition, they have never been comfortable with the special emphasis these programs place on food. In 1974 Nancy Amedei, who later served as director of FRAC, told the Senate Nutrition Committee, "We know what is wrong with the food programs, they don't work. . . . They are lousy programs. We should not have them in the first place."[27] "Redistributing income," rather than handing out food or stamps, was Amedei's solution to the problem of poverty. The final report of the National Nutrition Policy Study, which was sponsored by the Senate Nutrition Committee, chaired by FRAC's chief litigator, and approved by leading members of the "hunger lobby," made a similar argument: "All would agree that in-kind food programs are cumbersome, demeaning, inadequate, and usually inefficient." The food stamp program is so "basically flawed" that "no amount of program revision can ever enable it to solve this problem. The only solution is a just, dignified, guaranteed income maintenance program that ensures that no person lives without an adequate income." The report called for a "national commitment to move toward adequate income for all Americans."[28]

It is easy to understand the concerns of the reformers. A central assumption of nutrition programs is that the government needs to tell the poor how to spend their money. Using food stamps in grocery stores can be embarrassing and stigmatizing. Just as important, participation rates tend to be lower for voucher programs than for straight income transfers. Yet, as most food stamp advocates also realize, cutting the cord between these programs and nutrition threatens to undermine their political support. In 1981, a few years after elimination of the purchase requirement, a Gallop poll reported that 61 percent of respondents believed that the government spent too much on food stamps. In fact, in that year food stamps was the most unpopular of the government programs listed by the pollsters.[29] Hugh Heclo has speculated that "insofar as the food stamp program has gradually been perceived as income support rather than a food program, it has become politically suspect."[30]

"Talk about hunger, but slowly cash out food programs" has long been the political strategy of food stamp advocates. In 1975 Senator George McGovern remarked,

> We are moving toward the concept of a single flat income maintenance guarantee. Now, very frankly, when you eliminate the purchase price [for food stamps], you are taking a step in that direction, and it is probably more palatable to the Congress and the American people than talking about a guaranteed income. Nobody is more painfully aware of the hazards of that approach than I am.[31]

McGovern was referring to his ill-fated "demi-grant" proposal, which Republicans derided during the 1972 presidential campaign. During that campaign Senator McGovern developed a reputation for political ineptness. Yet his years of congressional work in building the food stamp program show that he was remarkably adept at fashioning welfare reform that is "palatable" to the American public. What made the program palatable, of course, was the ostensible focus on nutrition, which slowly faded as the program matured.

Committee Jurisdiction

One of the most important consequences of the program's link with food and nutrition is that it falls within the jurisdiction of the House and Senate Agriculture committees. This arrangement dates back to 1939, when Secretary of Agriculture Henry Wallace established the first food stamp program. Initially, stamps could be used only to purchase surplus commodities. Although the program served 4 million people by 1941, Congress never passed authorizing legislation or even appropriated money for this purpose. Funding came from section 32 of the Agricultural Adjustment Act, which allowed the secretary of agriculture to use money raised from customs on agricultural products to "encourage the domestic consumption" of surplus farm commodities. From the late 1930s to the mid-1960s the two Agriculture committees tolerated executive branch initiatives on food stamps but did nothing to promote the program. Their principal concern was that the program not divert resources from farm programs aiding their rural constituents. After Secretary Wallace unilaterally terminated the original program in 1943, the Agriculture committees did nothing to resuscitate it. During the 1950s and early 1960s, the leading congressional supporter of food stamps, Representative Leonor Sullivan, was not even a member of the Agriculture Committee.

In 1961 President Kennedy used his first executive order to establish a program similar to that of 1939–43. He, too, relied on funds from section 32 rather than take the risk of asking Congress for money. When Kennedy proposed authorizing legislation in 1963, the House Agriculture Committee's disinterest turned into hostility. Its potent "conservative coalition" of Southern Democrats and Republicans refused to act on the bill. Representative Sullivan and the Democratic leadership retaliated by blocking House action on a tobacco research bill dear to the heart of some committee members. They made clear their intention to hold the tobacco bill hostage in the Rules Committee until the Agriculture Committee reported out the president's food stamp legislation. This was the first of many collisions between food stamp supporters and the conservative coalition on the Agriculture committees.

The events of 1964 seem at first glance to support the most common explanation for the success of the food stamp program, logrolling. According to the conventional wisdom, the representatives of farm states who dominate the Agriculture committees have struck deals with urban members: they support food stamps in exchange for urban votes for commodity bills.[32] By combining forces, each faction achieves a goal neither could attain on its own. For many years food stamp and commodity bills have been brought to the floor together in order to facilitate negotiation between urban and rural interests.

John Ferejohn's careful analysis of legislative bargaining on food stamps has exposed the shortcomings of the logrolling thesis. He shows that the commodity bill has needed food stamps far more than food stamp legislation has needed the commodity bill. Indeed, the food stamp program has always been popular enough on the floor to command a majority on its own.[33] Commodity bills, in contrast, have been in trouble in Congress since the mid-1960s. The principal obstacles for food stamp advocates lay in forcing the House committee to send a bill to the floor and in preventing committee members from gutting it in conference.

After food stamp supporters retaliated against the obstructionist committee in 1964, committee members learned to take advantage of a program they had originally disdained. In exchange for reporting out food stamp legislation, committee leaders received promises from food stamp advocates to support commodity bills on the floor. A few Republicans and conservative Democrats on the committees continued to complain that a welfare program belonged neither within their jurisdiction nor in the USDA. But their more pragmatic colleagues refused to kill the goose that was laying golden eggs. For strategic reasons, committee members not only accepted expansion of the program but strenuously resisted efforts to transfer the food stamp program to other committees.

This was not logrolling in the ordinary sense of mutual cooperation between legislators seeking benefits for their constituents. Rather, it was "mutual hostage taking between hostile interests."[34] As Ferejohn explains, "The food stamp program was 'used' by the Agriculture committee and the Democratic leadership to secure votes for a controversial farm program. Had it come up for a vote by itself, it would have passed anyway without any special need to court the votes of farm state Democrats."[35]

Membership changes in the early 1970s made the Agriculture committees less southern, conservative, and hostile to food stamps. Yet the committees remained a stumbling block for those favoring expansion of the program. In the Senate, George McGovern and his allies were often able to rewrite the committee's bill on the floor. After losing several fights, conservatives on the committee became more willing to strike a deal with McGovern rather than risk a showdown on the floor.

The House was a harder nut to crack. In 1970 Thomas Foley, then a relatively junior member of the committee, tried to convince House Agriculture to approve a bill similar to one McGovern had steered through the Senate. Foley later described the effort as "a catastrophic failure. The vote was always 25-2."[36] Foley took his proposal to the floor. After a confusing sequence of parliamentary maneuvers, Foley lost by the narrow vote of 172-183. The conference committee eventually split the difference between the House bill and the more generous Senate bill.

As this example shows, food stamp bills were often delicate compromises constructed to survive votes in the two Agriculture committees, on the House and Senate floor, and in conference. Neither committee could expect its bill to emerge from the floor unscathed. The more conservative majorities on the committees had to negotiate with program supporters in order to win enough votes for food stamp and commodity bills. McGovern and Foley had to compromise with others on the committee in order to get any bill at all. This is obviously much different from education for the handicapped, where the two education committees had a relatively free hand in developing legislative proposals.

Another consequence of the peculiar legislative jurisdiction of the food stamp program is that the two Agriculture committees have a legislative style much different from entrepreneurial "policy" committees such as House Education and Labor and Senate Human Resources. They are classic "constituency committees," used to working closely with the USDA. Their overriding concern is passing legislation to help the farmers in their districts. Consequently, all members of the committee, Republicans and Democrats, liberals and conservatives, recognize

> the importance of developing a balanced package of subsidies for producers in the various constituencies. Without such a package, most subsidies for producers of individual commodities would not gain majority support in the House. A strong chair responsible for creating a package with majority support [is] viewed by members as an expedient means to servicing constituency interests and their own political goals.[37]

The committees' norms and structure—weak subcommittees and strong chairmen—are designed to promote compromise and accommodation of competing interests and to restrain the type of unbridled advocacy that could lead to defeat on the floor. Committee members have been accustomed to working out differences quietly among themselves and, when necessary, with the USDA. They are not used to dealing with the courts, nor are they comfortable with the uncertainty that litigation often produces. Even the program's strongest supporters on the committee view policymaking by the courts with suspicion.

From Discretion to Confrontation

The food stamp program provides a particularly vivid example of the changes in the American political system described in chapter 2. Both the original program of 1939–43 and the similar program established by President Kennedy in 1961 were products of New Deal politics. Initiative came from the executive branch: the former was the work of Secretary Henry Wallace; the latter rested on JFK's executive order. Not until 1964 did Congress pass authorizing legislation or even appropriate funds for the program. Careerists in the USDA wrote all the national program guidelines on eligibility and benefit levels and turned administration over to state and local governments. The federal administrators who ran the program hoped eventually to replace their small, project-based program with one featuring universal geographic coverage, uniform eligibility requirements, and higher benefit levels. But they feared antagonizing staunch food stamp foes such as House Agriculture Committee Chairman Robert Poage and Appropriations Subcommittee Chairman Jamie Whitten, who wielded significant influence on agricultural matters.

In 1967 food stamp politics changed dramatically. The previous quiet "inside" strategy centered in the executive branch became a boisterous "outside" strategy that cast administrators as the problem, not the solution. Liberal Democrats in Congress worked with the press and the hunger lobby to force the president to take more aggressive action under the existing law and to propose legislation expanding the program. Once this legislation was in place, the hunger lobby took its case to court. Food stamps—neither the program nor its politics—was never the same again.

The emotional tenor of the new politics of food stamps is captured by two descriptions written by participants in the events of the day. According to journalist Nick Kotz, who did as much as anyone to publicize the problem of hunger and to blame it on public officials, "the politics of hunger in affluent America" is "the story of how some leaders left their air-conditioned sanctuaries, discovered hunger among the poor, and determined to make it a national issue; of others who knew about hunger but lied; of still others who learned about hunger but voted for fiscal economy at the expense of the poor."[38]

As a key aid to President Nixon, Daniel Patrick Moynihan frequently found himself at odds with the hunger lobby. He later wrote, "The more government did to meet the nutrition needs of the poor, the more impassioned grew the insistence that it was not doing enough." According to Moynihan, "The style of the hunger movement was attack, and it attacked whoever was in office, almost regardless of what the officeholder did."[39]

The issue of hunger began its rise to prominence when the Subcommittee on Employment, Manpower, and Poverty of the Senate Committee on Labor and Public Welfare traveled to Mississippi to investigate the incidence of malnutrition. Senator Joseph Clark chaired the subcommittee, but freshman Senator Robert Kennedy was the main media attraction. The trip inspired the Field Foundation to send physicians to the South to gather more evidence. Media coverage increased substantially when these physicians testified before the subcommittee. Their testimony was well suited for newspapers and TV. Not only did it come from authoritative sources, but it provided graphic personal portraits of extreme poverty in the rural South.

This coverage quickly snowballed. The *Washington Post, Newsweek,* and the *Christian Science Monitor* sent reporters to the South to see for themselves. The reporters came back with heart-rending stories. CBS's documentary "Hunger in America" opened with a shot of a baby allegedly dying of malnutrition.[40] The more attention the hunger issue received, the more sense it made for welfare reformers to focus their energy on food stamps. The Field Foundation, working with Walter Reuther and Robert Kennedy, pulled a number of activists together to form the Citizens' Board of Inquiry into Hunger and Malnutrition in the United States. The Citizens' Board published its exposé, *Hunger, U.S.A.,* in 1968. Shortly thereafter the Senate passed a resolution establishing the Select Committee on Nutrition and Human Needs. That same year the Poor Peoples' Campaign came to Washington and made expansion of the food stamp program a key demand. The fact that the USDA's building lay right across the street from the Poor People's encampment, Resurrection City, made it a particularly inviting target. When President Nixon paid his first visit to the Department of Agriculture, hunger was what he talked about.

Not by chance did the issue of hunger rise to prominence in 1967: these events were tied to much broader political developments. With congressional support for poverty programs waning and with President Johnson devoting more time and money to Vietnam, liberal Democrats were looking for ways to revitalize the war on poverty. They first tried to goad Johnson into proposing a major expansion of the program. When this failed, food stamps became one of the issues that defined the increasingly bitter rift within the Democratic party. The two men who did most to draw attention to hunger were Robert Kennedy—the leader of the "dump-Johnson" forces in 1968—and George McGovern—whose name later became synonymous with the "new politics" wing of the Democratic party.

One of the ironies of food stamps politics is that it fared much better under Richard Nixon than under Lyndon Johnson. Nixon certainly had no more sympathy for the poor than did Johnson. But he was significantly more susceptible to the claim that he was indifferent to the plight of the needy. Food stamp advocates took full advantage of this vulnerability. After Nixon's election, Democrats in Congress could join together to blame the Republican administration for inaction:

> Nixon's election provided a real tonic to congressional Democrats, for it reduced their internal tensions and integrated the party—and thereby the institution—against a Republican administration. The Senate liberals, in particular, were able to immerse themselves in the occupational therapy of unembarrassed opposition to the White House.[41]

With Richard Nixon in the White House, "partisan politics began to sharpen the Democratic food aid reformers' attacks."[42]

If Robert Poage's Agriculture Committee symbolized the old regime in Congress, George McGovern's Select Committee on Nutrition and Human Needs represented the liberal, media-oriented activism of the emerging Congress. Because the Senate Agriculture Committee retained control over food stamp legislation, investigating and publicizing the problem of malnutrition became the Select Committee's major function. As Martha Derthick has pointed out, committees that lack legislative jurisdiction are particularly prone to "fix blame for government's poor performance on the executive branch or the other political party." Committees that engage in this form of "exposure and attack" often discover "a spontaneous and powerful ally in the press, which ordinarily finds the cause of bureaucratic failures in the bureaucracy itself, a proximate, vulnerable, and easily caricatured target."[43]

No body fit this description better than the Senate Nutrition Committee. Committee hearings were carefully scripted with an eye to providing reporters with a simple, dramatic story. As one staff member put it, "Committee hearings are like a play. . . . You need some good guys and bad guys. You need a supporting cast, in this case the poor."[44] Documents leaked from the Nixon administration passed from journalists to committee staff and from staff to journalists. On one occasion, committee hearings were timed to coincide with a front-page story staffers had learned would appear in the *Washington Post*. On another, Nutrition Committee staff members provided the *New York Times* with leaked documents on the condition that the story be printed on page one. It was.[45]

Nick Kotz, who covered the issue for the *Des Moines Register* and the *Washington Post* and won a Pulitzer prize for his stories, served as a key link between the Senate Nutrition Committee and the media. His popular book, *Let Them Eat Promises: The Politics of Hunger in America,* constitutes a comprehensive and instructive demonology of food stamp politics. Senators Kennedy, McGovern, and Clark are presented as compassionate and far-sighted, Representatives Poage and Whitten as ignorant, racist autocrats. The most striking aspect of Kotz's analysis is the way blame for hunger spreads from congressional opponents to presidents and administrators who proposed modest increases and eventually to American government and society as a whole. Secretary of Agriculture Orville Freeman, generally viewed as a liberal Democrat in the Minnesota tradition, comes under special attack for timidly "knuckling under" to President Johnson and to "segregationists" like Poage and Whitten. In Kotz's writing, the USDA's fledgling program became the *cause* of hunger: "The apparatus of the state, including federal food programs, was used to keep rural Americans from obtaining social, political, or economic equality."[46]

Muckraking American journalists have long viewed themselves as locked in mortal, moral combat with the powerful. But this view of the world became especially compelling in the political environment of the late 1960s and early 1970s. Confidence in the government dropped precipitously as the inner cities burned and the United States sank deeper into the mud of Vietnam. With the aid of journalists such as Kotz and members of Congress such as McGovern, food stamp advocates managed to tap popular discontent with government in their effort to build a larger government program.

A New Program Emerges

Two months after President Nixon took office, Secretary of Agriculture Russell Hardin and Secretary of HEW Robert Finch presented him with an ambitious program devised by a task force of the White House Urban Affairs Council. They recommended that the president propose to Congress a $1.7 billion food stamp program with nationally uniform eligibility requirements. Hardin told Nixon, "This is the hottest item on the domestic front, and we must take the leadership ourselves."[47] Fiscal conservatives within the administration opposed the plan, as did supporters of the incipient family assistance plan, who recognized that FAP and food stamps were competing for funds, public attention, and the loyalty of reformers.

Nixon deferred action on the task force's proposal—at least until the Senate Nutrition Committee managed to force his hand. The committee got possession of virtually all the documents of the Urban Affairs Council and promptly scheduled hearings on the subject. Faced with the embarrassing prospect of explaining why the president had not approved a plan they had so strenuously supported, Hardin and Finch persuaded Nixon to send the legislation to Congress posthaste. The bill raised authorizations to $600 million in 1970 and $1.5 billion in 1971. It gave the USDA authority to set national eligibility standards and required all counties to participate in either the food stamp or commodity distribution programs. Nixon announced, "The moment is at hand to put an end to hunger in America itself for all time." While "gratified that the administration has now indicated its willingness to face up" to the problem of hunger, Senator McGovern chided the president for failing "to provide a commitment for enough funds."[48]

By September 1969 the Senate had passed a bill expanding the food stamp program even more than Nixon had recommended. In a sequence that was to be repeated several times in subsequent years, Senator McGovern's forces defeated the Senate Agriculture Committee on the floor. The "McGovern substitute," which passed 54–40, increased authorizations to $2.5 billion by 1972, lowered the purchase price to 25 percent, and provided free stamps for the very poor. The bill required the USDA to use the "low-cost food plan" (then valued at $134 a month for a family of four) rather than the "economy food plan" (then valued at $106), which Secretary Hardin had just instituted. The House, in contrast, waited until the summer of 1970 to produce a bill. Committee Chairman Poage was in no hurry to expand the program, and he hoped to use the food stamp bill to ensure passage of the 1970 commodity bill.

Meanwhile, a new round of press reports—this time to the effect that the Nixon administration would be attacked in the upcoming White House Conference on Food, Nutrition, and Health for failing to act decisively on food stamps—spurred the White House to expand the existing program administratively. Secretary Hardin unilaterally adopted several key parts of the legislation stalled in the House committee. Most important were the reduction of the purchase price and sizable increases in benefits, especially for the poorest recipients. Hardin justified this action by pointing to a special one-year increase in the program's authorization. Late in 1969 Congress had, at Nixon's request, raised the authorization for fiscal 1970 in order to make room for a food stamp appropriation already accepted by the conference committee on the agriculture appropriations bill. Previously, Hardin had argued that this increase was necessary to fund the existing program; now he argued that it authorized a significant expansion of the program. Representatives Poage and Whitten objected to these regulations—which one member of Congress aptly called "legislation on an appropriation"—but did not make a concerted effort to block them.[49]

In August 1970, the House Agriculture Committee finally reported a bill that incorporated most of the changes proposed by Nixon in 1969 and instituted by Hardin in 1970. The committee bill authorized the USDA to create a nationally uniform program. But it also included several provisions that infuriated liberals. Most controversial were the bill's work requirement for some recipients and the requirement that the states pay part of the cost of benefits. Unlike the Senate, the House committee allowed the USDA to continue using the less expensive economy food plan and refused to permit free stamps for the very poor. As the session drew to a close, the committee bill survived a close vote on the House floor.

The bundle of compromises that emerged from the conference committee established the framework for seven more years of political dispute over the program. The authorization for 1971 was $1.75 billion, more than the Nixon administration wanted but less than the Senate bill. The conferees rejected state cost sharing but accepted a weakened version of the House committee's work requirement. They adopted the Senate provision on free stamps for the very poor, kept the maximum purchase price at 30 percent, and delegated authority to the USDA to set the purchase price for various income levels. They rejected the Senate's more expensive low-cost food plan but added an annual cost-of-living adjustment.

Despite their success in creating an enlarged, nationally uniform program, food stamp advocates were disappointed by their near-miss in the House. They decried the new work requirement, which McGovern called "a declaration of serfdom for America's hungry poor." McGovern and Foley tried unsuccessfully to have the conference report sent back to committee. When they failed, one activist announced that the hunger lobby was "making plans now to pressure the Administration and Congress into approving higher funding levels and eliminating that onerous work requirement."[50] Food stamp advocates did not rest; they simply focused their attention on a new arena.

The Battle Continues

The Department of Agriculture was left with the politically sensitive job of settling many of the issues the 1970 act failed to resolve. In preparing its new regulations, the department for the first time followed the notice-and-comment rulemaking procedures spelled out in the Administrative Procedure Act. Administrators in the Food and Nutrition Service conferred informally with staff from the Senate Nutrition Committee, the two Agriculture committees, and FRAC before publishing final rules. While in previous years USDA regulations had attracted little outside attention, now administrators received lots of conflicting advice. The dispute over the USDA's 1971 regulations was a prelude to the extensive litigation of the early 1970s.

The Senate Nutrition Committee and FRAC were pleased with the USDA's interpretation of the controversial work requirement but were disturbed by other sections of the regulations. The new rules raised the purchase price slightly for 1.7 million recipients near the income ceiling. They did not allow recipients to take deductions for educational or work expenses. And they eliminated automatic eligibility for recipients of state public assistance. This meant that about 350,000 public assistance recipients whose income exceeded national eligibility standards would be dropped from the program. Most of these households lived in high-benefit states such as New York and California.[51]

The hunger lobby geared up for another attack on the Department of Agriculture. A flurry of newspaper articles called attention to the fact that some current recipients would have their food stamp benefits cut and others would become ineligible. The Nutrition Committee held hearings to investigate and to make clear its understanding of "congressional intent." For its lead witness, the committee chose FRAC's chief attorney, who charged that "the administration's proclamations about ending hunger are only rich in rhetoric, meager in performance," and that the rules would "create and perpetuate the tragic nightmare of hunger, and its attendant miseries." Senator McGovern charged that the rules subverted the will of Congress, which was to increase participation and benefits.[52] McGovern and FRAC persuaded more than twenty senators and a number of governors to write to the USDA urging changes in the rules.

On deductions, the 1970 act was completely silent. It stated only that the secretary of agriculture "shall establish uniform national standards of eligibility." On the purchase price, too, the compromise constructed by the conference committee left the department with substantial discretion: "such charge shall represent a reasonable investment on the part of the household, but in no event more than 30 percentum of the household's income." On the third issue, blanket eligibility for public assistance recipients, the USDA argued that it had no choice but to establish a single set of eligibility requirements. "If we automatically accept as eligible all of those who are on public assistance rolls," a USDA official warned the committee, "we will wind up with a lack of uniformity."[53] Long-time food stamp supporter Representative Leonor Sullivan went to the House floor to defend the department on this issue: "I point out that Congress required that the income eligibility standards be uniform all over the country. . . . So while it is easy to blame the Department of Agriculture for its insensitivity in setting up the new regulations . . . we should place the blame where it belongs—right here in Congress."[54]

Although the USDA's Food and Nutrition Service was willing to modify the new regulations, the Office of Management and Budget was not. OMB soon relented on the two less costly items, deductions and public assistance eligibility. But on the purchase price—which OMB estimated would cost $200 million to $300 million—it held fast. Senator McGovern responded by introducing legislation to overturn the purchase price rules. FRAC filed suit. None of their efforts bore fruit until the *New York Times* published a story claiming that the USDA had "impounded" $200 million in food stamp funds. Strictly speaking, this was inaccurate; the food stamp program was now an entitlement program rather than one based on annual appropriations. But the threat of further Senate hearings on the politically sensitive impoundment issue forced OMB and the USDA to relent. In the words of one department official, "It was plain old political pressure. We couldn't stand the heat."[55]

After their victories in 1970 and 1971, food stamp advocates continued to lobby for changes that would boost benefits and increase participation. When the act came up for reauthorization in 1973, they won two important victories. The first was a mandate that all states replace commodity programs with food stamps by mid-1974. The second was a semiannual rather than annual cost-of-living adjustment. Their timing on the latter was perfect: the new adjustment took effect just before food prices began to skyrocket. Although the Senate passed a number of other changes recommended by McGovern, these liberalizing amendments died in conference.

With spending on food stamps rising from less than $600 million in 1970 to $1.6 billion in 1971 and $2.2 billion in 1973, it was hard to argue that the federal government was ignoring the problem of hunger. By 1975 the program had come under intense attack from conservatives, who called for a halt to what they termed the "food stamp stampede." Deflecting this assault rather than expanding the program suddenly became its supporters' preoccupation.

Although food stamp advocates shifted from an "inside" to an "outside" strategy in the late 1960s, they remained uncomfortably dependent on the executive branch. In 1969–70 it took both unilateral administrative action by Agriculture Secretary Hardin and legislation sponsored by President Nixon to push a bill through Congress. The 1970 act addressed a few major issues—authorization levels, the ceiling for the purchase price, the cost-of-living adjustment—but made no attempt to spell out all eligibility rules or even to specify benefit levels. On many of these issues Congress remained badly divided. The history of the 1971 regulations demonstrated the extent of discretion remaining in the hands of administrators and the success of the Senate Nutrition Committee in influencing department policy. But in 1974 the Ford administration became more aggressive in using regulations to reduce spending, and food stamp advocates seldom had enough votes in Congress to overturn them. Food stamp advocates then turned to the courts for help. As chapter 10 shows, for a while this strategy met with remarkable success.

CHAPTER TEN

From Litigation to Legislation

We think it plain that the Food Stamp Act requires the Secretary to distribute the food stamp coupons in such a way that all, or at least virtually all, recipients are given the "opportunity to obtain a nutritionally adequate diet." . . . The purposes of the Food Stamp Act—the health and well-being of our populace—are too important, and the legislative intent that those purposes be achieved for substantially all recipients too clear, for us to allow their administrative evisceration.
                                            —Judge Skelly Wright in *Rodway* v. *USDA*, 1975

The Committee determined by unanimous voice vote to delete the nutritional adequacy standard from the purposes of the Act. . . . Thus, litigation along the lines of Rodway would be impossible to sustain under the Committee bill.
                                            —House Agriculture Committee Report, 1977

IN 1968 a young lawyer at the Columbia Center for Social Welfare Policy and Law—the same organization that had initiated the litigational assault on AFDC—began to look for ways to expand food programs for the poor. Ronald Pollack's initial goal was to ensure that a nutrition program was in operation in every part of the country. His prospects for winning food stamp cases, though, were not bright. In the late 1960s the statute required counties to apply to the U.S. Department of Agriculture for participation in the program. The number of county programs the USDA could approve was limited by the size of the federal appropriation.

At the Columbia center, Pollack learned the importance of bringing the right type of plaintiff to court. His strategy was to find "plaintiffs whose situations would become so desperate if the court did not rule in their favor that a judge could not help but think that the regulation under question was arbitrary or irrational."[1] Even if this tactic failed inside the courtroom, it could still generate publicity and shame state and county officials into expanding food programs. This form of litigation meshed well with food stamp advocates' general strategy of attack and exposure. From the beginning, Pollack stressed that "much of the necessary work that must be done to reform the program is political in nature" and that "attorneys must frame their litigation in a political context."[2]

Pollack's first effort was to file twenty-six suits throughout the country demanding that all counties establish either a food stamp program or a commodity distribution program. He won in two key states, California and Texas. The federal judge in Texas stated that "the denial of Federal food assistance benefits on the basis of county of residence is contrary to the Congressional purpose and intent in the formulation of the Food Stamp and Commodity Distribution Programs," which is "to aid needy families."[3] Although this decision was later overturned by the Fifth Circuit, within two years nearly every county in Texas participated in one of the programs.[4] This was the first of a long string of victories for Pollack.

With help from the federal Office of Economic Opportunity, Pollack founded the Food Research and Action Center, which for many years both coordinated food stamp litigation and served as the headquarters of the "hunger lobby." For FRAC, lobbying and litigating were closely intertwined. This was most apparent in its successful effort to block restrictive regulations announced by the Ford administration in 1976. FRAC persuaded twenty-six state attorneys general, fifty-three labor unions, and twenty-two church groups to join its suit. Its primary objective in this case, *Trump* v. *Butz*, was to allow Congress to wait until 1977 to restructure the program.[5] This case also demonstrated FRAC's knack for generating publicity: the dramatic court decision enjoining the administration from implementing the cutbacks was featured on the evening news and in *Time* magazine. Shortly after winning this pivotal case, Pollack left FRAC. He may well have recognized that the era of significant food stamp litigation had come to an end.

The Dance of Litigation

Not only did aid to families with dependent children and food stamp litigation share a common point of origin, but judges drew upon AFDC case law in their food stamp opinions. For example, they frequently applied to the food stamp program the rules on available income first developed in AFDC cases. Nonetheless, AFDC and food stamp litigation differed in two important respects. First, most food stamp cases involved challenges to federal regulation, not state rules. On the one hand, this meant that FRAC could change national policy simply by winning one case. On the other hand, federal judges generally showed greater deference to federal administrators than they did to the states.

Fortunately for FRAC, the heyday of food stamp litigation, 1971–76, was also the high-water mark of legislative-executive conflict and popular distrust of the "imperial" presidency. One key case, *Bennett* v. *Butz*, was decided by a district court judge who had previously ordered the Nixon administration to release impounded pollution control funds.[6] The judge equated failure to expand participation in entitlement programs with the impoundment of appropriated sums. In several cases, the challenged regulations had been forced upon the USDA's Food and Nutrition Service by the White House and Office of Management and Budget. This added to judges' sense that political pressure had displaced agency expertise in the rulemaking process.

A second difference between food stamps and AFDC is that there were no blockbuster food stamp decisions similar to the *King-Townsend-Carleson* trilogy. The Supreme Court did not decide a single statutory case until 1977.[7] Not only were the important cases resolved by the lower courts, but each one dealt with a discrete part of the program. Judicial expansion came in undramatic increments. The following review of federal cases covers three elements of this segmented case law: the diet plan, certification and outreach, and the definition of income and deductions.

The Diet Plan

Food stamp benefits are based on the diet plan established by the USDA. Few elements of the program have such a direct and substantial effect on the program's impact and cost. The 1970 act stated that the value of the stamps given to each household "shall be in such amount as the Secretary determines to be the cost of a nutritionally adequate diet." In his testimony on the bill, Secretary Hardin informed both committees that the USDA would continue to use the economy food plan, which it had first instituted in 1969. In *Rodway* v. *USDA*, a decision that generated a great deal of controversy in Congress, the D.C. Circuit ordered the USDA to reconsider the adequacy of the economy food plan. Judge Skelly Wright argued that the language and legislative history of the 1970 act demonstrated that this law "marked a major shift in the policy of the Food Stamp Act, a shift from supplementing the diets of low-income households to *guaranteeing* those households the opportunity for an adequate diet. Congress plainly intended . . . to assure that no eligible family need go malnourished."[8] The right to a "nutritionally adequate diet" became a leitmotif of food stamp opinions.

The *Rodway* litigation grew out of FRAC's challenge to the regulations issued shortly after passage of the 1970 law. Early in 1971 FRAC filed suit in the federal district court for the District of Columbia claiming that the department's rules on the purchase price contravened congressional intent. Before the court had a chance to decide the case, the department agreed to roll back the price increase (see chapter 9). FRAC then reconstituted the case, focusing this time on coupon allotments. It argued that the economy food plan did not adequately reflect the cost of a "nutritionally adequate diet" for recipients with special dietary needs. FRAC's attorneys argued that the USDA should either create new categories for those with special needs or raise benefits across the board. They preferred the latter and knew that officials of the Food and Nutrition Service considered the first option an administrative nightmare.

At the center of this litigation was a vital element of the compromise crafted in Congress in 1970. Senator McGovern persuaded the Senate to endorse an alternative diet plan, the low-cost food plan, which would raise benefits by about 30 percent. The House committee stuck with the economy food plan. On the House floor, Representative Foley argued that the economy food plan "is too risky a measure of the purchasing power needed to insure against malnutrition." He complained that the committee's bill "makes no significant changes" in either the diet plan or the purchase price; it "leaves them both to the Secretary's discretion."[9] His amendment to replace the economy food plan with the Senate's low-cost plan was narrowly defeated. The 1970 conference report announced the following agreement:

> The House bill established the value of the coupon allotment to food stamp recipients at a level which the Secretary finds will provide a "nutritionally adequate diet." The Department informed the Committee that this is currently $106 per month for a family of four. The Senate amendment proposed to establish a "low cost food plan" standard which the Department stated would require $134 per month for a family of four.
>
> The conference substitute retains the House standard, but adopts the language of the Senate amendment requiring the Secretary of Agriculture to make an annual adjustment to reflect increases for food in the "Cost of Living" index.[10]

The statute made explicit reference to the cost-of-living adjustment, but not to the economy food plan.

The *Rodway* case bounced back and forth between the district and circuit courts. Initially, the district court dismissed FRAC's belated challenge to the diet plan. The D.C. Circuit reversed. The appellate court conceded that "Congress was aware that the Secretary planned to use the Economy Food Plan" and noted that "Senator McGovern advanced many of the arguments here urged by appellants." But, it held, the district court still has a responsibility to make sure that the secretary's decision had a "rational basis."[11]

On remand, the district court judge again ruled in favor of the USDA. According to the court, the secretary did not abuse the discretion granted to him since he abided by the compromise announced in the conference report. Moreover, the district court argued, no government program can be expected to take account of all special circumstances.[12] Again the D.C. Circuit disagreed. This time, Judge Wright found that the department had violated its own procedural requirements by failing to request comments on the diet plan when it reaffirmed its commitment to the economy food plan in 1971. FRAC had not raised this procedural point until the second oral argument before the circuit court.

In order to "expedite the administrative process," Judge Wright presented his reading of the act's substantive requirements. He maintained that the compromise announced in the conference report did not settle the issue of whether the economy food plan did in fact guarantee a "nutritionally adequate diet" for all recipients:

> While there are frequent references to the Plan in the legislative history, Congress was acting only on the Secretary's representations that the Plan would be the basis for a nutritionally adequate diet. It did not attempt to evaluate those representations, and it did not incorporate them into the statutory standard. Thus the Secretary must find support for the Plan in fact, not in the legislative history.[13]

The court would judge the secretary's plan solely on the basis of whether it provided "virtually all recipients" with enough stamps to pay for a nutritionally adequate diet. Neither cost nor administrative convenience could justify exceptions. "The nation's poor and low-income families who are so dependent on the relief promised by the Food Stamp Act deserve no less."[14]

Six months later, the USDA completed its new analysis, cited extensive evidence, and promulgated a thrifty food plan nearly identical to the preexisting economy food plan. The USDA refused to create a variety of special categories. Secretary Earl L. Butz told the Senate Agriculture Committee that instituting "individualized allotments, recently suggested by the court, is enormously complicated and would undercut our other proposals to assure timely accurate certification."[15] FRAC never had a chance to challenge the new regulations in court because in 1977 Congress removed from the statute all references to a "nutritionally adequate diet."

There can be little doubt that the USDA *did* take into consideration the fact that adopting a new food plan would raise program costs significantly. The food stamp budget had grown particularly rapidly in 1975–76, and the program was politically vulnerable. Budget cuts, not expansion, loomed on the horizon. Even the program's friends in Congress viewed increasing the coupon allotment as politically unwise at that time. The *Rodway* litigation did not have any lasting effect on the composition of the diet plan. But it highlights the importance of the "right to a nutritionally adequate diet" in food stamp litigation. It also illustrates the tension between the courts' rights-based vision of the program and Congress's abiding concern about the program's cost.

Outreach and Certification

Low participation rates plagued the food stamp program for many years. The number of recipients often dropped sharply when counties switched from commodity distribution to stamps.[16] By the mid-1970s, only about half of all eligible households were receiving stamps. These low participation rates were of great concern to food stamp advocates. They saw elimination of the purchase requirement as the best way to increase participation. But this required legislation, and its proponents could not muster a majority in Congress until 1977. A second strategy was to simplify the application process. The ultimate goal of reformers was a "self-certification" system in which verification followed rather than preceded distribution of benefits. In 1975 a self-certification bill passed the Senate but died in the House.

A third approach was commonly called "outreach," which meant state and local governments would publicize the food stamp program and encourage low-income households to apply. Outreach began in the mid-1960s as an effort by the USDA to encourage grocery stores to accept food stamps and to provide recipients with education on nutrition. A little-noted provision in the 1970 act required states to "undertake effective action" to "inform low-income households concerning the availability and benefits of the food stamp program and insure the participation of eligible households."

The USDA considered outreach a peripheral matter. Advertising and community organizing were not part of its organizational mission. Secretary Butz was particularly opposed to using department money to encourage people to apply for welfare benefits. "Butz was just death on outreach," officials who worked under him recalled.[17] The department required the states to submit outreach plans but did little to supervise their activities.

FRAC saw outreach as a means of increasing participation in the food stamp program, mobilizing poor people, and building its own organization. It filed more than twenty suits to force the USDA and the states to mount larger outreach efforts. The key court decision was *Bennett* v. *Butz*, written by Judge Miles Lord of Minnesota, a man known for his confrontational style and controversial decisions.[18]

Ironically, in *Bennett* v. *Butz* the program's appropriations "cap," which program advocates had long tried to eliminate, worked to FRAC's advantage. Congress had appropriated $2.5 billion for food stamps for fiscal 1973. The department predicted that the program would have a $302 million surplus by the end of the year. Congressional supporters of the program were trying to have this surplus carried over to the next fiscal year. Judge Lord attributed the surplus to the department's failure to undertake outreach activities. He prohibited the department from returning the money to the treasury and ordered it to put together a new outreach program. Judge Lord not only converted the appropriations cap into a spending floor but equated the perennial problem of low participation rates with the failure to expand outreach.

Judge Lord's opinion frequently cited Senate Nutrition Committee studies on low participation rates. Looking at Senate floor statements and at the announced purpose of the 1970 act, he discovered a "strong legislative mandate" for "effective outreach." That law, he maintained, "was passed to place under Congressional directive and control a program previously administered on a wholly discretionary basis by the Secretary." The secretary's lack of action on outreach was a threat to "the rule of law."[19] Yet the judge gave no indication of what sort of outreach program the rule of law required. In essence, he told the department and the states to try harder.

Bennett v. *Butz* had two immediate consequences. First, it helped FRAC negotiate consent agreements with many of the twenty-two states it had sued. These states hired more staff, ran media campaigns, and engaged in various forms of community organizing, sometimes by contracting out to existing advocacy groups (including FRAC itself). Second, the department wrote new outreach requirements, which—after being amended by Judge Lord—became effective in 1975. These rules required states to hire full-time outreach coordinators, to establish contact with community groups, and to target certain sectors of the population (the elderly, migrant workers, those not speaking English) for special attention. All the states submitted new outreach plans within a few months. But state efforts remained meager except where FRAC and Legal Services threatened further legal action.[20] In the meantime, outreach became a bête noire of conservative members of Congress, who saw it as a miniature community action program and a cause of the "food stamp stampede."

Probably the most important long-term consequence of *Bennett* v. *Butz* was to encourage court supervision of the details of the certification process. According to a federal judge in Connecticut, a state cannot satisfy the outreach requirement "by merely imparting such information." Rather, it "must operate a food stamp program which actively *insures* participation by placing as few obstacles as possible in the way of those applying for benefits."[21]

The courts reviewed a wide variety of state and federal administrative practices to see whether they created excessive barriers to participation. This required judges to delve into the intricate administrative details of the program. Among other issues, federal courts decided the amount of verification states could require for reported income; timetables for processing benefits for those facing emergencies; the option of telephone applications and home interviews for those unable to travel to food stamp offices; the provision of new stamps to those who report the loss or theft of their initial allotment; and automatic forwarding of previous underpayments. In some of these cases the courts were enforcing Food and Nutrition Service rules that the service was unable or unwilling to enforce by itself. But the courts were also quite willing to overturn federal rules they considered too restrictive. This is one area in which the courts remained active even after passage of the 1977 amendments.[22]

Income and Deductions

Food stamp legislation enacted before 1970 made no effort to define the key term "income" or to explain which deductions (if any) were permitted. Before 1970 federal administrators had unilaterally created a variety of deductions for such things as special medical costs, work expenses, child care, and "excess shelter cost." FRAC and Legal Services attorneys asked the courts to expand these deductions, to narrow the definition of countable income, and to prevent the Nixon and Ford administrations from imposing more restrictive accounting rules. Between 1971 and 1976 the federal courts issued a large number of decisions on deductions and income that had the effect of increasing benefits substantially for many households. In essence, the courts held that the Food and Nutrition Service had broad authority to create deductions and exemptions, but not to narrow them in later years.

Most food stamp recipients also receive some other form of government benefits. A central question in many court cases was whether to count these benefits as "income" under the food stamp program. On the one hand, including all these benefits in the calculation of income gives the most accurate picture of the need of various recipients. On the other hand, counting benefits such as energy assistance payments or housing subsidies reduces food stamp benefits. This in effect reduces the redistributive effect of other programs without reducing their cost—a combination that seldom pleases the clientele and political sponsors of these other programs. Disputes over the status of various forms of government benefits is a good example of the "policy congestion" discussed in chapter 2.

A case that came before the Ninth Circuit provides a typical example. The USDA had counted as "income" benefits paid under the Alaskan Native Claims Settlement Act. The court overturned this decision. "Our study of the Settlement Act and the legislative history surrounding its enactment," the court stated, "convinces us that Congress did not intend that the distributions of funds to individual Alaska Natives . . . should displace the food stamp assistance to which the Natives would otherwise have been entitled."[23]

Another court ruled that federal work training grants cannot be treated as income since such a policy would discourage participation in training programs.[24] Several courts ruled that home energy assistance grants cannot be considered income for the purpose of calculating benefits under the food stamp program. According to the Eighth Circuit, "The framers of the energy legislation intended that food stamp benefits should not be diminished by reason of energy payments."[25] The courts have held that educational grants "specially earmarked" by other statutes for payment of tuition or books are excluded from income.[26] Utility reimbursements, the Third Circuit held, cannot be counted as income since they are "energy assistance," not "housing assistance."[27] Federal judges have allowed administrators to count AFDC benefits, including those for unborn children.[28] But they have barred the states from reducing general assistance grants to those receiving food stamps.[29] It is probably impossible to discover an underlying logic to these cases. Each decision constitutes an ad hoc reading of the intent of the Food Stamp Act and other entitlement statutes.

This seat-of-the-pants approach was clearly evident in *Anderson* v. *Butz*, probably the most important case categorizing government benefits.[30] A district court in California and the Ninth Circuit ruled that housing subsidies provided by the Department of Housing and Urban Development cannot be counted as income under the food stamp program. The judges relied on the "Ichord amendment," a little-noted provision added to the 1973 reauthorization bill on the House floor.[31] On its face, the Ichord amendment seemed to broaden rather than narrow the act's definition of income. It required the secretary to include as income "payments in kind received from an employer by members of a household, if such payments are in lieu of or supplemental to household income." It further stipulated that "such payments in kind shall be limited only to housing provided by such employer to such employee."[32] In *Anderson* the court argued that to include employer-provided housing subsidies is to exclude all other forms of housing subsidies, particularly those provided by the government. To buttress this reading of legislative intent, the court cited floor statements made by Senator McGovern a full two years after passage of the Ichord amendment—indeed, after Legal Services had filed this law suit.

The Sixth Circuit later came down on the other side of the issue.[33] It argued that the *Anderson* court had "exalt[ed] form over substance" by equating in-kind benefits (which are hard to quantify) with vendor payments (which are not). An *exception* to the ban on counting *in-kind* benefits, the court claimed, does not constitute an *exclusion* of *vendor* payments. USDA attorneys believed that the Supreme Court would side with them in this conflict between the circuits and recommended appealing the *Anderson* decision. But by this time the Carter administration had decided it preferred the policy established by the Ninth Circuit. Congress later agreed.[34]

The federal courts also left their mark on rules for calculating the income of migrant workers. In *Gutierrez* v. *Butz*, FRAC and Legal Services challenged a federal regulation that allowed the states to devise their own procedures for estimating the income of migrant workers. The federal district court for the District of Columbia found these regulations to be "an inadequate and feeble response to the problems of migrant workers." The rules fail "to guarantee that migrant families will be provided the opportunity guaranteed them by the Food Stamp Act of attaining a nutritionally adequate diet."[35] The court ordered the USDA to issue new, nationally uniform rules in conformity with the understanding of "available income" developed by the courts in AFDC cases. This had the effect of reducing the recorded income of migrants and increasing their food stamp benefits.

In this and many other cases, FRAC argued that administrators should deduct from gross income any expenditures that did not increase the recipient's "food purchasing power." After prevailing in the lower courts, FRAC met with a stinging defeat in the Supreme Court on this issue. *Knebel* v. *Hein* upheld a standardized work-expense deduction.[36] This ruling was unexpected not only because FRAC had won so many cases in the lower courts, but also because the Court had struck down a similar AFDC regulation just three years before. In *Shea* v. *Vialpando* the Court held that income devoted to work expenses is not "available" for meeting other needs and thus cannot be counted as income for AFDC purposes.[37] *Shea* invalidated uniform work-expense ceilings and required states to approve deductions on an individual basis.

In *Knebel* v. *Hein* a unanimous Court found that the Food Stamp Act, unlike the AFDC section of the Social Security Act, included a "broad delegation of authority" to the secretary of agriculture. Although the statute did not require a standardized deduction for transportation expenses, neither did it prohibit the secretary from imposing one. Since "allowing a deduction for all transportation expenses would create significant administrative costs as well as risk of disparate treatment," the secretary of agriculture had acted reasonably in setting a single, uniform work-expense deduction. Moreover, because the central assumption of the food stamp program was that households would spend 70 percent of their funds on nonfood purchases, it made little sense to deduct from income *all* funds not available for purchasing food.

Knebel v. *Hein* pulled the rug out from under FRAC litigational strategy. If federal judges followed the Supreme Court's lead of deferring to federal administrators, then poverty lawyers had little hope of winning many food stamp cases. Fortunately for FRAC, its most important case reached the bench just before the Supreme Court announced this decision. In *Trump* v. *Butz* the lower court refused to defer to the USDA. By the time *Knebel* was decided, *Trump* v. *Butz* had already left an indelible mark on the program.

Playing the *Trump* Card

A curious feature of food stamp litigation is that the pivotal *Trump* ruling was never published in the official reports. In the winter of 1976 the Ford administration announced new food stamp regulations that the USDA estimated would remove over 5 million people from the rolls and cut annual costs by more than $1 billion. The administration saw these rules both as a way to reduce the program's cost and as a mechanism for forcing Congress to revamp the entire program.[38] Both Judge Howard Corcoran, who issued a temporary restraining order in late May 1976, and Judge John Lewis Smith, who issued a temporary injunction in June, maintained that they were merely preserving the status quo until Congress could finish work on the legislation before it. The effect of their decisions, though, was to bring congressional action to a halt: without the threat of retrenchment, program supporters had no reason to support pending legislation. After the second court ruling, the House Democratic leadership decided not to send the House committee's bill to the floor.

The *Trump* case provides a vivid illustration of how court decisions can affect congressional negotiations. "Given the mood of the country," program supporters "much preferred to take the chance that a better bill might emerge after public anger about the program subsided and, possibly, after a Democrat replaced President Ford."[39] When the Ford administration threatened the benefits of millions of recipients, food stamp advocates felt they had to strike a legislative deal that would undo some of the damage done by the new rules. Legislative retrenchment appeared all but certain. Once the courts had invalidated these rules, though, program advocates were free to wait until 1977—which proved to be a very good year for food stamps.

The story of *Trump* v. *Butz* really starts in 1975. The economy was then in a deep recession, food prices were increasing at a surprising rate, and the cost of the food stamp program was rising by more than a billion dollars a year. Secretary of the Treasury William Simon charged that the program had become a "haven for cheats and rip-off artists."[40] President Ford described food stamps as "scandal-ridden" and claimed "the need to control the growth and abuse of the Food Stamp program is broadly recognized."[41] The press, once the program's best friend, suddenly turned against it. The *Washington Star, U.S. News and World Report*, and *Reader's Digest* all ran major stories attacking "a program that has literally run amok." Members of Congress received thousands of angry letters from their constituents.[42] Alarmed by the "softening of congressional support" for food stamps, "even ardent supporters of the program admitted that some changes needed to be made."[43]

Since the program's cost regularly exceeded its spending cap, Congress had to pass large supplemental appropriations. This provided an opening for the program's critics. The House Appropriations Subcommittee on Agriculture, chaired by long-time food stamp foe Jamie Whitten, took the administration to task for allowing "the abuses of the program, which have been so widely reported."[44] Claiming that the 1970 amendments gave the department broad discretion to set eligibility standards, the subcommittee "earmarked $100,000 of the fiscal year 1976 appropriation for the specific purpose of revising program regulations so as to minimize existing misuse and unwanted expenditures." The subcommittee estimated that $1 billion could be saved through rule changes "subject to action by the Department." It expected the new regulations to be "in full force" by February 1, 1976.

The Ford administration needed little urging from Congress to go after the program. Shortly after the November 1974 elections, Ford unveiled a broad plan to curtail federal spending. One element was to increase the food stamp purchase price to the 30 percent maximum for all households. This initial attempt to cut food stamps proved to be a serious political mistake, since it would have its greatest effect on the program's most popular clientele, the elderly. Moreover, Ford announced these measures just as the "Watergate babies" elected in 1974 were taking their seats. The new rules were soon portrayed as another example of the "imperial presidency" in action. Congress quickly passed legislation blocking the rule for one year. At the same time, House Democrats conceded that the program had serious flaws and promised a thorough congressional reevaluation.[45]

Throughout 1975 food stamp costs continued to mount, media stories on "fraud and abuse" multiplied, and President Ford proposed legislation significantly tightening eligibility and reducing benefits. A contingent of 120 House Republicans wanted to go even further than the administration. They proposed legislation to cut the number of recipients by more than one-third. Other members of Congress favored further expansion. Most legislators wanted to reduce "fraud and abuse" without cutting benefits for the needy. With both the House and the Senate deeply divided, food stamp legislation went nowhere.

Impatient with Congress's failure to act and worried about Ronald Reagan's challenge for the Republican presidential nomination, President

Ford announced a second set of food stamp regulations. These rules increased the purchase price for most households without harming the elderly. They also broadened the definition of income, strengthened the work requirement, created a standard deduction, and instituted stricter reporting procedures.[46] The White House announced these changes just four days before the hard-fought New Hampshire primary.

Before these rules went into effect, the administration had to make concessions in order to get a bill through Congress. Now the shoe was on the other foot: program supporters had to make concessions in order to pass a bill that would modify the new regulations. The new situation was evident in April, after the rules had been proposed but before the court invalidated them. Senators McGovern and Dole had previously insisted that any new legislation include an amendment to eliminate the purchase requirement. President Ford had promised to veto such a bill. The amendment lost by a tie vote in the Senate Agriculture Committee. Although McGovern and Dole were confident they could muster just over fifty votes for the amendment on the floor, they did not have nearly enough support to override a presidential veto. Under pressure to reach a compromise, McGovern and Dole negotiated a deal with committee chairman Herman Talmadge, who adamantly opposed the change. This plan removed half a million people from the rolls—far fewer than the administration's regulations—and increased benefits for the poorest recipients. McGovern and Dole abandoned their major legislative goal, elimination of the purchase requirement.[47]

The House seemed likely to approve a more restrictive bill. The Agriculture Committee's thirty-six markup sessions produced a welter of close votes. After months of angry debate, the committee finally reported out a bill by the narrow margin of 21–19. The bill was a cornucopia of compromises. While it lowered the purchase price, it also broadened the definition of income, curtailed outreach, restricted student eligibility, banned strikers, and required states to pay 2 percent of program costs. The committee's attempt to write an asset limitation rule created a provision so complex that almost everyone considered it impossible to administer. Committee leaders claimed its bill would cost several hundred million dollars less per year than the one endorsed by the Senate.[48]

Attached to the committee report were an array of dissenting views. Eight supporters of the program described the bill as "basically a conservative piece of legislation" and served notice that they would propose amendments on the floor. Two liberal Democrats called for the bill's defeat. Nine Republicans on the committee characterized the bill as "a cruel hoax upon taxpayer hopes and demands for real reform."[49] They, too, vowed to take their case to the floor.

The House Democratic leadership did not want to bring this bill to the floor. No one was particularly happy with the revisions, and no one knew what would happen on the floor. Moreover, party leaders were reluctant to force the large class of freshman Democrats to vote on such a controversial matter just before the election.[50] Although party leaders and program advocates recognized that the program needed a thorough overhaul, they preferred to do so without President Ford setting the agenda or wielding a veto. The only thing keeping the bill alive during 1976 was the threat of the administration's cuts.

Delaying the new regulations became food stamp advocates' top priority. "If it had not been for the court decision," one of their strategists later explained, "we would have had to have a bill."[51] Publicly, FRAC maintained that the rules were "clearly in violation of the Food Stamp Act."[52] Privately, FRAC's lawyers recognized that their legal arguments were weak and that their task was more political than legal. Their strategy was to demonstrate broad opposition to the rules, to raise a number of procedural arguments, and, above all, to create enough doubts in the judge's mind about the propriety of unilateral administrative cuts to persuade him to freeze the status quo ante.

FRAC put together a long list of supporters and combed the administrative record for procedural irregularities. After winning an initial seven-day temporary restraining order from one judge, it flooded the court with additional information on the possible consequences of the rules. The second judge issued a preliminary injunction, which was never lifted.

The rationale for enjoining the regulations was murky at best. The court stressed that the 1976 supplemental appropriations bill—which had earmarked $100,000 "to revise regulations as authorized by existing law"—did not give the administration broad authority to restructure the food stamp program. Of course, neither the department nor the Appropriations Committee ever claimed it did. The USDA maintained that the new rules had been issued "in response to the directions" of the House committee, but under authority granted by the 1970 act.[53] The crux of the court's argument was that policy issues as important as these should be made by Congress, not the executive branch. This meant that eligibility rules and benefit levels established administratively in 1969–71 could not be tightened administratively in 1976. Such asymmetrical judicial limitations on executive discretion were later rejected by the Supreme Court in *Knebel* v. *Hein*.

Republicans on the House Agriculture Committee recognized that the court decisions ended their hope of getting food stamp legislation in 1976. They complained that the "poorly worded opinion" had "frustrated President Ford's attempt to reform the Food Stamp Program as directed by Congress in the Supplemental Appropriations Act."[54] Food stamp advocates, in contrast, breathed a collective sigh of relief. As one put it, "Now we could stall and get through the election."[55]

The gamble paid off. Unlike 1976, 1977 was a very good year for the food stamp program. With the economy improving, participation rates reached a two-and-one-half-year low. No longer could critics refer to the "food stamp stampede" and a program whose budget was "out of control." President Carter's choice for secretary of agriculture, Representative Bob Bergland, had been one of the most reliable supporters of the program on the House Agriculture Committee. Carter endorsed elimination of the purchase requirement, which he saw as a step toward comprehensive welfare reform. In 1976 President Ford's threatened veto had all but removed this issue from the legislative debate; a year later, this important policy passed with remarkable ease. The vote was 64–31 in the Senate and 317–102 in the House. According to *Congressional Quarterly*, "the most far-reaching revision of the food stamp program since it became permanent in 1964" had "an easy trip through Congress."[56] With the help of the courts, the program's supporters had converted an almost inevitable legislative setback into a substantial congressional victory.

The Attack on the Courts

Passage of the 1977 amendments constituted a refounding of the food stamp program. Elimination of the purchase requirement was the cornerstone of the reformulation. This change alone brought in nearly 3 million new recipients.[57] The amendments replaced the variable purchase price with a uniform benefit reduction rate of 30 percent. They completely revamped the method for calculating income, ended automatic eligibility for public assistance recipients, placed a ceiling on gross income, tightened work requirements, restricted eligibility for students and aliens, and established new rules on assets. While the 1970 act had left a wide variety of matters to agency discretion, the 1977 law was remarkably specific.

For example, it spelled out ten categories of excluded income, told administrators when applicants must be given registration forms, and even specified that benefits must be rounded to the nearest whole dollar. In addition, the accompanying 850-page House report explained in minute detail how administrators should interpret each section of the new law. According to one congressional staff member, the report was designed to "control every piece of regulation ever issued."[58]

Well aware of the role court decisions had played in expanding the program between 1970 and 1977, House Republicans suspected that the lengthy bill and the "gargantuan" committee report would provide further grist for the litigation mill. In previous years they had warned that "lofty aims and impractically stated goals normally are seized upon by judges to expand and liberalize federal assistance programs."[59] Committee Republicans were especially angry about *Trump*, *Rodway*, and *Bennett* v. *Butz*. They expected the 1977 amendments to produce more of the same.

As it turned out, the Republicans' suspicions were misplaced. The major sponsor of the 1977 law in the House, Agriculture Committee Chairman Thomas Foley, gave his staff clear instructions: they should strive to minimize rather than encourage court intervention.[60] Although Foley disagreed with committee Republicans on many policy matters, he shared their evaluation of the courts:

> Since the passage of the last major program changes in January 1971, well over 100 lawsuits have been brought in every State in the country by attorneys of organizations receiving Federal funds. The intent of Congress was not as explicitly expressed as it might have been in 1969, 1970, and 1971, but whatever intent there was has often been distorted in my judgement by the process of litigation.[61]

Foley saw this as an affront to Congress and as a violation of the separation of powers: "The Constitution bestows upon the Congress the power to create policy and program in the form of laws and upon the executive branch the responsibility to execute them. The courts have the right to interpret the laws, not write them." The 1977 law was designed to "eliminate the words and phrases that were conducive to litigation in the past." While some ambiguities might remain, Foley asked federal judges to "construe this new food stamp law in light of our intent to trust its management to the Department of Agriculture operating in good faith and under the guidance of our legislative dictates." To a remarkable extent, the 1977 amendments succeeded in removing food stamp issues from the courtroom.

The Scorecard

Examination of the 1977 amendments show how important court decisions had been in the development of the food stamp program. Restructuring the act involved ratifying, modifying, and overturning a large number of court rulings. The House report is so full of legal references that it often reads like a law review article. For example, several elements of the law's new certification process had initially been developed in *Tyson* v. *Norton* and other lower court cases. Congress codified the *Anderson* decision on HUD rent subsidies. In explaining the House bill's provision on estimating the income of migrant farm workers, the committee report stated, "the holding of *Gutierrez* would become law." The new law changed the purpose of outreach from "ensuring" participation to "encouraging" it.[62]

In three areas—the diet plan, income and deductions, and certification periods—the 1977 act removed statutory language that had sparked litigation in the past. Most important, the new law removed all references to "a nutritionally adequate diet." Not only was the act's "declaration of policy" amended so that the purpose of the program was to "permit low-income households to obtain a *more* nutritious diet," but the new law referred explicitly to the USDA's thrifty food plan. This change was proposed in full committee by Chairman Foley—overturning a subcommittee's recommendation—and adopted unanimously.[63] In explaining this endorsement of the thrifty food plan, the House report emphasized the difference between the committee's approach and that of the D.C. Circuit in *Rodway*:

> The Committee recognizes that in doing so, some households with special nutritional needs may not receive an allotment which, strictly speaking, provides for a fully adequate diet. In view of the enormous complexity of determining allotments keyed to individual household circumstances and because the Thrifty Food Plan allotments would supply the overwhelming majority of households with the chance to purchase an adequate diet, the Committee felt that the use of standardized allotments based on the Thrifty Food Plan was the most reasonable solution.[64]

Not only did the committee focus on normal rather than extreme cases, but it placed the diet plan within the context of a redesigned program.

With the elimination of the purchase requirement, the program "is no longer, if it ever was, in and of itself sufficient to provide all the nutrition a participating household should have in order to remain healthy." As a result of these changes, the committee report claimed, "litigation along the lines of *Rodway* would be impossible to sustain."[65]

By all accounts, Representative Foley was infuriated by the *Rodway* decision—despite the fact that he had led the attack on the economy food plan in 1970. To Foley, the economy food plan was part of the deal adopted in conference: he and Senator McGovern lost on the food plan but won on indexation. The courts had no business undoing a compromise clearly enunciated in the conference report. Just as important, increasing the cost of the program by 20 or 30 percent in the difficult years of 1975–77 would have been a political blunder of major proportion. In his floor statement on the 1977 conference bill, Foley emphasized that the "thrifty food plan is up to the Secretary to calculate not the courts." Removal of any hint of a judicially protected right to a "nutritionally adequate diet" was part of the grand congressional compromise Foley helped to engineer.

Another key element of this restructuring was that it replaced the patchwork of income exemptions and deductions that had evolved through years of administrative rulemaking and judicial interpretation with a simpler, more coherent framework:

> The old system of Secretarial discretion within the parameters of Congressional goals would be abandoned in favor of Congressionally set income limitations implementing the broadly-stated Congressional goal. This should also prevent frequent judicial invalidation of the Department's income regulations and instructions as inconsistent with Congressional goals and/or the even broader judicially-developed interpretation of the Act's purpose as guaranteeing households the right to obtain a nutritionally adequate diet. The courts would have to measure the validity of future administrative regulations and instructions against specific Congressional definitions and guidelines directed to "income," not vague goals and purposes of the statute as a whole.[66]

The House committee report praised the Supreme Court's ruling in *Knebel* v. *Hein* and listed a number of lower court decisions inconsistent with its new rules. The committee emphasized that "there is no basis, if the Committee bill becomes law, for a court to contrast the Secretary's regulations with the purposes of this Act."[67]

The 1977 amendments also changed the procedures for affording recipients due process hearings. On the one hand, Congress took steps to safeguard their right to receive benefits in a timely fashion. The new law set rigid time limits for processing applications and explicitly prohibited states from imposing additional eligibility requirements. On the other hand, Congress made it easier for administrators to remove ineligible recipients from the rolls. Under the new law, eligibility ceased at the end of each three-month certification period. It was up to each household to reapply at least fifteen days before the end of each certification period. The statute provides that "if such household is found to be ineligible or to be eligible for a smaller allotment during the new certification period it shall not continue to participate and receive benefits on the basis authorized for the preceding certification period *even if it makes a timely request for a fair hearing*."[68] This means, in effect, that recipients do not receive the pretermination hearing mandated for welfare recipients by the Supreme Court in *Goldberg* v. *Kelly*.

In explaining this change, the committee report embraced the narrow understanding of entitlements examined in chapter 3. The food stamp program was no longer "a program of permanent or continuing eligibility subject to periodic review" but "a program of distinct and separate entitlements known as certification periods." The end of the certification period, the report added, is "the definitive cut-off of the right to participate in the absence of recertification." This procedure "reinforces the limited nature of the property interest conferred by certification—an entitlement for one certification period and one certification period only."[69]

The provision on certification periods was first proposed by Foley in a full committee markup session and passed by voice vote.[70] This was a particularly clear sign that a rift had developed between food stamp litigators and their principal patron in the House. The fact that the federal courts eventually upheld the constitutionality of the provision shows that they, too, were moving toward a more circumscribed understanding of welfare entitlements.[71]

Explaining the Congressional Response

Such congressional rebukes to the judiciary are relatively rare. In some policy areas, most notably special education and civil rights, Congress has encouraged the courts to play a major policymaking role. In other areas, including disability insurance and AFDC, Congress has modified court decisions without making any effort to reduce future litigation. Given the fact that the sponsors of the 1977 amendments benefited enormously from the delay caused by *Trump* and that they agreed with the courts on a number of substantive issues, the attack on the courts is particularly surprising. How did it happen?

The principal reason the House committee went to great lengths to write a specific bill and an even more detailed report was to limit the discretion of the *executive*. In 1976 the House committee created a special food stamp study group staff with a budget of $200,000 to review the operation of the program and provide alternatives to the proposals of the Ford administration. The working assumption of Chairman Foley, his allies, and his extensive staff was that whenever they failed to pin a matter down in the statute or the committee report, they would leave the Ford administration free to implement its more restrictive policies. Although the administrators in charge of the USDA in 1977 were far more sympathetic to the program than were those in office in 1976, committee leaders were reluctant to return to a broad delegation of authority. Not only was the Carter administration still something of an unknown, but no one knew how long Democrats would control the White House.

This does not explain, though, why Congress removed the broad prefatory language that so worried Republicans or why it went even further in 1977 than in 1976. The attack on the courts was not simply a by-product of congressional efforts to constrain the executive branch. Despite the litigational successes of FRAC, congressional supporters of the program had a special reason to be wary of court involvement: they feared it undermined political support for food stamps.

The wholesale restructuring of the act in 1977 was a response to the precipitous decline in the program's political support. Lacking a well-organized constituency, the program was particularly dependent on public opinion. Support for the program was shaken by skyrocketing costs, high error rates, and the public's perception that the program was serving large numbers of people who were not really needy. For example, the rules in effect before 1977 allowed a few participating households to take large itemized deductions. According to the 1977 Senate Report, "this potential for 'pyramiding' deductions . . . destroys public confidence in the program and evoked the consternation of the American public last year when it read that households might be eligible with incomes up to $16,000 per year."[72] The program's congressional sponsors recognized that they had to address the problems identified by critics in order to rebuild the food stamps' political base. Cost-cutting measures such as limiting deductions, reducing error rates, and denying eligibility to students not only addressed public complaints but made more money available for those with very low incomes.

Court decisions were the source of a number of the program's political black eyes. The Supreme Court's decision in *USDA* v. *Murry* had preserved the eligibility of college students, some of whom had easy access to parental resources. The outreach program mandated by *Bennett* v. *Butz* became a red flag for conservatives. Most important, court rulings on income and deductions allowed a few households with income well above the poverty line to qualify for benefits. Neither the courts nor FRAC was sensitive to the political fallout of these policies. The program's political patrons were.

From the perspective of members of Congress engaged in negotiations over food stamps, court decisions were also dangerously disruptive and unpredictable. Unexpected cost increases were almost certain to precipitate another round of budget cutting. This is why some members of Congress viewed the *Rodway* litigation with such apprehension: a change in the diet plan would swamp all the small adjustments made in deductions or the definition of income. To the extent the courts fiddled with one element of the program, Congress would be forced to fiddle once again with many of the others—a prospect no one relished.

This points to a larger gap between the perspective of Congress and that of the courts, one that relates to the ambiguous nature of the food stamp program. The long congressional debate over the program in the mid-1970s led attentive members of Congress to think of food stamps not in terms of an abstract "right to a nutritionally adequate diet," but rather in terms of "who gets what." Each possible change in the program was "costed out" and compared with the alternatives. If there was room under the budget ceiling for one more deduction, should it take the form of a deduction for excess shelter costs that would help recipients in the Northeast or a deduction for medical care that would help the elderly? Or should the amount be spread around more broadly by increasing the standard deduction? Lowering the gross income ceiling might provide enough savings to allow for an additional cost-of-living adjustment. Counting low-income energy assistance payments as income would hurt those in the Frost Belt. Counting the value of school lunch benefits, in contrast, would most affect those in the poorest southern states. Once the purchase price was eliminated, the nutritional side of the program became even less important and distributional issues more prominent. To give federal judges control over the latter clearly went against the congressional grain.

Those well versed in the operation of the program had yet another reason for reducing judicial intervention. By 1976 most program advocates in Congress and public interest groups recognized that the complexity of the program had contributed substantially to lengthy delays in certification and to distressingly low participation rates. In the words of the 1977 Senate report,

> This complexity leads to delay in providing assistance, denials of aid when a needy household's circumstances do not precisely match the program's rules, the provision of assistance to some who do not need it, and high rates of error in program administration. . . . [It] places unnecessary burdens both on the welfare agencies that administer the program and applicants and recipients who must comply with lengthy documentation.[73]

During the recession of 1974–75 these problems became so acute that the lines at food stamp offices sometimes stretched for blocks. Combining elimination of the purchase requirement with program simplification promised not just to reduce fraud and error but also to increase participation rates and eliminate such long delays. That is why standard deductions and uniform income ceilings and benefit reduction rates received the support of most program advocates, even though these changes would reduce benefits for some current recipients.

The courts, in contrast, had emphasized individualized treatment, which is usually the enemy of administrative simplification. In both food stamp and AFDC cases, judges insisted (absent clear and convincing statutory language to the contrary) that administrators look at the peculiar details of each case rather than apply hard and fast rules about income or eligibility. Individualized due process hearings constitute the clearest example of the conflict between judicialization and simplification.

The distinctive legislative styles of the House and Senate Agriculture committees made them particularly uneasy with policymaking by the courts. As explained in chapter 9, these two bodies are classic "constituency committees" accustomed to working closely with the USDA. Each committee's norms and structure are designed to restrain advocacy, promote accommodation of competing agricultural interests, and thus produce bills that will command majority support on the floor. The House committee's standard operating procedure was evident in its handling of the 1977 act: committee leaders used lengthy full committee markup sessions to strike a series of compromises that built a comfortable majority on the floor. In this political environment, ignoring a previous agreement—something FRAC and the D.C. Circuit seemed to be doing in *Rodway*—threatened not just the next food stamp bill but committee harmony on all agricultural legislation.

One of the main reasons Thomas Foley was selected to replace the ousted Robert Poage as chairman of the House Agriculture Committee in 1974 was that Foley's style fit the committee, even if his ideology did not. Foley was known as a liberal who was also a "hard-nosed compromiser," "a broker between the NFU [National Farmers Union], organized labor, and the DSG [Democratic Study Group] on farm issues," and a leader who had learned "how to balance the interests of grain producers in the Midwest, milk producers of the Northeast and cotton growers of the South."[74] Foley's determination to reduce the role of the courts reflected the legislative style of the committee he led and his strongly held views about the constitutional role of Congress.

Postscript: From the Reagan Revolution to the Hunger Resolution

In retrospect, the years 1977–78 were the calm before another storm over food stamps. The combination of legislative change, unprecedented inflation, and economic stagnation led food stamp program expenditures to rise once again. Not only did elimination of the purchase requirement bring in half a million more recipients than expected, but less than half the 1.3 million households that the department had predicted would become ineligible actually left the program.[75] Spending for fiscal years 1979, 1980, and 1981 shot above the authorization caps established in 1977. Each time Congress considered legislation raising authorization levels, program critics had an opportunity to remind their colleagues of the extent of budget growth and to demand a quid pro quo for raising the cap.

In 1979 Congress adopted a number of provisions to reduce fraud and error. At the same time, it increased the housing and medical care deductions, guaranteeing even larger cost overruns in coming years. In 1980 spending soared to $9 billion, nearly $3 billion over the cap. The Carter administration waited until the last moment to ask for a new authorization, leading Republicans to charge that it was purposely creating an emergency to discourage congressional scrutiny of the program.

Recognizing they could not ignore the growing discontent on the floor, USDA officials and Democratic leaders recommended replacing the semi-annual cost-of-living adjustment with an annual one, tightening rules on assets and fraud, and giving the states the option of using retrospective accounting. For the first time ever, Congress passed legislation that curtailed rather than expanded the food stamp program.

These changes did little to cure the program's budgetary and political woes. The 1980 elections dealt the program a number of serious blows. George McGovern and several other liberal Democratic senators went down to defeat, leaving the Senate in the hands of the Republicans. Perpetual critic Jesse Helms became chairman of the Senate Agriculture Committee. Thomas Foley left the House Agriculture Committee to become majority whip. Most important, Ronald Reagan was elected president. Early in 1981 *Congressional Quarterly* reported, "Pressure for major changes has been building up over the last few years. Recent food stamp legislation . . . has been enacted in a 'crisis atmosphere' that discouraged radical changes. Critics were told to hold off their amendments until reauthorization, and now that time has come."[76]

Few programs sustained as many cuts as food stamps did in the first two years of the Reagan presidency. In the end, Congress enacted slightly larger reductions—$6 billion over a three-year period—than the Reagan administration had requested. The changes included delays in cost-of-living adjustments for the diet plan and deductions; a reduction in the earned income deduction; prohibition of funding for outreach; mandatory retrospective accounting and monthly reporting; and a variety of provisions to reduce fraud and error. By one estimate, legislative changes reduced food stamp expenditures by nearly 14 percent.[77]

It did not take long for the political pendulum to swing once again. In 1982 the country entered a severe recession. For reasons that are not entirely clear—but are the subject of heated debate—the number of people requesting commodity assistance and eating at soup kitchens increased substantially. Press accounts of hunger in America appeared on the front page and the evening news. The Reagan administration came under attack for perpetuating hunger, just as the Nixon administration had a decade and a half before. After the Democrats picked up a number of congressional seats in the midterm election, Congress paid little attention to the administration's proposals on food stamps. In 1983 the House and Senate passed a resolution urging the administration to protect food programs from further cuts.

In 1985 Congress approved a set of amendments that would increase spending by about $250 million over a three-year period. In both 1986 and 1987 Congress approved a variety of small rule changes that made food stamps more widely available. The Hunger Prevention Act of 1988 expanded deductions and increased the value of the diet plan above the rate of inflation. The cost of this change was estimated to be $288 million in fiscal 1989, growing to nearly $600 million in 1991. *Congressional Quarterly* reported that the "largest expansion of the food stamp program since 1977" had "moved through Congress with nearly no opposition."[78] Another set of incremental increases were adopted in 1991, yet another in 1993.[79] In short, Congress restored the funding cuts from the program at the beginning of the decade and then added more. These legislative changes combined with slow economic growth to produce a sharp rise in the number of recipients and the cost of the program.

A notable feature of food stamp politics during the 1980s was that highly charged disputes were resolved by Congress rather than by administrators or judges. No longer did the executive branch exercise substantial unilateral control over policy, as it did from the New Deal to 1970. Nor did the courts have much influence on the program, in marked contrast to the period from 1970 to 1977. Because the 1977 amendments established most of the program's parameters, all efforts to modify these parameters had to be addressed to Congress. The food stamp program shows that even on a contentious issue Congress can speak with clarity. In such instances, Congress does not need the courts to keep federal administrators in line.

Conclusion

Why did the right to a "nutritionally adequate diet" lack the appeal of the right to a "free appropriate education"? The reason is not that members of Congress lacked sympathy for those who receive food stamps. Although the program has had a multitude of critics, Congress has expanded benefits on a regular basis. The legislation that did the most to reduce the role of the courts and remove statutory references to nutritional rights also provided food stamp advocates with some of their most important victories in the history of the program.

One notable difference between the right to a nutritionally adequate diet and the right to a free appropriate public education is their impact on the federal budget. When a federal court decides a handicapped student needs a special tutor or residential placement, state and local school systems bear the additional cost. When the courts expanded food stamp benefits, the federal government paid the full amount. As federal spending rose, the program became more vulnerable in Congress. The fact that food stamps must be reauthorized periodically and that the program occasionally needed a supplemental appropriations increased the opportunities for attack. Unexpected judicial expansion worried program supporters as much as it angered opponents.

Just as important, the right to a nutritionally adequate diet became anachronistic as the program developed. Those familiar with the operation of the program recognized that it was an effective welfare supplement, equalizer, and gap-filler, but that it had only a minor effect on most recipients' nutritional intake. Behind the rhetoric about combating hunger lay sophisticated calculations about how to target benefits to the most needy—and, of course, to one's constituents.

Finally, with special education the courts' insistence on individualized treatment fit well both with the professional norms of service providers and with the statute's emphasis on meeting the unique needs of each child. The arguments for individualized treatment are less compelling in the food stamp program since the program gives recipients substantial control over how to use their added purchasing power. Those familiar with the program recognized that individualized determination of such items as dietary need or work expenses complicates the application process, and that this complexity produces delay and lowers participation rates. Extensive court intervention tended to undercut the uniformity and simplicity for which the program's supporters had long strived.

PART V

Conclusions

CHAPTER ELEVEN

Statutory Interpretation and Political Institutions

In each of the three programs examined in this book, the federal courts' interpretation of statutes had a substantial effect on public policy: it expanded the scope of the programs and shifted power from the states to the federal government. Judicial decisions following *King* v. *Smith* greatly reduced the states' control over eligibility standards for aid to families with dependent children, opened the program to a much larger number of families, and increased benefits to many recipients. Two rulings by federal district courts provided the model and the political catalyst for the Education of All Handicapped Children Act (EAHCA) of 1975. Subsequent court interpretation of such key terms as "free appropriate public education" and "related services" imposed rigorous demands on state and local school systems. During the 1970s a variety of judicial interpretations of the Food Stamp Act raised benefits, broadened eligibility, and prevented the Ford administration from imposing spending cuts. These rulings left a substantial imprint on the 1977 Food Stamp Act, which established the program in its present form. In each area, critical decisions were based on judicial doctrines that first emerged in the late 1960s and early 1970s. Although the Rehnquist court has chipped away at some of these doctrinal innovations, others have survived unscathed.

The significance of the court decisions examined in this book lies not just in their direct effect on welfare programs, but also in the opportunities they created for subsequent action in other political arenas. The financial demands placed on state and local governments by the *PARC* and *Mills* decisions sent school officials scurrying to Washington to ask for federal financial assistance. Advocates for the disabled then insisted that schools demonstrate their compliance with the dictates of these two court rulings before receiving federal money. Similarly, the intense legislative negotiations over food stamps in 1975–77 took place in the shadow of court decisions. The district court's injunction in *Trump* v. *Butz* allowed the program's supporters to wait until 1977—the first year of Jimmy Carter's presidency—to overhaul the Food Stamp Act. Instead of cutting food stamps, as Congress was virtually certain to do in 1976, legislators expanded the program in a variety of important ways. The Supreme Court's initial decisions on AFDC freed the Department of Health, Education, and Welfare to take a much tougher line against the states. "Once the courts had spoken," one government attorney explained, "the federal administrators could then respond by framing a rule embodying the judicially-enunciated principle, perhaps even embellishing it a bit." Within this new political context, reform could "proceed in an ever-ascending spiral with no single participant in the process having the capacity to block progressive developments."[1]

"New policies," E. E. Schattschneider pointed out many years ago, "create a new politics."[2] Judicial action on AFDC and education of the handicapped altered public expectations about the responsibilities of the federal government. No longer were these matters for the states to decide. In addition, court decisions increased the number of people eligible for government benefits. As every politician knows, benefits once granted are hard to retract. Above all, by establishing a new policy status quo, the courts shifted what might be called the political burden of proof within Congress. No longer was the burden on those favoring national uniformity and program expansion to build a coalition broad enough to pass new legislation. Now the burden was on their opponents to pass legislation to overturn the courts. Given the obstacles to constructing winning coalitions in Congress, this shift often proved decisive.

The findings of the three case studies run directly counter to the argument Gerald Rosenberg makes in his book, *The Hollow Hope*. Rosenberg maintains that the "structural constraints" that are "built into the American judicial system" make the courts "virtually powerless to produce change." Indeed, "U.S. courts can *almost never* be effective producers of significant social change." The "lure of litigation," Rosenberg warns, not only steers reformers toward "an institution that is constrained from helping them," but also "siphons off crucial resources and talent, and runs the risk of weakening political efforts." Thus, social reform litigation may actually impede progress by "providing only an illusion of change."[3]

One of the reasons the courts have been so influential is that legal reformers are more politically astute than Rosenberg and most other court watchers have realized. Far from naifs who relied exclusively on litigation, the reformers studied in this book recognized the need to combine litigation with other forms of lobbying and to build broad political alliances. The "hunger lobby" and the groups representing the disabled proved particularly adept at developing close ties with congressional subcommittees and key officials in federal agencies. They consciously used litigation to force, delay, and focus legislative and administrative action.

Unlike most academic commentators, these litigators also recognized the opportunities offered by statutory interpretation, particularly by the lower courts. Students of the judiciary who limit their attention to the overtly constitutional rulings of the Supreme Court will look at the post-1970 case law on AFDC, food stamps, and education of the handicapped and see a judiciary reluctant to challenge the status quo. That is to say, they will miss the most interesting and significant part of the story. The lesson of the case studies is that in order to understand the ways in which the federal courts have affected public policy and the operation of government institutions, one must look outside the confines of constitutional law as conventionally defined.

This does not mean one should forsake study of the Constitution for the more mundane topic of public policy. The American Constitution is more than simply a list of individual rights recognized by the courts. A catalog of rights, James Madison warned, is a mere "parchment barrier." He and the other framers believed that the only reliable way to protect individual liberty is by "contriving the interior structure of the government" so that "its several constituent parts may, by their mutual relations, be the means of keeping each other in their proper places."[4] For many years, constitutional law was primarily about the powers and duties of government institutions, not the legal rights of individuals.[5]

The two most important features of the government the framers created are federalism and the separation of powers. The presumptions the courts employ in statutory interpretation cases play a pivotal—but generally ignored—role in shaping these two features of the constitutional system. Are state AFDC rules valid unless they conflict with explicit federal restrictions, or are state rules invalid unless explicitly authorized by federal law? Must federal legislation authorize suits by beneficiaries against the states, or will the courts recognize "implied" private rights of action? Should judges accept the food stamp rules established by the executive unless they are directly contrary to explicit statutory language? Or should they search for other indications of congressional intent? The answers the courts provide to such questions probably have more significance for the operation of U.S. governmental institutions than do better-known, more overtly constitutional rulings of the Supreme Court.

Separation of Powers

All too often students of statutory interpretation focus on only two branches of government, Congress and the courts. The case studies in this book show why it is necessary to place statutory interpretation within the context of the division of power and responsibility among all *three* branches of government. Despite the courts' profound influence on the development of AFDC, special education, and food stamps, administrators rather than judges have borne primary responsibility for turning general laws into specific program guidelines. In each program, Congress granted administrators broad authority to establish eligibility requirements and benefit levels. Indeed, it is hard to imagine how any of these programs could operate without specialized bureaucracies armed with extensive rulemaking power. No country has ever built a welfare state without first constructing a large and powerful administrative apparatus. A defining characteristic of the administrative state is "that most statutes are not direct commands to the public enforced exclusively by courts, but are delegations to administrative agencies to issue and enforce such commands."[6]

In each of the three programs, Congress also authorized federal courts to hear suits challenging administrative rulings. Rarely does Congress exercise its power to preclude judicial review of agency action. For many years, the Veterans Administration was the only large federal bureaucracy insulated from judicial oversight, and even it lost this special status in 1988. Thus in virtually all welfare and regulatory programs both judges and administrators claim authority to ascertain the meaning of statutory language. Consequently, "the central question of statutory interpretation" is "whether administrative agencies or courts should exercise greater authority over statutory interpretation."[7]

American courts have never provided a clear answer to this central question. For years they have vacillated between two competing conceptions of their role. The first view harkens back to Chief Justice John Marshall's famous words in *Marbury* v. *Madison*: "It is emphatically the province and duty of the judicial department to say what the law is."[8] "A pure question of statutory construction," the Supreme Court announced more than a century and a half later, is "for the courts to decide."[9] This was the predominant view for the first century and a half of the American republic. So small and weak was the national bureaucracy for most of American history that the courts' role as preeminent interpreter of federal law remained unchallenged.

The alternative view took shape as the federal judiciary struggled to come to terms with the legacy of the New Deal. This approach gives the courts a far more limited role: to reverse only those agency interpretations that clearly violate the statute. As Chief Justice Warren put it, "When faced with a problem of statutory construction, this Court shows great deference to the interpretation given the statute by the officers or agency charged with its administration."[10] In *Chevron* v. *NRDC*, one of the most important decisions of the 1980s, the Supreme Court announced that when "the statute is silent or ambiguous with respect to the specific issue," the sole question before the court is whether the agency adopted a "permissible construction of the statute." A reviewing court "may not substitute its own construction of a statutory provision for a reasonable interpretation made by the administrator of an agency."[11]

These competing views are at the heart of the contemporary debate over statutory interpretation. Judges who believe that administrators have primary responsibility for filling statutory gaps see less need to go beyond the "clear meaning" of the words in the statutory text than do those who insist that judges establish the meaning of the law. The latter will usually look at a law's history, purpose, and general spirit to give specific meaning to vague phrases and statutory silences.

The approach adopted by particular judges is likely to reflect their evaluation of the administrative agencies that come before them. Judges who believe that most administrators are trustworthy and attentive to congressional concerns will be reluctant to second-guess agency interpretations. Judges who fear that administrators are parochial, myopic, malicious, or excessively loyal to the White House will insist upon more rigorous judicial review. All judges are likely to give more credence to the interpretations put forth by agencies they consider competent and honest than those they consider bumbling and disingenuous.

What, then, do the case studies reveal about *administrative* interpretation of statutes? First and most obviously, they indicate the enormous volume and importance of administrative rules and guidelines. The AFDC program was in place for more than thirty years before the federal courts offered any opinion about the meaning of title IV. Federal rules took the form of the bulky *Handbook on Public Assistance*. Included in the *Handbook* were more than 600 "State Letters," which explained to the states how to comply with federal law.[12] In 1968 HEW pruned these guidelines and published them in the *Federal Register*. Today, they cover 300 pages of the *Code of Federal Regulations*—despite the fact that AFDC remains a program that leaves many important decisions to the states.[13]

Rulemaking by federal administrators has been even more important in the nationally uniform food stamp program. The entire structure of the program—from the food plan to the calculation of income to the complex set of deductions—was devised by career civil servants in the Department of Agriculture. From 1939 to 1977, administrative regulations did not merely fill in the gaps in legislation; administrators created a program with virtually no statutory guidance. Congress later validated what these administrators had done.[14] After enactment of the 1977 Food Stamp Amendments, the department devoted nearly a year and a half to the task of revising all its food stamp rules. The Department of Agriculture now has approximately 450 pages of formal regulations on the program.[15]

Enactment of the Education for All Handicapped Children Act, too, required an enormous rulemaking effort by the executive branch. In 1976 twelve "writing teams" began work on these rules. After holding numerous public hearings and receiving more than 16,000 comments, the Department of Education promulgated 150 pages of regulations.[16] The department now has almost 500 pages of regulations on education of the handicapped.[17] This does not include either state rules or the thousands of individualized decisions made by state and local officials every year, only a fraction of which are reviewed by federal judges.

Second, noticeably absent from the case studies is a "runaway" bureaucracy oblivious to the intent of Congress. Investigation of these three policy areas turned up no examples of federal agencies violating a clear congressional directive or trying to sabotage congressionally established policies. Almost every important dispute revolved around the question of how administrators had interpreted ambiguous phrases or gaps in the statute. Ironically, the most obvious distortion of both statutory language and legislative history came in the *courts'* interpretation of the AFDC title of the Social Security Act.

This is not to say that members of Congress and the executive branch always agreed on how to carry out these programs. The Senate Finance Committee was highly critical of the liberal eligibility policies of HEW in the 1968–72 period. Democratic party and committee leaders opposed the Ford administration's effort to reduce food stamp expenditures in 1975–76. The Reagan administration ran into a torrent of congressional criticism when it proposed relaxing some rules on education of the disabled. The 1970s and 1980s were years in which divided government was the norm; conflict between Congress and the president was frequent and heated. Yet when Congress did manage to write clear, detailed legislation, administrators almost always complied. One of the key lessons of the food stamp program is that specific legislation diminishes the importance of litigation. Litigation increases not when administrators act lawlessly but when both administrators and judges are compelled to read between the lines of statutes produced by factious legislators.

Third, the case studies show how attentive administrators are to all sorts of "signals from the Hill." As political scientist Herbert Kaufman has pointed out, members of Congress have an "awesome arsenal" to employ against administrators who ignore their wishes. Bureau chiefs are "constantly looking over their shoulders at the legislative establishment relevant to their agencies."[18] Particularly in the 1970 and 1980s, members of Congress devoted a substantial amount of time and effort to learning what the executive branch was doing and persuading administrators to listen to them rather than the White House.[19]

During the first thirty years of the Social Security Act, federal administrators pushed for more uniform, more generous, and less punitive state AFDC rules but remained acutely aware of congressional opposition to federal control of state programs. These administrators had lost too many fights in Congress to risk antagonizing those members who paid attention to the issue. Statutory changes such as the codification of the Flemming ruling and the 1967 cost-of-living adjustment were delicate legislative compromises, and HEW acted with understandable caution in putting them into effect. What eventually emboldened HEW, precipitated attacks from congressional conservatives, and insulated federal administrators from informal congressional controls was the sudden change in the courts' interpretation of title IV. HEW policy shifted again in 1972 when the Nixon administration fastened on an administrative strategy for reducing welfare costs. This switch drew predictable applause from Senator Long and his allies and equally predictable attacks from congressional liberals. Since 1970 the absence of congressional consensus on welfare issues has virtually guaranteed that any administrative policy will have vocal critics and defenders.

The informal powers of Congress were particularly evident in the refounding of the food stamp program in 1969–71. Publicity generated by the Senate Select Committee on Nutrition and Human Needs induced the Nixon administration to establish a drastically enlarged, nationally uniform program. In hearings held shortly after passage of the 1970 act, the committee again succeeded in forcing the administration to revise important rules on benefits and eligibility. The Nutrition Committee "took a group of regulations, most of them not nearly as malicious as they were made out to be, and gave them the appearance of pettiness and cruelty. The administrators conceded on almost every disputed point in the final regulations."[20]

The Nutrition Committee was not the sole source of congressional pressure. Senior members of the House Agriculture Committee pushed for tougher work rules. Moreover, in 1976 the House Appropriations Committee "earmarked $100,000 of the fiscal year 1976 appropriation for the specific purpose of revising program regulations so as to minimize existing misuse and unwanted expenditures."[21] This was one of the factors that encouraged the Ford administration to announce the set of regulations eventually enjoined in *Trump* v. *Butz*. During the Carter years, the Food and Nutrition Service worked very closely with the staff of the House and Senate Agriculture committees in revising food stamp regulations.

For many years, congressional committees took the lead in pushing for more federal aid for the disabled. The Bureau of Education for the Handicapped was created by Congress over the objection of the Johnson administration. The first director of the bureau was the staff director of the House subcommittee that had written the legislation. The EAHCA was put together by the House and Senate Education committees and became law despite opposition from the Nixon and Ford administrations. In 1982 the House Education and Labor Committee used a combination of hearings, publicity, and appropriations riders to force the Reagan administration to withdraw its controversial EAHCA regulation. The committee assigned one staff member to work full time monitoring regulations issued under the act. After failing in its initial effort to relax these requirements, the Reagan administration never again sought to make major changes in the program.

Since much of the current debate over statutory interpretation has focused on judges' use of legislative history, it is important to note that administrators have powerful reasons for paying careful attention to committee reports. A series of events in the summer of 1988 brings home this point. For many years, the appropriations committees have written lengthy reports "earmarking" funds for one purpose or "directing" their use for another.[22] The appropriations committees do not need to rely on the courts to enforce these directives. Administrators must go back to these committees every year, and few agency officials dare incur the wrath of the appropriations committees by ignoring their suggestions.

In 1988 James Miller, director of the Office of Management and Budget, wrote to all agency heads informing them that such committee report language is not legally binding and requiring them to receive OMB clearance before spending earmarked funds. Members of Congress were appalled and ready to fight. One conservative Republican stated, "I think he declared war on the Congress."[23] *Congressional Quarterly* reported that "a number of agencies heads who actually preferred the flexibility given them in non-binding report language began to resist Miller's efforts to cut off their informal working relationship with congressional committees." The head of the Veterans Administration informed Miller that his agency would continue to comply with committee reports: "My obligations to this agency and to this nation's veterans preclude me from taking action which, in the long term, will only negatively impact on them."[24]

Miller quickly gave up. His spokeswoman claimed, "We have made our point. We wanted to call attention to Congress and the public that report language was not legally binding."[25] But obviously Congress had made its point even more emphatically: ordinarily the language of appropriations reports is politically binding.

The case studies indicate not only that Congress has significant control over administrative policy but also that administrators usually have a more extensive and subtle understanding of a law's evolution than do judges. "Legislative history," states a veteran of two federal agencies, "has a centrality and importance for agency lawyers that might not readily be conceived by persons who are outside government." Federal judges deal with particular statutes intermittently at most. But agency officials "essentially *live* the process of statutory interpretation." Agency officials work with Congress day after day, revising legislation, negotiating yearly appropriations, vetting nominees for political posts, and listening to members' complaints about the consequences of agency decisions. They regularly consult not just committee reports and floor statements, "but also transcripts of relevant hearings, correspondence, and other informal traces of the continuing interactions that go on between an agency and Capitol Hill as a statute is being shaped in the legislative process, and perhaps afterwards in course of implementation."[26]

If this assortment of congressional contacts and controls reduces the threat of runaway bureaucracy, it simultaneously increases the danger of congressional parochialism. Members will try—sometimes with success—to win special benefits for their constituents. Just as serious is the problem of unrepresentative committees. Informal congressional control over administrative policy is usually exercised by members of committees or subcommittees with jurisdiction over the program in question. Members gravitate to committees dealing with issues in which they have a strong interest. Most members of the agriculture committees, for example, come from farm states and strongly support the continuation of agricultural subsidies. Democrats on the education committees are more liberal than other Democrats and are especially energetic supporters of federal aid to education. In short, members of committees and subcommittees show "a marked tendency to regard themselves as advocates for 'their' programs and thus to oversee within this context."[27]

Since the early days of the Republic, committees have created a paradox for Congress.[28] On the one hand, Congress needs specialized committees in order to avoid subservience to the executive. On the other hand, as Arthur Maass has put it, "committees tend inevitably to challenge the whole House for control of the legislature's business." They threaten to "become master rather than servant of the House."[29] Any realistic assessment of the consequences of judicial interpretation of statutes must place court action within the context of both extensive administrative interpretation of legislative enactments and extensive oversight of administrators by specialized components of Congress. This does not mean that all efforts to restrain the executive will redound to the benefit of congressional committees. Indeed, in two of the three case studies, committee leaders believed that active court involvement reduced their influence. It does mean, though, that when court action changes the balance of power *between* the president and Congress, it will also have a substantial effect on the distribution of influence *within* these two branches.

Federalism

In 1920 Justice Oliver Wendell Holmes, Jr., remarked that although the United States would not come to an end if the Supreme Court lost its authority to declare an act of Congress unconstitutional, "the Union would be imperiled if we could not make that declaration as to the laws of the several states. For one in my place sees how often a local policy prevails with those who are not trained to national views."[30] Judicial insistence that national views prevail over local policy is a recurrent theme in the court decisions examined in this book. In two of the case studies—AFDC and education for the handicapped—the vast majority of cases pitted recipients against state and local governments. At the nub of almost every AFDC case was the issue of the extent of state control over eligibility rules and benefit levels. The EAHCA instructs federal courts to ride herd on state and local school systems to ensure that they provide handicapped children with an "appropriate education" and "related services" in the "least restrictive environment." Interestingly, the federal judiciary played a smaller role in food stamps than in the two programs that leave significant discretion in the hands of state and local officials. Federal courts are clearly more willing to overturn the decisions of local and state officials than the rulings of federal administrators.

The history of AFDC and education of the handicapped demonstrates how important federal courts have become both as creator and as enforcers of federal mandates on the states. Starting in the 1960s, the federal courts fashioned a variety of legal doctrines that enhanced their ability to enforce the conditions attached to federal grants. Federal judges questioned the fairness of interstate variation. Egalitarianism, the central theme of the Warren court, required equal treatment of those equally in need. Just as important, many judges' experience with civil rights cases left them with little faith in state and local officials' willingness to treat racial minorities fairly. Lawyers representing welfare recipients and disabled children were quick to link their issues with civil rights. The first AFDC cases they brought to court were those from the deep South that revealed discriminatory administration of welfare programs. Attorneys for the disabled frequently compared segregation and exclusion of the disabled with discrimination against racial minorities.

The willingness of the courts to come to the aid of these litigants was enhanced by the evident shortcomings of administrative mechanisms for enforcing federal mandates. The threat of a funding cutoff, everyone recognized, was seldom adequate to force states to comply with particular federal rules. HEW officials did not relish the prospect of shutting down an entire state AFDC program because the state had excluded some eligible families. Imposing this sanction would not only harm the needy but would invite congressional action on behalf of the target state.

Only federal courts have the power to issue injunctions, which have two key advantages over administrative enforcement. First, to use a military analogy, an injunction constitutes a surgical strike against state programs, not dropping a nuclear bomb. The threat is more credible precisely because it is more limited in scope. Second, while administrators can merely halt funding, courts can order states to *increase* expenditures. This order is backed by the threat of contempt of court against officials who fail to comply. In *Federalist* 78, Hamilton argued that the courts are the "least dangerous branch" because they control neither the purse nor the sword. Ironically, in many disputes involving grant-in-aid programs only the courts wield the sword (the power of contempt) and thus can exercise effective control over the purse strings of the states.

Those familiar with the extensive case law on AFDC and education of the handicapped will recognize that since 1968 the federal courts have been doing far more than enforcing rules enumerated by Congress. Rather, the judiciary set about to create an elaborate federal common law of entitlement programs. This proved a daunting undertaking. The common law of property, contracts, and torts had slowly evolved over hundreds of years. Federal common law on AFDC and education of the handicapped, in contrast, had to be invented virtually overnight. Congress had never attempted to establish national eligibility rules for AFDC. It established a few minimum requirements and left the rest to the states. By inverting the thirty-five-year-old presumption of state control, the Supreme Court threw into question the validity of virtually every state eligibility rule. Recipients and Legal Services clamored for change; administrators at all levels clamored for guidance and certainty. All this occurred while the program was undergoing explosive growth. The Education for All Handicapped Children Act told schools to provide an "appropriate education" without explaining what this meant. As one appeals court judge bitterly exclaimed, "This is not legislation; it is not even news!"[31]

The difficulty of creating a federal common law in both areas often led judges to turn to federal administrators for advice. Even when federal administrators did not intervene, judges would often ask for their opinion.[32] Many federal administrators saw the federal courts as useful allies in their sometimes contentious dealings with the states: now they had a way to enforce their regulations without resorting to the ineffective and counterproductive funding cutoff. Indeed, they did not even need to go through the politically difficult task of writing formal regulations. They could simply explain to judges their position on a controversial issue and let the judges take the political heat.

Judges, though, did not feel bound to follow the advice of administrators. This was particularly evident during the Nixon, Ford, and Reagan administrations, when federal administrators were most likely to side with the states. One of the most puzzling features of the courts' interpretation of these laws has been judges' willingness to endorse the regulations promulgated by federal administrators in some instances and to ignore them in others. For example, in two 1970 AFDC decisions, *Rosado* v. *Wyman* and *Lewis* v. *Martin*, the Supreme Court relied heavily on HEW's interpretation of title IV. One year later, the Court rejected the department's reading of the statute in both *Townsend* v. *Swank* and *Wyman* v. *James*. It disagreed with HEW in *Carleson* v. *Remillard* (1972), *Shea* v. *Vialpando* (1974), *Philbrook* v. *Glodgett* (1975), and *Van Lare* v. *Hurley* (1975), but deferred in *Dublino* (1973) and *Burns* v. *Alcala* (1975). Only in the late 1970s and 1980s did the Supreme Court become more predictable in AFDC cases, routinely agreeing with federal administrators.

Recognizing that when push came to shove judges had the final word, many federal administrators refused to make hard political choices. This was especially apparent in education of the handicapped. Caught between two clienteles, school systems and advocates for the disabled, the fledgling Department of Education rid itself of hot potatoes by throwing them to the judiciary. The department euphemistically called this approach "minimum regulation–future rulemaking." The Eleventh Circuit has noted that "administrative regulations have tended to follow the opinions of the federal courts rather than to serve as authority for them."[33]

The most prominent feature of the congressional response to court decisions on AFDC and education of the handicapped has been the feebleness of the effort to defend state governments. Shortly after the Supreme Court entered the fray over AFDC, prominent conservatives such as Ways and Means Chairman Wilbur Mills and ranking member John Byrnes lost confidence in the states. Senator Russell Long and his allies remained devoted to state control, but could not build a majority large enough to reestablish policies in place before *King* v. *Smith*. Senator Long himself led efforts to federalize parent support programs and to establish a national workfare program. Although Ronald Reagan for many years defended state control of welfare programs, his administration sponsored a variety of restrictions on the states aimed at reducing program costs and mandating work for recipients. As welfare costs rose in the late 1960s and early 1970s, many states became more interested in ridding themselves of these troublesome programs than in defending decentralization. During the Carter administration, the intergovernmental lobby was one of the strongest proponents of a uniform program run by the federal government.

Passage of the EAHCA shows how willing Congress has become to impose new requirements on the states without providing sufficient funds to pay for them. Accustomed to getting new federal money and ignoring statutory "strings," state and local school officials were important supporters of the act. Only later did they realize that it contained many teeth but no assurance of sufficient federal money to pay for excess costs. When the Reagan administration proposed easing special education rules, it faced a bruising attack from the two education committees and the media. The National School Board Association, which had encouraged the administration to make the changes, stood back and let the White House and the Department of Education take the fall. Despite carping about the costs of special education, state and local governments have not mounted a sustained effort to reduce federal demands. Public officials have focused their efforts on increasing federal funding rather than attacking the federal mandates that are so important to advocacy groups.[34]

The political attractiveness of mandates did not abate in the 1980s. In 1986 Congress amended the EAHCA to require more services for preschool children, a requirement likely to cost the states about half a billion dollars a year. Federal medicaid requirements added in 1988 and 1989 will cost the states more than $2.5 billion annually.[35] Despite the Reagan administration's deregulation efforts, "the pace of administrative rulemaking and of new regulatory and preemptive enactments picked up as the decade progressed. The end result was an accumulation of new requirements roughly comparable to the record-setting pace of the 1970s."[36] The huge federal budget deficit has made the strategy of passing costs along to the states particularly appealing to members of Congress. It is likely, therefore, that this trend will continue in the 1990s.

What *has* changed over the past decade is the Supreme Court's position on federalism. The Court's majority has become less willing to find binding commands in federal statutes. According to Chief Justice Rehnquist, "if Congress intends to impose a condition on the grant of federal moneys, it must do so unambiguously." "By insisting that Congress speak with a clear voice," he maintains, "we enable the States to exercise their choice knowingly, cognizant of the consequences of their participation."[37] Justice Sandra Day O'Connor has argued that this "clear statement rule is not a mere canon of statutory interpretation. Instead, it derives from the Constitution itself. The rule protects the balance of power between the States and the Federal Government struck by the Constitution."[38] In a number of recent cases, the Court has adopted a narrow construction of federal mandates.[39] In a few instances, Congress has responded by amending the act in question in order to make clear that it intended to bind the states.[40] This is a pattern that is likely to recur in coming years.

Judicial Presumptions

The reader who has come this far no doubt will readily concede that the court rulings discussed in this book were not the product of the mechanical application of generally accepted canons of construction. One of the reasons that statutory interpretation has languished in the intellectual doldrums for so long is that court opinions seem so ad hoc, so devoid of general principles. In most instances, how a case comes out depends on where the judge comes in. That is, the set of presumptions a judge brings to the enterprise very often determines the outcome. Sometimes judges explicitly defend these presumptions. Usually they do not.

This chapter has already called attention to the importance of judges' assumptions about federalism and the role of administrative agencies. Equally important is a judge's tacit understanding of the nature of entitlements in the welfare state. Chapter 3 identified two competing conceptions of entitlements that undergird most of the court decisions examined in this book. According to the first, an entitlement is nothing more or less than a government benefit defined by a law or regulation. When "statutory entitlements" are at stake, Justice Brennan once wrote, "claimants have an interest only in their benefit level as correctly determined under the law."[41] Recipients must be willing to take what Justice Rehnquist

called "the bitter"—all limitations, both procedural and substantive—
with "the sweet"—namely, goods, services, and cash. Such an entitlement, in the words of a report produced by the Senate Finance
Committee, "is no more substantial and has no more legal effect than any
other benefit conferred by a generous legislature."[42]

The second, broader view establishes the presumption that statutory
entitlements should be delivered to *all* those in need and will be adequate
to meet these needs *in full*. As Justice Douglas once put it, the amount
clients receive should be "commensurate with their actual need."[43] Often
this presumption is justified on the basis of the general purpose of the
statute—to aid needy dependent children; to provide citizens with the
opportunity to receive a nutritionally adequate diet; to ensure that all
disabled children receive a "free appropriate public education" that meets
"their unique needs." This interpretive approach in effect creates a rebut-
table presumption of eligibility. As one lower court judge put it, if
Congress had meant to leave some needy children "without any means of
subsistence . . . there is good reason to suppose that it would have made
its intent more explicit."[44]

Judges who adopt this broad understanding of entitlements confront
the difficult task of determining who is "in need" and precisely what sort
of assistance they need from government. They usually respond by adopting what Jerry Mashaw has called the "professional treatment" model of
justice: "Justice lies in having the appropriate professional judgement
applied to one's particular situation in the context of a service relationship."[45] In all three case studies, the courts placed great weight on the
norms and diagnoses of professionals. This was most evident in education
for the handicapped, where judges are "likely to treat professional judgments as particularly persuasive, especially where such judgments are
those of teachers or other personnel who have worked with the handicapped child over an extended period."[46] Similarly, the D.C. Circuit
indicated that the composition of the food stamp diet plan should be
established by experts on nutrition, not on the basis of a compromise
negotiated by administration officials and members of Congress.[47] Court
rulings on AFDC repeatedly rejected a "punitive" and "moralistic" view
of welfare in favor of the "sophisticated and enlightened approach" of
social welfare professionals.

Mashaw points out that in the professional treatment model, "the
incompleteness of facts, the singularity of individual contexts, and the
ultimately intuitive nature of judgement are recognized, if not exalted."[48]

In many of the cases examined in this book, judges have emphasized the need for individualized treatment of clients and prohibited administrators from using hard-and-fast eligibility rules. Again, this is clearest with education of the handicapped. For example, most judges found a 180-day limit on the school year "incompatible with the Act's emphasis on the individual" because it "imposes with rigid certainty a program restriction which may be wholly inappropriate to the child's educational objective."[49] In both food stamp and AFDC cases, the courts repeatedly struck down regulations that assumed certain categories of income were available to recipients. They demanded an individualized assessment of whether these funds were "actually available" to recipients. For example, the Supreme Court ruled that states cannot impose any across-the-board limits on work expenses but must assess the reasonableness of deductions on a case-by-case basis.[50]

Legislative Histories

Understanding the importance of judicial presumptions on federalism, the separation of powers, and the nature of entitlements allows one to recognize recurrent patterns in what at first seems to be a sea of ad hoc judicial decisions. Recognizing the significance of these presumptions also shows how statutory interpretation raises fundamental issues about the proper role and structure of government. What does *not* exhibit much independent significance in the cases examined in this book, it should be noted, is the use of legislative history. To put the matter baldly, judges tend to throw in references to legislative history primarily to buttress positions adopted on other grounds. Legislative history is the tail, not the dog. Given the amount of attention devoted to legislative history in current debates over statutory interpretation, this finding is rather surprising.

The central feature of the courts' use of legislative history in these three programs is its arbitrariness. The case studies provide ample evidence for Judge Harold Leventhal's aphorism that citing legislative history is akin to "looking over a crowd and picking out your friends."[51] Legislative language that supports judges' preexisting understanding of federalism, the separation of powers, and entitlements is repeated in judicial opinions. Language that contravened this understanding is conveniently ignored. Examples of the selective use of legislative history are legion. Even his defenders concede that Chief Justice Warren's rendition of the history of AFDC seriously distorts both the structure of the statute and the mood of the amending Congresses. Five years later, the Court justified an exception to the rule established in *King* v. *Smith* on the basis of an equally suspect use of legislative history.[52] Judge Wright's decision in *Rodway* put great weight on the act's broad statement of purpose, ignoring a specific statement by the House and Senate conferees. In *Rowley*, the Court ignored numerous statements in the legislative record about the need for aggressive judicial review of state and local school decisions. Perhaps the low point in the misuse of legislative history came when a federal judge relied on a speech delivered by Senator George McGovern to confirm an unconventional interpretation of a House floor amendment that had passed two years before that speech.[53]

If these examples buttress Justice Scalia's warnings about the possible misuse of legislative history, they undermine his claim that the use of legislative history serves to strengthen the hand of committee leaders and staff. In neither AFDC nor the food stamp program had the legislative history relied upon by the court been manufactured or manipulated by the members or staff of committees with legislative jurisdiction over the programs. Indeed, these four committees—House Ways and Means, Senate Finance, and the two Agriculture committees—were frequently angered by court rulings. They complained that the courts had ignored or misinterpreted such key pieces of legislative history as the conference report on the 1970 food stamp amendments and the 1975 report on supplemental food stamp appropriations—not to mention the long series of congressional statements on state control of the AFDC program. In each of these instances the courts prevented the agency in question from following the directives of congressional committees.

In EAHCA cases, some federal courts did rely on the reports produced by the House Education and Labor Committee and the Senate Committee on Education and Public Welfare. Particularly important in a number of cases was the statement in the conference report that judges should make an "independent" assessment of the adequacy of individualized educational programs. In *Rowley*, though, a majority on the Supreme Court chose to ignore this element of legislative history, ordering the lower courts to show greater deference to the decisions of local schools. Many lower courts subsequently found other justifications for strict judicial scrutiny of state and local decisions. Judges frequently cited congressional statements about providing disabled children with "equal," "equivalent," and "full" educational opportunity, but such congressional descriptions were so vague and diverse as to give little useful guidance.[54] One comes away from these decisions with the strong sense that references to legislative history were little more than window dressing designed to provide additional support for positions arrived at by other means.

Judicial Cacophony

Another notable feature of the judicial interpretation of these three statutes is the high degree of variation both over time and among the many federal courts. The Supreme Court has difficulty giving direction to the lower courts, which decide the overwhelming preponderance of statutory cases. Most questions of statutory interpretation never reach the Supreme Court. The authority of the Supreme Court is particularly weak when disagreements among the justices prevent them from constructing consistent lines of decision. But even when the Supreme Court speaks unambiguously, there is no assurance the lower courts will comply. Disagreements between the Supreme Court and the lower courts and among the circuits can persist for years, even decades.

In two of the three programs, the Supreme Court waited years before reviewing lower court decisions. Virtually all the important food stamp decisions examined in chapter 10 were issued before the Supreme Court handed down *Knebel* v. *Hein*, its sole stab at interpreting the act. Not only did the USDA have to contend with conflicting rulings by the circuits, but seriatim court decisions on income and deductions created a cumbersome patchwork of eligibility rules that Congress ultimately jettisoned. In education of the handicapped the Supreme Court was similarly tardy in explaining what the law required of local school systems. The lower courts differed wildly in their interpretation of "free appropriate public education." Seven years after passage of the federal law, the Supreme Court endorsed a relatively narrow definition of the term, stressing the need for federal judges to defer to the decisions of local school systems. But the *Rowley* decision did little to constrain lower court judges or to bring more consistency to judicial decisions. Previous patterns of judicial behavior reappeared in new guise, and the Supreme Court never revisited the issue.

The Supreme Court decided a surprisingly large number of AFDC cases—twelve statutory cases between 1968 and 1975 alone. In this instance, reinterpretation of the act started at the top rather than percolating up from the bottom. The lower courts, though, were not only willing to comply, but often went further than the Supreme Court. In its 1975 decision on pregnancy benefits, the Supreme Court reversed the decisions of five of the six circuit courts that had ruled on the issue. The Supreme Court's control over the lower courts' interpretation of title IV was limited by its own failure to adopt a consistent line of interpretation. The Court first took a hard line against state discretion, then repudiated what it called this "departure from ordinary principles of statutory interpretation." For many years thereafter the Court resolved conflicts among the circuits (and conflicts among its own precedents) by issuing narrow opinions that gave little guidance to the lower courts. Neither state welfare officials nor HEW knew what to expect next. Not until the mid-1980s did the Court finally settle on a consistent line of interpretation.

Such judicially created fragmentation of authority is apparent in other policy areas as well. Describing the consequences of the legal battle over disability insurance in the early 1980s, Martha Derthick reports that henceforth "there were to be two disability determination processes—one bureaucratically controlled and nationally uniform in application, the other judicially controlled and potentially varying among the circuits."[55] One reason the Social Security Administration resisted court intervention so tenaciously was that judicial review threatened its strongly held belief that policy should be uniform throughout the nation. Disability insurance is an extreme example, but not an isolated one. In a variety of areas, "the infrequency of Supreme Court review combines with the formal independence of each circuit's law from that of the other circuits to permit a gradual balkanization of federal law."[56] In short, while the federal courts clearly have reduced the authority of the states, they have not always made welfare programs more nationally uniform.

Variation flowing from disagreements among federal courts is harder to justify than the traditional variation among the states. The principal argument for strong state and local governments has always been that they are closer to the average citizen than is the federal government. These "small republics" foster public participation, reflect the preferences of local populations, and provide opportunities for experimentation. It is hard to see how the new form of decentralization furthers these goals. The territories covered by the First, Fourth, Seventh, or Eleventh circuits are hardly small republics that facilitate citizen participation. (How many citizens know what circuit they are in or who their judges are? What recourse would they have even if they knew?) Nor are citizens likely soon to benefit from investigation of the long-term consequences of contrasting circuit court interpretations of federal statutes. Given the conceit that judges merely announce what the law requires, conflicts among circuit and district courts are more a source of embarrassment than of experimentation. This serious problem has generally been ignored by legal scholars, whose preoccupation with the Supreme Court has exaggerated the judiciary's ability to bring coherence and consistency to the law.

The combination of judicial activism and judicial decentralization exhibited in these three programs exemplifies one of the key developments examined in chapter 2: American politics has been nationalized, but authority at the national level is more fragmented than ever before. The central government has become more powerful but less capable of speaking with a single voice. In the 1970s and 1980s, this new fragmentation created unexpected opportunities for innovation and expansion of the public domain. As the case studies show, lower courts and congressional subcommittees proved highly responsive to impassioned pleas for government assistance. Each institution built on the work of the other, producing major policy change without presidential leadership or strong parties. At the same time, this new form of decentralization made it difficult for the federal government to establish coherent policies, coordinate related programs, establish spending limits and priorities, or even reach agreement on procedures for writing a budget. Ironically, the "gridlock" that pundits and politicians so often decry is inseparable from institutional developments that have often produced rapid policy change.

CHAPTER TWELVE

The Court-Congress Connection

To STUDENTS of statutory interpretation, no problem is more vexing than affixing a single meaning or intent to legislation that is the product of many hands. This task is especially difficult in the United States, where the legislative process is complex and legislative coalitions are diverse and shifting. Under the Constitution, laws must ordinarily receive the approval of three institutions—the House, the Senate, and the president—each of which has its own electoral base. Congressional rules and traditions require that each bill also receive the assent of a number of specialized committees. Any one of these can usually veto proposed legislation. Adding to the fragmentation of legislative power is the notorious weakness of American parties. Members of Congress are independent entrepreneurs who owe little to parties and have little to fear from them. As a result, congressional leaders cannot rely on party loyalty alone to build winning coalitions. Most important bills must be drafted and redrafted, amended and amended again to build a coalition large enough to overcome the multiple vetoes in the legislative process. The fluidity and fragility of legislative majorities is a major theme of the literature on Congress.[1]

The Many Faces of Congress

The members of Congress who make up these motley coalitions have diverse reasons for supporting the proposed legislation. Sometimes disagreement produces ambiguous statutory language. At other times congressional compromises are spelled out in detailed statutes that resemble treaties negotiated by warring countries. It is not unusual for such compromises to be cobbled together in the middle of the night by members of a conference committee (or their staff) eager to complete their work before Congress adjourns.[2] Some legislative agreements remain informal, explained in committee reports or worked out quietly between key members of Congress and executive branch officials. The subtlety and complexity of congressional politics is seldom reflected in court opinions. Indeed, if judges tried to capture the full texture of congressional debates and negotiations, it is hard to see how they would have time to decide all the cases that come before them.

Congressional factiousness was particularly apparent with aid to families with dependent children. In 1935 Congress quickly reached an agreement on the program by handing over to the states almost all the important policy decisions. Since then it has been hard to build a congressional consensus either on the extent of federal control or on the substance of federal requirements. In their study of welfare reform in the 1970s, Lawrence Lynn and David Whitman sound a theme that appears in almost every examination of the topic: "critics of the system were united in their distaste for the 'mess,' but they were by no means united in their views of 'reform,' which meant quite different things to different people." The "mutually contradictory demands" of "powerful congressional conservatives, welfare rights organizations, labor unions, academicians, administrators of welfare programs, and financially hard-pressed state and local governments" constituted "a policymaking dilemma of major proportions."[3]

Congress managed to pass several incremental adjustments to title IV, most notably in 1967, 1981, and 1988. Both the 1967 amendments and the 1988 Family Support Act were delicately balanced compromises that combined expanded benefits with new restrictions on eligibility. Some liberals considered the amendments too restrictive; some conservatives considered them too expensive. In both instances, compromise legislation nearly unraveled at the last moment. The thrust of the 1981 changes was more clear-cut: they were designed to cut costs and restrict eligibility. Several of these changes, though, were rescinded later in the decade. Years of "tireless tinkering" with AFDC (to use Gilbert Steiner's apt phrase) has produced lots of political turmoil but little lasting agreement on how to structure the program.

Congress has done considerably more than tinker with the food stamp program. Over the past twenty-five years annual spending on food stamps has gone from $100 million to almost $30 billion. This dramatic expansion has not come without controversy. From the late 1960s to the mid-1980s Congress was constantly fighting about the program. Votes were often razor thin. Congressional moods shifted rapidly from ending hunger to cutting waste, and then back again.

The fickleness of both congressional and public opinion was most evident in the mid-1970s. After years of growth and favorable publicity, the program suddenly came under attack. In 1976 Congress came close to passing legislation cracking down on what the program's critics called the "food stamp stampede." The House Agriculture Committee was so divided that many issues were decided by a margin of one or two votes. The committee's bill eventually died in the Rules Committee because party leaders neither liked the bill nor believed it had enough support to survive on the floor. For reasons explained in chapter 10, program advocates fared much better in 1977. But to achieve their principal goal, elimination of the purchase requirement, they still had to accept a number of provisions restricting eligibility. The 1977 act was a complex bundle of compromises worked out over two years of negotiations. Even this agreement did not last long. Within the next few years food stamps became the American public's least favorite welfare program. The food stamp program was one of the biggest losers in the initial stages of the "Reagan revolution." This retrenchment was soon followed by renewed concern about hunger in America and gradual expansion of the program after 1985.

Education of the handicapped has not been nearly as volatile as AFDC or food stamps. The original legislation passed by wide margins with little concerted opposition. The few subsequent changes in the act have incited little controversy. The popularity of the law is in large part a result of the fact that members of Congress have not been forced to take positions on hard issues. The law does not specify the level of services schools must provide to disabled students; it merely requires that these students receive an "appropriate" education. Just as important, the law does not commit the federal government to pay all the costs incurred by the schools or even a predetermined percentage of these expenses. The federal government appropriates about $2 billion a year and expects state and local school systems to pick up the rest of the tab—which amounts to about $25 billion annually.

A clear lesson of the case studies is that it is misleading to attribute to legislation a single overriding purpose, spirit, or direction. Most legislation emerging from Congress is a complex amalgam of conflicting goals and multiple constraints that reflect the nature of the underlying legislative coalitions. Some members voted for the Education for All Handicapped Children Act because they believed it would provide disabled students with a wide variety of new services. Others thought it would increase federal funding without imposing extensive federal control over local school systems. Many believed Congress should act because the courts had clearly established the rights of the disabled; a few thought Congress should act because the Supreme Court might reverse lower court decisions. Similarly, some members of Congress voted for expansion of the food stamp program because they thought it would improve the nutrition of poor families. Others voted for it because they recognized it would increase the amount of money poor families had to spend on items other than food. Some members considered the 1967 amendments to the AFDC statute a wake-up call to the states: either you crack down on welfare or we will. Others may have voted for it because it offered new services to recipients. Most probably voted for it because these AFDC amendments were attached to a larger social security bill. In short, it is essential to keep in mind that Congress is "a 'they,' not an 'it.' "[4]

Like most citizens, members of Congress want to help the "truly needy" without rewarding the "merely greedy"; to promote "family values" while protecting the privacy of recipients; to promote work without forcing those unable to work to take a job. And they want to accomplish all this without spending too much money. How legislators and administrators manage to establish acceptable trade-offs among these competing goals—none of which is overriding—is the essence of welfare politics. When judges arbitrarily elevate one goal above all others, they not only present a distorted view of legislative politics but hand one faction a victory in the judicial process it was unable to win in the legislative process. As Justice Kennedy has put it, "The problem with spirits is that they tend to reflect less the views of the world whence they come than the views of those who seek their advice."[5]

In recent years some legal scholars (egged on by economists) have argued that legislation should be seen as the result of deals negotiated by self-interested pressure groups. Others maintain that judges should instead treat legislation as the product of deliberation about shared public values.[6] Neither of these two images of the legislative process finds much support in the three case studies. One remarkable aspect of congressional action on the three programs is how little effort traditional interest groups have put into them. Business groups had virtually no direct influence on any of the programs. Contrary to the conventional wisdom, farm groups did little to support food stamps. The Chamber of Commerce contributed to the Ford administration's effort to cut food stamps in the mid-1970s, but it lost. Groups that did exert some influence include the National Association for Retarded Citizens, the Council for Exceptional Children, various elements of the "intergovernmental lobby," and the loose coalition of churches, labor unions, and advocacy groups called the "hunger lobby." A leading characteristic of this array of groups is that their interest is neither purely economic nor particularly well-defined. With little money to spread around and relatively few members, their chances for success depended on their ability to attract public attention and to appeal to a diffuse constituency.

Many of the legislators described in these cases acted not on the basis of their desire to be reelected or to maintain their power in Congress but on the basis of strongly held beliefs about the public interest. Neither Russell Long nor Thomas Foley took a leading role on AFDC and food stamps to curry favor with interest groups or their constituents. What the debates over these three programs show, however, is not deliberation about *shared* values, but the collision of *competing* values. AFDC and food stamps were lightning rods for ideological combat. Some members favored generous benefits because they viewed poverty as the result of external social forces. Others favored work requirements, low benefits, and restrictive eligibility requirements because they saw poverty as the result of poor decisions made by the indigent. Some had no qualms about imposing "middle-class morality" on recipients; others considered this vindictive and a serious violation of the recipients' right to privacy. As Madison pointed out in *Federalist* 10, property is not the only source of faction. "A zeal for different opinions concerning religion, concerning government, and many other points" has "divided mankind into parties" and "inflamed them with mutual animosity." All too often those who talk about the importance of recognizing "public values" seek to impose their own preferences without providing a justification.[7] Recognizing the importance of ideology should make one even more attentive to divisions within Congress and the hazards of attributing to that body a single purpose or intent.

The Fortune of Reversals

One of the ironies of statutory interpretation is that the very features of the American political system that make it difficult for judges to discern the meaning of statutes also tend to protect court rulings from congressional revision. Legislative coalitions must be large and diverse to overcome the multiple veto points in the legislative process. Legislators who like the policies established by the judiciary are often able to veto legislation designed to override court rulings. This was particularly evident with AFDC. Time and time again, the Senate would pass legislation that returned to the states the authority they had before *King* v. *Smith.* Again and again, the House would reject the Senate's amendments. Congress's failure to act during the 1970s did not signify its acceptance of the courts' rulings, but rather reflected its inability to put forth a majority coalition in support of any position. Recognizing that it is much easier to block legislation than to enact laws, American courts for years have endorsed the principle that Congress's failure to reject a previous line of decisions does not indicate its acceptance of these rulings. Unfortunately, this canon—like so many others—is often honored in the breach.[8]

Several recent articles based on rational choice analysis have demonstrated that Congress will often have difficulty overriding a court decision even if the decision clearly violates an agreement made by the prevailing legislative coalition and even if all the members of that coalition remain in Congress.[9] The reason for this is relatively straightforward: at least one element of the original coalition may prefer the court's ruling to the initial legislative agreement. The remaining members of the coalition may not be able to find an adequate replacement for the defectors.

The food stamp program provides a vivid example of this point. As explained in chapter 10, in 1970 the House and the Senate differed on whether to use the economy food plan or the low-cost food plan to set benefit levels. The Senate favored the more generous low-cost plan. By a narrow margin, the House endorsed the economy food plan previously established by the Department of Agriculture. The conferees reached a compromise: their agreement "retains the House standard, but adopts the language of the Senate amendment requiring . . . an annual adjustment to reflect increases for food in the 'Cost of Living' index."[10] The D.C. Circuit's decision in *Rodway* put this agreement in jeopardy. It seemed likely that the court would eventually require the U.S. Department of Agriculture to increase its payments to some recipients. Many members of the House—especially those who had participated in the 1970 conference—were angered by the decision. Legislation to reinstate the economy food plan, though, faced a formidable obstacle—the Senate. Not only had the Senate previously supported the more generous diet plan, but a bill reinstating the economy plan would first go to a subcommittee chaired by Senator McGovern, the chief proponent of the low-cost plan. Having already prevailed on the cost-of-living adjustment, McGovern no longer had any reason to acquiesce to the economy food plan.

Congress took no action on the matter until it completed its comprehensive overhaul of the program in 1977. The 1977 amendments endorsed the Department of Agriculture's food plan and removed the general language relied upon in *Rodway*. As chapter 10 explained, this was one small part of the grand compromise engineered in 1977. Senator McGovern and his allies were willing to give in on a number of issues, including the diet plan, as long as they prevailed on elimination of the purchase requirement. In other words, the court decision created a status quo that could be altered only when defectors received a significant side payment.[11]

In general, whenever court decisions create a new policy status quo, they alter the bargaining power of factions within Congress. This was particularly clear with the *Trump* decision. Before *Trump*, food stamp program advocates had no choice but to reach an accord with President Ford. After *Trump*, they were free to wait for a new president, a new Congress, and a healthier economy.

One might conclude from this that Congress seldom modifies or reverses the courts. For many years this was the prevailing wisdom among the handful of people who considered the matter. Yet in each of the three policy areas Congress passed new legislation in response to court rulings. In 1981, 1982, and 1984 Congress overturned a number of long-standing AFDC decisions. The Handicapped Children Protection Act reversed the Supreme Court's decision on attorneys' fees. Two years later, Congress reversed another Supreme Court decision on education of the disabled that had limited parents' rights to collect damages from the states.[12] The 1977 food stamp amendments revised a large number of court rulings on eligibility and benefits.

Evidence compiled by William Eskridge shows that since 1975 Congress has overridden at least 100 Supreme Court rulings and 300 lower court decisions. These legislative responses were by no means limited to minor or technical issues. Among the Supreme Court decisions overturned were high-profile cases on endangered species, pregnancy benefits, employment discrimination, racial gerrymandering, and private colleges' duty to comply with the Civil Rights Act.[13]

What do the case studies show about when Congress is likely to pass legislation in response to judicial rulings? First, the preferences of committee leaders are particularly important. These strategically located members of Congress have the power not only to protect the court decisions they like, but also to move along legislation modifying decisions they dislike. All the overrides examined in the case studies were championed by committee leaders in at least one chamber. Full committee and subcommittee chairs on both the Senate Human Resources Committee and the House Education and Labor Committee strongly opposed the two Supreme Court decisions limiting disabled children's access to federal courts. They quickly ushered remedial bills through Congress. House Agriculture Committee chair Thomas Foley was intent upon overturning several food stamp decisions and reducing the role of the courts in the future.

Committee leaders' ability both to push legislation and to veto it was a crucial part of the AFDC story. Russell Long repeatedly offered amendments. Often these amendments would show up late in the session attached to tax bills dear to the heart of the president or the Ways and Means Committee. Usually, though, Ways and Means conferees insisted that these provisions be removed.

The two faces of committee power can also be seen in the congressional response to civil rights decisions. During the 1970s and 1980s the Democrats on the House Judiciary Committee were more liberal than the average Democrat on civil rights issues. The committee took no action when the Burger court read the Civil Rights Act to require extensive affirmative action programs. When the Rehnquist court later adopted an interpretation that threatened existing affirmative action programs, the committee quickly reported out a bill that eventually became the Civil Rights Act of 1991.[14]

A second, less obvious characteristic of the overrides examined in this book is that almost all of them were attached to larger financing bills. All the AFDC reversals were contained in budget reconciliation bills. The food stamp overrides were part of legislation reauthorizing the program. The provision reversing *Dellmuth* v. *Muth* was a little-noted piece of a larger bill reauthorizing the Education for the Handicapped Act. Only the Handicapped Children Protection Act was a free-standing piece of legislation.

Reauthorizations provide committee leaders with convenient vehicles for moving their proposals through Congress. Like appropriations, they are hard to veto: when these bills fail to pass, programs shut down— something few members of Congress want. If, as seems to be the case, the number of overrides has increased since the 1970s, the trend is probably linked to the popularity of short-term authorizations. Before 1970 most authorizations were long term and open-ended. Title IV of the 1935 Social Security Act, for example, established the AFDC program in perpetuity and placed no ceiling on spending. Authorizations for the food stamp program, in contrast, lapsed after three or four years and often set specific budget ceilings. At one time, specific, short-term authorizations were the exception. Today they are the norm.[15] When Congress routinely reviews and reauthorizes programs, it frequently runs into court decisions. Not all the policies established by court rulings will survive the reauthorization process, especially when Congress faces strong pressures to reduce federal spending.

In the 1980s omnibus budget reconciliation bills played a prominent role in congressional politics. Reconciliation bills bundled together a large number of budget cuts and tax increases. These packages were the product of extensive, often secretive negotiations between White House officials and congressional leaders. They usually came to the House floor under a rule allowing few amendments. Members were forced to vote yes or no on the entire package. Each of these factors reduced the influence of authorizing committees, particularly in the Democratic House. This was most evident in 1981 when the House rejected a package put together by committee chairs in favor of one constructed by the Office of Management and Budget and a handful of House Republicans. As pointed out in chapter 6, reconciliation bills gave President Reagan and his congressional allies an unusual opportunity to overcome opposition from the House Ways and Means Committee on AFDC issues. To the extent that reconciliation bills continue to be used to reduce the deficit and centralize power within Congress, they will remain an attractive mechanism for critics of the courts to overturn or modify benefit-expanding judicial rulings.

Committee Variation

In his well-known book *Congressmen in Committees*, Richard Fenno sorted congressional committees into three categories according to the goals of their members and showed how these committees differ in their structure, norms, and procedures. Members seek positions on what Fenno called "prestige" or "power" committees in order to gain influence within Congress. They join "constituency" committees to help themselves get reelected, and "policy" committees to pursue whatever they define as "good public policy." Since winning on the floor is particularly important to members of prestige and constituency committees, they put a premium on developing a consensus within the committee before reporting out a bill. These committees develop norms of loyalty and reciprocity. Policy committees are less obsessed with success on the floor, far more decentralized, and more tolerant of entrepreneurial activities by their members. Constituency committees and policy committees tend to be more egalitarian and participatory than prestige committees, which emphasize apprenticeship, fiscal restraint, and deference to committee leaders.[16]

The case studies in this book suggest that the three types of committees also develop distinctive relations with the courts. House Education and Labor and Senate Labor and Public Welfare are two of the policy committees examined by Fenno. The Senate Select Committee on Nutrition and Human Needs was an exaggerated version of the entrepreneurial policy committee. These committees frequently framed issues in terms of rights and encouraged the courts to play a major role in policymaking. House Ways and Means and Senate Finance are prototypical prestige committees. They were wary of giving the courts a major role or of establishing open-ended welfare rights. The House and Senate Agriculture committees are classic constituency committees. They are less familiar with the courts than either policy or prestige committees. Like prestige committees, they jealously guard their control over the programs within their jurisdiction and hesitate to allow the courts to resolve policy disputes.

It is not hard to see why policy committees are the most favorably inclined toward judicial intervention. The norms and structure of these committees encourage unbridled program advocacy. Their strongest loyalties are not to the committee or to Congress as an institution, but to particular policies and the groups that support them. Committee members and staff often work closely with groups that combine litigation with lobbying, like the Food Research and Action Center and the Council for Exceptional Children. Members of policy committees recognize that extensive judicial involvement in policymaking often results in higher benefits and more lenient eligibility rules. Lacking budgetary responsibilities, they are less concerned about the fiscal consequences of their actions than are members who sit on prestige or constituency committees.[17]

Prestige committees are the mirror image of policy committees. Their uneasiness with policymaking through litigation is readily understandable in light of their desire to retain control over policy and their commitment to a powerful legislative branch. Both the process by which members are assigned to these committees and internal committee norms discourage the open, unrestrained program advocacy that characterizes policy committees. Moreover, prestige committees tend to develop closer relations with members of the executive branch than with advocacy groups. Not only do they deal with administrative officials regularly, but few administrators dare antagonize members of these powerful committees. Committee members have much more confidence in their ability to control executive branch officials than their ability to control judges.

Of particular concern to members of prestige committees is the effect court decisions can have on spending. Aggressive judicial review almost always raises the cost of welfare programs. The rules of standing and jurisdiction virtually ensure this: the vast majority of cases are brought by recipients who argue they were denied benefits promised by the statute; taxpayer suits are not accepted by the federal judiciary. Moreover, judges focus not on the program as a whole, but on the particular individuals before them. Many of these plaintiffs have compelling personal stories that engage judges' sympathies. Advocacy groups try to make sure that these are the cases that come to court first. Judges who increase benefits or expand eligibility are under no obligation to raise the necessary revenues. That difficult task is left to Congress. As a rule, then, the more responsible a committee is for financing a program, the less likely it will be endorse or encourage aggressive judicial review.

Senate Finance and House Ways and Means have jurisdiction over social security and health care programs because, for the most part, these programs are financed through earmarked taxes. This means that the committees that can claim credit for expanding benefits must also accept blame for raising taxes.[18] Two events that transpired in April 1992 help explain why the two revenue committees are wary of policymaking through litigation. On April 2, the overseers of the social security trust fund informed Congress that the disability fund might run dry as early as 1995—not 2015, as previously estimated. They warned that the fund would need an additional $80 billion over the next ten years to keep reserves at a safe level. Two weeks later, the Bush administration reached a final settlement with plaintiffs in New York State who had participated in the extensive litigation of the early 1980s.[19] The ultimate cost of this agreement is likely to run into the billions of dollars. This, too, must come from the disability trust fund. When litigation raises costs above projections, it is committee members who face the politically unpalatable task of either hiking taxes or cutting benefits. This fact has been at the center of years of conflict between the courts and the revenue committees over disability policy.[20]

At first glance, it seems puzzling that constituency committees are so hostile to court intervention and a rights-based approach to policymaking. Why did the House Agriculture Committee—not just its anti–food stamp Republican minority, but even its pro–food stamp Democratic chairman, Thomas Foley—make a concerted and ultimately successful effort to curtail court intervention? Why did the House Veterans Affairs Committee for many years oppose *any* judicial review of veterans' benefits? Why did they not see judicial review as a way to increase benefits for their constituents?

A large part of the answer lies in the way in which these programs are funded. Although the principal goal of members of constituency committees is to get as much as possible for their clientele, they are acutely aware of the dangers of asking for too much. Not only do farm bills, rivers and harbor bills, and highway bills cost a good deal of money, but almost all of this money comes directly from the U.S. treasury. Costs are not shifted to subnational governments or the private sector, but show up all too visibly in the federal budget. As a consequence, such bills frequently encounter trouble on the floor. They become especially vulnerable when the federal government runs high deficits.

Members of constituency committees recognize that in order to put together a bill that can survive on the House and Senate floor and not invite a presidential veto they must develop a carefully balanced package that provides something—but not too much—for each of the committees' constituencies: "floor success is of critical instrumental value" to members of constituency committees since they are "anxious to deliver tangible benefits to their districts."[21] This requires restraint, mutual accommodation, and a willingness to defer to committee leaders.

As explained in chapter 10, it had long been the House Agriculture Committee's habit of working out extensive compromises before the farm bill reached the floor and spelling these compromises out in the statute. Moreover, the committee worked closely with the USDA on a wide variety of matters. Its members dealt with judges only sporadically and tended to view them as space invaders who came to earth unexpectedly to announce inexplicable decisions. Most important, committee members— especially the food stamp program's patrons—had to cope with the fiscal consequences of these court rulings when the act came up for reauthorization. Even the program's strongest supporters have been bothered by the unpredictable way in which the courts have expanded eligibility and benefits. They feared that budget-busting decisions would expose the program to further attack, and they jealously guarded their own prerogative to set spending priorities.

Similar concerns seem to have been behind the House Veterans Affairs Committee's long-standing opposition to judicial review. The system in place between 1933 and 1986 gave a special role to the traditional service organizations—the Veterans of Foreign Wars, Disabled American Veterans, and American Legion—in handling appeals before administrative law judges. The effort to end the statutory preclusion of judicial review was spearheaded by the Vietnam Veterans of America (VVA), which disagreed with the traditional groups both on ideological grounds and on the appropriate balance between spending on Vietnam era veterans and those who fought in previous wars. The VVA not only deeply distrusted the veterans' bureaucracy, but believed the courts would be more sympathetic to claims about Agent Orange and posttraumatic stress syndrome. If judicial review does direct more money to Vietnam vets (as the VVA hopes), then traditional groups may well get less, a prospect not likely to please committee members.[22]

These findings square with other studies of court-Congress interaction. According to Robert Katzmann's detailed examination of transportation for the disabled, House Education and Labor and Senate Labor and Human Resources were "right-oriented" committees that encouraged the courts to play an active role in policymaking. The House Public Works Committee (a constituency committee) and the two appropriations committees (prestige committees) were highly critical of this approach. They preferred to allocate specific amounts of federal funds for specific forms of public transportation, an approach that left little room for court intervention.[23] The House Education and Labor Committee also played a key role in passage of the vaguely worded, much litigated Age Discrimination Act of 1975.[24] Several studies of the House and Senate Judiciary Committees have demonstrated that these "policy" committees have been particularly likely to endorse a rights-based approach to policymaking.[25]

In a 1992 article, Mark Miller examined the attitudes of members of various committees toward the courts. He found that members of the "power-oriented" House Energy and Commerce Committee are "more likely than other members to express negative attitudes toward the courts," that they "get furious when the courts make policy instead of waiting for Congress to take action," and that they have few qualms about overturning court decisions. In contrast, the House Judiciary Committee "treats the courts with a great deal of deference, almost bordering on mystical respect." Members of House Interior, a constituency committee, do not think of the courts as important actors. Indeed, they do not seem to "think about the courts at all" except when constituents complain about "the effects of particular decisions on their specific interests or well-being."[26] These views are strikingly similar to those evidenced by the three types of committees examined in this book.

Judicial Review: The View from Congress

Statutory interpretation is usually studied from the point of view of the judge. From this perspective, the central question is, How should judges decide what this legislation means? Since members of Congress have a big stake in how judges read statutes, it is worth examining statutory interpretation from their perspective as well. For members of Congress, the key question is, How can we structure administrative rulemaking and judicial review to get the types of policy outcomes we want? The preceding section suggests that where one stands on this issue depends on where one sits within Congress.

Legislators have a variety of mechanisms for controlling the extent and direction of court involvement in policymaking. Most important, they establish the powers of administrative agencies and the scope of judicial review. Congress can specify that the courts will have the final word on certain matters and that the role of administrative agencies is simply advisory. Examples include antitrust policy under the Sherman Act and employment discrimination policy under title VII of the Civil Rights Act. At the other extreme, Congress can preclude judicial review altogether. In between lie a wide variety of shades of judicial review. In addition, Congress can either require that administrative remedies be exhausted or allow for quick judicial review. It can specify who has standing to sue, where suits must be brought, and what remedies are available. It can allow the prevailing party to collect attorneys' fees from the loser or require all parties to pay for their own lawyers. Congress also determines the types of cases the Legal Services Corporation can handle.

The amount of attention these issues receive varies from program to program and from time to time. The role of the federal courts became a major issue in the final negotiations over the Education for All Handicapped Children Act. Advocates for the handicapped and their congressional allies wanted to encourage substantial judicial oversight of school decisions. Various groups representing state and local school systems favored a more lenient standard. The former prevailed. In contrast, judicial review was hardly mentioned when Congress passed title IV of the Social Security Act. The statute authorized the states to contest decisions of the federal government to withhold funds but made no provision for suits by recipients. Food stamp legislation provides extensive guidance on legal challenges by stores denied participation in the program but says little about suits by recipients. For this reason, lawyers filing suit on behalf of AFDC and food stamp recipients must rely on generic jurisdictional statutes. These laws, it should be noted, fall within the purview of the Judiciary committees, which have tried to make it easier for recipients to obtain federal judicial review of state rules.[27]

When members of Congress compose judicial review provisions, they face a dilemma. On the one hand, aggressive judicial review can serve as a mechanism for keeping agencies attentive to the wishes of Congress and its committees. The advantages of judicial oversight loom particularly large to members of Congress during periods of divided government: judges, unlike administrators, are not subject to control by the White House and the Office of Management and Budget. On the other hand, there is no guarantee that the interpretations announced by judges will conform to the preferences of the prevailing coalition. As the case studies demonstrate, this is not just an abstract possibility. Once Congress asks judges to guard against administrative error, who is left to guard against malfeasance by the judicial guardians?[28]

From the point of view of members of Congress, there is a particularly serious disadvantage associated with having judges make key decisions: the informal, post hoc controls that members of Congress so frequently use against administrators cannot be employed against the judiciary. Members are much better informed about the activities of federal agencies—most of which have their headquarters in Washington—than about the decisions of the far-flung lower courts.[29] Committee members and their staff confer regularly with administrators; they seldom talk to judges or their clerks. Members of Congress can write indignant letters to administrators and grill them in televised hearings. They can threaten them with budget cuts. They can refuse to confirm political appointees or extract promises from them in confirmation hearings. They can make life unpleasant for administrators when the act comes up for reauthorization. None of these sanctions can be used against judges. When members of Congress dislike a court decision, their sole recourse is passing new legislation—which is seldom an easy task.

Most members of Congress and their staff recognize their limited ability to influence judicial interpretation of statutes. As one House Energy and Commerce staffer put it, "You get much different information about court decisions than about agency decisions. To overturn agency decisions, all we need to do is to ask current or former agency staff. But we can't ask judges how to overturn court decisions."[30] Another staff member was even more direct:

> Congress is better able to coerce agencies than the courts to correct policy problems. Congress can use its influence on the executive branch through letter writing, telephone calls, and budget threats. I am unaware of the use of any threats by Congress against the judicial branch or any level of courts.[31]

Clearly Senator Russell Long and Representative Thomas Foley had more clout with HEW and the USDA than they did with the judiciary.

By far the best method members of Congress have for dealing with the dilemma of judicial review is writing detailed statutes. While there are instances in which courts and agencies have ignored clear statutory commands, these are relatively rare. The difficulty with this solution, of course, is that legislators are not always able to come into agreement on controversial topics or to foresee all major issues.

The second-best alternative is writing detailed committee reports and floor statements. These, too, are addressed to both agencies and courts—though primarily to the former. Writing a report or making a speech is far easier than enacting a statute. Since the cost of creating legislative history is low, though, many members will engage in the activity. When members disagree with one another—as is often the case—the result is a cacophony of signals from the Hill. As the endgame over the 1991 Civil Rights Act demonstrates, it is easy for everyone to play the legislative history game and to present their own idiosyncratic interpretation of legislative intent. But it is hard to predict whose version of legislative intent the courts will eventually fasten upon. This makes legislative history an unreliable instrument for those who seek to affect public policy.

Given the fact that members usually have greater control over agencies than over courts, why do they sometimes give a leading policymaking role to the latter? Under what circumstances are they most likely to do so? The preceding section suggested one part of the answer: members will encourage judicial review when they favor program expansion and bear little responsibility for footing the bill.

Aggressive judicial review will be particularly useful to members who seek to control the activities of subnational governments. Members of Congress do not have nearly as much influence with state officials as they have with administrators in Washington. Moreover, the federal courts have a unique ability to force state and local governments to comply with national standards and have often pushed hard to make grant-in-aid programs more nationally uniform. Members of Congress who want to protect state autonomy are likely to advocate a circumscribed role for the courts. Before the 1960s such members were dominant; today they are not.

Members of Congress are also likely to take into account the track record of various courts on particular issues. For example, in the 1950s and 1960s many federal district court judges in the South were less than enthusiastic about school desegregation and enforcement of federal civil rights laws. When the Johnson administration and Congress constructed the Voting Rights Act in 1965, they gave unusual powers to the federal district court in the District of Columbia, effectively bypassing federal courts in the deep South. During the 1960s and 1970s federal judges—particularly those on the D.C. Circuit—showed a strong commitment to environmental protection. Recognizing this, members of Congress who advocated more stringent environmental regulation sought to create open-ended "citizen suit" provisions and to expand the jurisdiction of the D.C. Circuit. Industry lobbyists opposed citizen suits and favored granting district courts outside the District of Columbia the authority to review rules of the Environmental Protection Agency.

Trying to predict the sympathies of federal judges, though, is risky business. The Supreme Court's position on a number of issues—including affirmative action, federalism, and the amount of deference owed to administrators—has changed significantly over the past ten years. The D.C. Circuit underwent a similar change after President Reagan appointed to that court judges such as James Buckley, Robert Bork, Antonin

Scalia, Clarence Thomas, and Kenneth Starr. The behavior of lower court judges is even harder to forecast.

At times, committee norms, fiscal concerns, and careful calculations about the likely consequences of judicial review may simply be overwhelmed by widely shared and strongly held beliefs about the nature of individual rights. Congress eventually passed legislation allowing judicial review of the Veterans Administration because few could justify denying servicemen their "day in court." In the words of Senator John Glenn, the key sponsor of the judicial review provision, "I do not see why we have businessmen, Social Security recipients, welfare beneficiaries, immigrants and criminals that have rights that veterans do not." Senator Gary Hart argued that "the insulation of any agency from the scrutiny of the courts runs counter to our most cherished constitutional principles."[32] The chair of the American Bar Association's Committee on Veterans described preclusion of review as "astonishing." "It's deeply rooted in the American psyche that you should be able to go into the American courthouse."[33] Most members of Congress did not endorse judicial review in order to weaken an "iron triangle" or to shift benefits from World War II veterans to Vietnam vets (as the Vietnam Veterans of America hoped and the traditional service organizations feared), but to protect a right most viewed as fundamental. Why some rights gain such special status and others do not is the subject of the final chapter.

CHAPTER THIRTEEN

The Political Appeal of Welfare Rights

THE THREE case studies show not just that members of Congress occasionally see the judiciary as a useful instrument for producing the policies they want, but that members of Congress are often drawn to a rights-based approach to policymaking. Americans, it seems, have a proclivity to define public issues in terms of individual rights. "The language of rights," Ronald Dworkin wrote more than a decade ago, "now dominates political debate in the United States." More recently, Mary Ann Glendon has observed that "discourse about rights has become the principal language that we use in public settings to discuss weighty questions of right and wrong." While Dworkin urges us to "take rights seriously," Glendon argues that this mode of discourse "impedes compromise, mutual understanding, and the discovery of common ground," "ignores both social costs and the rights of others," and creates a "near-aphasia concerning responsibilities." Regardless of how one evaluates the trend, it is clear that "rights talk" has a powerful hold, not just on judges and lawyers but also on politicians and public opinion.[1]

The rights examined in this book are demands for government goods and services rather than demands for protection against government intrusion—entitlements, rather than liberties. The history of these three programs illustrates how the traditional American emphasis on individual rights has melded with the modern welfare state. If the older view of rights as individual liberty delayed and stunted the growth of the welfare state, then the newer view of rights as entitlements has helped it to flourish. In 1944 Franklin Roosevelt put forth an "Economic Bill of

Rights" to supplement the "sacred Bill of Rights of our Constitution." Although these economic rights were never formally added to the Constitution, Roosevelt's formulation has left an indelible mark on American political culture.[2]

The federal courts have not tried to define this new set of rights by themselves. Reading substantive rights to government benefits into the equal protection or due process clauses of the Constitution, the Supreme Court recognized, would stretch judicial capacity to the breaking point. But that does not mean that the courts have simply left the task to the other branches. Statutory interpretation has proven a powerful mechanism for shaping, expanding, and protecting these "programmatic rights."[3]

The case studies not only demonstrate the significance of "rights talk" in the development of welfare policy, but they also show that the paradigm of individual rights has permeated some programs much more than others. Today, benefits under all three programs are rights in the narrow sense that they cannot be denied without reason and without judicial review. But the three programs differ greatly in the extent to which they have come to incorporate a broad, need-based understanding of welfare rights.

At one extreme lies special education. The right to an "appropriate education" based on an "individualized educational program" is central to the Education for All Handicapped Children Act. Schools are expected to spend whatever it costs to provide handicapped children with the education they need. At the other end of the spectrum lies aid to dependent families with children. From its inception, AFDC has been a categorical program: only one category of the needy—single-parent families—qualifies for benefits. Most states provide AFDC families with only a part of the "standard of need" they have established. Far from withering away, behavioral conditions on eligibility have become more prevalent in recent years. The food stamp program falls somewhere between special education and AFDC. All needy households are eligible. The program is designed to provide these households with the resources necessary to purchase a minimally adequate diet. Yet the 1977 Food Stamp Act removed all reference, direct and oblique, to an individual right to a "nutritionally adequate diet." It also eliminated pretermination hearings, substituted uniform rules for a more individualized determination of need, and discouraged court intervention.

What explains the differential political appeal of the rights paradigm? It is tempting to argue that strong clients establish rights and that weak clients are left with mere claims. Until recently, though, who would have described the disabled as a strong clientele? A decade and a half ago, the disabled were frequently described as an extremely insular and powerless minority.[4] All of the claimants examined in this book were originally weak in the sense that they did not have the capacity to mobilize large numbers of voters, to make sizable campaign contributions, or to withhold resources coveted by government officials.

Addressing three questions helps one understand the strength of the rights paradigm in the case studies and, quite likely, in other policy areas as well. First, how plausible is it to argue that experts can define clients' need in some objective fashion? Second, how visible and traceable are program costs? Finally, how likely is it that providing benefits will encourage unwanted behavior?

The Claim of Objectivity

In all three cases, the rights of beneficiaries were closely tied to professional norms. This was most evident with education of the handicapped, where the leading professional association participated in early litigation, drafted the initial version of federal legislation, and coordinated lobbying activities. Virtually every study of the EAHCA has stressed the importance of the parent-professional alliance for building and sustaining the program. The EAHCA explicitly incorporates a basic tenet of special education professions, namely, that each child has unique needs that can be determined only through extensive analysis of the individual. The act, Senator Robert Stafford has said, codifies "the best and most progressive professional practice of all who are involved in the instructional development of exceptional children."[5] When courts have overturned the decisions of local administrators, it is almost always because they have found the plaintiff's experts more convincing than those of the school system. Most special education teachers and specialists recognize that federal legislation increases the resources available to them, enhances their autonomy, and adds to their political clout within the school system.

Central to the success of the food stamp program was the widespread belief that experts can establish in an objective manner how much it costs to buy a nutritionally adequate diet. Both the thrifty food plan (which establishes the basic benefit package) and the official poverty line (which sets the income ceiling) were widely perceived not as artificial constructs but as objective minimums for an acceptable existence. This attribute makes them easier for program advocates to defend and harder for program critics to attack. Neither legislators nor the administration wish to be seen as having done away with nutritionally adequate diets for the truly needy.[6]

The food stamp program is one of the few means-tested programs to include a cost-of-living adjustment. This, too, reflects the belief that experts can determine how much it costs to eat properly. Recognizing the political importance of presenting food stamps as a scientifically based nutrition program, program advocates have vociferously attacked those who question its nutritional benefits.

The claim of objectivity is not as strong for food stamps as for special education. Since the program distributes scrip rather than services, there exists no army of service providers who can claim intimate knowledge of the particular nutritional needs of each client. Basing benefits on the particular dietary needs and spending habits of each of the millions of families who qualify for food stamps would not only be an administrative nightmare but would also intrude upon families' privacy and inhibit them from applying for benefits. To a large extent, beneficiaries control their own nutritional fate because they buy their own food. Elimination of the purchase requirement added to recipients' freedom: after 1977 they could chose to spend more on heat or medical care or housing and less on food. Program advocates have long been caught between their desire to maintain the public perception that food stamps is a feeding program and their reluctance to focus exclusively on the nutritional needs of the poor.

In the 1960s welfare rights advocates tried to establish a broader right to an "adequate subsistence." Although this nomenclature was novel, many of the concrete objectives of legal reformers had long been on the agenda of social welfare professionals: elimination of residency requirements, suitable-home provisions, and workfare; extending aid to two-parent families; raising benefit levels; and establishing nationally uniform eligibility rules and benefit schedules. Why did this "right to an adequate subsistence" prove less politically potent than the "right to a nutritionally adequate diet" or the right to an "appropriate education"? Part of the reason, one suspects, is the low status of social work as a profession. More fundamentally, it is hard to argue that any profession or government agency can provide an objective answer to the question, How much does an adequate subsistence cost? As useful and ubiquitous as it is, the government's official poverty line lacks the technical veneer of the thrifty food plan. Few would argue that it is impossible to subsist on an income below the poverty line. How *well* the poor should live appears to most people to be a political question rather than a technical one. Indeed, those who believe the poor have contributed to their own plight—because they fail to work or have given birth to children they cannot afford to rear—want to be sure that recipients do *not* live well.

The difficulty of establishing in an objective fashion the cost of an adequate existence also helps explain why, in litigation over benefit levels, poverty lawyers tended to stress comparative issues. AFDC families, they argued, should not receive less than households receiving old age assistance; states should pay no less than the "standard of need" they themselves have established. Lacking clear standards for assessing these claims, the courts eventually washed their hands of the entire matter. So, too, in effect, did Congress: time and time again, it defeated efforts to establish a nationally uniform benefit level for AFDC. Indeed, almost all federal income maintenance programs avoid the issue of "adequate subsistence" by basing benefit levels on prior earnings or by delegating the determination to the states.

Students of the American welfare state have frequently noted that means-tested programs that provide goods and services tend to be more politically popular than those that provide cash. Sometimes this is because the groups that provide the services constitute a powerful lobby. But this is not always the case. Neither farmers nor retailers have made much effort to push food stamps. Certainly, no one would attribute enactment of medicare and medicaid in 1965 to the support of the American Medical Association. Nonetheless, the public's belief that doctors can prescribe the proper treatment for the ills of the body gives the "right to adequate health care" an appeal that the "right to an adequate subsistence" lacks. The argument that some professions can identify and measure the needs of potential beneficiaries is not by itself enough to turn a claim into a right. But it certainly helps.

Distribution of Costs

Rights can quickly become very expensive. Other things being equal, the greater the responsibility of legislators for providing funding for a program, the less likely they will be to acknowledge broad rights or to give courts a large policymaking role. Members of Congress are more likely to create such rights when subnational governments or the private sector bear the cost than when the cost is recorded in the federal budget.

Here the contrast between education of the disabled and food stamps is illuminating. Both programs grew rapidly during the 1970s. Both received strong support from Congress and the courts. In the early 1980s both were the target of budget cutting by the Reagan administration. Special education remained a sacred cow, but food stamps encountered hard times. Why?

The food stamp program is a creation of the federal government, which bears sole responsibility for its cost. Food stamp spending generally rises during economic hard times, when federal revenues are dropping and the costs of many other programs are increasing. This explains why attacks on the program reached their zenith during the recessions of 1974–75 and 1981–82. Reducing food stamp costs is relatively simple because the program's rules are clearly stated and nationally uniform. Congress can drop cost-of-living adjustments or deductions, broaden the definition of income, or set a gross income ceiling.

The EAHCA, in contrast, imposed new responsibilities on school systems already engaged in the task of educating disabled children. State and local school systems pay over 90 percent of the total cost of special education and 100 percent of marginal costs. Although spending on special education has risen faster than any other part of the state and local education budget over the past two decades, it still constitutes little more than one-tenth of the total spending of these school systems. Just as important, the decentralized nature of decisionmaking for special education makes it hard to evaluate the fiscal consequences of legislative changes. That means it will be hard for legislators to take credit for saving taxpayers' money—or for taxpayer groups to blame legislators for failing to reduce costs. Most efforts to reduce costs will meet with substantial resistance from professional and parent groups—who view the act as their Magna Carta—but will generate little interest among the taxpaying public.

On questions of finance, AFDC falls between these two extremes. The federal government pays about half the cost of the program. Members of Congress often complain about rising AFDC costs and at times have attributed part of the increase to court decisions. States, though, retain substantial control over benefit levels. The Supreme Court's decision in *Rosado* v. *Wyman* left them free to reduce the percentage of the "standard of need" they pay to recipients.[7] In the early 1970s many states did just that, either moving to a percentage reduction system or allowing inflation to eat away at the real value of benefits. When federal spending on AFDC leveled off in 1972, the sense of crisis rapidly dissipated. If Legal Services had won the *Rosado* case, AFDC costs would have risen sharply, and some sort of major revision of the federal law would undoubtedly have followed. In other words, the courts managed to retain extensive control over eligibility standards because they did not try to dictate benefit levels.

Fault and Responsibility

No one argues that disabled children acquire disabilities in order to receive special treatment in school. Indeed, the idea is laughable. Not so amusing is the possibility that wider availability of AFDC benefits might lead teenage girls to have more babies or males of all ages to desert their offspring. Nor can one quickly dismiss the possibility that AFDC and food stamp recipients might work fewer hours or be less diligent in looking for a job. As many writers have pointed out, in the American welfare state the "deservingness" of beneficiaries is linked to an assessment of fault: it is not one's fault to be old or congenitally disabled, but it *might* be one's fault to be unemployed or a single parent.

The categorical welfare system is designed to distinguish—albeit in a very rough and imprecise manner—between those who are poor for reasons beyond their control and those who have contributed to their own impoverishment. That benefits provided by "upper-tier" contributory programs—especially old age insurance and medicare—should be considered "rights" has never been controversial. It is worth noting that the legislation providing benefits to those who served their country in World War II is known as the GI Bill of Rights. The political appeal of rights is substantially weaker in means-tested programs, where questions of fault, responsibility, and incentives remain at center stage.

Of the three programs examined in this book, the problem of incentive is greatest for AFDC. Frequently this issue has dominated the political debate. Critics have argued that the program encourages fathers to desert their children and mothers to substitute welfare for work. In the late 1960s and early 1970s many people believed it was possible to design a guaranteed income that would assist those unable to work, preserve work incentives, and keep families together. Most accounts of the failure of comprehensive welfare reform stress the enormous political damage done by studies linking "income by right" to reduced work effort and higher rates of family breakup.[8] During the 1980s, there were renewed efforts to modify the program to punish some forms of behavior—dropping out of school or having children out of wedlock—and reward others.

For several reasons, the problem of perverse incentives is less severe for the food stamp program than for AFDC. Because all households, including single individuals, are eligible for benefits, the food stamp program does not create incentives for family breakup or for bearing children out of wedlock. Ever since 1970 the program has included an explicit work requirement and a large work incentive. Each of these factors has helped make food stamps more politically popular than AFDC and more readily recognized as a basic right of Americans.

Public opinion on all these matters—personal fault and responsibility, the objectivity of professional judgments, and acceptable levels of public spending—obviously changes over time. In a wide variety of areas, ranging from torts and workers' compensation to labor and environmental law, American law has shifted fault from the individual to society and concomitantly increased the opportunities for appeal to the judiciary.[9] These changes have led Lawrence Friedman to argue that one of the "superprinciples" of modern legal culture is "the general expectation that somebody will pay for any and all calamities that happen to a person, provided only that it is not the victim's 'fault,' or at least not solely his fault."[10] The broad understanding of entitlements employed by judges in many AFDC, food stamp, and EAHCA cases is one corollary of Friedman's superprinciple.

Not all the movement, though, is in one direction. The "new consensus" on welfare policy described in chapter 6 is largely a reassertion of traditional social norms. Indeed, AFDC eligibility policy has become steadily more restrictive over the past twenty years. Food stamp politics has been more cyclical, alternating between alarm over hunger and concern about "waste, fraud, and abuse." The right to a "free appropriate public education" has had a smoother ride. But states that for years had been the leader in expanding rights of the disabled now are looking for ways to contain escalating costs, which will inevitably require circumscribing those rights as presently defined.[11] In short, although each of these three programs has grown significantly over the past three decades, one does not find inevitable or uninterrupted movement toward an expansion of entitlements.

A comparison of the Democratic platforms of 1972 and 1992 suggests that disquiet with a broad, need-based understanding of entitlements is not limited to conservative Republicans. In 1972 expansion of welfare rights was at the heart of the Democratic party's platform. The party was "determined to make economic security a matter of right." The basic rights of Americans, the platform asserted, include "the right to a decent job and an adequate income, with dignity," "the right to quality, accessibility and sufficient quantity in tax-supported services and amenities—including educational opportunity, health care, housing and transportation," and "the right to legal services, both civil and criminal, necessary to enforce secured rights."[12] The 1992 Democratic platform, in contrast, said significantly less about rights and far more about responsibilities. "Our future as a nation," the platform contended, "depends upon the daily assumption of personal responsibility by millions of Americans from all walks of life." In particular, "people who bring children into this world have a responsibility to care for them and give them values, motivation and discipline."[13] One of the themes of the party's standard-bearer, Bill Clinton, was the "new covenant," which emphasized reciprocal responsibilities. In his acceptance speech Clinton told the assembled delegates, "We offer opportunity. We demand responsibility." Government, Clinton proclaimed, should offer "more empowerment and less entitlement."[14]

Underlying many key court decisions and much of the legal scholarship on statutory interpretation is the assumption that one can identify the direction of progress in these programs, and that progress means moving toward a need-based understanding of entitlements. Adopting a "sophisticated and enlightened" approach toward welfare meant jettisoning the heritage of the Elizabethan poor laws, making government programs nationally uniform, less punitive, and noncategorical. "Although poverty may once have been considered an inevitable part of the human condition," one district court judge wrote in a food stamp case, "the modern perspective is that it is a social problem to be eradicated."[15]

The distinction between "the modern" and "the outmoded" is a constant refrain in much of the legal commentary on statutory interpretation. Judges should use interpretation to deal with "the problem of legal obsolescence," to "keep anachronistic laws from governing us," to "take account of the need for statutes to evolve over time," to "create new substantive values to reflect new thinking about justice," and to revise "outmoded statutes" to make them "consistent with current public mores."[16] The most frequent criticism of the Rehnquist court's interpretation of civil rights laws is that its rulings set the clock back, which means, presumably, that they have tried to halt the inevitable movement toward racial equality and justice.

In an essay written shortly before his death, Alexander Bickel wrote of the Warren court, "What informed the enterprise was the idea of progress. There was . . . an aspiration to a transcendent consistency with a preferred past, a striving for fidelity to a true line of progress." Belief in "man-made progress was the new faith, and the supremacy of judges as its carriers and executors was not denied."[17] Since 1970 the "idea of progress" has become less pronounced in constitutional law but has remained deeply embedded in statutory interpretation. As many of the cases discussed in this book show, judges view their task not merely as enforcing the terms of past legislative compromises, but as nudging statutes along their proper evolutionary course. Once the intellectual vanguard points the way, the public and its elected officials will eventually shed their prejudices and tag along.

Yet in all three policy areas the meaning of progress remains illusive. The more closely one looks at these programs, the more apparent their insoluble dilemmas and painful trade-offs become. One advantage of studying the programmatic consequences of court decisions is that it forces one to link legal abstractions with real-world problems. In the splendid isolation of the judge's chamber or the professor's office, it is easy to talk blithely about the direction of history. But in the trenches of governance, reasonable, honest, and well-meaning men and women continue to disagree about which direction is forward.

NOTES

Chapter 1

1. *Bob Jones University* v. *United States*, 461 U.S. 574, 585–86 (1983).

2. *Grove City College* v. *Bell*, 465 U.S. 555 (1984); and P.L. 100-259. The history of the legislation is summarized in *Congressional Quarterly Almanac, 1984*, vol. 40, pp. 239–43, and *1988*, vol. 44, pp. 63–68.

3. These developments are discussed in detail in Jerry L. Mashaw, "Disability Insurance in an Age of Retrenchment: The Politics of Implementing Rights," in Theodore R. Marmor and Jerry L. Mashaw, eds., *Social Security: Beyond the Rhetoric of Crisis* (Princeton University Press, 1988), pp. 166–67; Martha Derthick, *Agency under Stress: The Social Security Administration in American Government* (Brookings, 1990); Edward Berkowitz, *Disabled Policy: America's Programs for the Handicapped* (Cambridge University Press, 1987), chaps. 3, 4; and Susan Gluck Mezey, *No Longer Disabled: The Federal Courts and the Politics of Social Security Disability* (Greenwood Press, 1988).

4. *Wards Cove Packing Co.* v. *Antonio*, 490 U.S. 642 (1989).

5. *Griggs* v. *Duke Power*, 401 U.S. 424, 431 (1971).

6. *Wards Cove* v. *Antonio*, 660.

7. Quoted in *Congressional Quarterly Almanac, 1990*, vol. 46, p. 472.

8. *Congressional Quarterly Almanac, 1991*, vol. 47, p. 259.

9. *Congressional Record*, daily ed., October 25, 1991, pp. S15233–35 (Kennedy); October 29, 1991, pp. S15315–24 (Hatch); November 7, 1991, pp. H9526–32 (Edwards); November 7, 1991, pp. H9533–35 (Ford); November 7, 1991, pp. H9543–49 (Hyde); October 30, 1991, pp. S15472–78 and November 5, 1991, p. S15953 (Dole).

10. *Congressional Record*, daily ed., October 29, 1991, p. S15325.

11. 105 Stat. 1075, sec. 105(b).

12. "Statement on Signing the Civil Rights Act of 1991," *Public Papers of the Presidents of the United States: George Bush*, bk. 2 (Government Printing Office, 1992), p. 1504.

13. *EDF* v. *Ruckelshaus*, 439 F.2d 584 (D.C. Cir. 1971). The changes wrought by this case are described in Angus MacIntyre, "A Court Quietly Rewrote the Federal Pesticide Statute: How Prevalent Is Judicial Statutory Revision?" 7 *Law and Policy* 249 (1985).

14. See R. Shep Melnick, *Regulation and the Courts: The Case of the Clean Air Act* (Brookings, 1983), chap. 4; Khristine L. Hall, "The Control of Toxic Pollutants under the Federal Water Pollution Control Act Amendments of 1972," 63 *Iowa Law Review* 609 (1978); and Frederick R. Anderson, *NEPA in the Courts: A Legal Analysis of the National Environmental Policy Act* (Washington: Resources for the Future, 1973).

15. Abigail M. Thernstrom, *Whose Votes Count? Affirmative Action and Minority Voting Rights* (Harvard University Press, 1987).

16. Among the few political science investigations devoted principally to statutory interpretation are Robert A. Katzmann, ed., *Judges and Legislators: Toward Institutional Comity* (Brookings, 1988); Beth Henshen, "Statutory Interpretations of the Supreme Court: Congressional Response," *American Politics Quarterly*, vol. 11 (October 1983), p. 441; Harry P. Stumpf, "Congressional Response to Supreme Court Rulings: The Interaction of Law and Politics," 14 *Journal of Public Law* 377 (1965); John R. Schmidhauser, Larry L. Berg, and Albert Melone, "The Impact of Judicial Decisions: New Dimensions in Supreme Court-Congressional Relations, 1945–1968," 49 *Washington University Law Quarterly* 209 (1971); and McIntyre, "A Court Quietly Rewrote the Pesticide Statute." Several studies contain detailed and useful examinations of courts' interpretation of particular statutes, particularly Robert A. Katzmann, *Institutional Disability: The Saga of Transportation Policy for the Disabled* (Brookings, 1986); Jerry L. Mashaw and David L. Harfst, *The Struggle for Auto Safety* (Harvard University Press, 1990); Mashaw, *Bureaucratic Justice: Managing Social Security Disability Claims* (Yale University Press, 1983); Thernstrom, *Whose Votes Count?*; Martin Shapiro, *Law and Politics in the Supreme Court* (Free Press, 1964), and the studies of disability insurance cited in note 3.

17. Aristotle, *Politics*, bk. 3, trans. H. Rackham (Harvard University Press, 1967), p. 229.

18. Martin Shapiro, *Courts: A Comparative and Political Analysis* (University of Chicago Press, 1981), p. 118.

19. On the difference between English and American practices, see, for example, Reed Dickerson, *The Interpretation and Application of Statutes* (Little, Brown, 1975), chap. 10; Patricia M. Wald, "Some Observations on the Use of Legislative History in the 1981 Supreme Court Term," 68 *Iowa Law Review* 195, 196–206 (1983); and Kenneth W. Starr, "Observations about the Use of Legislative History," 1987 *Duke Law Journal* 371, 373–74 (1987).

20. Patrick S. Atiyah and Robert S. Summers, *Form and Substance in Anglo-American Law: A Comparative Study in Legal Reasoning, Legal Theory, and Legal Institutions* (Clarendon Press, 1987), pp. 100–01. The following para-

graphs draw heavily from this book, particularly chaps. 1, 4, 11; and from Patrick S. Atiyah, "Judicial-Legislative Relations in England," in Katzmann, ed., *Judges and Legislators*, pp. 129–61.

21. Chief Justice John Marshall in *Marbury* v. *Madison*, 1 Cranch 137, 177 (1803), emphasis added.

22. *Barlow* v. *Collins*, 397 U.S. 159, 166 (1970).

23. *INS* v. *Cardoza-Fonseca*, 480 U.S. 421, 446 (1987). For a more detailed examination of the Supreme Court's changing position on this matter, see chapter 3.

24. Atiyah and Summers, *Form and Substance*, p. 102.

25. *Kelly* v. *Robinson*, 479 U.S. 36, 43 (1986). Justice Lewis Powell quoted from a 1986 case, which in turn quoted a 1956 case that itself quoted a 1949 case.

26. *Griffin* v. *Oceanic Contractors, Inc.*, 458 U.S. 564, 577 (1982) (Stevens dissenting). For example, in *United States* v. *Locke*, 471 U.S. 84, 93, 119 (1985), Stevens claimed that when Congress wrote a statute requiring claims to be filed "before December 31," it really meant that claims must be filed no later than the end of business hours on December 31. Justice Marshall's majority opinion, though, insisted that the statute meant what it said, that is, that the claim must be filed no later than December 30.

27. *Church of the Holy Trinity* v. *United States*, 143 U.S. 457, 459 (1892).

28. *Steelworkers* v. *Weber*, 443 U.S. 193, 201 (1979). For other instances of the Court's use of the *Holy Trinity* case, see *K Mart Corp.* v. *Cartier, Inc.*, 486 U.S. 281, 300 n. 2 (1988); and *California Federal Savings and Loan Association* v. *Guerra*, 479 U.S. 272, 284 (1987).

29. *Public Citizen* v. *Department of Justice*, 491 U.S. 440, 454 (1989), citations and internal quotation marks omitted. The Hand quotation comes from *Cabell* v. *Markham*, 148 F.2d 737, 739 (2d Cir. 1945), emphasis added.

30. Guido Calabresi, *A Common Law for the Age of Statutes* (Harvard University Press, 1982), p. 1.

31. Atiyah and Summers, *Form and Substance*, pp. 299–306; and Atiyah, "Judicial-Legislative Relations in England," pp. 147–59.

32. *Rosado* v. *Wyman*, 397 U.S. 397, 412 (1970).

33. *Calvert Cliffs' Coordinating Committee* v. *AEC*, 449 F.2d 1109, 1111 (D.C. Cir. 1971).

34. *Murray* v. *The Charming Betsy*, 2 Cranch 64, 118 (1804).

35. *Hooper* v. *California*, 155 U.S. 648, 657 (1895).

36. *DeBartolo Corp.* v. *Florida Gulf Coast Trades Council*, 485 U.S. 568, 575 (1988); *Machinists* v. *Street*, 367 U.S. 740 (1961); *Bill Johnson's Restaurants Inc.* v. *NLRB*, 461 U.S. 731 (1983); *St. Martin Evangelical Lutheran Church* v. *South Dakota*, 451 U.S. 772 (1981); and *Regan* v. *Wald*, 468 U.S. 222 (1984).

37. *NLRB* v. *Catholic Bishop of Chicago*, 440 U.S. 490, 509 (1978). Judge Richard A. Posner makes a similar point in *Federal Courts: Crisis and Reform* (Harvard University Press, 1985), p. 285.

38. For an extended discussion of the nature and consequences of these conflicting sources of law, see Atiyah and Summers, *Form and Substance*, pp. 59–69.

39. See Peter L. Strauss, "One Hundred Fifty Cases Per Year: Some Implications of the Supreme Court's Limited Resources for Judicial Review of Agency Action," 87 *Columbia Law Review* 1093 (1987); and chapter 11.

40. Commonwealth Club Address, September 23, 1932, in Franklin D. Roosevelt, *Public Papers and Addresses*, vol. 1 (Random House, 1938), p. 756. On the significance of Roosevelt's claim, see Sidney M. Milkis, "The Presidency, Policy Reform, and the Rise of Administrative Politics," in Sidney Milkis and Richard Harris, eds., *Remaking American Politics* (Westview, 1989), pp. 148-87.

41. *Gray v. Powell*, 314 U.S. 402, 413 (1941).

42. *NLRB v. Hearst Publications*, 322 U.S. 111, 130 (1944). Also see Justice Frankfurter's majority opinion in *O'Leary v. Brown-Pacific-Maxon, Inc.*, 340 U.S. 504 (1951).

43. James M. Landis, "A Note on 'Statutory Interpretation,'" 43 *Harvard Law Review* 886, 891 (1930).

44. The best accounts of these changes are Richard B. Stewart, "The Reformation of American Administrative Law," 88 *Harvard Law Review* 1669 (1975); and Martin Shapiro, *Who Guards the Guardians? Judicial Control of Administration* (University of Georgia Press, 1988). On the use of legislative history, see Jorge L. Carro and Andrew R. Brann, "The U.S. Supreme Court and the Use of Legislative Histories: A Statistical Analysis," 22 *Jurimetrics Journal* 294 (1982); and Note, "Intent, Clear Statements, and the Common Law: Statutory Interpretation in the Supreme Court," 95 *Harvard Law Review* 892 (1982). This is discussed in greater detail in chapter 3.

45. Melnick, "The Courts, Congress, and Programmatic Rights," in Milkis and Harris, eds., *Remaking American Politics*, pp. 188-212.

46. State of the Union Address, 1944, in Roosevelt, *Public Papers and Addresses*, vol. 13 (Random House, 1950), p. 41; and campaign address of October 28, 1944, in Alan Pifer and Forrest Chisman, eds., *The Report of the Committee on Economic Security of 1935: 50th Anniversary Edition* (Washington: National Conference on Social Welfare, 1985), pp. 150-56.

47. *Chevron v. NRDC*, 467 U.S. 837, 843–44 (1984), emphasis added.

48. The extent of compliance and noncompliance with the *Chevron* standard is discussed at length in Peter H. Schuck and E. Donald Elliott, "To the *Chevron* Station: An Empirical Study of Federal Administrative Law," 1990 *Duke Law Journal* 984 (1990); and Richard J. Pierce, "Two Problems in Administrative Law: Political Polarity on the District of Columbia Circuit and Judicial Deterrence of Agency Rulemaking," 1988 *Duke Law Journal* 300 (1988). As chapters 5 and 8 will show, over the past ten years the lower courts have become more deferential in AFDC cases, but not in cases involving education of the handicapped.

49. See chapter 3.

50. The quotations come from *Blanchard v. Bergeron*, 489 U.S. 87, 98 (1989) (Scalia concurring). Also see his opinions in *INS v. Cardoza-Fonseca*; *Hirschey v.*

FERC, 777 F.2d 1, 7–8 (D.C. Cir. 1985); and *Conroy* v. *Aniskoff*, 123 L. Ed 2d 229 (1993).

51. *Statutory Interpretation and the Uses of Legislative History*, Hearings before the Subcommittee on Courts, Intellectual Property, and the Administration of Justice, House Committee on the Judiciary, 101 Cong. 2 sess. (GPO, 1990), pp. 6–7.

52. *West Virginia University Hospital* v. *Casey* 113 L. Ed 2d 68, 92 (1991).

53. Quoted in Joan Biskupic, "Scalia Takes a Narrow View in Seeking Congress's Will," *Congressional Quarterly Weekly Report*, March 24, 1990, p. 913.

54. *Statutory Interpretation and the Uses of Legislative History*, Hearings, p. 2.

55. Karl N. Llewellyn, "Remarks on the Theory of Appellate Decision and the Rules or Canons about How Statutes Are to be Construed," 3 *Vanderbilt Law Review* 395, 401, 405 (1950).

56. Felix Frankfurter, "Some Reflections on the Reading of Statutes," 47 *Columbia Law Review* 527, 530 (1947). The authors of a current casebook note that "almost everyone . . . seems to use the canons to support their interpretations of statutes," yet "almost everybody thinks the canons are bunk." William Eskridge, Jr., and Philip P. Frickey, *Cases and Materials on Legislation* (West, 1988), p. 639.

57. Daniel A. Farber, "Statutory Interpretation and Legislative Supremacy," 78 *Georgetown Law Review* 281 (1989). The recent law review literature is enormous. Collections of essays on the subject can be found in 89 *Columbia Law Review* 369 (1989); 1987 *Duke Law Journal* 362 (1987); and 78 *Georgetown Law Journal* 281 (1989). Other prominent works include William N. Eskridge, Jr., "Public Values in Statutory Interpretation," 137 *University of Pennsylvania Law Review* 1007 (1989); Eskridge, "Dynamic Statutory Interpretation," 135 *University of Pennsylvania Law Review* 1479 (1987); Cass Sunstein, *After the Rights Revolution* (Harvard University Press, 1990); Sunstein, "Interpreting Statutes in the Regulatory State," 103 *Harvard Law Review* 405 (1989); Frank Easterbrook "Statutes' Domains," 50 *University of Chicago Law Review* 533 (1983); Patricia Wald, "The Sizzling Sleeper: The Use of Legislative History in Construing Statutes in the 1988–89 Term of the United States Supreme Court," 39 *American University Law Review* 277 (1990); Colin S. Diver, "Statutory Interpretation in the Administrative State," 133 *University of Pennsylvania Law Review* 549 (1985); Daniel A. Farber and Philip P. Frickey, "Legislative Intent and Public Choice," 74 *Virginia Law Review* 423 (1988); and Richard A. Posner, "Statutory Interpretation—In the Classroom and in the Courtroom," 50 *University of Chicago Law Review* 800 (1983). Posner provides a lengthy bibliography at the end of "Legislation and Its Interpretation: A Primer," 68 *Nebraska Law Review* 431 (1989).

58. One recent exception is William N. Eskridge, Jr., "Overriding Supreme Court Statutory Decisions," 101 *Yale Law Review* 331 (1991). Eskridge shows that Congress frequently responds to court interpretations of federal statutes,

overturning on average more than ten a year. This is the most ambitious attempt so far to collect data on the congressional response to court decisions.

Chapter 2

1. Robert Kagan, "Adversarial Legalism and American Government," *Journal of Policy Analysis and Management*, vol. 10, no. 3 (1991), p. 392.

2. Steven S. Smith, *Call to Order: Floor Politics in the House and Senate* (Brookings, 1989), chaps. 2, 5.

3. Five collections of essays provide detailed descriptions of these changes: Anthony King, ed., *The New American Political System* (American Enterprise Institute, 1978); King, ed., *The New American Political System*, 2d version (American Enterprise Institute, 1990); Sidney Milkis and Richard Harris, eds., *Remaking American Politics* (Westview, 1989); R. Shep Melnick, Robert A. Kagan, Paul J. Quirk, and John W. Ellwood, "Symposium on the New Politics of Public Policy," *Journal of Policy Analysis and Management*, vol. 10 (Summer 1991), pp. 363-433; and John E. Chubb and Paul E. Peterson, eds., *The New Direction in American Politics* (Brookings, 1985).

4. James Q. Wilson, "American Politics, Then and Now," *Commentary*, vol. 67 (February 1979), p. 41.

5. Robert A. Katzmann, *Institutional Disability: The Saga of Transportation Policy for the Disabled* (Brookings, 1986), pp. 106-20.

6. A large literature describes these changes in Congress. See, for example, Lawrence C. Dodd and Bruce I. Oppenheimer, eds., *Congress Reconsidered*, 3d ed. (CQ Press, 1985); Thomas E. Mann and Norman J. Ornstein, eds., *The New Congress* (American Enterprise Institute, 1981); James L. Sundquist, *The Decline and Resurgence of Congress* (Brookings, 1981); and Gary Orfield, *Congressional Power: Congress and Social Change* (Harcourt Brace Jovanovich, 1975).

7. Richard P. Nathan, *The Administrative Presidency* (Wiley, 1983); and Sidney M. Milkis, *The Presidents and the Parties: The Transformation of the American Party System since the New Deal* (Oxford University Press, 1993), chaps. 9-11.

8. These changes are described in Joel D. Aberbach, *Keeping a Watchful Eye: The Politics of Congressional Oversight* (Brookings, 1990); and Christopher H. Foreman, Jr., *Signals from the Hill: Congressional Oversight and the Challenge of Social Regulation* (Yale University Press, 1988).

9. *INS v. Chadha*, 462 U.S. 919 (1983); and Louis Fisher, "Judicial Misjudgments about the Lawmaking Process: The Legislative Veto Case," *Public Administration Review*, vol. 45 (November 1985), p. 705.

10. Robert Salisbury, "Interest Groups in Washington," in King, ed., *The New American Political System*, 2d version, pp. 208-09.

11. Quoted in Hedrick Smith, *The Power Game: How Washington Works* (Ballantine, 1989), p. 445.

12. Anthony King develops this theme in "The American Polity in the 1990s," in King, ed., *The New American Political System*, 2d version, pp. 287-305.

13. Heclo, "One Executive Branch or Many?" in Anthony King, ed., *Both Ends of the Avenue: The Presidency, the Executive Branch, and Congress in the 1980s* (American Enterprise Institute, 1983), pp. 32–33.

14. This is best illustrated in Robert Katzmann's insightful study of the legislative history of section 504, *Institutional Disability*, chap. 2.

15. James Q. Wilson, *Bureaucracy: What Government Agencies Do and Why They Do It* (Basic Books, 1989), chaps. 3, 9, 18.

16. Environmental and Energy Study Institute and the Environmental Law Institute, "Statutory Deadlines in Environmental Legislation: Necessary But Need Improvement," Washington, September 1985, p. 11.

17. Clean Air Act, P.L. 101-594, sec. 163(b)(1).

18. *Regulatory Federalism: Policy, Process, Impact and Reform* (Washington: Advisory Commission on Intergovernmental Relations, 1984), p. 1, emphasis in original.

19. Thomas J. Anton, *American Federalism and Public Policy: How the System Works* (Random House, 1989), p. 187.

20. Voting Rights Act, 42 U.S.C. 1973(c); Endangered Species Act of 1973, 16 U.S.C. 1540(g); Clean Air Act, 42 U.S.C. 1857h-2; Federal Water Pollution Control Act, 33 U.S.C. 1365; Energy Policy and Conservation Act, 42 U.S.C. 6305; Noise Control Act of 1972, 42 U.S.C. 4911; Futures Trading Act, 7 U.S.C. 25; Toxic Substances Control Act, 15 U.S.C. 2618(a); Consumer Product Safety Commission, 15 U.S.C. 2062; and Occupational Safety and Health Act, 29 U.S.C. 660(a).

21. Robert A. Dahl, *Pluralist Democracy in the United States: Conflict and Consent* (Rand McNally, 1967), p. 156. Dahl first presented this argument in "Decision-Making in a Democracy: The Role of the Supreme Court as a National Policymaker," 6 *Journal of Public Law* 279 (1957).

22. See Jonathan D. Casper, "The Supreme Court and National Policy Making," *American Political Science Review*, vol. 70 (March 1976), pp. 50–63; and William Lasser, "The Supreme Court in Periods of Critical Realignment," *Journal of Politics*, vol. 47 (November 1985), pp. 1174–87.

23. Martin Shapiro, "The Supreme Court from Early Burger to Early Rehnquist," in King, ed., *The New American Political System*, 2d version, p. 60.

24. This is most evident for the second most important court in the country, the D.C. Circuit. See Richard J. Pierce, Jr., "Two Problems in Administrative Law: Political Polarity on the District of Columbia Circuit and Judicial Deterrence of Agency Rulemaking," 1988 *Duke Law Journal* 300 (1988).

25. Archibald Cox, *The Court and the Constitution* (Houghton Mifflin, 1987), p. 182.

26. Philip B. Kurland, *Politics and the Constitution and the Warren Court* (University of Chicago Press, 1970), p. 98.

27. "The Rootless Activism of the Burger Court," in Vincent Blasi, ed., *The Burger Court: The Counter-Revolution That Wasn't* (Yale University Press, 1983), p. 211. Martin Shapiro sounds a similar theme in "The Supreme Court from Early Burger to Early Rehnquist," p. 59.

28. Donald L. Horowitz, *The Courts and Social Policy* (Brookings, 1977), p. 13.

29. *Wyatt* v. *Stickney*, 325 F. Supp. 781 (M.D. Ala. 1971).

30. See Phillip J. Cooper, *Hard Judicial Choices: Federal District Court Judges and State and Local Officials* (Oxford University Press, 1988); Robert C. Wood, ed., *Remedial Law: When Courts Become Administrators* (University of Massachusetts Press, 1990); and John J. DiIulio, Jr., *Courts, Corrections and the Constitution: The Impact of Judicial Intervention on Prisons and Jails* (Oxford University Press, 1990).

31. Richard Stewart, "The Reformation of American Administrative Law" 88 *Harvard Law Review* 1667 (1975); and Antonin Scalia, "Vermont Yankee, the D.C. Circuit, and the Supreme Court," in Philip B. Kurland and Gerhard Casper, eds., *1978 Supreme Court Review* (University of Chicago Press, 1979), p. 345.

32. W. John Moore, "Righting the Courts," *National Journal*, January 25, 1992, p. 200. See also David M. O'Brien, "The Reagan Judges: His Most Enduring Legacy?" in Charles O. Jones, ed., *The Reagan Legacy: Promise and Performance* (Chatham House, 1988), pp. 60–101; and Al Kamen and Ruth Marcus, "The Next Species for the Endangered List: Liberal Judges," *Washington Post National Weekly Edition*, February 6–12, 1989, p. 31. Ronald Reagan surpassed Carter's record by appointing 379 judges to the various levels of the federal court system.

33. *Rodway* v. *USDA*, 514 F.2d 809 (D.C. Cir. 1975).

Chapter 3

1. *Overview of Entitlement Programs: Background Material and Data on Programs within the Jurisdiction of the Committee on Ways and Means, 1991 Green Book*, Committee Print, House Committee on Ways and Means, 102 Cong. 1 sess. (Government Printing Office, 1991), p. 1511.

2. Quoted in R. Kent Weaver, "Controlling Entitlements," in John E. Chubb and Paul E. Peterson, eds., *The New Direction in American Politics* (Brookings, 1985), p. 308, emphasis added.

3. *Goldberg* v. *Kelly*, 397 U.S. 254, 262 n. 8, 265 (1970).

4. *Shapiro* v. *Thompson*, 394 U.S. 618 (1969).

5. On gender, see *Weinberger* v. *Wiesenfeld*, 420 U.S. 636 (1975); *Califano* v. *Goldfarb*, 430 U.S. 199 (1977); and *Califano* v. *Westcott*, 443 U.S. 76 (1979). On illegitimacy and marital status, see *Weber* v. *Aetna Casualty and Surety Co.*, 406 U.S. 164 (1972); *Jimenez* v. *Weinberger*, 417 U.S. 628 (1974); *U.S. Department of Agriculture* v. *Moreno*, 413 U.S. 528 (1973); and *New Jersey Welfare Rights Organization* v. *Cahill*, 411 U.S. 619 (1973).

6. Susan E. Lawrence, *The Poor in Court: The Legal Services Program and Supreme Court Decision Making* (Princeton, 1990), pp. 98–104.

7. The key cases were *Dandridge* v. *Williams*, 397 U.S. 471 (1970); and *Jefferson* v. *Hackney*, 406 U.S. 535 (1972).

8. There is a huge literature on this subject. Among the best-known and most useful law review articles are Charles A. Reich, "The New Property," 73 *Yale Law Journal* 733 (1964), and "Individual Rights and Social Welfare: The Emerging Legal Issues," 74 *Yale Law Journal* 1245 (1965); William W. Van Alstyne, "The Demise of the Right–Privilege Distinction in Constitutional Law," 81 *Harvard Law Review* 1439 (1968), and "Cracks in the 'New Property': Adjudicative Due Process in the Administrative State," 62 *Cornell Law Review* 445 (1977); Rodney A. Smolla, "The Reemergence of the Right–Privilege Distinction in Constitutional Law: The Price of Protecting Too Much," 35 *Stanford Law Review* 69 (1982); Arthur B. LaFrance, *Welfare Law: Structure and Entitlement: In a Nutshell* (West Publishing, 1979), pp. 82–94; and Rand E. Rosenblatt, "Legal Entitlement and Welfare Benefits," in David Kairys, ed., *The Politics of Law: A Progressive Critique* (Pantheon Books, 1982).

9. Pre-1960 court action is described in Louis L. Jaffe, *Judicial Control of Administrative Action* (Little, Brown, 1965), pp. 176–92; and *West's Federal Digest, 1940–1960* (West Publishing, 1960), pp. 39–61. On war risk insurance, see Deborah A. Stone, *The Disabled State* (Temple University Press, 1984), pp. 72–75.

10. Quoted in Martha Derthick, *Policymaking for Social Security* (Brookings, 1979), p. 31.

11. See, for example, the following cases: *Walker* v. *Altmeyer*, 137 F.2d 531 (2d Cir. 1943); *O'Leary* v. *Social Security Board*, 153 F.2d 704 (3d Cir. 1946); *U.S.* v. *LaLone*, 152 F.2d 43 (9th Cir. 1945); *Social Security Board* v. *Warren*, 142 F.2d 974 (8th Cir. 1944); and *Schroeder* v. *Hobby*, 222 F.2d 713 (10th Cir. 1955). It should be noted that the client-serving ethos of the Social Security Board helps explain why so few of its decisions were overturned. In close cases the board usually sided with alleged beneficiaries.

One famous social security case, *Flemming* v. *Nestor*, 363 U.S. 603 (1960), is frequently cited as evidence of the vitality of the rights-privilege distinction. The issue in this case, though, was not whether Nestor had been deprived of a benefit conferred by statute, but whether Congress could by statute deny him a benefit that he claimed he had earned by contributing payroll taxes to the social security trust fund. Ironically, if Nestor and the liberal dissenters on the Court had prevailed in their argument that benefits should be based on contribution, the redistributive aspects of the social security system would have been seriously threatened.

12. I have borrowed the term "gatekeeper" from Deborah Stone. Her book *The Disabled State* (pp. xi, 3–28) provides a particularly good description of this form of highly discretionary entitlement program.

13. *Lietz* v. *Flemming*, 264 F.2d 311, 314 (6th Cir. 1959).

14. Richard B. Stewart, "The Reformation of American Administrative Law," 88 *Harvard Law Review* 1669 (1975).

15. Martha Derthick, *Agency under Stress: The Social Security Administration in American Government* (Brookings, 1990), chap. 7.

16. *National Welfare Rights Organization* v. *Finch*, 429 F.2d 725 (D.C. Cir. 1970).

17. Cases in which these requirements were applied to welfare programs include *National Welfare Rights Organization* v. *Mathews*, 533 F.2d (D.C. Cir. 1976); *Maryland* v. *Mathews*, 415 F. Supp. 1206 (D.D.C. 1976); and *Rodway* v. *USDA*, 514 F.2d 809 (D.C. Cir. 1975) (discussed at length in chapter 10).

18. Stewart, "Reformation of American Administrative Law," p. 1712.

19. Martin Shapiro, *Who Guards the Guardians? Judicial Control of Administration* (University of Georgia Press, 1988), p. 54. This point is also developed in R. Shep Melnick, "The Politics of Partnership," *Public Administration Review* vol. 45 (November 1985), pp. 653–60.

20. *Environmental Defense Fund* v. *Ruckelshaus*, 439 F.2d 584, 598 (D.C. Cir. 1971).

21. *Arizona* v. *Hobby*, 221 F.2d 498 (D.C. Cir. 1954). Remarkably, the judge who wrote this decision was none other than David Bazelon, the author of the *Environmental Defense Fund* v. *Ruckelshaus* opinion quoted above.

22. Note, "Making the Old Federalism Work: Section 1983 and the Rights of Grant-in-Aid Beneficiaries," 92 *Yale Law Journal* 1001, 1003 (1983).

23. *J. I. Case Co.* v. *Borak*, 377 U.S. 426 (1964).

24. Ibid., 432, 433, emphasis added.

25. Richard B. Stewart and Cass R. Sunstein, "Public Programs and Private Rights," 95 *Harvard Law Review* 1195, 1196 (1982).

26. *Maine* v. *Thiboutot*, 448 U.S. 1 (1980).

27. *Cannon* v. *University of Chicago*, 441 U.S. 677, 741 (1979) (Powell dissenting).

28. Stewart and Sunstein, "Public Programs and Private Rights," 1196–97.

29. Motion for leave to file brief amicus curiae and brief amicus curiae of the Columbia Center on Social Welfare Policy and Law, *Jefferson* v. *Hackney* (N.D. Tex. Civil Action 3-3012-b), p. 6. The center was very concerned about the fact that the district court had enjoined the state of Texas from receiving federal funds until the state complied with the court order.

30. Another Supreme Court decision, *Rosado* v. *Wyman*, 397 U.S. 397 (1970), also made it easier for recipients to pursue their claims in federal court. The Court ruled that those challenging state rules need not exhaust administrative remedies before initiating litigation. Given the limited resources of Legal Services and recipient organizations and the length and complexity of administrative proceedings, this was extremely important. See LaFrance, *Welfare Law*, pp. 49–60.

Not until 1979 did the Court discuss the nature of relief appropriate in entitlement cases. *Califano* v. *Westcott* found unconstitutional a provision that established different employment rules for mothers and fathers. It then ordered the states to extend benefits to those families in which the mother was unemployed. Four dissenters agreed that the law violated the Fourteenth Amendment, but argued that the proper remedy was to enjoin "any further payment of benefits under the provision found to be unconstitutional" (94). The majority maintained that "equitable considerations surely support" the lower courts' choice of "extension rather than invalidation" (90). This is a good brief statement of the general attitude of the federal courts on remedies.

31. *King* v. *Smith*, 392 U.S. 309, 312 n. 3 (1968), emphasis added.

32. *Hagans* v. *Lavine*, 415 U.S. 528, 534–35 n. 5, 537, 541 (1974).

33. Alan W. Houseman, "A Short Review of Past Poverty Law Advocacy," *Clearinghouse Review*, vol. 23 (April 1990), p. 1516.

34. *Citizens to Preserve Overton Park* v. *Volpe*, 401 U.S. 402, 412 n. 29 (1971). This led legal scholar Reed Dickerson to remark that "the courts' currently widespread use of federal legislative materials is professionally shocking . . . even those who have become inured to American excesses were recently jolted when the Supreme Court came close to turning a piece of Canadian ridicule into a principle of American jurisprudence." Reed Dickerson, *The Interpretation and Application of Statutes* (Little, Brown, 1975), pp. 163-64.

35. Jorge L. Carro and Andrew R. Brann, "The U.S. Supreme Court and the Use of Legislative Histories: A Statistical Analysis," 22 *Jurimetrics Journal* 294, 303 (1982).

36. Patricia M. Wald, "Some Observations on the Use of Legislative History in the 1981 Supreme Court Term," 68 *Iowa Law Review* 195 (1983), emphasis in original.

37. Patricia M. Wald, "The Sizzling Sleeper: The Use of Legislative History in Construing Statutes in the 1988–89 Term of the United States Supreme Court," 39 *American University Law Review* 277, 288 (1990), emphasis deleted.

38. *Schwegmann Bros.* v. *Calvert Distillers Corp.*, 341 U.S. 384, 396 (1951).

39. Wald, "Some Observations," 214, 216.

40. Abner J. Mikva, "A Reply to Judge Starr's Observations," 1987 *Duke Law Review* 380, 383, 386 (1987), emphasis added.

41. See Robert A. Katzmann, "Summary of Proceedings," in Katzmann, ed., *Judges and Legislators: Toward Institutional Comity* (Brookings, 1988), pp. 170–75.

42. *Brown* v. *Bates*, 363 F. Supp. 897, 902–03 (N.D. Ohio 1973), emphasis added.

43. Sylvia Law, "Poverty and the Good Society," 12 *Cardozo Law Review* 1817, 1821 (1991).

44. *Social Security Amendments of 1970*, S. Rept. 91-1431, 91 Cong. 2 sess. (GPO, 1970), p. 357.

45. *Arnett* v. *Kennedy*, 416 U.S. 134, 153–54 (1974). This was a plurality rather than a majority opinion. Rehnquist also presented this view in his majority opinion in *Califano* v. *Boles*, 443 U.S. 282 (1979).

46. *Atkins* v. *Parker*, 472 U.S. 115, 146 (1985).

47. *Holman* v. *Block*, 823 F.2d 56, 59 n. 4 (4th Cir. 1987). The other cases are *Banks* v. *Block*, 700 F.2d 292 (6th Cir. 1983), and *Jackson* v. *Jackson*, 857 F.2d 951 (4th Cir. 1988).

48. *Banks* v. *Block*, cert. denied, 464 U.S. 934 (1983).

49. Smolla, "Reemergence of the Right-Privilege Distinction," pp. 90–94; and Van Alstyne, "Cracks in the 'New Property.'"

50. Reich, "Individual Rights and Social Welfare," 1256.

51. Ibid., 1255–56. Reich's article entitled "The New Property" is far and away the most frequently cited article ever published by the prestigious *Yale Law*

Journal. His "Individual Rights and Social Welfare" is number ten. Fred R. Shapiro, "The Most-Cited Articles from the *Yale Law Journal*," 100 *Yale Law Journal* 1449 (1991).

52. *American Constitutional Law,* 1st ed. (Foundation Press, 1978), p. 1118.

53. *King* v. *Smith,* 330. Susan Lawrence's figures show that *King* v. *Smith* is one of the most frequently cited of the Supreme Court's welfare decisions. *The Poor in Court,* p. 129.

54. *Doe* v. *Shapiro,* 302 F. Supp. 761, 765 (D. Conn. 1969).

55. *Jamroz* v. *Blum,* 509 F. Supp. 953, 959 (N.D. N.Y. 1981).

56. *Rush* v. *Smith,* 573 F.2d 110, 118 (2d Cir. 1978).

57. *Board of Regents* v. *Roth,* 408 U.S. 564, 588–89 (1972), Marshall dissenting. This statement is made all the more striking by the fact that the case did not involve just any government job, but a state university's failure to renew the contract of a nontenured faculty member.

58. *New York* v. *Dublino,* 413 U.S. 405, 432, 431 (1973).

59. *Miller* v. *Youakim,* 440 U.S. 125, 133–34 (1979). Justice Marshall wrote for a unanimous court. This case is discussed in chapter 5.

60. *USDA* v. *Moreno,* 413 U.S. 528, 534 (1973), emphasis in original.

61. *Van Lare* v. *Hurley,* 421 U.S. 338, 348 (1975).

62. *Bowen* v. *Gilliard,* 483 U.S. 587, 610 (1987). For an extended and critical review of Brennan's opinions on privacy and the family, see Robert K. Faulkner, "Difficulties of Equal Dignity: The Court and the Family," in Robert A. Goldwin and William A. Schambra, eds., *The Constitution, the Courts, and the Quest for Justice* (American Enterprise Institute, 1989), pp. 93–114.

Justice Marshall adopted Brennan's line of reasoning in several food stamp cases. He argued that a rule that included parents and all their children within the eligible "household" violates the due process clause of the Fifth Amendment because it inhibited "members of a family from dining as they choose." Echoing Justice Douglas's well-known words about protecting the privacy of the "marital bedroom," Marshall stated, "The Government has thus chosen to intrude into the family dining room—a place where I would have thought the right to privacy exists in its strongest form." *Lyng* v. *Castillo,* 477 U.S. 635, 645 (1986). In another food stamp case he argued that a law prohibiting strikers' families from receiving benefits was unconstitutional because "their need for nourishment is in no logical way diminished by the striker's action" and passage of the ban is based entirely on "public animus toward strikers." *Lyng* v. *Automobile Workers,* 485 U.S. 360, 377, 383 (1988). In an earlier case he argued that the government may not "wield its economic whip" when "the effect is to cause a deprivation to needy dependent children in order to correct an arguable fault of their parents." *Dandridge* v. *Williams,* 525.

63. Henry J. Aaron, "Six Welfare Questions Still Searching for Answers," *Brookings Review,* vol. 3 (Fall 1984), pp. 13–14.

64. Ibid., p. 13.

65. Bill Cavala and Aaron Wildavsky, "The Political Feasibility of Income by Right," *Public Policy,* vol. 18 (Spring 1970), pp. 321–54; and Herbert McClosky and John Zaller, *The American Ethos: Public Attitudes toward Capitalism and*

Democracy (Harvard University Press, 1984), pp. 84, 109, 226. Also see Sidney Verba and Gary R. Orren, *Equality in America: The View from the Top* (Harvard University Press, 1985).

66. Quoted in Lawrence M. Mead, *The New Politics of Poverty: The Non-working Poor in America* (Basic Books, 1992), p. 59.

67. *Chevron* v. *NRDC*, 467 U.S. 837 (1984).

68. *Pennhurst State School* v. *Halderman*, 451 U.S. 1 (1981); and *Atascadero State Hospital* v. *Scanlon*, 473 U.S. 234 (1985).

69. See, for example, *Middlesex County Sewage Authority* v. *National Sea Clammers Association*, 453 U.S. 1 (1981); and *Touche Ross and Co.* v. *Redington*, 442 U.S. 560 (1979).

Chapter 4

1. *Overview of Entitlement Programs: Background Material and Data on Programs within the Jurisdiction of the Committee on Ways and Means, 1992 Green Book*, Committee Print, House Committee on Ways and Means, 102 Cong. 2 sess. (Government Printing Office, 1992), p. 657 (hereinafter cited as *1992 Green Book*).

2. Margaret Weir, Ann Shola Orloff, and Theda Skocpol, *The Politics of Social Policy in the United States* (Princeton University Press, 1988), p. 4.

3. The figures on benefit levels come from the *1992 Green Book*, pp. 638–39. Since 1961 states have had the option of providing benefits to families in which the primary wage earner is present in the home but unemployed. Less than 10 percent of AFDC households fall within the AFDC-UP (unemployed parent) category (*1992 Green Book*, p. 653). The principal reason is that to qualify as "unemployed" one must show a substantial previous attachment to the work force. In 1988 Congress mandated AFDC-UP for all states. As a result, the number of AFDC-UP families will probably increase somewhat over the next few years.

4. Charles Murray, *Losing Ground: American Social Policy, 1950–1980* (Basic Books, 1984), chaps. 12, 13. Some of the weaknesses of Murray's influential argument are pointed out by David Ellwood and Lawrence Summers in "Is Welfare Really the Problem?" *The Public Interest*, no. 83 (Spring 1986), pp. 57–78; and Christopher Jencks, *Rethinking Social Policy: Race, Poverty, and the Underclass* (Harvard University Press, 1992), chap. 2.

5. *Shapiro* v. *Thompson*, 394 U.S. 618 (1969); and *Goldberg* v. *Kelly*, 397 U.S. 254 (1970). The former struck down state residency requirements; the latter called for pretermination hearings.

6. *Dandridge* v. *Williams*, 397 U.S. 471, 486 (1970). Two years later the Supreme Court reiterated this argument in *Jefferson* v. *Hackney*, 406 U.S. 535 (1972). The initial success and ultimate failure of this effort at constitutionally based welfare reform is described in Samuel Krislov, "The OEO Lawyers Fail to Constitutionalize a Right to Welfare: A Study in the Uses and Limits of the Judicial Process," 58 *Minnesota Law Review* 211 (1973).

7. *Rosado* v. *Wyman*, 397 U.S. 397 (1970). This litigation is discussed in detail in chapter 5. On the jurisdictional issues, see chapter 3.

8. *Lewis* v. *Martin*, 397 U.S. 552 (1970). This case is discussed in chapter 5.

9. *King* v. *Smith*, 392 U.S. 309 (1968).

10. *Carleson* v. *Remillard*, 406 U.S. 598, 601 (1972).

11. Ira C. Lupu, "Welfare and Federalism: AFDC Eligibility Policies and the Scope of State Discretion," 57 *Boston University Law Review* 1, 20–21 (1977).

12. Edwin E. Witte, *The Development of the Social Security Act* (University of Wisconsin Press, 1962), p. 164.

13. "Report of the Committee on Economic Security," reprinted in *The Report of the Committee on Economic Security of 1935: 50th Anniversary Edition* (Washington: National Conference on Social Welfare, 1985), p. 27.

14. Frances Perkins, *The Roosevelt I Knew* (Harper Colophon, 1946), p. 284.

15. Gilbert Y. Steiner, *Social Insecurity: The Politics of Welfare* (Rand Mc-Nally, 1966), chap. 2 and p. 114; and Lester M. Salamon, *Welfare: The Elusive Consensus: Where We Are, How We Got There, and What's Ahead* (Praeger, 1978), p. 72.

16. Wilbur J. Cohen, "The Social Security Act of 1935: Reflections Fifty Years Later," in *The Report of the Committee on Economic Security of 1935: The 50th Anniversary Edition*, p. 9.

17. *Social Security Bill*, S. Rept. 74-628, 74 Cong. 1 sess. (GPO, 1935), p. 36; and *Social Security Bill*, H. Rept. 74-615, 74 Cong. 1 sess. (GPO, 1935), p. 24.

18. *Social Security Bill*, S. Rept. 74-628, pp. 4, 19.

19. Martha Derthick describes the powerful ethos of the Social Security Administration in *Policymaking for Social Security* (Brookings, 1979), chap. 1.

20. Steiner, *Social Insecurity*, p. 133.

21. Steiner, *Social Insecurity*, pp. 96–97.

22. Martha Derthick, *Influence of Federal Grants: Public Assistance in Massachusetts* (Harvard University Press, 1970), p. 74.

23. The most complete discussion of suitable-home provisions and HEW policy on them is Winifred Bell, *Aid to Dependent Children* (Columbia University Press, 1965).

24. *Public Welfare Amendments of 1962*, S. Rept. 87-1589, 87 Cong. 2 sess. (GPO, 1962), cited in *U.S. Code Congressional and Administrative News* (1962), p. 1971.

25. Steiner, *Social Insecurity*, p. 101.

26. Martin Rein and Hugh Heclo, "What Welfare Crisis?—A Comparison among the United States, Britain, and Sweden," *The Public Interest*, no. 33 (Fall 1973), p. 61; and *Overview of Entitlement Programs: Background Material and Data on Programs within the Jurisdiction of the Committee on Ways and Means, 1991 Green Book*, Committee Print, House Committee on Ways and Means, 102 Cong. 1 sess. (GPO, 1991), p. 621.

27. Commencement address at Howard University, June 4, 1965, in Richard and Beatrice K. Hofstadter, *Great Issues in American History: From Reconstruction to the Present Day, 1864–1981* (Vintage, 1982), p. 463.

28. Gilbert Y. Steiner, *The State of Welfare* (Brookings, 1971), pp. 111–13.

29. Daniel P. Moynihan, "The Crisis in Welfare," in *Coping: Essays on the Practice of Government* (Random House, 1973), pp. 151–54. This article was first presented at a conference in March 1967.

30. Steiner, *The State of Welfare*, pp. 106–10.

31. Martha Derthick, *Uncontrollable Spending for Social Services Grants* (Brookings, 1975), p. 24.

32. Irene Lurie, "Legislative, Administrative, and Judicial Changes in the AFDC Program, 1967–71," in *Studies in Public Welfare*, Committee Print, Joint Economic Committee, 92 Cong. 2 sess. (GPO, 1972), p. 73.

33. "Back to Barbarism," *Washington Post*, August 18, 1967, p. A20; and Moynihan, "Crisis in Welfare," p. 134.

34. *Congressional Record*, daily ed., August 17, 1969, p. H10668.

35. The role of the Columbia center and its relations with Legal Services are discussed by Martha F. Davis, *Brutal Need: Lawyers and the Welfare Rights Movement, 1960–1973* (Yale University Press, 1993); Martin Garbus, *Ready for the Defense* (Farrar, Straus and Giroux, 1971); Susan E. Lawrence, *The Poor in Court: The Legal Services Program and Supreme Court Decision Making* (Princeton University Press, 1990), esp. pp. 22–25, 40–57; and Earl Johnson, Jr., *Justice and Reform: The Formative Years of the OEO Legal Services Program* (New York: Russell Sage Foundation, 1974).

36. Steiner, *The State of Welfare*, p. 114.

37. Davis, *Brutal Need*, p. 84.

38. Charles F. Grosser and Edward V. Sparer, "Legal Services for the Poor: Social Work and Social Justice," *Social Work*, vol. 11 (January 1966), p. 81. Grosser was a professor of social work at Columbia and assistant director of Mobilization for Youth. Also see Sparer, "The Place of Law in Social Work Education: A Commentary on Dean Schottland's Article," 17 *Buffalo Law Review* 733 (1968).

39. Edward V. Sparer, "The Role of the Welfare Client's Lawyer," 12 *UCLA Law Review* 361, 375 (1965).

40. Edward V. Sparer, "The Right to Welfare," in Norman Dorsen, ed., *The Rights of Americans: What They Are—What They Should Be* (Pantheon, 1971), p. 65.

41. Ibid., p. 67.

42. Ibid., pp. 76, 77.

43. Ibid., p. 71.

44. Sparer, "Role of the Welfare Client's Lawyer," 366–67.

45. Sparer, "Right to Welfare," pp. 66–67.

46. Johnson, *Justice and Reform*, pp. 23–25, 34–35, 132–34, 180–82. Susan Lawrence, in *The Poor in Court*, notes that the center often had difficulty persuading local attorneys to follow their lead and that this contributed to some key defeats. See, for example, the discussion of *Wyman* v. *James* in chapter 5. By focusing almost entirely on constitutional law and ignoring statutory interpretation, though, she seriously understates the significance of the center and its strategy.

47. Lee Albert, "Choosing the Test Case in Welfare Litigation: A Plea for Planning," *Clearinghouse Review*, vol. 1 (November 1968), pp. 4–6, 28.

48. Ibid., p. 28.

49. Quoted in Lawrence, *The Poor in Court*, p. 54. For use of this strategy in food stamp cases, see chapter 10.

50. Edward V. Sparer, "A Friendly Critique," 36 *Stanford Law Review* 509, 562–63 (1984), emphasis in original.

51. Nick Kotz and Mary Lynn Kotz, *A Passion for Equality: George A. Wiley and the Movement* (Norton, 1977).

52. Sparer, "Right to Welfare," p. 90.

53. These battles are discussed in Warren E. George, "Development of the Legal Services Corporation," 61 *Cornell Law Review* 681 (1976). The Agnew quotation appears on pp. 694–95. The Long quotation comes from *Child Support and the Work Bonus*, Hearings before the Senate Committee on Finance, 93 Cong. 1 sess. (GPO, 1973), p. 111. The Reagan quotation appears in the *Los Angeles Times*, September 30, 1982, p. 5.

54. Quoted in Lawrence, *The Poor in Court*, p. 117.

55. *Social Security Amendments of 1970*, S. Rept. 91-1431, 91 Cong. 2 sess. (GPO, 1970), p. 436.

56. *Annual Report of the Department of Health, Education, and Welfare, Fiscal Year 1968: Secretary's Introduction*, p. 66, quoted in Steiner, *The State of Welfare*, p. 90.

57. St. John Barrett, "The New Role of the Courts in Developing Public Welfare Law," 1970 *Duke Law Journal* 1, 23 (1970).

58. Ibid., p. 8.

59. *Social Security Amendments of 1970*, S. Rept. 91-1431, pp. 364–65.

60. *Social Security Amendments of 1972*, S. Rept. 92-1230, 92 Cong. 2 sess. (GPO, 1972), p. 454.

Chapter 5

1. *Smith* v. *Board*, 259 F. Supp. 423, 424 (D.D.C. 1966).

2. *Arizona* v. *Hobby*, 221 F.2d 478 (D.C. Cir. 1954).

3. Susan E. Lawrence, *The Poor in Court: The Legal Services Program and Supreme Court Decision Making* (Princeton University Press, 1990), p. 103.

4. Motion for leave to file brief amicus curiae and brief amicus curiae of the Columbia Center on Social Welfare Policy and Law, *Jefferson* v. *Hackney* (N.D. Tex., Civil Action 3-3012-b), p. 4.

5. *Shapiro* v. *Thompson*, 394 U.S. 618 (1969).

6. *Goldberg* v. *Kelly*, 397 U.S. 254 (1970).

7. *Dandridge* v. *Williams*, 397 U.S. 471 (1970).

8. *King* v. *Smith*, 392 U.S. 309 (1968); *Townsend* v. *Swank*, 404 U.S. 282 (1971); and *Carleson* v. *Remillard*, 406 U.S. 598 (1972).

9. Three law review articles on judicial interpretation of title IV are particularly useful: Ira Lupu, "Welfare and Federalism: AFDC Eligibility Policies and the Scope of State Discretion," 57 *Boston University Law Review* 1, 20–21 (1977); Fred C. Doolittle, "State-Imposed Nonfinancial Eligibility Conditions in AFDC: Confusion in Supreme Court Decisions and a Need for Congressional Clarification," 19 *Harvard Journal on Legislation* 1 (1982); and Frank S. Bloch, "Cooperative Federalism and the Role of Litigation in the Development of Federal AFDC Eligibility Policy," 1979 *Wisconsin Law Review* 1 (1979). Bloch's article is based on his informative Ph.D. dissertation, "The Role of Litigation in the Development of Federal Welfare Policy: A Study of Legal Challenges to State Administration of Aid to Families with Dependent Children Programs as Politics of Redistributive Policy," Brandeis University, 1977.

10. *Burns* v. *Alcala*, 420 U.S. 575, 580 (1975).

11. *Miller* v. *Youakim*, 440 U.S. 125, 133–34 (1979).

12. Quoted in Martha F. Davis, *Brutal Need: Lawyers and the Welfare Rights Movement, 1960–1973* (Yale University Press, 1993), p. 107.

13. Quoted in Lawrence E. Lynn, Jr., and David deF. Whitman, *The President as Policymaker: Jimmy Carter and Welfare Reform* (Temple University Press, 1981), pp. 24, 27.

14. The story of the litigation is recounted in Martin Garbus, *Ready for the Defense* (New York: Farrar, Straus and Giroux, 1971), chap. 2; and Davis, *Brutal Need*, chap. 5.

15. *King* v. *Smith*, 277 F. Supp. 31, 38–39 (M.D. Ala. 1967). The author of the opinion was Judge Frank Johnson, who had several other confrontations with George Wallace. Judge Johnson desegregated the public schools of Montgomery and ordered the state to upgrade its facilities for the retarded and the mentally ill. He later ruled that Alabama's entire welfare system was operated in a racially discriminatory manner and should be placed in receivership. *Whitfield* v. *Oliver*, 399 F. Supp. 348 (M.D. Ala. 1975).

16. Garbus, *Ready for the Defense*, pp. 194–95.

17. *King* v. *Smith*, 392 U.S. 309, 320, 324–35. The 1962 amendments (and their total failure to reduce the welfare caseload) are discussed in Gilbert Y. Steiner, *The State of Welfare* (Brookings, 1971), pp. 35–50.

18. *Social Security Amendments of 1967—Conference Report, Congressional Record*, December 14, 1967, p. 36785. The National Welfare Rights Organization called the act "a betrayal of the poor, a declaration of war upon our families and a fraud on the future of our nation." Quoted in Davis, *Brutal Need*, pp. 119–20.

19. *King* v. *Smith*, 392 U.S. 309, 328, 329 (emphasis added).

20. Ibid., 330.

21. Lee Albert, "Choosing the Test Case in Welfare Litigation: A Plea for Planning," *Clearinghouse Review*, vol. 1 (November 1968), p. 5.

22. One expert on the administration of welfare program has noted, "Unreported support contributions are likely to escape detection. . . . Since support contributions usually are in cash, goods, or services and vary in frequency and amount, proof of their existence is difficult to find." Sharon Galm, "Welfare—An

Administrative Nightmare," *Studies in Public Welfare*, Committee Print, Joint Economic Committee, 92 Cong. 2 sess. (Government Printing Office, 1972), p. 8. The House report on the welfare reform bill of 1971 explained that it was imputing income of "parents (or their spouses) living in the same household" to the family because "if income were not imputed in the case of the father or stepfather who is living in the same household with the children, it would be extremely difficult to prove that the father or stepfather were actually contributing to the support and maintenance of the children if he should allege that he was not." *Social Security Amendments of 1971*, H. Rept. 92-231, 92 Cong. 1 sess. (GPO, 1971), p. 185.

23. *Lewis* v. *Martin*, 397 U.S. 552 (1970).

24. *Lewis* v. *Stark*, 312 F. Supp. 197 (N.D. Cal. 1968).

25. *Lewis* v. *Martin*, 558, 559, emphasis added.

26. *Van Lare* v. *Hurley*, 421 U.S. 338, 346 (1975).

27. Ibid., 348, emphasis added.

28. *Taylor* v. *Lavine*, 497 F.2d 1208, 1218 (2d Cir. 1974). (*Van Lare* was consolidated with this case.)

29. *Bowen* v. *Gilliard*, 483 U.S. 587, 632 (1987). This case is discussed in detail below.

30. *Townsend* v. *Swank*, 286.

31. Ibid., 288, 292 n. 8, 291, emphasis in original..

32. *Carleson* v. *Remillard*, 601, 604.

33. *Wyman* v. *James*, 400 U.S. 309 (1971).

34. Ibid., 322–23, 319.

35. Doolittle, "State-Imposed Nonfinancial Eligibility Conditions," p. 16.

36. N.Y. *State Department of Social Services* v. *Dublino*, 413 U.S. 405 (1973).

37. Ibid., 413–14.

38. 39 Fed. Reg. 16363 (1974).

39. 39 Fed. Reg. 26912 (1974).

40. See Paul Peterson and Mark Rom, *Welfare Magnets: A New Case for a National Standard* (Brookings, 1990), esp. pp. 90–110.

41. Both the legislative history and the early stages of litigation are described in Robert Rabin, "Implementation of the Cost of Living Adjustment for AFDC Recipients: A Case in Welfare Administration," 118 *University of Pennsylvania Law Review* 1143 (1970).

42. "Special grants" became controversial in the late 1960s when welfare rights activists began to encourage recipients to demand payments for such things as furniture and winter clothes. This was part of a larger strategy to flood the welfare system with so many demands that it would come crashing down. See Frances Fox Piven and Richard Cloward, *Regulating the Poor: The Functions of Public Welfare* (Vintage, 1971), esp. chap. 10. The response of the state of New York was predictable, at least to those lacking revolutionary zeal. The state replaced special grants—which could be used as an organizing tool and brought administrative chaos—with uniform "flat" grants. The issue that led to protracted

litigation in New York and elsewhere was how to compare a flat grant with a system that had allowed for special grants.

43. This extensive litigation is described in Davis, *Brutal Need*, pp. 124–32.

44. *Rosado* v. *Wyman*, 304 F. Supp. 1356, 1374, 1378–79 (E.D. N.Y. 1969).

45. *Rosado* v. *Wyman*, 397 U.S. 397, 412–13, 414 n. 17 (1970).

46. Edward V. Sparer, "The Right to Welfare," in Norman Dorsen, ed., *The Right of Americans: What They Are—What They Should Be* (Pantheon, 1971) p. 79.

47. These decisions are discussed in Bloch, "Cooperative Federalism and the Role of Litigation," pp. 56–72, 90–115.

48. *Saddler* v. *Winstead*, 332 F. Supp. 130, 135 (N.D. Miss. 1971).

49. 42 U.S.C. 602 (a)(17)(A), added in 1967.

50. *Doe* v. *Shapiro*, 302 F. Supp. 761, 765 (D. Conn. 1969).

51. The one decision upholding state rules was *Saiz* v. *Goodwin*, 325 F. Supp. 23 (D.N.M. 1971), reversed in *Saiz* v. *Goodwin*, 450 F.2d 788 (10th Cir. 1971). The cases striking down state requirements include *Doe* v. *Harder*, 310 F. Supp. 302 (D. Conn. 1970); *Meyer* v. *Juras*, 327 F. Supp. 759 (D. Ore. 1971); *Taylor* v. *Martin*, 330 F. Supp. 85 (N.D. Cal. 1971); *Doe* v. *Schmidt*, 330 F. Supp. 159 (E.D. Wisc. 1971); *Doe* v. *Swank*, 332 F. Supp. 61 (N.D. Ill. 1971); *Woods* v. *Miller*, 318 F. Supp. 510 (W.D. Pa. 1970); *Saddler* v. *Winstead; Doe* v. *Lavine*, 347 F. Supp. 357 (S.D. N.Y. 1972); *Doe* v. *Ellis*, 350 F. Supp. 375 (D.S.C. 1972); *Doe* v. *Gillman*, 347 F. Supp. 483 (N.D. Iowa 1972) and 479 F.2d 646 (8th Cir. 1973); *Storey* v. *Roberts*, 352 F. Supp. 473 (M.D. Fla. 1972); *Doe* v. *Flowers*, 364 F. Supp. 953 (N.D. W.Va. 1973); *Doe* v. *Carleson*, 356 F. Supp. 753 (N.D. Cal. 1973); and *Shirley* v. *Lavine*, 365 F. Supp. 818 (N.D. N.Y. 1973). The Supreme Court issued a brief affirmance of some of these decisions in *Shirley* v. *Lavine*, 420 U.S. 730 (1975).

52. *Solman* v. *Shapiro*, 300 F. Supp. 409 (D. Conn. 1969).

53. *Nolan* v. *deBoca*, 603 F.2d 810 (10th Cir. 1979).

54. *Archibald* v. *Whaland*, 555 F.2d 1061 (1st Cir. 1977).

55. *Rosen* v. *Hursh*, 464 F.2d 731 (8th Cir. 1972). While the courts adopted a narrowed interpretation of "parent" in most cases, one court adopted a very broad interpretation of the term when it helped a child qualify for benefits. In *Curry* v. *Dempsey*, 520 F. Supp. 70 (W.D. Mich. 1981), the district court ruled that needy children living with court-appointed guardians could be considered to be living with their "parents" because guardians assume a parental position toward their wards.

56. Regarding SSI payments, see, for example, *Johnson* v. *Harder*, 438 F.2d 7 (2d Cir. 1975); *Howard* v. *Madigan*, 383 F. Supp. 351 (D.S.D. 1973); *Nelson* v. *Likins*, 510 F.2d 414 (8th Cir. 1975); *Elan* v. *Hanson*, 384 F. Supp. 552 (N.D. Ohio 1974); and *Riddick* v. *D'Elia*, 626 F.2d 1084 (2d Cir. 1980). Regarding child support payments, see *Gilliard* v. *Craig*, 331 F. Supp. 587 (W.D. N.C. 1971), affirmed without opinion by the Supreme Court, 409 U.S. 807 (1972); and *Swift* v. *Toia*, 461 F. Supp. 578 (S.D. N.Y. 1978). Regarding sibling earnings, see *Reyna* v. *Vowell*, 470 F.2d 494 (5th Cir. 1972); *Rodriguez* v. *Vowell*, 472 F.2d 622 (5th Cir. 1973); and *MCRO* v. *Stanton*, 371 F. Supp. 298 (N.D. Ind. 1973).

Regarding income from work-study programs, see *Brown* v. *Bates*, 363 F. Supp. 897 (N.D. Ohio 1973). Regarding educational loans, see *Jamroz* v. *Blum*, 509 F. Supp. 953 (N.D. N.Y. 1981).

57. *Gurley* v. *Wohlgemuth*, 421 F. Supp. 1337 (E.D. Pa. 1976). Also see *Owen* v. *Parham*, 350 F. Supp. 589 (N.D. Ga. 1972); and *Martinez* v. *Maher*, 485 F. Supp. 1264 (D. Conn. 1980).

58. *Kaisa* v. *Chang*, 396 F. Supp. 375 (D. Ha. 1975).

59. *National Welfare Rights Organization* v. *Mathews*, 533 F.2d 637, 648 (D.C. Cir. 1976).

60. *Buckner* v. *Maher*, 424 F. Supp. 366 (D. Conn. 1976).

61. *Anderson* v. *Burson*, 300 F. Supp. 401 (N.D. Ga. 1968).

62. *Woolfork* v. *Brown*, 325 F. Supp. 1162 (E.D. Va. 1971), upheld by the Fourth Circuit, 456 F.2d 652 (1972). A second set of work rules was struck down by the same district court in *Woolfork II*, 358 F. Supp. 524 (1973). Other examples are *Bueno* v. *Juras*, 349 F. Supp. 91 (D. Ore. 1972); and *New York Department of Social Services* v. *Dublino*, 348 F. Supp. 290 (W.D. N.Y. 1972). The same district court that had previously struck down two sets of work rules in Virginia invalidated a third set after the Supreme Court had decided *Dublino*. In this case the Fourth Circuit overruled the district court. *Woolfork* v. *Brown*, 393 F. Supp. 263 (E.D. Va. 1975) and 538 F.2d 598 (4th Cir. 1976).

63. *McLean* v. *Mathews*, 458 F. Supp. 285 (S.D. N.Y. 1977).

64. *Davis* v. *Reagan*, 485 F. Supp 1255, 1260 (S.D. Iowa 1980), affirmed by the Eighth Circuit 630 F.2d 1299 (1980).

65. After years of litigation, the Supreme Court upheld HEW rules leaving this decision to the states. *Batterton* v. *Francis*, 432 U.S. 416 (1977).

66. These decisions were upheld by the Supreme Court in *Shea* v. *Vialpando*, 416 U.S. 251 (1974), discussed below.

67. *Perez* v. *Chang*, 438 F. Supp. 238 (D. Ha. 1977).

68. *Maryland* v. *Mathews*, 415 F. Supp. 1206 (D.D.C. 1976); *J.A.* v. *Ritti*, 377 F. Supp. 1046 (D.N.J. 1974); *Cooper* v. *Laupheimer*, 316 F. Supp. 264 (E.D. Pa. 1970); *Owen* v. *Roberts*, 377 F. Supp. 45 (M.D. Fla. 1974); and *Holly* v. *Lavine*, 553 F.2d 845 (2d Cir. 1977). See also Sherry Leiwant and John Hasen, "Caselaw on AFDC Verification Problems," *Clearinghouse Review*, vol. 20 (July 1987), pp. 215–22.

69. Much of this litigation is described in Bloch, "Cooperative Federalism and the Role of Litigation," pp. 126–48; and in Arthur B. LaFrance, *Welfare Law: Structure and Entitlement in a Nutshell* (West, 1979), pp. 351–65.

70. The lower court decisions are cited in *Parks* v. *Hardin*, 504 F.2d 861, 863 n. 4 (5th Cir. 1974).

71. *Carver* v. *Hooker*, 501 F.2d 1244, 1247 (1st Cir. 1974); *Parks* v. *Hardin*, 504 F.2d 861, 872 (5th Cir. 1974); and *Wilson* v. *Weaver*, 449 F.2d 155, 158 (7th Cir. 1974).

72. *Gurley* v. *Wohlgemuth*, 1347.

73. *Simpson* v. *Miller*, 535 F. Supp. 1041, 1048, 1050 (S.D. Ill. 1982).

74. *Burns* v. *Alcala*, 580.

75. *Shea* v. *Vialpando*, 260, 266.

76. 607(b)(2)(c)(ii).

77. *Philbrook* v. *Glodgett*, 421 U.S. 707, 718 (1975). One year later the House and Senate adopted compromise legislation that required those who qualify for both programs to apply first for unemployment compensation but allowed them to receive AFDC as well if their income remained below the state's standard of need. P.L. 94-566, sec. 508.

78. *Quern* v. *Mandley*, 436 U.S. 725, 743 (1978).

79. *Blum* v. *Bacon*, 457 U.S. 132, 142 (1982).

80. *Miller* v. *Youakim*, 133–34.

81. *Turner* v. *Prod*, 707 F.2d 1109, 1110 (9th Cir. 1983).

82. The lower court decisions are listed in ibid., 1110 n. 1, and in *Heckler* v. *Turner*, 470 U.S. 184, 188 n. 2 (1984).

83. *Heckler* v. *Turner*, 200.

84. Ibid., 212. Three years later the court echoed these themes in *Lukhard* v. *Reed*, 481 U.S. 368 (1987).

85. *Sullivan* v. *Stroop*, 496 U.S. 478, 481–82, 485, 496 (1990).

86. *Bowen* v. *Gilliard*, 483 U.S. 587 (1987).

87. Ibid., 596, 604.

88. Ibid., 610–11, 627, 629, 632.

89. *Malloy* v. *Eichler*, 860 F.2d 1179 (3d Cir. 1988); and *Georgia Department of Medical Assistance* v. *Bowen*, 846 F.2d 708 (11th Cir. 1988).

90. *Wilcox* v. *Ives*, 864 F.2d 915 (1st Cir. 1988).

91. *Tambe* v. *Bowen*, 839 F.2d 108 (2d Cir. 1988).

92. *Figueroa* v. *Sunn*, 884 F.2d 1290 (9th Cir. 1989).

93. *Mangrum* v. *Griepentorg*, 702 F. Supp. 813 (D. Nev. 1988). The district court argued that since *Lukhard* v. *Reed* was a plurality opinion, its dicta did not need to be followed.

94. *Boettger* v. *Bowen*, 714 F. Supp. 272 (E.D. Mich. 1989).

95. On the new conditions of eligibility, see Julie Kosterlitz, "Behavior Modification," *National Journal*, February 1, 1992, pp. 271–75; and Kitty Dumas, "States Bypassing Congress in Reforming Welfare," *Congressional Quarterly Weekly Report*, April 11, 1992, pp. 950–53.

96. Barbara Sard, "The Role of the Courts in Welfare Reform," *Clearinghouse Review*, vol. 22 (August–September 1988), p. 367. Fred Doolittle describes the California litigation in "Ronald Reagan and Conservative Welfare Reform," copy on file with Department of Politics, Brandeis University, July 1986. The Massachusetts decision is described in "Justice to Hear Welfare Order Arguments," *Boston Globe*, January 7, 1987, p. 19.

97. Donald L. Horowitz, *The Courts and Social Policy* (Brookings, 1977), p. 41.

98. Albert, "Choosing the Test Case in Welfare Litigation," pp. 5, 28.

99. Horowitz, *The Courts and Social Policy*, pp. 35, 37.

100. See the discussion of 1981–82 AFDC legislation in chapter 6 and 1977 food stamp legislation in chapter 11.

101. Again the courts' answer was no. See, for example, *J.A.* v. *Riti*; and *Bradford* v. *Juras*, 331 F. Supp. 167 (D. Ore. 1971). Judge Friendly provides an

incisive discussion of how the early Supreme Court decisions raise difficult questions about antifraud rules in *Rush* v. *Smith*, 573 F.2d 110 (2d Cir. 1978).

102. Lupu, "Welfare and Federalism," p. 23.

103. Galm, "Welfare—An Administrative Nightmare," pp. 31–32.

104. Vincent Blasi, "The Rootless Activism of the Burger Court," in Vincent Blasi, ed., *The Burger Court: The Counter-Revolution That Wasn't* (Yale University Press, 1983), p. 211.

Chapter 6

1. Quoted in Vincent J. Burke and Vee Burke, *Nixon's Good Deed: Welfare Reform* (Columbia University Press, 1974), p. 74.

2. A number of studies of FAP and PBJI have described the difficulty of getting a variety of actors to agree on comprehensive reform. Among the most useful are the following: Christopher Leman, *The Collapse of Welfare Reform: Political Institutions, Policy, and the Poor in Canada and the United States* (MIT Press, 1980); Lawrence E. Lynn, Jr., and David deF. Whitman, *The President as Policymaker: Jimmy Carter and Welfare Reform* (Temple University Press, 1981); Theodore R. Marmor and Martin Rein, "Reforming 'The Welfare Mess': The Fate of the Family Assistance Plan, 1969–72," in Allan P. Sindler, ed., *Policy and Politics in America* (Little, Brown, 1973); Daniel P. Moynihan, *The Politics of A Guaranteed Income* (Vintage, 1973); Dennis Coyle and Aaron Wildavsky, "Requisites of Radical Reform: Income Maintenance Versus Tax Preferences," *Journal of Policy Analysis and Management*, vol. 17 (Fall 1987), pp. 1–16; Burke and Burke, *Nixon's Good Deed*; M. Kenneth Bowler, *The Nixon Guaranteed Income Proposal: Substance and Process in Policy Change* (Ballinger, 1974); and Henry J. Aaron, *Why Is Welfare So Hard to Reform?* (Brookings, 1973).

3. Quoted in Julie Rovner, "Congress Clears Overhaul of Welfare System," *Congressional Quarterly Weekly Report*, October 1, 1988, p. 2699.

4. *Overview of Entitlement Programs: Background Material and Data on Programs within the Jurisdiction of the Committee on Ways and Means, 1991 Green Book*, Committee Print, House Committee on Ways and Means, 102 Cong. 1 sess. (Government Printing Office, 1991), pp. 1415–17, 771, 901.

5. Robert Greenstein, "Universal and Targeted Approaches to Relieving Poverty: An Alternative View," in Christopher Jencks and Paul E. Peterson, eds., *The Urban Underclass* (Brookings, 1991), p. 440.

6. Quoted in Bowler, *Nixon Guaranteed Income Proposal*, p. 109.

7. Quoted in Martha Derthick, *Agency under Stress: The Social Security Administration in American Government* (Brookings, 1990), p. 88.

8. Quoted in Bowler, *Nixon Guaranteed Income Proposal*, p. 112.

9. Quoted in Leman, *Collapse of Welfare Reform*, p. 101. In 1978 *Congressional Quarterly* reported that "interest groups representing the nation's governors, state legislators, county officials and mayors lobbied aggressively for

Carter's legislative package." *Congressional Quarterly Almanac, 1978*, vol. 34, p. 666. Also see Lynn and Whitman, *President as Policymaker*, p. 230.

10. *Congressional Quarterly Almanac, 1972*, vol. 28, p. 901.

11. Gilbert Y. Steiner reviews these common (but, as he shows, unsubstantiated) assumptions in *The Futility of Family Policy* (Brookings, 1981), pp. 97–111.

12. Nathan Glazer, *The Limits of Social Policy* (Harvard University Press, 1988), p. 35.

13. Quoted in Lynn and Whitman, *President as Policymaker*, p. 248.

14. See, for example, Eleanor Holmes Norton, "Restoring the Traditional Black Family," *New York Times Magazine*, June 2, 1985, p. 79. James Q. Wilson discusses the significance of this shift in "The Rediscovery of Character: Private Virtues and Public Policy," *The Public Interest*, no. 81 (Fall 1985), pp. 3–16; and "The Family Values Debate," *Commentary*, vol. 95 (April 1993), pp. 24–31.

15. Quoted in Lynn and Whitman, *President as Policymaker*, p. 106.

16. See Lawrence M. Mead, *Beyond Entitlement: The Social Obligations of Citizenship* (Free Press, 1986), chaps. 5, 6; and Mead, *The New Politics of Poverty: The Nonworking Poor in America* (Basic Books, 1992), chaps. 8, 9.

17. Bill Cavala and Aaron Wildavsky, "The Political Feasibility of Income by Right," *Public Policy*, vol. 18 (Spring 1970), pp. 321, 324–26. Also see the other sources cited in chapter 3, note 65.

18. Steven Smith and Christopher Deering, *Committees in Congress* (CQ Press, 1984), p. 97.

19. *Congressional Quarterly Almanac, 1978*, p. 601.

20. Richard F. Fenno, *Congressmen in Committees* (Little, Brown, 1973), p. 159. See also John Manley, *The Politics of Finance: The House Committee on Ways and Means* (Little, Brown, 1970), p. 297.

21. The quotations are from Fenno, *Congressmen in Committees*, pp. 183–84; and Smith and Deering, *Committees in Congress*, p. 160.

22. *Congressional Quarterly Almanac, 1970*, vol. 26, pp. 1030–41.

23. *Social Security Amendments of 1972*, S. Rept. 92-1230, 92 Cong. 2 sess. (GPO, 1972), p. 16.

24. *Social Security Amendments of 1970*, S. Rept. 91-1431, 91 Cong. 2 sess. (GPO, 1970), p. 4 (hereinafter cited as *1970 Report*). Large sections of the 1970 report were incorporated into the 1972 report.

25. *1970 Report*, p. 50.

26. *Congressional Record*, August 6, 1971, p. 30547.

27. *1970 Report*, pp. 357–59. Moynihan wrote that the committee "gave any who cared to learn a lesson in what repressive legislation could be like. . . . This was done by voice votes, with Ribicoff reportedly the only opposition." *Politics of a Guaranteed Income*, p. 535. Although Senator Harris led the efforts to kill these provisions on the Senate floor, he apparently missed the markup session.

28. *1970 Report*, p. 361.

29. Because *Shapiro* v. *Thompson* and *Goldberg* v. *Kelly* were constitutional rulings, they could not be overturned by legislation. But the bill proposed elaborate mechanisms for blunting their effect. See *1970 Report*, pp. 359–61.

30. Steiner, *Futility of Family Policy*, p. 150.

31. For a full description of this legislation and Long's subsequent efforts to force HEW to administer it aggressively, see ibid., pp. 111–28.

32. *Congressional Quarterly Almanac, 1977,* vol. 33, p. 161; *Adoption Assistance and Child Welfare Act of 1979,* S. Rept. 96-336, 96 Cong. 1 sess. (GPO, 1979); and *Adoption Assistance and Child Welfare Act of 1980,* Conf. Rept. 96-900, 96 Cong. 2 sess. (GPO, 1980), p. 65. The 1979 Senate bill also included provisions to count the income of stepparents and to prorate the shelter allowance of ineligible relatives. In 1980 the House finally accepted the latter but not the former.

33. Fred Doolittle, "Ronald Reagan and Conservative Welfare Reform," copy on file with Department of Politics, Brandeis University, July 1986, chap. 1.

34. Ronald Reagan, "Conservative Blueprint for the 1970s," *Human Events,* October 4, 1975, reprinted in *Congressional Record,* October 1, 1975, p. 31186.

35. Quoted in Doolittle, "Ronald Reagan and Conservative Welfare Reform," chap. 2.

36. Ibid., chap. 3. Most of these court cases, including those heard by the California courts, are discussed in Fred Doolittle and Michael Wiseman, "The California Welfare Reform Act: A Litigation History," Working Paper 71, University of California, Berkeley, Institute of Business and Economic Research, Department of Economics, Income Dynamics Project, August 1976.

37. Doolittle, "Ronald Reagan and Conservative Welfare Reform," chap. 4.

38. Ronald Randall, "Presidential Power versus Bureaucratic Intransigence; The Influence of the Nixon Administration on Welfare Policy," *American Political Science Review,* vol. 73 (September 1979), pp. 795–810. Swoap, too, served on the staff of the Senate Finance Committee.

39. For a good overview of the welfare provisions in the 1981 reconciliation bill, see Tom Joe and Cheryl Rogers, *By the Few, For the Few: The Reagan Welfare Legacy* (Lexington Books, 1985), chap. 4.

40. Quoted in Doolittle, "Ronald Reagan and Conservative Welfare Reform," chap. 7.

41. Ibid.

42. *Engelman* v. *Amos,* 404 U.S. 23 (1971), affirming *X* v. *McCorkle,* 333 F. Supp. 1109 (D. N.J. 1970). Also see *McGraw* v. *Berger,* F.2d 719 (2d Cir. 1976).

43. *Administration's Proposed Savings in Unemployment Compensation, Public Assistance, and Social Services Programs,* Hearings before the Subcommittee on Public Assistance and Unemployment Compensation of the House Committee on Ways and Means, 97 Cong. 1 sess. (GPO, 1981), p. 7. It should be noted that "assuming the role of stepparent" is another name for the rules on "men assuming the role of spouse" rejected by the courts a decade before.

44. *Deficit Reduction Act of 1984: Explanation of Provisions Approved by the Committee on March 21, 1984,* Committee Print, Senate Committee on Finance, 98 Cong. 2 sess. (GPO, 1984), vol. 1, pp. 982–83; and *Deficit Reduction Act of 1984,* H. Conf. Rept. 98-801, 98 Cong. 2 sess. (GPO, 1984), pp. 1394–95.

45. Nathan Glazer, "The Social Policy of the Reagan Administration: A Review," *The Public Interest,* no. 75 (Spring 1984), pp. 87.

46. Julie Rovner, "Congress Clears Overhaul of Welfare System," *Congressional Quarterly Weekly Report*, October 1, 1988, p. 2701.

47. Quoted in Mead, *New Politics of Poverty*, p. 201.

48. Robert D. Reischauer, "Welfare Reform: Will Consensus Be Enough?" *Brookings Review*, vol. 5 (Summer 1987), pp. 3, 4, 6.

49. Michael Novak and others, *The New Consensus on Family and Welfare: A Community of Self-Reliance* (American Enterprise Institute, 1987), p. 82.

50. Mead, *New Politics of Poverty*, pp. 22–23.

51. Joel Handler, "The Transformation of Aid to Families with Dependent Children: The Family Support Act in Historical Context," 16 *New York University Review of Law and Social Change* 457, 466 (1987–88).

52. Rovner, "Congress Clears Overhaul of Welfare System," p. 2699. Paul E. Peterson and Mark Rom note that the "new consensus" has "skirted a number of difficult questions, all related to money." *Welfare Magnets: A New Case for a National Standard* (Brookings, 1990), p. 1.

Chapter 7

1. Robert T. Stafford, "Education for the Handicapped: A Senator's Perspective," 3 *Vermont Law Review* 71, 74–76 (1978).

2. Judith D. Singer and John A. Butler, "The Education for All Handicapped Children Act: Schools as Agents for Social Reform," *Harvard Educational Review*, vol. 57 (May 1987), p. 125. Other informative discussions of the importance of the EAHCA include the following: Paul E. Peterson, "Background Paper," in *Making the Grade: Report of the Twentieth Century Fund Task Force on Federal Elementary and Secondary Education Policy* (Twentieth Century Fund, 1983), pp. 119–26; David L. Kirp, "Professionalization as a Policy Choice: British Special Education in Comparative Perspective," in Jay Chambers and William Hartman, eds., *Special Education Policies: Their History, Implementation, and Finance* (Temple University Press, 1983), pp. 74–112; and Jack Tweedie, "The Politics of Legalization in Special Education Reform," in ibid., pp. 48–73.

3. Information from U.S. Department of Education, Office of Special Education and Rehabilitative Services, November 9, 1993.

4. Peterson, "Background Paper," p. 119; and John C. Pittenger and Peter Kuriloff, "Educating the Handicapped: Reforming a Radical Law," *The Public Interest*, no. 66 (Winter 1982), p. 73.

5. The first case is *Timothy W. v. Rochester*, 875 F.2d 954 (1st Cir. 1989). The other cases are discussed in chapter 8.

6. *School Board of the County of Prince William v. Malone*, 762 F.2d 1210 (4th Cir. 1985).

7. *Honig v. Doe*, 484 U.S. 305 (1988).

8. *Students of California School for the Blind v. Honig*, 736 F.2d 538 (9th Cir. 1984), emphasis in the original. The six dissenters had requested that the

decision be reconsidered *en banc*. *Students of California School for the Blind* v. *Honig*, 745 F. 2d 582, 584 (9th Cir. 1984).

9. *The Pennsylvania Association for Retarded Children (PARC)* v. *Commonwealth of Pennsylvania*, 343 F. Supp. 279 (E.D. Pa. 1972); and *Mills* v. *Board of Education of the District of Columbia*, 348 F. Supp. 866 (D.D.C. 1972).

10. *San Antonio School District* v. *Rodriguez*, 411 U.S. 1 (1973).

11. David Neal and David L. Kirp, "The Allure of Legalization Reconsidered: The Case of Special Education," 48 *Law and Contemporary Problems* 63, 68 (1985). David Kirp has written or coauthored several insightful articles on this subject. I have learned a great deal from this work, which includes David Kirp, William Buss, and Peter Kuriloff, "Legal Reform of Special Education: Empirical Studies and Procedural Proposals," 62 *California Law Review* 40 (1974); David L. Kirp and Donald N. Jensen, "What Does Due Process Do?" *The Public Interest*, no. 73 (Fall 1983), pp. 75–90; and Kirp, "Professionalization as a Policy Choice." In 1980 David Kirp, David Neal, and Jack Tweedie conducted interviews with a number of people involved with passage of the act. I am grateful to them for sharing with me the tapes of these interviews.

12. Quoted in Kirp, "Professionalization as a Policy Choice," p. 95. Australia, too, has followed the British model. Betsy Levin, "Equal Educational Opportunity for Children with Special Needs: The Federal Role in Australia," 48 *Law and Contemporary Problems* 213 (1985).

13. Richard A. Weatherly, *Reforming Special Education: Policy Implementation from State Level to Street Level* (MIT Press, 1979), p. 137. See also Paul E. Peterson, Barry G. Rabe, and Kenneth K. Wong, *When Federalism Works* (Brookings, 1986), pp. 181–84.

14. Mark G. Yudof, "Education for the Handicapped: *Rowley* in Perspective," *American Journal of Education*, vol. 92 (February 1984), p. 165.

15. A number of works explore the history, legal arguments, and implementation of the *PARC* and *Mills* cases: Leopold Lippman and I. Ignacy Goldberg, *Right to Education: Anatomy of the Pennsylvania Case and Its Implications for Exceptional Children* (Teachers College Press, 1973); Frederick J. Weintraub and others, eds., *Public Policy and the Education of Exceptional Children* (Washington: Council for Exceptional Children, 1976); Erwin L. Levine and Elizabeth M. Wexler, *PL 94-142: An Act of Congress* (Macmillan, 1981), chap. 2; and Kirp, Buss, and Kuriloff, "Legal Reform of Special Education," p. 40.

16. *Education for All Handicapped Children, 1975*, Hearings before the Subcommittee on the Handicapped of the Senate Committee on Labor and Public Welfare, 94 Cong. 1 sess. (Government Printing Office, 1975), p. 312.

17. *Education for the Handicapped Act Amendments of 1975*, S. Rept. 94-168, 94 Cong. 1 sess. (GPO, 1975), p. 17.

18. William H. Wilkin and David O. Porter, *State Aid for Special Education: Who Benefits?* (U.S. Department of Health, Education and Welfare, National Institute of Education, 1977), p. 1.

19. Quoted in Tweedie, "Politics of Legalization," p. 53. Tweedie's article provides a good explanation of the strategy of advocates for the handicapped.

20. Peterson, Rabe, and Wong, *When Federalism Works*, p. 56.

21. *PARC* v. *Commonwealth of Pennsylvania*, 295, 297.

22. Kirp, Buss, and Kuriloff, "Legal Reform of Special Education," p. 84.

23. *Mills* v. *Board of Education of the District of Columbia*, 878.

24. Ibid., 880, 881, 878.

25. *Hobson* v. *Hansen*, 269 S. Supp. 401 (D.D.C. 1967). Donald L. Horowitz provides a detailed examination of this case in *The Courts and Social Policy* (Brookings, 1977). In another important case growing out of desegregation litigation—*Larry P.* v. *Riles*, 343 F. Supp. 1306 (N.D. Cal. 1972)—a federal district court in California enjoined the use of IQ tests for assignment of minority students to classes for the retarded. NAACP lawyers argued the case for the plaintiffs.

26. The first and most famous case is *Wyatt* v. *Stickney*, 325 F. Supp. 781 (M.D. Ala. 1971), which, appropriately enough, pitted Governor George Wallace of Alabama against Judge Frank Johnson, the man who had previously ordered the integration of Alabama's school and welfare system.

27. Lippman and Goldberg, *Right to Education*, chap. 4; and Thomas K. Gilhool, "Education: An Inalienable Right," in Weintraub and others, eds., *Public Policy and the Education of Exceptional Children*, pp. 14–21. The Pennhurst facility not only spawned the *PARC* case, but eventually became the focus of important institutional reform litigation, with three cases culminating in Supreme Court opinions: *Pennhurst State School and Hospital* v. *Halderman*, 451 U.S. 1 (1981); *Youngberg* v. *Romeo*, 457 U.S. 307 (1982); and *Pennhurst State School and Hospital* v. *Halderman*, 465 U.S. 89 (1984).

28. *Brown* v. *Board of Education*, 347 U.S. 483 (1954).

29. *San Antonio* v. *Rodriguez*, 411 U.S. 1, 20 (1973), emphasis in original. The Court emphasized several times the difference between "an absolute denial of educational opportunities" and "relative differences in spending levels." The Court also stressed that in the Texas case "no charge fairly could be made that the system fails to provide each child with an opportunity to acquire the basic minimal skills necessary for the enjoyment of the rights of speech and of full participation in the political process" (3). Advocates for the handicapped did claim their clients suffered such an absolute denial and were left without minimal skills.

30. Gilhool, "Education: An Inalienable Right," p. 18.

31. The state's quick surrender led one sympathetic observer to claim that "the federal court did not resolve a dispute between contesting parties, but instead ratified an agreement between advocates for children's services and professional service agencies to raid state treasuries for greater funds on behalf of their shared clientele." Richard A. Burt, "Beyond the Right to Habilitation," in Michael Kindred and others, eds., *The Mentally Retarded Citizen and the Law* (Free Press, 1976), p. 420. On the general theme of government lawyers' occasional interest in losing cases, see Donald L. Horowitz, *The Jurocracy* (Lexington Books, 1977), pp. 84–90.

32. Kirp, Buss, and Kuriloff, "Legal Reform of Special Education," p. 63.

33. *Education for the Handicapped Act Amendments of 1975*, S. Rept. 94-168, p. 8.

34. These studies are described in William H. Clune and Mark H. Van Pelt, "A Political Method of Evaluating the Education for All Handicapped Children Act of 1975 and the Several Gaps of Gap Analysis," 48 *Law and Contemporary Problems* 7, 15–16 (1985).

35. Robert A. Katzmann, *Institutional Disability: The Saga of Transportation Policy for the Disabled* (Brookings, 1986), p. 111.

36. Gilhool, "Education: An Inalienable Right," p. 20. Also see Frederick J. Weintraub and Mary A. McCaffrey, "Professional Rights and Responsibilities," in Weintraub and others, eds., *Public Policy and the Education of Exceptional Children*, pp. 333–43.

37. Alan Abeson, "Litigation," in Weintraub and others, eds., *Public Policy and the Education of Exceptional Children*, p. 240.

38. *PARC* v. *Commonwealth of Pennsylvania*, 299, emphasis in original.

39. *Harrison* v. *Michigan*, 350 F. Supp. 846 (E.D. Mich. 1972); and *Tidewater Society for Autistic Children* v. *Virginia*, 426-72-N (E.D. Va. December 26, 1972).

40. Tweedie, "Politics of Legalization," p. 54. Tweedie's findings are based on extensive interviews with participants.

41. *San Antonio* v. *Rodriguez*, 33, 42. The Court quotes a key phrase from *Dandridge* v. *Williams*.

42. Kirp, Buss, and Kuriloff, "Legal Reform of Special Education," pp. 81, 96.

43. For developments at the state level, see Lippman and Goldberg, *Right to Education*, pp. 54–56; Weatherly, *Reforming Special Education*, chap. 2; A. B. Harmon, "The Kentucky Right to Education Litigation," in Weintraub and others, eds., *Public Policy and the Education of Exceptional Children*, p. 308; and David Riley, "The Ins and Outs of Legislative Reform: Vermont's S. 98," in ibid., p. 316. According to Riley, one attorney testifying in favor of CEC-sponsored legislation in Vermont told a legislative committee, "The consequences of the court order in Pennsylvania were complete and total chaos, confusion, and exorbitant, unnecessary expense." The message was clear: pass this bill or we will sue you—and create chaos.

44. Quoted in Tweedie, "Politics of Legalization," p. 55.

45. The first quotation comes from Albert Shanker, quoted in Mark C. Weber, "The Transformation of the Education of the Handicapped Act: A Study in the Interpretation of Radical Statutes," 24 *U.C. Davis Law Review* 349, 365 n. 94 (1990); the second from Weatherley, *Reforming Special Education*, p. 1; and the third from George Will, quoted in Yudof, "Education for the Handicapped," p. 166.

46. "Additional Views" of Representatives Albert Quie, Alphonzo Bell, John Erlenborn, John Buchanan, Larry Pressler, and George Goodling, in *Education for all Handicapped Children Act of 1975*, H. Rept. 94-332, 94 Cong. 1 sess. (GPO, 1975), p. 60.

47. Senate Republican leader Dole is paralyzed in the right arm. Hubert Humphrey had a retarded grandson, Weicker a child with Down's syndrome. President Kennedy's interest in mental retardation apparently came from the fact

that he had a retarded sister. Columnist George Will, too, has a child with Down's syndrome. His wife served as director of the Office of Special Education and Rehabilitative Services. When two Reaganites in the Department of Education called for the act's repeal, Will attacked their "dangerous subordination of individual rights to calculations of social utility" and accused the officials of "betraying a President who supports it [the EAHCA]." George F. Will, "Unfeeling Bureaucrats Who Badger the Handicapped," *Boston Globe*, April 26, 1985, p. 15. The point is not to accuse Will and others of conflict of interest, but to show how this issue cuts across partisan and ideological lines.

48. The classic description of the House committee during this period is Richard F. Fenno's *Congressmen in Committees* (Little, Brown, 1973). See also Levine and Wexler, *PL 94-142*, pp. 42–48; and Hugh Davis Graham, *The Uncertain Triumph: Federal Education Policy in the Kennedy and Johnson Years* (University of North Carolina Press, 1984), p. 119.

49. Eugene Eidenberg and Roy D. Morey, *An Act of Congress: The Legislative Process and the Making of Education Policy* (Norton, 1969).

50. Levine and Wexler, *PL 94-142*, p. 33.

51. Gary Orfield, *Congressional Power: Congress and Social Change* (Harcourt Brace Jovanovich, 1975), 124–25. Chapters 7 and 8 of Orfield's book provide a good overview of this change.

52. Katzmann, *Institutional Disability*, pp. 36–37.

53. Tweedie, "Politics of Legalization," p. 58. See also Benjamin D. Stickney and Lawrence R. Marcus, *The Great Education Debate: Washington and the Schools* (Springfield, Ill.: Charles C. Thomas, 1984), p. 36.

54. *Congressional Record*, May 20, 1974, p. 15268. Maryland's spending on special education rose from $65 million in fiscal 1973 to $170 million in fiscal 1980. Pittenger and Kuriloff, "Educating the Handicapped," p. 92.

55. *Congressional Record*, May 20, 1974, p. 15272.

56. *Education for the Handicapped Act Amendments of 1975*, S. Rept. 94-168, pp. 1428, 1450.

57. Levine and Wexler, *PL 94-142*, p. 99.

58. Neal and Kirp, "The Allure of Legalization Reconsidered," p. 74; and Clune and Van Pelt, "A Political Method," pp. 13–14.

59. Quoted in "Aid to Education of Handicapped Approved: President's Statement," *Congressional Quarterly Almanac*, 1975, vol. 31, p. 656.

60. Edward I. Koch, "The Mandate Millstone," *The Public Interest*, no. 61 (Fall 1980), pp. 42–57.

61. Peterson, Rabe, and Wong, *When Federalism Works*, p. 56.

Chapter 8

1. Peter J. Kuriloff, "Is Justice Served by Due Process?: Affecting the Outcome of Special Education Hearings in Pennsylvania," 48 *Law and Contemporary Problems* 48, 94 (1985). Jane David and David Greene come to a similar conclu-

sion in "Organizational Barriers to Full Implementation of PL 94-142," in Jay Chambers and William Hartman, eds., *Special Education Policies: Their History, Implementation, and Finance* (Temple University Press, 1983), p. 128.

2. This quotation comes from the dissenting opinion in *Georgia Association of Retarded Children* v. *McDaniel*, 716 F.2d 1565, 1582–83 (11th Cir. 1983).

3. *Hendrick Hudson District Board of Education* v. *Rowley*, 458 U.S. 176 (1982).

4. The rulemaking process is described in Erwin L. Levine and Elizabeth M. Wexler, *PL 94-142: An Act of Congress* (Macmillan, 1981), chap. 5. Proposed regulations appeared in 41 Fed. Reg. 56966–67 (1976), and final regulations in 42 Fed. Reg. 42474–75 (1977). Despite the fact that the proposal came in the waning days of the Ford administration and the final rules were issued during the Carter administration, there are few major differences between the two sets of regulations.

5. Paul E. Peterson, Barry G. Rabe, and Kenneth K. Wong, *When Federalism Works* (Brookings, 1986), p. 154.

6. 42 Fed. Reg. 42475. The statement originally appeared in the proposal, 41 Fed. Reg. 56967.

7. *Department of Labor, Health, Education, and Welfare, and Related Agencies Appropriation for 1981, Part 6: Department of Education*, Hearings, House Committee on Appropriations, 96 Cong. 2 sess. (Government Printing Office, 1980), p. 1253.

8. 47 Fed. Reg. 33836 (1982).

9. Subcommittee on Select Education of the House Committee on Education and Labor, *Oversight Hearings on Proposed Changes in Regulations for the Education for All Handicapped Children Act*, 97 Cong. 2 sess. (GPO, 1982); Harrison Donnelly, "Congress Fights Loosening of Regulations," *Congressional Quarterly Weekly Report*, September 4, 1982, p. 2197; Marjorie Hunter, "Bell Ends Plan to Erase Some Rules for Education of the Handicapped," *New York Times*, September 30, 1982, p. A1; "Education Regulations," *Congressional Quarterly Almanac*, 1982, vol. 38, pp. 486–87; and *Regulations Concerning the Education of the Handicapped Act*, H. Rept. 97-906, 97 Cong. 2 sess. (GPO, 1982).

10. P.L. 98-199, sec. 608(b).

11. The Pennsylvania Commissioner of Education estimated that this ruling could cost his state alone $200 million to $500 million a year. *Oversight of PL 94-142—The Education for All Handicapped Children Act, Part I*, Hearings before the Select Subcommittee on Education of the House Education and Labor Committee, 96 Cong. 1 sess. (GPO, 1980), p. 227.

12. *Battle* v. *Pennsylvania*, 629 F.2d 269, 280 (3d Cir. 1980).

13. *Alamo Heights Independent School District* v. *State Board of Education*, 790 F.2d 1153, 1158 (5th Cir. 1986).

14. See, for example, *Georgia Association of Retarded Children* v. *McDaniel*, 1574. For a dissenting view, see *Stacy G.* v. *Pasadena Independent School District*, 695 F.2d 949, 955 (5th Cir. 1983). The Supreme Court's call for judicial caution in *Rowley* had little effect on the lower courts in extended school year

cases. Among the post-*Rowley* decisions are the following: *Georgia Association for Retarded Children; Alamo Heights; Crawford* v. *Pittman,* 708 F.2d 1028 (5th Cir. 1983); *Yaris* v. *Special School District,* 558 F. Supp. 545 (E.D. Mo. 1983), aff'd 728 F.2d 1055 (8th Cir. 1984); and *Stanton* v. *Board of Education of Norwich Central School District,* 581 F. Supp. 190 (N.D. N.Y. 1983). *Anderson* v. *Thompson,* 495 F. Supp. 1256 (E.D. Wisc. 1980); and *Phipps* v. *New Hanover County Board of Education,* 551 F. Supp 732 (E.D. N.C. 1982) came before *Rowley.*

15. *Alamo Heights,* 1158.

16. The many cases on suspension and expulsion are summarized in *Handicapped Students and Special Education* (Rosemount, Minn.: Data Research, Inc., 1991), pp. 67–75; and in Center for Law and Education, *Special Education: An Overview of Federal Law and Recent Legal Developments* (Cambridge, Mass., 1987), pp. 163–94.

17. *S-1* v. *Turlington,* 635 F.2d 342, 347 (5th Cir. 1981).

18. *Kaelin* v. *Grubbs,* 682 F.2d 595 (6th Cir. 1982).

19. *Stuart* v. *Nappi,* 443 F. Supp. 1235 (D. Conn. 1978).

20. *School Board of the County of Prince William* v. *Malone,* 762 F.2d 1210 (4th Cir. 1985).

21. *Victoria L.* v. *District School Board of Lee County, Florida,* 741 F.2d 369 (11th Cir. 1984).

22. *Honig* v. *Doe,* 484 U.S. 305, 324–25 (1988), emphasis in original.

23. Both the California Superintendent of Public Instruction and the National School Boards Associations, the two parties that tried to persuade the Supreme Court to find a "dangerousness" exception in the act, decided not to ask Congress to amend the law. They were in part appeased by the Court's recognition of the option of seeking a court order to remove a dangerous child—an option not specified by the act. Nadine Cohodas, "Right to Bar Handicapped Students Limited," *Congressional Quarterly Weekly Report,* January 23, 1988, p. 159.

24. *Vogel* v. *School Board of Montrose,* 491 F. Supp. 989 (W.D. Mo. 1980); *Robert M.* v. *Benton,* 634 F.2d 1138 (8th Cir. 1980); *Helms* v. *McDaniel,* 657 F.2d 800 (5th Cir. 1981); *Kotowicz* v. *Mississippi,* 630 F. Supp. 925 (S.D. Miss. 1986); and *Mayson* v. *Teague,* 749 F.2d 652 (11th Cir. 1984). For a discussion of the issues raised in this case, see Donal M. Sachen, "*Mayson v. Teague*: The Dilemma of Selecting Hearing Officers," 16 *Journal of Law and Education* 187 (1987).

25. *Mayson* v. *Teague,* 658–59.

26. Sec. 1401(a)(17), emphasis added.

27. Judith Welch Wegner, "Variations on a Theme: The Concept of Equal Educational Opportunity and Programming Decisions under the Education for All Handicapped Children Act of 1975," 48 *Law and Contemporary Problems* 169, 200 (1985). For a summary of cases, see *Handicapped Students and Special Education,* pp. 66–75; and Thomas B. Mooney and Lorraine M. Aronson, "Solomon Revisited: Separating Educational and Other than Educational Needs in Special Education Residential Placements," 14 *Connecticut Law Review* 531 (1982).

28. *North* v. *District of Columbia Board of Education*, 471 F. Supp. 136, 141 (D.D.C. 1979).

29. *Kruelle* v. *New Castle County School District*, 642 F.2d 687, 693 (3d Cir. 1981). This case and *North* v. *D.C. Board* have become the main precedents on related services.

30. *Abrahamson* v. *Hershman*, 701 F.2d 223, 228 (1st Cir. 1983).

31. *Parks* v. *Pavkovic*, 753 F.2d 1397 (7th Cir. 1985). This opinion was written by Judge Richard Posner, hardly a flaming liberal. Also, *Christopher T.* v. *San Francisco Unified School District*, 553 F. Supp. 1107 (N.D. Cal. 1982).

32. James Stark, "Tragic Choices in Special Education: The Effect of Scarce Resources on the Implementation of Pub.L. 94-142," 14 *Connecticut Law Review* 477, 495–96 (1982).

33. *Darlene L.* v. *Illinois State Board of Education*, 568 F. Supp. 1340 (N.D. Ill. 1983); *McKenzie* v. *Jefferson*, 566 F. Supp. 404 (D.D.C. 1983); *TG* v. *Board of Education*, 576 F. Supp. 420 (D.N.J. 1983), aff'd 738 F.2d 425 (3d Cir. 1984); *Doe* v. *Anrig*, 692 F.2d 800 (1st Cir. 1982); and *Papacoda* v. *Connecticut*, 528 F. Supp. 68 (D. Conn. 1981).

34. *Espino* v. *Besteiro*, 520 F. Supp. 905 (S.D. Tex. 1981), aff'd 708 F.2d 1002 (5th Cir. 1983).

35. *Department of Education, State of Hawaii* v. *Katherine D.*, 531 F. Supp. 517 (D. Hawaii 1982). But in *Detsel* v. *Board of Education*, 637 F. Supp. 1022 (N.D. N.Y. 1986), the judge ruled that the act did not require school officials to provide constant monitoring of a student to keep her lungs clear.

36. *Irving Independent School District* v. *Tatro*, 468 U.S. 883, 893 (1984).

37. Note, "Enforcing the Right to an 'Appropriate' Education: The Education for All Handicapped Children Act of 1975," 92 *Harvard Law Review* 1103, 1127 (1979). A number of judges cited this article, including the district court in *Rowley*, discussed below.

38. Mark G. Yudof, "Education for the Handicapped: *Rowley* in Perspective," *American Journal of Education*, vol. 92 (February 1984), p. 165.

39. *Hendrick Hudson District Board of Education* v. *Rowley*.

40. Wegner, "Variations on a Theme," p. 179. Katherine Bartlett notes that "a fundamental disagreement about the basic purpose and thrust of this legislation" has "created confusion and inconsistency" in the case law. "The Role of Cost in Educational Decisionmaking for the Handicapped Child," 48 *Law and Contemporary Problems* 7, 18 (1985).

41. *Bales* v. *Clark*, 523 F. Supp. 1366, 1370 (E.D. Va. 1981).

42. *Pinkerton* v. *Moye*, 509 F. Supp. 107, 113 (W.D. Va. 1981). See also *Age* v. *Bullit*, 673 F.2d 145 (6th Cir. 1982).

43. Wegner provides an extensive list of cases adopting a more aggressive approach in "Variations on a Theme," pp. 180–81, nn. 45, 46, 48.

44. *Kruelle* v. *New Castle County School Board*, 692.

45. *Gladys J.* v. *Pearland Independent School District*, 520 F. Supp. 869, 879 (S.D. Tex. 1981).

46. *Espino* v. *Besteiro*, 911.

47. *Rowley* v. *Board of Education of Hendrick Hudson Central School District*, 483 F. Supp. 528, 535 (S.D. N.Y. 1980).

48. *Rowley* v. *Board of Education of Hendrick Hudson*, 632 F.2d 945, 948 (2d Cir. 1980). Judge Mansfield dissented. He argued that "no support for this definition [of appropriateness] is to be found in the Act, its legislative history, or in regulations promulgated thereunder," and that the standard employed by the district court had been "borrowed from a law review note" (the *Harvard Law Review* article cited above in note 37) (*Rowley* v. *Board of Education*, 952).

49. *Hendrick Hudson District Board of Education* v. *Rowley*, 188–89, 206.

50. Ibid., 192, 200, 207, emphasis added.

51. Ibid., 215, 216.

52. Mark Weber, "The Transformation of the Education of the Handicapped Act: A Study in the Interpretation of a Radical Statute," 24 *U.C. Davis Law Review* 349, 353–54 (1990). Weber praises the lower courts for ignoring the Supreme Court and saving "the Act's original, radical message." According to another law review note, a key feature of the standard of review announced in *Rowley* is "the ease with which it can be manipulated." Shawn Elizabeth Carroll, "Defining Appropriate Education for the Handicapped: The *Rowley* Decision," 27 *Saint Louis University Law Journal* 685, 702 (1983).

53. Sy DuBow and Sarah Geer, "Special Education Law since *Rowley*," *Clearinghouse Review*, vol. 17 (January 1984), p. 1005. See, for example, *Adams by Adams* v. *Hansen*, 632 F. Supp. 858 (N.D. Cal. 1985). Immediately after citing *Rowley*, the judge stated, "The court must make an independent determination of the appropriateness of the child's placement, and need not defer to the findings of administrative agencies" (865).

54. In a concurring opinion, Judge Levin Campbell commented, "The thrust of this is hard to square with *Rowley*." *Doe* v. *Anrig*, 806, 813, emphasis in the original.

55. See, for example, *Abrahamson* v. *Hershman*, another ruling of the First Circuit. Immediately after quoting the Supreme Court's command to give "due weight" to the determinations of state officials, the court quoted the 1975 conference report, which called for an "independent" judicial appraisal of the evidence (230). Another example is *Springdale School District* v. *Grace*, 656 F.2d 300 (8th Cir. 1981), and 693 F.2d 41 (8th Cir. 1982). One review article notes, "Interestingly, the court of appeals found no justification for altering its reasoning, thus arriving at the same decision using both standards [of review]." Cathy Broadwell and John Walden, ' "Free Appropriate Public Education' after *Rowley*: An Analysis of Recent Court Decisions," 17 *Journal of Law and Education* 35, 42 (1988).

56. *Hall* v. *Vance City Board of Education*, 774 F.2d 629, 635–36 (4th Cir. 1985).

57. *Polk* v. *Central Susquehanna Intermediate Unit* 16, 853 F.2d 171, 182–83 (3d Cir. 1988).

58. For another example of this line of reasoning, see *Blazejewski* v. *Board of Education of Allegheny Central School*, 560 F. Supp. 701 (W.D. N.Y. 1983); and other cases discussed in Weber, "Transformation of the Education of the Handi-

capped Act," pp. 379–88; and in Dixie Snow Huefner, "Judicial Review of the Special Educational Program Requirements under the Education for All Handicapped Children Act: Where Have We Been and Where Should We Be Going?" 13 *Harvard Journal of Law and Public Policy* 2, 494–500 (1991).

59. *Roncker* v. *Walter*, 700 F.2d 1058, 1062–63 (6th Cir. 1983).

60. Weber points out that the court's reasoning "cannot disguise the fact that the implications of *Roncker* run far to the contrary of *Rowley*" and cites a number of other cases that follow the *Roncker* decision. "Transformation of the Education of the Handicapped Act," p. 391.

61. *David D.* v. *Dartmouth School Committee*, 775 F.2d 411, 419 (1st Cir. 1985).

62. The other circuit cases are *Geis* v. *Board of Education*, 774 F.2d 575 (3d Cir. 1985); and *Students of California School for the Blind* v. *Honig*, 736 F.2d 538 (9th Cir. 1984).

63. See Janet Hook, "House Committee OKs Aid for Handicapped Preschoolers," *Congressional Quarterly Weekly Report*, September 20, 1986, p. 2221; and Hook, "Congress Clears Legislation on Education for Handicapped," *Congressional Quarterly Weekly Report*, September 27, 1986, p. 2322.

64. *Smith* v. *Robinson*, 468 U.S. 992 (1984).

65. *Alyeska Pipeline Serv. Co.* v. *Wilderness Society*, 421 U.S. 240 (1975).

66. The quotations come from, respectively, Senators Lowell Weicker, Edward Kennedy, and John Kerry, *Congressional Record*, daily ed., July 30, 1985, pp. S10398, S10399.

67. *Congressional Record*, daily ed., November 12, 1985, p.H9969.

68. *Handicapped Children's Protection Act of 1985*, Hearings before the Subcommittee on the Handicapped, Senate Committee on Labor and Human Resources, 99 Cong. 1 sess. (GPO, 1985), p. 47.

69. *Dellmuth* v. *Muth*, 491 U.S. 223, 230 (1989).

70. Education of the Handicapped Act Amendments of 1990, P.L. 101-476.

71. Quoted in Milton Budoff, Alan Orenstein, and Carol Kervick, *Due Process in Special Education: On Going to a Hearing* (Cambridge, Mass.: Ware Press, 1982), p. 199. Several other studies have also found that administrators are eager to settle cases on terms favorable to parents in order to avoid the ordeal of a hearing. Peterson, Rabe, and Wong, *When Federalism Works*, p. 127; and Paul T. Hill and Doren L. Madley, *Educational Policymaking through the Civil Justice System* (Santa Monica: Rand, 1982), pp. vi–vii.

72. Budoff and others, *Due Process in Special Education*, p. 119.

73. R. Douglas Arnold, *The Logic of Congressional Action* (Yale University Press, 1990), p. 48.

Chapter 9

1. "Program Information Report, May, 1993," supplied by U.S. Department of Agriculture, Food and Nutrition Service, Data Base Monitoring Branch, p. 1.

2. G. William Hoagland, "Perception and Reality in Nutrition Programs," in John C. Weicher, ed., *Maintaining the Safety Net: Income Redistribution Programs in the Reagan Administration* (American Enterprise Institute, 1984), p. 45.

3. "1993 Budget-Reconciliation Act," *Congressional Quarterly Weekly Report*, September 18, 1993, p. 2491.

4. Paul E. Peterson and Mark C. Rom, "The Case for a National Welfare Standard," *Brookings Review*, vol. 6 (Winter 1988), p. 28.

5. *Overview of Entitlement Programs: Background Material and Data on Programs within the Jurisdiction of the Committee on Ways and Means, 1992 Green Book*, Committee Print, House Committee on Ways and Means, 102 Cong. 2 sess. (Government Printing Office, 1992), pp. 1631–36, table 10 (hereinafter cited as *1992 Green Book*). See also Paul E. Peterson and Mark C. Rom, *Welfare Magnets: A New Case for a National Standard* (Brookings, 1990), pp. 166–67.

6. *Food Stamps: The Statement of Hon. William E. Simon, Secretary of the Treasury, with a Staff Analysis*, Committee Print, Senate Select Committee on Nutrition and Human Need, 94 Cong. 1 sess. (GPO, 1975), p. 109. The program's role as a welfare supplement and welfare equalizer is examined in Richard D. Nathan, "Food Stamps and Welfare Reform," *Policy Analysis*, vol. 2 (Winter 1976), pp. 61–70.

7. P.L. 91-671. Since Congress completed work on the legislation in 1970, it is commonly known as the 1970 act. Because President Nixon signed the bill in early 1971, it is occasionally referred to as the 1971 act. This book uses the former appellation.

8. *Gutierrez v. Butz*, 415 F. Supp. 827, 830 (D.D.C. 1976).

9. *Knebel v. Hein*, 429 U.S. 288 (1977).

10. *Congressional Record*, September 16, 1977, p. 29568.

11. Food Research and Action Center, "Food Research," *Clearinghouse Review*, vol. 14 (January 1981), p. 982. FRAC warned that litigation might increase under the Reagan administration. While food stamp advocates did challenge many administrative rulings in the early 1980s, they did not win any important cases for the reason explained in the text. The change after 1977 is evident in FRAC's annual review of legal developments in the *Clearinghouse Review*.

12. Quoted in Daniel P. Moynihan, *The Politics of a Guaranteed Income: The Nixon Administration and the Family Assistance Plan* (Vintage, 1973), p. 124.

13. *Report of the President's Task Force on Food Assistance* (Washington, January 1984), p. 2.

14. Cited in Robert Y. Shapiro and others, "Public Assistance," *Public Opinion Quarterly*, vol. 51 (Spring 1987), p. 123.

15. Descriptions of the "hunger lobby" are contained in Jeffrey Berry, *Feeding Hungry People: Rulemaking in the Food Stamp Program* (Rutgers University Press, 1986), pp. 90–93; Bill Keller, "Facing the Reagan Ax: Special Treatment No Longer Given Advocates for the Poor," *Congressional Quarterly Weekly Report*, April 18, 1981, pp. 659–64; Linda E. Demkovich, "FRAC: A Lean, Mean Hunger Machine Fueled by Research, Action, Controversy," *National Journal*, January 28, 1984, pp. 169–73; and a series of articles by Steven V. Roberts that

appeared in the *New York Times*, ' "Antihunger' Lobbyists Start Their Rounds," March 11, 1981, p. B5; "Food Stamp Backers Drafting Strategy," March 29, 1981, p. 30; and "Congressional Battle on Food Stamps Is Joined and Is Already Half Over," April 8, 1991, p. A25.

16. There are surprisingly few writings on the politics of food stamps. By far the best book is Berry's *Feeding Hungry People*. Berry focuses on the administrative process between 1967 and 1975 but also provides important insights into the legislative process. Sections of this and the following chapter draw upon his work. Three government sources provide an extensive history and analysis of the program: *Food Stamp Act of 1976*, H. Rept. 94-1460, 94 Cong. 2 sess. (GPO, 1976) (hereinafter cited as *1976 House Report*); *Food Stamp Act of 1977*, H. Rept. 95-464, 95 Cong. 1 sess. (GPO, 1977) (hereinafter cited as *1977 House Report*); and *The Food Stamp Program: History, Description, Issues, and Options*, Committee Print 99-32, Senate Committee on Agriculture, Nutrition and Forestry, 99 Cong. 1 sess. (GPO, 1985). Chapter 5 of Kent Weaver's *Automatic Government: The Politics of Indexation* (Brookings, 1988) provides a perceptive analysis of budget politics. Nick Kotz's *Let Them Eat Promises: The Politics of Hunger in America* (Anchor, 1971) provides a vivid, if polemical, look at the program.

17. Nathan, "Food Stamps and Welfare Reform," p. 64.

18. "Available income" means total income minus deductions for such items as high housing costs, unusual medical expenditures, and work expenses. For most participating households available income is about two-thirds of total income.

19. *1992 Green Book*, p. 1624.

20. Congressional Budget Office, *The Food Stamp Program: Income or Food Supplementation?* (January 1977).

21. The findings of a few studies on the subject are reviewed in appendix D of the *Report of the President's Task Force on Food Assistance*, pp. 215–27. Most of these studies were conducted before elimination of the purchase requirement.

22. Ibid., p. 225.

23. George G. Graham, "Searching For Hunger in America," *The Public Interest*, no. 78 (Winter 1985), p. 13–15.

24. Maurice MacDonald, *Food, Stamps, and Income Maintenance* (Academic Press, 1977), p. 58. This book was written shortly before elimination of the purchase requirement. MacDonald noted that "eliminating the purchase requirement would weaken the already indirect link between the program's effects on recipient behavior and food consumption (or nutritional status)" (p. 122).

25. *1976 House Report*, p. 230.

26. *1977 House Report*, p. 243.

27. *National Nutrition Policy Study—1974: Part 3A, Appendix to Nutrition and Special Groups*, Hearings before the Senate Select Committee on Nutrition and Human Needs, 93 Cong. 2 sess (GPO, 1974), p. 1227. See also Kotz, *Let Them Eat Promises*, pp. 230–34.

28. *National Nutrition Policy Study: Report and Recommendations*, pt. 8, Committee Print, Senate Select Committee on Nutrition, 93 Cong. 2 sess. (GPO, 1974), pp. 54, 31, 11.

29. "Poll: Let the Ax Fall," *Newsweek*, February 23, 1981, p. 19. According to an ABC poll, by 1986 only 32 percent of respondents favored cuts in the program. Shapiro and others, "Public Assistance," p. 129.

30. Hugh Heclo, "The Political Foundation of Antipoverty Policy," in Sheldon Danzinger and Daniel Weinberg, eds., *Fighting Poverty: What Works and What Doesn't* (Harvard University Press, 1986), p. 339.

31. *Food Stamp Reform*, Hearings before the Subcommittee on Agriculture Research and General Legislation of the Senate Committee on Agriculture and Forestry, 94 Cong. 1 sess. (GPO, 1975), p. 201.

32. The leading work on this topic is Randall B. Ripley, "Legislative Bargaining and the Food Stamp Act, 1964," in Frederic N. Cleaveland, ed., *Congress and Urban Problems* (Brookings, 1969), pp. 279–310.

33. John Ferejohn, "Logrolling in an Institutional Context: A Case Study of Food Stamp Legislation," in Gerald C. Wright, Jr., Leroy N. Rieselbach, and Lawrence C. Dodd, eds., *Congress and Policy Change* (New York: Agathon Press, 1986), pp. 223–53. Even Randall Ripley, the original proponent of the logrolling thesis, agrees with Ferejohn on the crucial point: "It is likely that the food stamp bill could have passed the floor without being attached to any rurally oriented bill." "Legislative Bargaining," p. 310.

34. R. Kent Weaver, *Automatic Government: The Politics of Indexation* (Brookings, 1988), p. 101.

35. Ferejohn, "Logrolling," p. 233.

36. Quoted in John K. Iglehart, "Hunger Report/Rush-Hour Compromise Portends Fresh Quarrel in New Congress," *National Journal*, January 16, 1971, p. 114.

37. Steven S. Smith and Christopher J. Deering, *Committees in Congress* (CQ Press, 1984), p. 141.

38. Kotz, *Let Them Eat Promises*, p. xvi.

39. Moynihan, *Politics of a Guaranteed Income*, pp. 117, 120.

40. The child actually did not die of starvation. It had been born three months prematurely (weighing three pounds) after its mother suffered an auto accident. Agriculture Secretary Orville Freeman characterized "Hunger in America" as "a biased, one-sided, dishonest presentation," full of "errors of fact," "misinterpretations," and "misinformation." Quoted in Gilbert Y. Steiner, *The State of Welfare* (Brookings, 1971), p. 231. The House Agriculture Committee wrote an angry report attacking the misrepresentations of the documentary. *Hunger Study*, Committee Print, House Committee on Agriculture, 90 Cong. 2 sess. (GPO, 1968); and *Hunger Study Supplement (Supplement to Hunger Study, June 11, 1968)*, Committee Print, House Committee on Agriculture, 90 Cong. 2 sess. (GPO, 1968).

41. Michael Foley, *The New Senate: Liberal Influence on a Conservative Institution, 1959-72* (Yale University Press, 1980), p. 77.

42. Kotz, *Let Them Eat Promises*, p. 195.

43. Martha Derthick, *Agency under Stress: The Social Security Administration in American Government* (Brookings. 1990), pp. 160–61.

44. Quoted in Berry, *Feeding Hungry People*, p. 50.

45. Ibid., p. 159, n. 25.

46. Kotz, *Let Them Eat Promises*, pp. 65, 97, 54, 23.

47. Quoted in Moynihan, *Politics of a Guaranteed Income*, p. 121.

48. *Nutrition and Human Needs, Part 8—The Nixon Administration Program*, Hearings before the Senate Select Committee on Nutrition and Human Needs, 91 Cong. 1 sess. (GPO, 1969), pp. 2437-38.

49. The quotation comes from Berry, *Feeding Hungry People*, p. 63. On the history of the 1970 legislation, see ibid., pp. 59-64; *Congressional Quarterly Almanac, 1969*, vol. 25, pp. 823-31; *Congressional Quarterly Almanac, 1970*, vol. 26, pp. 764-67; and *Food Stamp Program*, Committee Print 99-32, pp. 32-42.

50. John Kramer, quoted in Iglehart, "Hunger Report," p. 113.

51. 36 Fed. Reg. 14102-20 (1971); and 37 Fed. Reg. 1180 (1972). Berry, *Feeding Hungry People*, pp. 68-76, provides a good review of the rulemaking process.

52. *Nutrition and Human Needs, 1971*, Hearings before the Senate Select Committee on Nutrition and Human Needs, 92 Cong. 1 sess. (GPO, 1971), pp. 759, 762, 786, 896.

53. Ibid., p. 975 (testimony of Richard Lyng).

54. Quoted in *Food Stamp Program*, Committee Print 99-32, p. 43.

55. Quoted in Berry, *Feeding Hungry People*, p. 74. See also Jack Rosenthal, "10% Impounded in Food Stamp Act," *New York Times*, January 12, 1972, p. A1.

Chapter 10

1. Jeffrey M. Berry, *Feeding Hungry People: Rulemaking in the Food Stamp Program* (Rutgers University Press, 1984), p. 93.

2. Ronald Pollack, "Legal Services and the Fight against Hunger," *Clearinghouse Review*, vol. 3 (June 1969), p. 38.

3. *Jay* v. *USDA*, 308 F. Supp. 100, 106, 105 (N.D. Tex. 1969). The California case was *Hernandez* v. *Hardit*, Civil Action 50333 (N.D. Cal. 1968).

4. *Jay* v. *U.S. Department of Agriculture*, 441 F. 2d 574 (5th Cir. 1971). The Fifth Circuit relied on the reasoning of the First Circuit in a similar case, *Tucker* v. *Hardin*, 430 F.2d 737 (1st Cir. 1970). The litigation is described in Earl Johnson, Jr., *Justice and Reform: The Formative Years of the Legal Services Program* (New York: Russell Sage, 1974), p. 205; and Martha F. Davis, *Brutal Need: Lawyers and the Welfare Rights Movement, 1960–1973* (Yale University Press, 1993), pp. 75-76.

5. *Trump* v. *Butz*, Civil Action 76-933 (May 1976). Unpublished.

6. *Bennett* v. *Butz*, 386 F. Supp. 1059 (D. Minn. 1974). Judge Lord's role in the impoundment controversy is described in Louis Fisher, *Presidential Spending Power* (Princeton University Press, 1975), pp. 179-81, 189-92.

7. The Supreme Court has decided several constitutional law cases involving food stamps. None of these rulings had an important long-term effect on operation of the program. *USDA* v. *Murry*, 413 U.S. 508 (1973) struck down a poorly

drafted provision in the 1970 act designed to deny food stamps to college students. A year later, Congress imposed a more carefully worded restriction that survived court review. The history of this legislation is reviewed in *Food Stamp Act of 1977*, H. Rept. 95-464, 95 Cong. 1 sess. (Government Printing Office, 1977), pp. 101–05 (hereinafter cited as *1977 House Report*). *USDA* v. *Moreno*, 413 U.S. 528 (1973) struck down another provision of the 1970 law, this one limiting eligibility to groups of "related" individuals. This restriction, added on the House floor, was designed to prevent "hippie communes" from receiving benefits. The Supreme Court ruled that under the equal protection clause "a bare congressional desire to harm a politically unpopular group cannot constitute a legitimate governmental interest." Since few "hippie communes" ever received food stamps, this issue quickly faded away. See *1977 House Report*, p. 143. In *Lyng* v. *Castillo*, 477 U.S. 635 (1986), the Court upheld the standard filing unit. Its decision was similar to *Bowen* v. *Gilliard*, discussed in chapter 5. Finally, in *Lyng* v. *Automobile Workers*, 485 U.S. 360 (1988), it upheld a provision denying food stamps to strikers.

8. *Rodway* v. *USDA*, 514 F.2d 809, 820 (D.C. Cir. 1975). The 1970 act added three separate references to a "nutritionally adequate diet." Its general statement of policy announced, "To alleviate such hunger and malnutrition, a food stamp program is herein authorized which will permit low-income households to purchase a nutritionally adequate diet through normal channels of trade" (sec. 2011). The 1964 act had stated that the purpose of the act was to "permit those households with low incomes to receive a greater share of the Nation's food abundance." Sec. 2013(a) of the 1970 act provided the secretary of agriculture with general authority "to formulate and administer a food stamp program under which, at the request of the State agency, eligible households within the State shall be provided with an opportunity to obtain a nutritionally adequate diet through the issuance to them of a coupon allotment." The statute had previously stated that the secretary was authorized to establish a program in which eligible households would be "provided with an opportunity more nearly to obtain a nutritionally adequate diet." Finally, sec. 2016(a) stated that the value of the coupon allotment "shall be in such amount as the Secretary determines to be the cost of a nutritionally adequate diet, adjusted annually to reflect changes in the price of food." This section of the statute had previously stated that the value of coupons "shall be in such amount as will provide such households with an opportunity more nearly to obtain a low-cost nutritionally adequate diet." Judge Wright stressed the fact that the 1970 act dropped the word "more nearly" from sections 2013 and 2016. He did not mention the fact that the 1970 law also added the words "as the Secretary determines," language that the USDA argued provided it with broad discretion.

9. *Congressional Record*, December 16, 1970, p. 42006.

10. *Amendments to the Food Stamp Act of 1964*, H.Rept. 91-1793, 91 Cong. 2 sess. (GPO, 1970), p. 9.

11. *Rodway* v. *USDA*, 482 F.2d 722, 728 n. 17 (D.C. Cir. 1973). The district court's memorandum was not published.

12. *Rodway* v. *USDA*, 369 F. Supp. 1094 (D.D.C. 1973).

13. *Rodway* v. *USDA*, 514 F.2d 809, 818 n. 16.

14. Ibid., 824. Judge Wilkey refused to join this part of the opinion, labeling it "dicta," adding, "whether it is all helpful dicta may be problematical" (824).

15. *Food Stamp Reform*, Hearings before the Subcommittee on Agriculture Research and General Legislation of the Senate Committee on Agriculture and Forestry, 94 Cong. 1 sess. (GPO, 1975), p. 624.

16. Gilbert Y. Steiner, *The State of Welfare* (Brookings, 1971), pp. 213–20.

17. Interview with Ronald Hill, Alberta Frost, and Ed Barron, USDA, June 12, 1986.

18. *Bennett* v. *Butz*.

19. Ibid., 1066, 1071.

20. *1977 House Report*, p. 345.

21. *Tyson* v. *Norton*, 390 F. Supp. 545, 552 (D. Conn. 1975), emphasis in original, upheld in *Tyson* v. *Maher*, 523 F.2d 972 (2d. Cir. 1975).

22. Examples include *Tyson* v. *Norton*; *Aiken* v. *Obledo*, 442 F. Supp. 628 (E.D. Cal. 1977); and *Bermudez* v. *USDA*, 348 F. Supp. 1279 (D.D.C. 1972). For a discussion of efforts to force states to process applications more quickly, see David B. Beumeyer, "Developments in Food Program Legislation and Case Law in 1986," *Clearinghouse Review*, vol. 20 (February 1987), pp. 1271–72.

23. *Hamilton* v. *Butz*, 520 F.2d 709, 712 (9th Cir. 1975).

24. *Turchin* v. *Butz*, 405 F. Supp. 1263 (D. Minn. 1976). This decision was criticized in *1977 House Report*, p. 28.

25. *Schmiege* v. *USDA*, 693 F.2d 55 (8th Cir. 1982).

26. *Shaffer* v. *Block*, 705 F.2d 805 (6th Cir. 1983).

27. *West* v. *Bowen*, 879 F.2d 1122 (3d Cir. 1989).

28. *McCoy* v. *Bergland*, 519 F. Supp. 796 (D.C. N.Y. 1981); *Allen* v. *Bergland*, 661 F.2d 1001 (4th Cir. 1981); and *Commonwealth of Massachusetts* v. *Lyng*, 893 F.2d 424 (1st Cir. 1990).

29. *Dupler* v. *City of Portland*, 421 F. Supp. 1314 (D. Me. 1976).

30. *Anderson* v. *Butz*, 428 F. Supp. 245 (N.D. Cal. 1975), and 550 F.2d 459 (9th Cir. 1977).

31. The amendment was proposed by Representative Richard Ichord, who had little other contact with the food stamp program. Through a typographical error, the Sixth Circuit referred to it as the "Ichabod Amendment." *Compton* v. *Tennessee*, 532 F.2d 561, 565 (6th Cir. 1976). This helped give the litigation a surreal aura.

32. *Anderson* v. *Butz*, 252.

33. *Compton* v. *Tennessee*, 532 F. 2d 561 (6th Cir. 1976).

34. Sec. 5(d)(1) of the 1977 amendments, discussed in *1977 House Report*, pp. 31–33.

35. *Gutierrez* v. *Butz*, 415 F. Supp. 827, 830 (D.D.C. 1976).

36. *Knebel* v. *Hein*, 429 U.S. 288 (1977).

37. *Shea* v. *Vialpando*, 416 U.S. 251 (1974).

38. "Food Stamp Restructuring," *Congressional Quarterly Weekly Report*, February 28, 1976, p. 498.

39. Berry, *Feeding Hungry People*, p. 92.

40. Quoted in Mary Link, "Food Stamp Program Faces Major Overhaul," *Congressional Quarterly Weekly Report*, February 21, 1976, p. 444.

41. "Income Assistance," *Congressional Quarterly Weekly Report*, January 24, 1976, p. 142; and "Food Stamps Text," *Congressional Quarterly Weekly Report*, October 25, 1975, p. 2260.

42. Berry, *Feeding Hungry People*, pp. 82–83.

43. Link, "Food Stamp Program Faces Major Overhaul."

44. *Supplemental Appropriations Bill, 1976*, H. Rept. 94-645, 94 Cong. 1 sess. (GPO, 1976), p. 7.

45. *Congressional Record*, February 4, 1975, pp. 2199–223.

46. 41 Fed. Reg. 8505 (1976); and 41 Fed. Reg. 18781 (1976).

47. Mary Link, "Senate Passes Food Stamp Reform Bill," *Congressional Quarterly Weekly Report*, April 10, 1976, pp. 807–09.

48. Mary Link, "House Food Stamp Bill Reported, but Appears Dead for This Session," *Congressional Quarterly Weekly Report*, September 18, 1976, pp. 2542–46. Many of the close votes in the committee's markup session are summarized in *Food Stamp Act of 1976*, H. Rept. 94-1460, 94 Cong. 2 sess. (GPO, 1976), pp. 650–55 (hereinafter cited as *1976 House Report*).

49. *1976 House Report*, pp. 633, 608.

50. Berry, *Feeding Hungry People*, p. 90.

51. Interview with Robert Greenstein, June 11, 1986.

52. Quoted in "Food Stamp Restructuring."

53. 41 Fed. Reg. 18781 (1976).

54. *1976 House Report*, p. 638.

55. Interview with Ronald Pollack, June 11, 1986.

56. Kathryn Waters Gest, "Food Stamp Program Overhauled by Congress," *Congressional Quarterly Weekly Report*, September 24, 1977, p. 2017.

57. *Food Stamp Act Amendments of 1980*, H. Rept. 96-788, 96 Cong. 2 sess. (GPO, 1980), pp. 33, 47.

58. Quoted in Berry, *Feeding Hungry People*, p. 111. John Kramer, who wrote much of the report, made a similar point in my interview with him on June 12, 1986. The USDA's explanation of its 1978 regulations makes over fifty references to the House report but virtually none to the Senate and conference reports. 43 Fed. Reg. 18874–958 (1978); and 43 *Federal Register* 47846–81 (1978).

59. *1976 House Report*, p. 703. Republicans on the committee had offered similar complaints about the courts in 1975. *Expedited Food Stamp Certification*, H. Rept. 94-428, 94 Cong. 1 sess. (GPO, 1975) pp. 39, 45, 75.

60. Several House staff members emphasized this in personal interviews with me. The real proof, though, is in the legislative pudding, which is examined below.

61. *Congressional Record*, September 16, 1977, p. 29568.

62. *1976 House Report*, pp. 267–75 (certification); p. 32 (rent subsidies); p. 77 (migrants); and pp. 340–47. Congress had trouble making up its mind on outreach. In 1976 the House committee first removed the requirement, then put it back. *Expedited Food Stamp Certification*, H. Rept. 94-428, pp. 333–35. In 1980

Congress made outreach optional for the states. The budget reconciliation act of 1981 went a step further, prohibiting federal money from being spent on outreach. P.L.-35, sec. 111(a), now sec. 11(e) (1) of the act.

63. 7 U.S.C. 2011. The vote is recorded in *1977 House Report*, p. 860.

64. Ibid., p. 246.

65. Ibid.

66. Ibid., p. 19.

67. Ibid., p. 27. The 1976 committee report had criticized the lower court decision eventually overturned by the Supreme Court. *1976 House Report*, p. 58.

68. Food Stamp Act, sec. 22(e)(4), emphasis added.

69. *1977 House Report*, pp. 282–83.

70. The vote is recorded in *1977 House Report*, p. 860.

71. *Banks v. Block*, 700 F.2d 292 (6th Cir. 1983), cert. denied 464 U.S. 934 (1983); *Holman v. Block*, 823 F.2d 56 (4th Cir. 1987); and *Jackson v. Jackson*, 857 F.2d 951 (4th Cir. 1988).

72. *Food and Agriculture Act of 1977*, S. Rept. 95-180, 95 Cong. 1 sess. (GPO, 1977), p. 116.

73. Ibid.

74. The first quotation comes from Representative Bob Bergland, the second from an unnamed lobbyist, and the third from political scientist Garrison Nelson. Alan Ehrenhalt, "House Agriculture: New Faces, New Issues," *Congressional Quarterly Weekly Report*, February 22, 1975, p. 379; and "The Turmoil and the Transition: Stage Set for New Speaker," *Congressional Quarterly Weekly Report*, May 27, 1989, p. 1226.

75. *Food Stamp Amendments of 1980*, H. Rept. 96-788, p. 47.

76. "Congress to Decide Fate of Food Stamps," *Congressional Quarterly Weekly Report*, February 7, 1981, pp. 277–78.

77. R. Kent Weaver, *Automatic Government: The Politics of Indexation* (Brookings, 1988), p. 325. G. William Hoagland provides a useful review of these budget cuts in "Perception and Reality in Nutrition Programs," in John C. Weicher, ed., *Maintaining the Safety Net: Income Redistribution Programs in the Reagan Administration* (American Enterprise Institute, 1984).

78. "House, Senate Agree on Hunger Bill," *Congressional Quarterly Weekly Report*, August 13, 1988, p. 2276.

79. Food, Agriculture, Conservation and Trade Amendments of 1991, P.L. 102-237, secs. 901–13. The omnibus budget bill that passed in August 1993 added $2.5 billion to the program over five years. *Congressional Quarterly Weekly Report*, August 7, 1993, p. 2142.

Chapter 11

1. St. John Barrett, "The New Role of the Courts in Developing Public Welfare Law," 1970 *Duke Law Journal* 1, 8 (1970).

2. E. E. Schattschneider, *Politics, Pressure, and the Tariff* (Prentice-Hall, 1935), p. 288.

3. Gerald N. Rosenberg, *The Hollow Hope: Can Courts Bring About Social Change?* (University of Chicago Press, 1991), pp. 338, 339, 341, emphasis in original.

4. James Madison, "No. 51," in Roy P. Fairfield, ed., *The Federalist Papers* (Johns Hopkins University Press, 1981), p. 159.

5. See Morton Keller, "Powers and Rights: Two Centuries of American Constitutionalism," in David Thelen, ed., *The Constitution and American Life* (Cornell University Press, 1988), pp. 15–34.

6. Colin S. Diver, "Statutory Interpretation in the Administrative State," 133 *University of Pennsylvania Law Review* 549, 551 (1985).

7. Ibid., 550–51.

8. *Marbury* v. *Madison*, 1 Cranch 137, 177 (1803).

9. *INS* v. *Cardoza-Fonseca*, 480 U.S. 421, 446 (1987).

10. *Udall* v. *Tallman*, 380 U.S. 1, 16 (1965).

11. *Chevron* v. *NRDC*, 467 U.S. 837, 843–44 (1984). For further description of these two lines of cases, see Diver, "Statutory Interpretation"; Antonin Scalia, "Judicial Deference to Administrative Interpretation of Law," 1989 *Duke Law Journal* 511 (1989); and the opinion of Judge Friendly in *Pittston Stevedoring Corp.* v. *Dellaventura*, 544 F.2d 35, 49–51 (2d Cir. 1976).

12. One such State Letter was more than 100 pages long. Martha Derthick, *The Influence of Federal Grants* (Harvard University Press, 1970), p. 228.

13. 45 C.F.R., pts. 200–307.

14. Jeffrey M. Berry, *Feeding Hungry People: Rulemaking in the Food Stamp Program* (Rutgers University Press, 1984), esp. chaps. 1–3.

15. 7 C.F.R., pts. 271–85.

16. 42 Fed. Reg. 42475 (1977).

17. 34 C.F.R., chap. 3, pts. 300–99.

18. Herbert Kaufman, *The Administrative Behavior of Federal Bureau Chiefs* (Brookings, 1981), pp. 47, 164. See also James Q. Wilson, *Bureaucracy: What Government Agencies Do and Why They Do It* (Basic Books, 1989), chap. 13; and Christopher H. Foreman, *Signals from the Hill: Congressional Oversight and the Challenge of Social Regulation* (Twentieth Century Fund, 1988).

19. Joel D. Aberbach, *Keeping a Watchful Eye: The Politics of Congressional Oversight* (Brookings, 1990), esp. chaps. 3, 8.

20. Berry, *Feeding Hungry People*, pp. 112–13.

21. *Supplemental Appropriations Act, 1976*, H. Rept. 94-645, 94 Cong. 1 sess. (Government Printing Office, 1976), p. 9.

22. Arthur Maass, *Congress and the Common Good* (Basic Books, 1983), pp. 138–41. Maass recalls one member of Congress telling him, "I'll let you write the statute if you let me write the committee report" (p. 139).

23. Senator James McClure, quoted in Joseph A. Davis, "War Declared over Report-Language Issue," *Congressional Quarterly Weekly Report*, June 25, 1988, p. 1752.

24. David Rapp, "OMB's Miller Backs Away from Report-Language Battle," *Congressional Quarterly Weekly Report*, July 9, 1988, p. 1928.

25. Quoted in ibid.

26. Peter L. Strauss, "When the Judge Is Not the Primary Official with Responsibility to Read: Agency Interpretation and the Problem of Legislative History," 66 *Chicago Kent Law Review* 321, 329 (1990). Strauss provides a vivid illustration of this point in "Revisiting *Overton Park*: Political and Judicial Controls over Administrative Actions Affecting the Community," 39 *UCLA Law Review* 1251 (1992).

27. Aberbach, *Keeping a Watchful Eye*, p. 162. Self-selection is not as common on the appropriations and revenue committees. This does not ensure, though, that these committees will be a cross-section of the parent body. For example, in the 1970s senators from the South and from rural areas dominated the Senate Finance Committee. Comprehensive welfare reform had more support on the Senate floor than on this committee.

28. For a particularly thoughtful discussion of this dilemma, see Joseph Cooper, *Origins of the Standing Committees and the Development of the Modern House*, vol. 56, no. 3, Rice University Studies (1970).

29. Maass, *Congress and the Common Good*, p. 42.

30. Justice Oliver Wendell Holmes, *Collected Legal Papers* (New York: Peter Smith, 1952), p. 295.

31. *Georgia Association of Retarded Children* v. *McDaniel*, 716 F.2d 1565, 1582 (11th Cir. 1983), Judge Hill dissenting.

32. In the first round of *King* v. *Smith*, for example, Judge Johnson ordered HEW to state its position. The department continued to waffle. See Martin Garbus, *Ready for the Defense* (Farrar, Straus and Giroux, 1971), p. 171. For another example of a court seeking HEW opinion and HEW refusing, see *Holley* v. *Lavine*, 553 F.2d 845 (2d Cir. 1977).

33. *Mayson* v. *Teague*, 749 F.2d 652, 657 n. 2 (11th Cir. 1984).

34. In his study of community development block grants, Donald Kettl found that public officials placed "regulatory issues relatively low on their agendas." They usually "saved their powder" for "the big and important battles, the debate over the authorization of new programs and the level at which they would be funded." Consequently, "there was no strong constituency to oppose the regulatory changes many other groups, particularly the public interest groups, wanted." *The Regulation of American Federalism* (Johns Hopkins University Press, 1983), pp. 110-11.

35. Timothy J. Conlan, "And the Beat Goes On: Intergovernmental Mandates and Preemption in an Era of Deregulation," *Publius*, vol. 21 (Summer 1991), pp. 53, 47.

36. Ibid., p. 44.

37. *Pennhurst State School and Hospital* v. *Halderman*, 451 U.S. 1, 17 (1981).

38. *Hilton* v. *South Carolina Public Railway Commission*, 112 S.Ct. 560, 567 (1991).

39. In addition to *Pennhurst* and *Hilton*, see *Gregory* v. *Ashcroft, Suter* v. *Artist M.*, and other cases cited in Charles Rothfeld, "Federalism in a Conservative Supreme Court," *Publius*, vol. 22 (Summer 1992), pp. 21–32.

40. See the discussion of *Dellmuth* v. *Muth*, chapter 8. Similarly, the Supreme Court's decision in *Atascadero State Hospital* v. *Scanlon*, 473 U.S. 234 (1985), was overturned by a section of the Rehabilitation Act Amendments of 1986, P.L. 99-506.

41. *Atkins* v. *Parker*, 472 U.S. 115, 146 (1985).

42. *Social Security Amendments of 1970*, S. Rept. 91-1431, 91 Cong. 2 sess. (GPO, 1970), p. 357. The Rehnquist quotation comes from *Arnett* v. *Kennedy*, 416 U.S. 134, 153–54 (1974).

43. *Dandridge* v. *Williams*, 397 U.S. 471, 490 (1970).

44. *Doe* v. *Shapiro*, 302 F. Supp. 761, 765 (D. Conn. 1969).

45. Jerry L. Mashaw, *Bureaucratic Justice: Managing Social Security Disability Claims* (Yale University Press, 1983), p. 29, emphasis omitted.

46. Judith Welch Wegner, "Variations on a Theme: The Concept of Equal Educational Opportunity and Programming Decisions under the Education for All Handicapped Children Act of 1975," 48 *Law and Contemporary Problems* 169, 188 (1985).

47. *Rodway* v. *USDA*, 514 F.2d 809 (D.C. Cir. 1975). For further discussion of the link between courts' use of statutory purpose and efforts to insulate the professional judgment of agency staff from political control, see Martin Shapiro, *Who Guards the Guardians? Judicial Control of Administration* (University of Georgia Press, 1988), chap. 5.

48. Mashaw, *Bureaucratic Justice*, p. 27.

49. *Battle* v. *Pennsylvania*, 629 F.2d 269, 280 (3d. Cir. 1980).

50. *Shea* v. *Vialpando*, 416 U.S. 251 (1974). Note that in *Knebel* v. *Hein*, 429 U.S. 288 (1977) the Supreme Court employed a presumption of administrative discretion and came to a much different conclusion on the same type of issue.

51. Quoted in Patricia M. Wald, "Some Observations on the Use of Legislative History in the 1981 Supreme Court Term," 68 *Iowa Law Review* 195, 214 (1983).

52. See discussion of *Dublino* in chapter 5.

53. *Anderson* v. *Butz*, 428 F. Supp. 245 (N.D. Cal. 1975), discussed in chapter 10. McGovern gave his speech after Legal Services filed suit. Given the close ties between Senator McGovern and food stamp litigants, it is unlikely that this was mere coincidence.

54. See Wegner, "Variations on a Theme," pp. 178–81.

55. Martha Derthick, *Agency under Stress: The Social Security Administration in the American Government* (Brookings, 1990), p. 149.

56. Peter L. Strauss, "One Hundred Fifty Cases Per Year: Some Implications of the Supreme Court's Limited Resources for Judicial Review of Agency Action," 87 *Columbia Law Review* 1093, 1105 (1987). Also see Richard Pierce, Jr., "Two Problems in Administrative Law: Political Polarity on the District of Columbia Circuit and Judicial Deterrence of Agency Rulemaking," 1988 *Duke Law Review* 300 (1988).

Chapter 12

1. Anthony King writes, "American politicians continue to try to create *majorities . . .* but they are no longer, or at least are not very often, in the business of building *coalitions. . . .* Building coalitions in the United States today is like building coalitions in the sand. It cannot be done." "The American Polity in the 1990s," in Anthony King, ed., *The New American Political System*, 2d version (American Enterprise Institute, 1990), p. 296. Also see Barbara Sinclair, "Coping with Uncertainty: Building Coalitions in the House and the Senate," in Thomas E. Mann and Norman J. Ornstein, eds., *The New Congress* (American Enterprise Institute, 1981), pp. 178–220. For a graphic example of the fragility of these majorities, see Timothy J. Conlan, Margaret T. Wrightson, and David R. Beam, *Taxing Choices: The Politics of Tax Reform* (CQ Press, 1990).

2. See, for example, Richard E. Cohen, *Washington at Work: Back Rooms and Clean Air* (Macmillan, 1992), chap. 10; Conlan, Wrightson, and Beam, *Taxing Choices*, chap. 8; and Bernard Asbell, *The Senate Nobody Knows* (Doubleday, 1978), pp. 431–52.

3. Laurence E. Lynn, Jr., and David deF. Whitman, *The President as Policymaker: Jimmy Carter and Welfare Reform* (Temple University Press, 1981), pp. 37, 40.

4. Kenneth A. Shepsle, "Congress Is a 'They,' Not an 'It': Legislative Intent as Oxymoron," *International Review of Law and Economics*, vol. 12 (June 1992), pp. 239–56.

5. *Public Citizen* v. *Department of Justice*, 491 U.S. 440, 473 (1989).

6. For the former view, see Frank H. Easterbrook, "Statutes' Domains," 50 *University of Chicago Law Review* 533 (1983); and Jonathan R. Macey, "Promoting Public-Regarding Legislation through Statutory Interpretation: An Interest Group Model," 86 *Columbia Law Review* 223 (1986). For the latter, see William N. Eskridge, Jr., "Public Values in Statutory Interpretation," 137 *University of Pennsylvania Law Review* 1007 (1989); and Cass R. Sunstein, "Interest Groups in American Public Law," 38 *Stanford Law Review* 29 (1985).

7. See Eskridge, "Public Values," pp. 1086–94; and Harvey Mansfield, Jr., *America's Constitutional Soul* (Johns Hopkins University Press, 1991), p. 13.

8. See the exchange between Justices Brennan and Scalia in *Johnson* v. *Transportation Agency, Santa Clara County*, 480 U.S. 616 (1987).

9. Matthew O. McCubbins, Roger G. Noll, and Barry R. Weingast state that "ex post reestablishment of a coalitional agreement, after a judicial opinion has upset the status quo, is likely to be difficult." "Structure and Process, Politics and Policy: Administrative Arrangements and the Political Control of Agencies," 75 *Virginia Law Review* 431, 445 (1989). Krishna K. Ladha develops this theme in "The Pivotal Role of the Judiciary in the Deregulation Battle between the Executive and Legislature," paper prepared for the National Bureau of Economic Research Conference on Political Economy, December 7 and 8, 1990.

10. *Amendments to the Food Stamp Act of 1964*, H. Rept. 91-1793, 91 Cong. 2 sess. (Government Printing Office, 1970), p. 9.

11. One finds a similar side payment in AFDC. As explained in chapter 6, in 1984 the Reagan administration proposed legislation establishing a "standard filing unit." This would have reversed a number of court rulings on "available income." The Senate passed the provision, but the House refused to concur. The impasse was resolved when the standard filing unit amendment was coupled with a $50 "pass through" of all child support payments. This gave recipients who also received child support payments a slight increase in benefits. *Deficit Reduction Act of 1964*, H. Rept. 98-861, 98 Cong. 2 sess. (GPO, 1984), p. 1407.

12. Education of the Handicapped Act Amendments of 1990, P.L. 101-476, overturning *Dellmuth* v. *Muth*, 491 U.S. 223 (1989).

13. William N. Eskridge, Jr., "Overriding Supreme Court Statutory Decisions," 101 *Yale Law Review* 331 (1991). Eskridge draws primarily on House and Senate reports published in *U.S. Code Congressional and Administrative News*. He notes, "This method has some gaps. Not all public laws generate committee reports, not all committee reports are reproduced in U.S.C.C.A.N. . . . and not all overrides of judicial decisions are reported in committee reports" (p. 337, n. 11). His list of decisions overridden does not include any of the Supreme Court's AFDC rulings reversed in 1981 or 1982; the committee reports did not mention the cases. Eskridge also misses most of the lower court decisions revised by the 1977 amendments to the Food Stamp Act. In addition, his list overlooks a number of court decisions reversed or significantly modified by the 1977 Clean Air Act Amendments, including *Train* v. *NRDC*, 421 U.S. 60 (1975); *Adamo Wrecking* v. *United States*, 434 U.S. 275 (1978); *Lubrizol Corp.* v. *EPA*, 562 F.2d 807 (D.C. Cir. 1977); and *NRDC* v. *EPA*, 489 F.2d 390 (5th Cir. 1974). These cases are discussed in R. Shep Melnick, *Regulation and the Courts: The Case of the Clean Air Act* (Brookings, 1983). Michael Solimine and James Walker have discovered fifty-five cases of congressional reversal of Supreme Court decisions between 1969 and 1988. "The Next Word: Congressional Response to Supreme Court Statutory Decisions," 65 *Temple Law Review* 425 (1992). They do not look at lower court decisions. Their research methods, like those of Eskridge, lead them to miss almost all the reversals of the Supreme Court's AFDC decisions. Their evidence provides additional support for two of the findings discussed below: the two revenue committees are particularly likely to overturn court rulings (p. 446), and most of the overrides are part of larger bills (p. 449).

14. Eskridge, "Overriding Supreme Court Statutory Decisions," 391–97; and chapter 1 of this volume.

15. Arthur Maass, *Congress and the Common Good* (Basic Books, 1983), chap. 7.

16. Richard F. Fenno, Jr., *Congressmen in Committees* (Little, Brown, 1973). Steven Smith and Christopher Deering provide an informative updating of Fenno's analysis in *Committees in Congress* (CQ Press, 1984); 2d ed. (CQ Press, 1990). Fenno argues that in the 1960s members of Senate Finance were not nearly as concerned with prestige and power as were their counterparts on House Ways and Means (p. 144). Smith and Deering indicate that over the next two decades Senate Finance became the most powerful and prestigious committee in the Senate

(1st ed., p. 115). If any Senate committee qualifies as a "prestige" or "power" committee, it is certainly Finance.

17. Another example of the Senate Labor and Public Welfare Committee's propensity to frame issues in terms of rights is the Developmental Disabilities Act of 1975. This act establishes a grant-in-aid program designed to help states upgrade state schools and community-based programs for the retarded. In 1975 the Senate committee attached to its reauthorization of the bill an extensive "Bill of Rights," which incorporated by reference 4,000 pages of regulations. States that failed to comply with these rules would lose not just developmental disability funds (which amounted to less than a billion dollars a year for the entire country), but medicare funds as well. The full Senate approved the committee bill without debate. The House, though, refused to go along with this substantial expansion of federal requirements. The final compromise included a Bill of Rights that lacked the specificity of the Senate bill (P.L. 94-473). Moreover, the statute failed to specify the penalty for failure to comply. The Third Circuit later ruled that Congress had passed this Bill of Rights under section 5 of the Fourteenth Amendment, and consequently it was binding on the states, regardless of whether they received federal funds under the act. The Supreme Court overruled the Third Circuit on the grounds that such vague legislative language was not sufficient to justify extensive intervention in state affairs. *Pennhurst State School and Hospital* v. *Halderman,* 451 U.S.1, esp. 18 (1981), overturning *Halderman* v. *Pennhurst,* 612 F.2d 84 (3d Cir. 1979).

18. To be sure, AFDC (and medicaid) funds come from general revenue. But committee members' concern about protecting the public fisc—and thus saving themselves the pain of recommending tax hikes—does not suddenly vanish when they shift their attention from big programs to smaller ones.

19. Susan Kellam, "Disability Fund Is Drying Up as 'Boomers' Swell Rolls," *Congressional Quarterly Weekly Report,* May 2, 1992, p. 1168; and Robert Pear, "US to Reconsider Denial of Benefits to Many Disabled," *New York Times,* April 19, 1992, p. A1.

20. As Patricia Dilley puts it, "Congressional reports for years had lambasted [the courts] for excessive activism and misinterpretation of the disability statute." "Social Security Disability: Political Philosophy and History," in Arthur T. Meyerson and Theodora Fine, eds., *Psychiatric Disability: Clinical, Legal, and Administrative Dimensions* (Washington: American Psychiatric Press, 1987) p. 381. Dilley's assessment of the conflict between the courts and the revenue committees is echoed by Deborah A. Stone, *The Disabled State* (Temple University Press, 1984), pp. 152–61; and by Jerry L. Mashaw, *Bureaucratic Justice: Managing Social Security Disability Claims* (Yale University Press, 1983), chaps. 1-3.

21. Fenno, *Congressmen in Committees,* p. 123.

22. For a glimpse at the politics of judicial review of the decisions of the Veterans Administration, see Paul C. Light, *Forging Legislation* (Norton, 1991); Kirk Victor, "A Different Drummer," *National Journal,* March 12, 1988, pp. 669–73; Richard Cowan, "Senate OKs Cabinet Status, Judicial Review for Vets," *Congressional Quarterly Weekly Report,* July 16, 1988, p. 1980; and

Michael Sherry, "Agent Orange and Congress: A New 'Generation Gap'?" *Congressional Quarterly Weekly Report*, December 16, 1989, pp. 3429–33.

23. Robert A. Katzmann, *Institutional Disability: The Saga of Transportation Policy for the Disabled* (Brookings, 1986), pp. 44–78.

24. Peter H. Schuck, "The Graying of Civil Rights Law: The Age Discrimination Act of 1975," 89 *Yale Law Journal* 27 (1979).

25. Eskridge, "Overriding Supreme Court Statutory Decisions"; Abigail M. Thernstrom, *Whose Votes Count? Affirmative Action and Minority Voting Rights* (Harvard University Press, 1987), chaps. 5, 6; and Susan Gluck Mezey, "Public Interest Litigation and the Civil Rights Attorneys Fees Awards Act: Attempting to Shut the Barn Door," paper prepared for the 1988 annual meeting of the American Political Science Association.

26. Mark C. Miller, "Congressional Committees and the Federal Court: A Neo-Institutional Perspective," *Western Political Quarterly*, vol. 45 (December 1992), pp. 957, 959, 956–57. Miller provides a lengthy and generally convincing justification for classifying Energy and Commerce as a "power committee" (pp. 953–54).

27. For example, the Federal Question Jurisdiction Amendment Act of 1980 (P.L. 96-486) eliminated the $10,000 floor for federal claims. This legislation was a response to a 1979 Supreme Court decision—*Chapman* v. *Houston Welfare Rights Organization*, 441 U.S. 600 (1979)—that had made it hard for welfare recipients to get into federal court. In the early 1970s and the early 1980s, there was considerable debate in Congress about Legal Service's role in bringing test cases. This issue fell within the jurisdiction of the House and Senate Education and Labor committees, which resisted imposing restrictions on Legal Services.

28. One committee staffer offered Mark Miller the following cynical evaluation of the performance of judges and administrators: "Congress sets the overall broad policy, agencies purposefully misinterpret congressional policy, and then the courts often aggravate the problem and further distort congressional intent" (Miller, "Congressional Committees and the Federal Court," p. 957). I thank Martin Shapiro for pointing out to me the importance of this dilemma. He provides an illuminating discussion of the dilemma in *Who Guards the Guardians? Judicial Control of Administration* (University of Georgia Press, 1988), esp. chaps. 4–6.

29. Robert A. Katzmann, "Bridging the Statutory Gulf between Courts and Congress: A Challenge for Positive Political Theory," 80 *Georgetown Law Journal* 653 (1992).

30. Quoted in Mark Miller, "Federal Court Decisions versus Federal Agency Decisions: How Congressional Committees Differ in Their Reactions," paper prepared for the 1990 annual meeting of the American Political Science Association, p. 28.

31. Ibid., p. 15.

32. Glenn quoted in Cowan, "Senate OKs Cabinet Status, Judicial Review for Vets." A staff member who worked with Glenn on this issue has written that "Glenn never talked about judicial review as anything but a right veterans should have." Light, *Forging Legislation*, p. 47. Light's book shows that little careful

consideration was given to the likely consequences of judicial review. Hart quoted in *Congressional Record*, daily ed. July 30, 1985, p. S10409.

33. Frederick Davis, quoted in *ABA Journal*, September 1, 1986, p. 29. Davis added this intriguing remark: "Without judicial review, the bureaucracy of the VA is subject to legislative intimidation." This suggests that some proponents of judicial review viewed it as a way to reduce informal congressional influence of the sort described earlier in the chapter. That would help explain the strenuous opposition of leaders of the House Veterans Affairs Committee. But apparently most members of Congress—including the entire Senate Veterans Affairs Committee—did not share this view.

Chapter 13

1. Ronald Dworkin, *Taking Rights Seriously* (Harvard University Press, 1978) p. 184; and Mary Ann Glendon, *Rights Talk: The Impoverishment of Political Discourse* (Free Press, 1991), pp. x, xi.

2. See Sidney M. Milkis, *The President and the Parties: The Transformation of the American Party System since the New Deal* (Oxford University Press, 1993), chaps. 7, 12. In a 1991 poll commissioned by the American Bar Association, almost three-fourths of the respondents said they would like the Constitution to guarantee adequate health care for all Americans. "Poll Finds Only 33% Can Identify Bill of Rights," *New York Times*, December 15, 1991, p. 33A.

3. See R. Shep Melnick, "The Courts, Congress, and Programmatic Rights," in Richard A. Harris and Sidney M. Milkis, eds., *Remaking American Politics* (Westview, 1989); and chapter 1.

4. See, for example, John Gliedman and William Roth, *The Unexpected Minority: Handicapped Children in America* (Harcourt Brace Jovanovich, 1980); and Michael J. Perry, *The Constitution, the Courts, and Human Rights: An Inquiry into the Legitimacy of Policymaking by the Judiciary* (Yale University Press, 1982).

5. Robert T. Stafford, "Education for the Handicapped: A Senator's Perspective," 3 *Vermont Law Review* 71, 73 (1978).

6. R. Kent Weaver, *Automatic Government: The Politics of Indexation* (Brookings, 1988), p. 116. Deborah Stone has noted that "the simplest, most common, and in some ways intuitively appealing definition of need is what is necessary for sheer physical survival. By this minimal standard, government should ensure that people have enough food and shelter to stay alive. The appeal of such a standard is obviously not its generosity, but its promise of objective, scientifically verifiable criteria of need." *Policy Paradox and Political Reason* (Scott, Foresman, 1988), pp. 69–70.

7. *Rosado v. Wyman*, 397 U.S. 397 (1970).

8. See Gilbert Y. Steiner, *The Futility of Family Policy* (Brookings, 1981), pp. 89–128.

9. See, for example, Lawrence Friedman, *Total Justice* (Russell Sage, 1985); Robert Kagan, "Adversarial Legalism," *Journal of Policy Analysis and Management*, vol. 10 (Spring 1991), pp. 369–406; and Peter Schuck, "The New Judicial Ideology of Tort Law," in Walter Olson, ed., *New Directions in Liability Law* (Academy of Political Science, 1988), pp. 4–17.

10. Friedman, *Total Justice*, p. 43.

11. See, for example, Joseph Berger, "Costly Special Classes Serving Many with Minimal Needs," *New York Times*, April 30, 1993, p. A1.

12. *National Party Platforms 1840–1972*, compiled by Donald Bruce Johnson and Kirk H. Porter (University of Illinois Press, 1973), pp. 784, 790.

13. 1992 Democratic Platform, reprinted in *Congressional Quarterly Almanac, 1992*, vol. 48, p. 61-A. "Responsibility" was one of the seven headings in the platform.

14. Quoted in ibid., p. 55-A. According to Al From and Will Marshall, who helped develop the "new covenant" theme, "The new politics of reciprocity is an alternative to the Right's politics of social neglect and the Left's politics of entitlement." In Will Marshall and Martin Schram, eds., *Mandate for Change* (Berkeley Books, 1993), p. xvii.

15. *Tyson v. Norton*, 390 F. Supp. 545, 559 (D. Conn. 1975).

16. The first two quotations come from Guido Calabresi, *A Common Law for the Age of Statutes* (Harvard University Press, 1982), p. 2; the third from William N. Eskridge, Jr., "Spinning Legislative Supremacy," 78 *Georgetown Law Journal* 319, 321 (1989); the fourth from Eskridge, "Public Values in Statutory Interpretation," 137 *University of Pennsylvania Law Review* 1007, 1090 (1989); the fifth from Daniel A. Farber, "Statutory Interpretation and Legislative Supremacy," 78 *Georgetown Law Journal* 281, 309 (1989). See also Cass R. Sunstein, *After the Rights Revolution: Reconceiving the Regulatory State* (Harvard University Press, 1990), pp. 174–77.

17. Alexander M. Bickel, *The Supreme Court and the Idea of Progress* (Harper and Row, 1970), pp. 13, 19.

Index

Aaron, Henry, 59–60

Abortion, 24, 101

Administrative interpretation of legislation, 8–9, 11, 14–15, 18, 238–44

Advisory Council on Public Welfare, 74

Affirmative action plans, 10

Age Discrimination Act of 1975, 27, 268

Agnew, Spiro T., 80

Agricultural Adjustment Act, 194

Agriculture, U.S. Department of (USDA), 185, 189, 190, 195, 196, 198, 200, 201–2, 203–4, 206, 208, 210–13, 214, 215, 216, 217, 220, 222, 226, 228, 230, 240, 261, 262

Aid to families with dependent children (AFDC): administrative interpretation of statutes and, 240, 241–42; benefit increases, 77, 94–97; caseworker home visits issue, 92–93; child support enforcement, 105–6, 123, 129–30; civil liberties of recipients and, 77–78; civil rights movement and, 73; college students, coverage for, 90–91; congressional amendments of 1967, 74–75; congressional amendments of 1970s, 120–24; congressional amendments of 1980s, 104, 105, 131–32; congressional factiousness and, 257, 259; congressional reaction to judicial interpretations, 128–29, 261, 262, 263, 270; congressional reform and, 119–20; conservative attack on welfare practices, 114–15, 120–30; cost distribution, 279–80; definition of needs, 78, 101–2, 277–78; as entitlement, 57, 250–51; executive initiatives of 1970s, 84–85, 112–19; executive initiatives of 1980s, 126–30; family maintenance issue, 116–17, 131; federal mandates imposed on states, 245, 246, 247–48; federal oversight of, 69–70, 116–17, 131; food stamp cases, comparison with, 207–8; growth in, 41, 73; income available to AFDC family, calculation of, 80, 89, 98–99, 102–3, 104–5, 109, 110–111, 123, 127; illegitimacy issue, 57, 85–88, 98, 122; interest groups and, 260; legislative histories and, 251–52; litigational strategy of reformers, 75–76, 78–80, 82; lower court activism, 97–102, 107; man-in-the-house issue, 88–90, 121–22, 130; origins of, 65, 67–68; perverse incentives issue, 66, 280–81; pregnant women, benefits for, 100–1, 102; Reagan's national reforms, 126–30; Reagan's reforms in California, 124–26; residency requirements issue, 77; standard filing unit rule, 105–6, 128; state control over, 68–69; state courts, litigation in, 107–8; state eligibility rules, 50–51, 66–67, 84–92; statutory cases versus constitutional cases, 85–86; statutory interpretation to effect major policy changes, lessons of, 108–11; suitable-home requirements and, 71–72; supporters and opponents in government, 80–82; Supreme Court rulings, 50–51, 57, 66–67, 83–84, 85–94, 96–97, 98, 102–6, 109, 110, 247; unemployment compensation issue, 103; uneven coverage, 65–

337